Pitt Latin American Series

A Revolution Aborted

The Lessons of Grenada

JORGE HEINE, *Editor*

UNIVERSITY OF PITTSBURGH PRESS

Published by the University of Pittsburgh Press, Pittsburgh, Pa. 15260

Copyright © 1990, University of Pittsburgh Press

Baker & Taylor International, London

Manufactured in the United States of America

Library of Congress Cataloging-in-Publication Data

A Revolution aborted : the lessons of Grenada / Jorge Heine, editor.
    p.   cm. — (Pitt Latin American series)
  Includes bibliographical references.
  ISBN 0-8229-3639-9. — ISBN 0-8229-5433-8 (pbk.)
  1. Grenada—Politics and government—1974– —Congresses.   2. New
Jewel Movement (Grenada)—Congresses.   I. Heine, Jorge.
II. Series.
F2056.8.R475   1990
972.9645—dc20   89-40583
                                                                     CIP

For Richard R. Fagen,
Teacher, Mentor, Friend

Contents

Acknowledgments

THIS BOOK is the product of a research program on Caribbean political and economic development issues of the Caribbean Institute and Study Center for Latin America (CISCLA) of Inter-American University of Puerto Rico, San Germán.[1]

If every multiauthored book implies overcoming a series of communication and coordination difficulties, the preparation of a symposium volume with contributions from a dozen authors spread throughout the Caribbean, Europe, and the United States has been a particularly daunting challenge. It could not have been done without the support of a number of institutions. A generous grant from the Ford Foundation made it possible to hold the initial San Germán conference, organized by CISCLA, at which first drafts of a majority of the chapters were delivered. That grant also allowed us to revise the original conference papers and to commission additional ones.

All of this has been possible because of CISCLA's support by Interamerican University, San Germán, something for which I would particularly like to express my appreciation to Chancellor Federico Matheu and to the then dean of studies, Bohdan Saciuk. I would also like to thank my two successors at CISCLA's helm, Dr. Gilberto Arroyo and Dr. Juan Hernández Cruz, whose commitment to the center's institutional continuity made it possible for me to discharge my responsibilities as an editor even after leaving CISCLA to join the University of Puerto Rico, Mayagüez. As has been the case with all of my previous books, without the extraordinary abilities and dedication of Sylvia Potter, CISCLA's administrative assistant, who coordinated this project from its very inception, this book could not have been completed.

Finally, I would like to dedicate this book to a man whose intellectual and human qualities have for long been a source of guidance and inspiration. Richard R. Fagen's unswerving commitment to understand the realities of Latin America and the Caribbean, his intellectual rigor, and his dedication to those of us who have been lucky enough to be his

1. A previous product of the same program is Jorge Heine and Leslie Manigat, eds., *The Caribbean and World Politics: Cross Currents and Cleavages* (New York: Holmes & Meier, 1988), which includes essays by several of the contributors to this book.

students make it difficult to express in words what those of us who received our professional training under his guidance feel for him. Suffice it to say that I consider this effort to understand the Grenadian Revolution to be part and parcel of the larger collective enterprise of analyzing the reality and the potential of socialism in the Americas, an endeavor to which Richard Fagen has made such a decisive contribution.

J.H.
Madrid, October 1989

A Revolution Aborted

... Aborted

"   St. George's after
th   rs, in the crucial
tur   aribbean"—from
Bish   d Anse beach on
25 C   ion had not only
killed

Th   nister Eric Gairy
in Gre   ....ional transfer of power to take place
in the Commonwealth Caribbean. In turn, the 1983 invasion of Grenada
by U.S. forces was the first time an English-speaking Caribbean territory
was occupied by U.S. troops, and the first occupation of a Caribbean
nation-state by the United States since 1965. Events on this small island
(133 square miles, population 90,000) located at the southern tip of
the Eastern Caribbean have thus had a remarkable impact on hemi-
spheric and even global affairs.

As the single most advanced effort to bring socialism to the English-
speaking Caribbean, regionally the Grenadian Revolution stands only
after the Haitian Revolution of 1804 and the Cuban Revolution of
1959 in the scope and degree of change brought to political institutions
(albeit obviously on a much smaller scale). Over and beyond this significance within the broader sweep of Caribbean history, the People's
Revolutionary Government (PRG) also embodies an important effort
at bringing about a transition to socialism in a small, underdeveloped
country. Although since the end of World War II the locus of revolution
has shifted to the Third World, and although there are now over some
twenty cases of such transitions in Asia, Africa, and Latin America (from
Vietnam to Mozambique, from Angola to Nicaragua), relatively few
efforts to develop some empirically based generalizations on that experience have been made.[1] What made the Grenadian Revolution and its
tragic denouement possible? Were Grenadian events a harbinger of
things to come in the Caribbean, or were they unique, the product of
a special combination of circumstances unlikely to be replicated elsewhere? Had the revolution reached a dead end by mid-1983, and was
the Fort Rupert massacre of 19 October only the subproduct of a social
and political process that had exhausted itself? Or rather, was it the case
of a successful effort at social and political change that was ultimately

aborted because of a failure of statecraft and the unlimited ambition of one man, Bernard Coard?

Over and beyond the specific features of the revolution, the Grenada experience has also raised a number of central theoretical and policy questions that go to the heart of the dilemmas faced by many small developing societies today. To what extent were some of the PRG's criticisms of the Westminster model of parliamentary democracy as applied to the Commonwealth Caribbean valid? Did the various mechanisms of grassroots democracy established by the PRG effectively deepen popular participation in the island's governance? What is the role of the vanguard party in the transition to socialism, and how can any emerging tensions between the party and the mass organizations be creatively harnessed? Which social sectors are likely to support a vanguard party committed to socialism in a society in which an urban working class is almost nonexistent?

It was precisely with the purpose of examining the Grenadian experience from a comparative perspective and to push beyond the events of the revolution to what we might call the lessons of Grenada that a conference, convened by the Caribbean Institute and Study Center for Latin America (CISCLA) of Inter American University was held in San Germán, Puerto Rico, on 17–19 October 1985. An important objective of the meeting was to obtain detailed, empirical assessments of a variety of issue areas—a prerequisite for any broader interpretive efforts. But the mix of participants and the agenda were designed to focus also on the wider questions of theory and policy raised by the revolution, its denouement, and its aftermath.

Drawing on the conference deliberations and other sources, this introductory essay is designed to provide the reader with an overview of some of the critical themes raised by the Grenadian Revolution.

THE TRANSITION TO SOCIALISM IN SMALL, DEVELOPING SOCIETIES

For better or for worse, the continued inability of capitalism to lift Third World countries out of the poverty and stagnation that has characterized much of the postcolonial world of Asia, Africa, Latin America, and the Caribbean has served as a powerful, if intermittent, lever pushing in the direction of socialism. Thus, despite the enormous obstacles to be faced in an often hostile international environment and the considerable barriers to be overcome in these efforts to gain control over their own economies and to assert some priorities not served by the market, a number of developing countries have continued to strive for the establishment of socialist relations of production, attempting to move toward some form of planned economy.

In this endeavor, the difficulties have not only been of a practical sort (finding the appropriate manpower, dealing with international marketing cartels, etc.) but, perhaps even more fundamentally, of a theoretical nature. For one thing, classical socialist theory emerged in, and was largely addressed to, nineteenth-century European societies, which were very different from today's Algeria, Jamaica, or South Yemen. The existence of a large, self-organized urban proletariat—identified by Marx as the key agent of revolution—is, needless to say, not a prominent feature of most African or Caribbean societies nowadays. For another, even Lenin's much more hands-on contributions on the role of the vanguard party and the need for alliances with the peasantry in societies with a relatively small working class were largely addressed to the question of how to *make* revolution, rather than to the no less important one of what to do on the morning *after* the revolution—in the case of Grenada on 14 March 1979.

The sort of class alliances to be forged, the pace at which to proceed in the desired direction, the type of political institutions needed for the transition period, the sort of relationship to establish with the metropolitan powers, and so forth, are all matters that cannot be resolved in abstract terms. They are questions to be answered by the revolutionary leadership in accordance with the specific, concrete circumstances they face in their own societies. For the revolution to survive, it is imperative that socialist theory be applied creatively to the regional and national circumstances that make, say, Zimbabwe different from Cuba.

Still, much as Marx was able to diagnose the condition of advanced European societies in the nineteenth century, it should be possible to draw some generalizations, however tentative, about the extant features of small, developing societies in the late twentieth century and their experiences as they attempt to traverse the uneasy road to socialism. It is only recently that this effort has started to be undertaken in any systematic fashion by Western social scientists. For obvious reasons, however, Soviet theoreticians have been grappling with this problem for much longer. Perhaps the most significant propositions to emerge from the work of Soviet specialists such as Ulyanovsky and Brutents are those related to the theory of the noncapitalist path.[2]

The theory of the noncapitalist path represents not so much an inductively derived body of theory constructed from the actual experience of Third World socialism but, rather, an effort to adapt classical Marxist theory to contemporary Third World realities. What it posits is the need, in the face of the relative weakness of the working class in many postcolonial societies of Asia and, particularly, Africa, to follow a rather different road from the classical proletarian revolution led by the vanguard of the working class first, followed by the dictatorship of the proletariat later. As the relative correlation of class forces in the society makes such approaches unworkable in the developing world, a much more incrementalist and cautious path is set forth.

Such a path implies the formation of a broad alliance of class forces, including not only the working class but also the peasantry, the petty bourgeoisie and even sectors of the national bourgeoisie. The tasks of this alliance will be essentially antiimperialist—directed at removing as much as possible imperialist influence and control over the economy, while, at the same time, embarking on the development of a mixed economy, the raising of the standard of living of the mass of the population, an increased participation of the people in political and economic decisionmaking, and an ambitious program of education of the people, which will also heighten their socialist consciousness.

A regime embarked on the noncapitalist path would not be directly engaged in the construction of socialism. It would simply by laying the foundations for it as it goes through a preceding national democratic stage—although the precise conditions under which the actual transition from national democracy to socialism will take place are left unspecified.

Although originally developed for Africa, in the early sixties,[3] the theory of the noncapitalist path was quickly embraced by a quite diverse array of parties and organizations throughout the developing world, including such improbable candidates as sectors of Chilean Christian Democracy in the late sixties.[4] It has fallen on particularly receptive ground in the English-speaking Caribbean, where a number of scholars and activists recognized it as a potentially powerful tool to overcome the obstacles to the construction of socialism in the West Indies.[5] And there is strong evidence to suggest that the theory of the noncapitalist path was indeed an important guide to action for the leadership of the Grenadian Revolution, although the revolution was in a number of respects more radical than the theory would seem to allow for.[6]

The Grenadian Revolution, then, constitutes not only an important case within the universe of efforts at transition to socialism in the Third World. It also embodies, much more specifically, an attempt to put into practice a particular *road* to socialism—the noncapitalist path. As such, a detailed examination of the Grenadian experience should be able to tell us much about the adequacy of the theory for Caribbean and other societies that share some of Grenada's characteristics.

THE GRENADIAN CASE

As the smallest and most densely populated of the Windward Islands, Grenada shares in the legacy of plantation society that is one of the defining features of the Caribbean region. The overwhelming majority of the population is of African descent, reflecting the massive importation of African slaves by British colonists in the seventeenth and eighteenth centuries to work on the sugar estates, which until the midnineteenth century provided the core of the island's economic activity. As elsewhere in the West Indies, a small part of the population is also of East Indian and Portuguese descent, the offspring of the indentured laborers from India and Madeira brought in to replace the slave labor lost in the wake of Emancipation.

Like all Caribbean societies, Grenada is an artificial society, in the sense that the social fabric was created anew by the European colonizers after the eradication of the indigenous Carib population. As M. G. Smith observed in his pioneering study *Social Stratification in Grenada,* an important social cleavage separates the Grenadian folk from the elite. While the former tend to be dark skinned, to have relatively little education, and to live in the countryside, the latter tend to be light skinned, to be better educated, and to live in the city—mostly in St. George's.[7] Unlike, say, Mexicans or Nigerians, Grenadians have no traditional culture to fall back on. Theirs is a Creole society, marked both by the imprint of the British colonizer and the African heritage kept alive by the common folk and ultimately defining its identity by the peculiar admixture of both elements in its Caribbean setting. In this, as in much else, Grenada is not too different from the rest of the West Indies. But there are a number of features specific to Grenada. One of them is the legacy of the French presence on the island, reflected in the French patois spoken until some years ago by the peasantry. Another, perhaps more important one is the strong influence of Catholicism; some two-thirds of the population is Catholic.

Grenada is also unique in two additional (and interrelated) aspects. It was among the earliest islands to move away from the cultivation of sugar as the mainstay of the economy. As early as 1870 sugar ceased to be the island's main economic crop, as cocoa, nutmeg, and bananas emerged as the planters' and the farmers' preferred crops. This has allowed Grenada to develop a more diversified economic base than many of the other islands. The inability of many of the larger estates to recruit enough labor after Emancipation also led to the breakup of many of them and the development of a small peasantry, which is perhaps the single most significant element of Grenadian social structure.[8] The rugged terrain, which did not lend itself easily to mechanized agriculture, the relatively high quality of the soil, and the ensuing sharecropping system, or *metayage*, all contributed to the emergence of a rather unique land-tenure pattern in which a relatively small number of estate owners, who controlled a considerable amount of land, coexisted with a large number of peasants owning small and often highly fragmented parcels

of land. One result of this is what Singham has referred to as an agropro-
letariat, a social grouping marked both by the ownership of land and
by the need to engage in wage labor.[9]

It is against this background that we have to analyze the emerging
pattern of crown colony politics, the successful challenge to it of Gairyism, and the ultimate displacement of Eric Matthew Gairy by the New
Jewel Movement in 1979.

GAIRY'S RULE AND THE WESTMINSTER MODEL

Eric Gairy's eccentricities, the band of thugs he surrounded himself with
in the seventies (the infamous Mongoose Gang), the repression he
engaged in to contain the increasing mobilization of the Grenadian
people against his misrule, and the repeated references to him by the
PRG as the dictator have all contributed to a widespread perception of
the Gairy era, roughly the period from 1951 to 1979, as one akin to the
dictaduras of a Somoza in Nicaragua, a Batista in Cuba, or a Duvalier
in Haiti. Yet there are fundamental differences between Gairy's rule and
the traditional Latin American dictatorships. For one thing, the role
initially played by Gairy in bringing about radical changes to the Grenadian polity (quite apart from his personal qualities as a leader) was,
objectively speaking, not different from the one played by Luis Muñoz
Marín in Puerto Rico, by Grantley Adams in Barbados, or by Eric
Williams in Trinidad—all men venerated as father figures in their respective countries today. For another, and despite his abuses, the basic
institutions of the Westminster system remained relatively intact during
Gairy's rule, with near-free elections being held regularly.

Rather than a prototypical Caribbean dictator in the mold of a Rafael
Leonidas Trujillo (which he clearly wasn't), Gairy therefore has to be
seen simply as a leader who took to its limits the wide latitude allowed
to the executive by the Westminster system. In that sense, Gairy was
much more like Antigua's Vere Bird, who has ruled Antigua with an
iron hand while fully respecting the formal strictures of parliamentary
democracy, than the tin god dictator he has been portrayed as.[10] In a
society where the constitutional structure has not been the product of
centuries of evolution and democratic practice, but simply resulted from
the unilateral imposition of a colonial power, there are few, if any,
countervailing forces to the unbridled exercise of authority of an all-
powerful executive.

Gairy was simply the most extreme expression of the peculiar mix of
democracy and authoritarianism that has been such a prominent feature
of West Indian political culture. The roots of this culture, of course, are
to be found, on the one hand, in the social relations emerging from
plantation society—social relations predicated on a rigid hierarchy and

unquestioning subordination to one's social superiors rather than on any notion of egalitarianism (which would have undermined an economic system based on the very premise of a few plantation owners and managers, mostly white, directing a large mass of slaves, overwhelmingly black); and, on the other hand, in the crown colony system of government, which deliberately excluded the local population from the political process, leaving it totally in the hands of the colonial administrators. The fact that universal suffrage was not introduced in Grenada until 1951 is perhaps the best indicator of how shallow the country's democratic roots really are.[11]

Moreover, as Arend Lijphart argues in his chapter, a number of features of the Westminister (or majoritarian) system established in Grenada (and in the rest of the Commonwealth Caribbean) have also contributed toward exacerbating this situation. From a rather different perspective as that of most critics of the Westminster system in the region, Lijphart, in a pioneering study of the effects of the Westminster system on electoral outcomes in the Eastern Caribbean, finds that one of the most detrimental results of it has been the systematic overrepresentation of parties winning a majority (or a plurality) in elections. In the case of Grenada, the observed exponent of overrepresentation linking vote-share to seat-share ratios was 4.61 in 1967, 5.26 in 1972, and 5.58 in 1976. Given the fact that legislatures in the Eastern Caribbean are very small to begin with, this tends to reduce the opposition to such a small number of legislators as to make the very notion of checks and balances an unattainable ideal.

As Selwyn Ryan shows in his chapter, this feature of the Westminster system became particularly apparent in the 1984 elections, when Eric Gairy's party received 36 percent of the popular vote but only one out of the fifteen seats being contested.

To these features of West Indian politics we must add another. The closed and static nature of societies such as Grenada meant that social mobility was highly restricted and limited. In this context, the emergence of democratic politics, the opening of the political system to black people, means also the sudden opening of unprecedented opportunities of social mobility for ambitious and able lower middle-class individuals. Politics represents perhaps the best chance to move from the lower ranks of the civil service or the teaching profession into the society's elite circles. The counterpart of this is, of course, that, in a small society, there is no going back. With no business experience to speak of, defeated politicians have nowhere to go once ousted from office. This, of course, puts a premium on doing whatever seems necessary to stay in office, and, just in case, to start feathering one's nest for the eventuality that things go wrong.

Gairy, then, was the leader who managed to accomplish in 1951 what none of his lighter skinned, middle-class politician colleagues, including the renowned journalist T. A. Marryshow, had managed to do: to channel and harness the energies and hunger for justice of the Grenadian peasant folk, to bring about the expansion of the political system, and, finally, to establish universal suffrage on the island. And Gairy's trade union (the Grenada Mental and Manual Workers Union, GMMU) and his subsequent Grenada United Labour Party (GULP) were instrumental in challenging the existing status quo, and in bringing a measure of respect for the Grenadian common people, something which Gairy continued to do from office for most of the fifties and sixties, as he carefully nurtured and cultivated his mostly rural following—the "hero" and his "crowd," in Singham's expression.

THE NEW JEWEL MOVEMENT DIAGNOSIS

Gairy, of course, was not only instrumental in bringing about universal suffrage to Grenada, he also played a key role in Grenada's gradual constitutional development—to associated statehood in 1967 and to full independence in 1974. The island was the first of the Windward and Leeward islands to accede to full sovereignty. But in the process of augmenting the powers of his office as chief (later prime) minister, Gairy seemed less and less prepared to engage in the power sharing, tolerance for dissent, and respect for the opposition that are supposed to be associated with parliamentary democracy. The former champion of Grenada's estate workers rights clamped down with a heavy hand on the demonstrations of an increasingly radicalized urban petty bourgeoisie and a younger generation of Grenadians. To this people Gairy's earlier triumphs meant little, his eccentricities (like his involvement with UFOs) seemed a national embarrassment, and the stagnation and poverty of the island offered only a dim future.

A number of young Grenadian professionals trained abroad, radicalized by their exposure to the plight of the West Indian communities in Britain and in the United States, and deeply affected by the black power "February revolution" that took place in Trinidad in 1970, started to organize a variety of groups to challenge Gairy. As Tony Thorndike discusses in his chapter, Maurice Bishop, Kendrick Radix, and the other leading members of Forum, MACE, and MAP quickly moved from the seeming sterility of black power ideology to a grassroots democracy perspective, inspired by such notions as Tanzania's *ujamaa* socialism and economic cooperativism.[12] Despite their interest in a wide variety of Third World currents of social and political thought, the JEWEL boys, as they would later come to be known, had no intention of limiting themselves to sitting around a table in a rum shop spinning theories of revolution. After getting involved in a variety of protest movements from 1970 to 1973, they founded the New Jewel Movement (NJM) in March 1973 and rapidly started to make a name for themselves as the most active and effective opponents of Gairyism.

A good proof of the down-to-earth approach to politics and how attuned to Grenadian realities the NJM leadership was is the New Jewel Movement Manifesto. Despite isolated digressions into academic jargon—including Harold Lasswell's definition of politics—the manifesto provides a vivid listing of the many difficulties faced by Grenada's common folk, including high inflation and unemployment rates, lack of educational facilities, and deficiencies in the health service and the transportation system. It then sets forth an extremely detailed program of social, economic, and political reconstruction of Grenada (going even into such matters as the court dress of lawyers and judges), anticipating many of the measures to be enacted later by the PRG.

It proposes the nationalization of the tourist, banking, and insurance sectors of the economy and ends on a note quite self-consciously modeled after the Communist Manifesto ("People of Grenada, you have nothing to lose but your continued exploitation"), but it is not a socialist program. Rather, it calls for developing Grenada with a much greater emphasis on self-reliance, making appropriate use of Grenada's own human and material resources. On the economic front, it stresses the development of what it calls the new tourism, owned and managed by Grenadians and using local products, as well as the development of the agricultural and fisheries sectors.Politically, its most startling and original proposal is its radical rejection of the existing Westminster system ("it fails to involve the people except for a few seconds once in every five years") and its proposed substitution by an elaborate system of people's assemblies (at the village, parish, and national levels) and a national government based on collective leadership (there would be no premier) elected by the National Assembly.

Implicit in many of the proposed measures is a strong critique of the Grenadian economic system as it had operated until then (as well as its insertion into the world economy). But there is no denunciation of capitalism per se or any effort to identify the underlying reasons for Grenada's poverty, over and beyond the incompetence of the politicians who ruled the country. More than anything, it is a call for action and a blueprint for change, inviting Grenadians to take their destiny into their own hands and to start to define their own, still somewhat blurred, national identity.

In finding their identity and political vocation while studying abroad, young men like Maurice Bishop, Unison Whiteman, and Bernard Coard were hardly alone. Many other West Indian radical politicians in the making underwent the same process in the late sixties and early seventies. What is unique about the NJM group is that they did not remain in the political wilderness, as many of their counterparts in the Eastern Caribbean do to this day. And the reasons for their success in reaching political power a scant six years after the formal founding of the NJM have as much to do with the complex changes Grenadian society underwent from the fifties to the seventies as with the strategy and tactics used by the JEWEL boys.

Sociologically, perhaps one of the most significant phenomena to occur in Grenada from the fifties onward was the gradual but steady expansion of the petty bourgeoisie. Based on the growth of the educational system, as well as on the emergence of tourism in the late fifties as an increasingly important economic activity, the numerically very small middle sectors in Grenadian society, located between the elite and the folk, started to become more and more a force to be reckoned with in Grenadian politics, particularly in and around St. George's. Gairy himself, in expanding the civil service (which he finally managed to get under his control with the advent of associated statehood in 1967), also contributed to the growth of this social class.[13]

The spark that ignited the growing resentment against Gairy in 1970 was a nurses' strike, and it is also indicative of the source of NJM support in the midseventies that the only two organizations that actively sympathized with the NJM within the Committee of Twenty-Two (the most important anti-Gairy front) were two teachers' unions, and that the first union actually organized from scratch by the NJM was the Bank Workers Union. Voting data from the 1976 elections and 1984 survey data indicate beyond doubt that support for the NJM (and later the PRG) was considerably higher among the younger, better educated, urban sectors of the population than among the older, poorer, less educated rural dwellers—which had been the bedrock of Gairy's support ever since he successfully defended the rights of estate workers in the early fifties.[14]

And this leads to the basic nature of the appeal exercised by the NJM and the reasons for its political success. For a variety of reasons, Grenadian nationalism had, until the seventies, been an extremely fragile and vulnerable sentiment. As a small island marked by heavy outmigration, Grenadians found themselves pulled in many directions. In addition to being Grenadian citizens, at one point or other they had been part of the British Empire, members of the West Indies Federation, and there was even one election (in 1962) largely fought on the issue of annexation to Trinidad and Tobago ("Go Trinidad"), a step then apparently favored by a majority of the electorate.

The black power movement, the emergence into nationhood of other West Indian territories in the sixties, and the militancy of the civil rights struggle in the United States all had a strong impact in the Eastern Caribbean, and particularly in Grenada, as more and more West Indians started to look for ways to find and affirm their personal and national identity. Though Gairy could have tried to tap into this burgeoning (albeit still undefined) search for a national identity, he was unable to do so. In fact, he was so reluctant to submit the issue of independence to the people's will that he bypassed the referendum he was supposed to hold on the subject. . He argued that the issue of independence had been settled in the 1972 general elections (where he introduced the issue vaguely and at the last minute) and asked the United Kingdom to grant independence without further ado. The way he phrased the whole affair ("Grenada does not have to support independence; independence will support Grenada") accurately reflects his rather uninspiring approach to the issue of national self-affirmation.

The root of the NJM's appeal to this still small but increasingly visible and powerful petty bourgeoisie—the teachers, bank clerks, nurses, high school students, and young professionals—was precisely its ability to tap into this search for a national identity. And the NJM's way of approaching it was just the opposite from the pompous and self-aggrandizing style used by Gairy (with expensive extravaganzas like the Eastern Caribbean Water Festival held in 1975) or his grotesque efforts to convince the United Nations to set up a center for the observation of unidentified flying objects in Grenada.

If the New Jewel Movement Manifesto started with a detailed inventory of the many unmet needs of Grenadians of all walks of life, it ended with an appeal to build a society in which questions such as Who are we? What is the nature of our condition? Why are we in that condition? would be at the center of the national agenda. They were the sorts of questions that the Grenada National Party (which had campaigned in 1962 under the banner of annexing Grenada to Trinidad) or Gairy's GULP were simply unable to ask, let alone attempt to answer.

THE NJM'S STRATEGY AND TACTICS

It is only in the context of that powerful nationalist appeal tied to the immediate material needs of the people that the NJM's rapidly growing support can be understood and appreciated. If organizationally the NJM evolved into a vanguard party, programmatically and operationally it remained a highly flexible and undogmatic, nationalist, antidictatorial movement. Its appeal cut across all segments of the Grenadian community but struck a particularly responsive chord in the younger generation and among the emerging petty bourgeoisie.

This willingness to challenge Gairyism on all fronts had already become evident before the formal founding of the party. For example, Unison Whiteman and Selwyn Strachan, both of the JEWEL, ran under the banner of the Grenada National Party in the 1972 elections, albeit losing badly. But this flexible approach to the political struggle would soon bloom and come into its own as Gairy clumsily clamped down on the swelling forces of the opposition to his rule.

From such seemingly minor (but symbolically powerful) issues as fighting for the public's access to a beach surrounded by the estate of an absentee landlord to the very issue of Grenadian independence, the NJM was quick to seize on issues that would command wide public attention. Although supporting Grenadian independence in principle, it strongly opposed and denounced the manner in which Gairy brought independence to Grenada; indeed the very independence celebrations were marred by strikes and demonstrations across the island against what was largely seen as a scheme by Gairy to augment his own powers.

Bishop and his colleagues also proved as adept in the wheeling and dealing with the far more senior leaders of the Grenada National Party as they were at stirring up the crowds at market square. Gearing up for the 1976 general elections, they outmaneuvered former Chief Minister Herbert Blaize in the negotiations for the formation of the Popular Alliance coalition. At the end of the day, the NJM secured three (versus the GNP's two) seats in the Grenadian Parliament. This still left Gairy with an absolute majority but catapulted Bishop into the position of leader of the opposition.

It was to be neither in the streets nor at York House, however, that the Gairy era would ultimately come to an end. It was in the barracks, in the valley of True Blue, where on 13 March 1979 the armed wing of the NJM overpowered Gairy's army while the prime minister was on his way to New York for a United Nations meeting.

And the NJM seizure of power cannot be understood as a Blanquist coup de main led by a small group of conspirators. If that had been the case, the enormous outpouring of support that followed Maurice Bishop's radio address announcing the establishment of the PRG would be incomprehensible. The uprising, rather, was simply the culmination of six years of political struggle in which Bishop and his colleagues had effectively managed to generate a considerable amount of support—in marked contrast with the listless and feeble opposition to Gairy exercised by the Grenada National Party. And it was this same flexibility, willingness to try what works (rather than whatever happened to be prescribed by ideology) that characterized the PRG in most of its programs and public policies.

As Paget Henry shows in his chapter on the cultural policies of the PRG, it was in the educational sphere where this flexibility came particularly to the fore, leading to some of the government's most significant achievements. Quite apart from the establishment of free secondary education and the enormous expansion of opportunities for

Grenadians to pursue university studies, this also involved a new approach to linguistic policy, enhancing the role of Grenadian Creole, innovative teacher training programs, and a wide-ranging literacy campaign. Perhaps surprisingly in a government led by a man educated in Catholic schools, no such flexibility obtained in the policy followed toward the established churches. As Henry points out, the rather dogmatic approach taken occasionally by the PRG on church-state relations created unnecessary obstacles and difficulties for the government in what is, after all, a profoundly religious society.

MOBILIZATION, PARTICIPATION, AND THE NATURE OF THE STATE

The most far-reaching changes brought about by the PRG were in the political sphere. The very establishment of a new government based on its revolutionary legitimacy rather than on elections was of course the first and most important of these changes. Directed by Prime Minister Maurice Bishop and seconded by Minister of Finance (later Deputy Prime Minister) Bernard Coard, the PRG was formed by a cabinet composed predominantly, though not exclusively, of NJM members. The government also established a new Supreme Court for Grenada and legislated, through cabinet-approved decrees, the people's laws.

The army was also dissolved and a new armed force was established, the People's Revolutionary Army (PRA), led by Commander Hudson Austin and staffed by many close associates of Bernard Coard. In addition, a people's militia was developed, in which civilians were trained to support the PRA in the case of an attack on the island.

The most original of the changes introduced, though, were those related to the new mechanisms of popular participation established at the village and parish level. In keeping with the grassroots democracy notions advanced in the NJM Manifesto in 1973, councils and assemblies were set up. The idea was that people would discuss their needs and aspirations at the community level and then transmit them to the leadership for appropriate action. The zonal and parish councils, open to all members of the community, were, in principle, to meet at least once a month.

As one former PRG cabinet member put it, "Prior to the revolution, once a year the minister of finance would present the budget in Parliament to fifteen people: there might have been another ten or twenty in the gallery. And that was it. The people have now changed all that. Now people know what a budget is. In every single village, technicians from the ministry would go to make the national presentation of the budget."[15] And these were not simple well-rehearsed exercises in public relations but important mechanisms of popular participation, which gave rise to some of the most important public policy initiatives of the PRG:

> The concept of the national transportation system, for example, did not originate with the PRG; it came from the people. It was mentioned at one meeting by the participants. The technicians mentioned it at other meetings, and there was a tremendous upsurge of support for the idea; it just caught like fire. We were talking about productivity, and people started to say "we are being late for work, children are late for schools," etc. We had been to OPEC and received some balance of payments support. We were going to use it for asphalt to repair roads, but decided to buy twenty-six buses from Japan, instead.[16]

As with any innovative political structure, there were problems in the implementation of the village and zonal councils, difficulties mentioned by Tony Thorndike in his chapter on people's power. The fact of the matter is, however, that the experience of the councils should remain as one of the most important experiments in grass roots democracy to have taken place in the Caribbean.

In addition to these participatory mechanisms, a number of mass organizations were also created to mobilize the Grenadian population, most prominently the National Women's Organization (NWO) and the National Youth Organization (NYO). Finally, Grenadian trade unionism also received a strong measure of support from the PRG through a variety of laws that effectively increased the number of unionized workers to some 10,000 by 1983, close to a third of the active labor force.

Rather than framing its politics within the logic and discourse of the Westminster system—as even West Indian governments ostensibly committed to socialism, as the Manley regime in Jamaica (1972–1980) and the Burnham regime in Guyana (1964–1985), have done—the PRG thus framed its political project within a radically different approach, one based on the principles of what Maurice Bishop referred to as "revolutionary democracy." As a perceptive Trinidadian commentator has observed: "In effect, the emphasis placed on the existence of free and fair elections as a measure of democratic freedoms serves to obscure the fact that elections ought to be merely the end of a complicated social process, and that in the Caribbean it is these crucial preconditions which are all too often missing."[17]

In mobilizing the people and actively involving them in the enormous task of national reconstruction, the PRG managed to start to build those very preconditions and develop that sense of national belonging that had so sorely been missing in the past. As one visiting Barbadian journalist put it on the first anniversary of the revolution:

Every home was also spik and span, rubbish and garbage neatly tucked away, trash removed and the roads cleaner than any I have seen in any other Caribbean island, including our own. Even as one drove off the beaten track, one saw continuing evidence of this enthusiasm and pride in the country.

For those who do not know Grenada, this may not be very important, but for those who have travelled there over the years, the destitution which is still there always had an air of abject helplessness about it which was most depressing. Today, the small and fragile houses of the poor are still evident, but their occupants now convey an air of expectancy, of feeling that better days are coming and that it will indeed be all right in the morning.[18]

THE POLITICAL ECONOMY OF THE TRANSITION

In marked contrast with other instances of transition to socialism in the Western Hemisphere, such as in Jamaica and Chile, the economy was not the Achilles' heel of the Grenadian Revolution. In fact, in the summer of 1983, only a few months before the public emergence of the factional struggle between Bishop and Coard, the World Bank and the International Monetary Fund had given their ringing endorsement to the policies followed by the PRG in the economic arena—a far cry from what such organizations would have voiced about the situation in Jamaica in 1980 or in Chile in the winter of 1973.

The relative success of the PRG in putting Grenada's economic house in order while moving toward socialism is particularly remarkable in view of the disastrous state of the public sector it encountered upon coming to power; the openness and vulnerability of the Grenadian economy; its tenure during a period (1979–1983) that started with the second oil shock and was marked by one of the biggest recessions experienced by the industrialized capitalist countries since the 1930s; and the damages suffered by the island's agriculture as a result of Hurricane Allen.

During the second half of the 1970s the Grenadian economy had started to recover somewhat from the serious difficulties it had undergone in the earlier part of the decade. But it was still an economy characterized by low investment rates, high unemployment, inflation, and a per capita income that in real terms was lower in 1979 than in 1970. One major problem was Grenada's extremely low absorptive capacity. As one study put it in 1979, "Actual development expenditures have fallen far short of the budgeted amount each year largely as a consequence of difficulties in project preparation, implementation and monitoring."[19]

It was in this context that the PRG attempted to steer a new course. Identifying agriculture, tourism, and fisheries as the three pillars of the island's economy, the PRG launched an ambitious program of economic reconstruction. The basic purpose of the program was to "shift the distribution of power and resources . . . so that the national economy (as opposed to the externally controlled sector) would become the primary source of growth and accumulation."[20]

Investment increased dramatically, from E.C. $9 million in 1979, to $110 million in 1982, reaching 50.2 percent of Grenada's gross domestic product, most of it public investment for infrastructural purposes (of which about 40 percent went to the international airport). Services, particularly in health and education but also in other areas, were drastically improved. Unemployment was reduced from an estimated 50 percent in 1979 to 15 percent in 1983. Perhaps most significantly, when compared to the Chilean, Jamaican, and Nicaraguan experiences, these vastly increased spending programs did not lead to the runaway inflation that has become almost a trademark of other Third World transitions to socialism. From 21.2 percent in 1980 and 18.8 percent in 1981, inflation actually declined to 7.8 percent in 1982 and 6.1 percent in 1983.

According to the Caribbean Development Bank, the average growth rate of Grenada for 1981–1983 (2.2 percent) was the third highest in all of the English-speaking Caribbean. There were no shortages of consumer goods in Grenada from 1979 to 1983, either; if anything, shortages that had existed in previous years of such basic staples as rice, for example, ceased to exist with the establishment of the National Marketing and Import Board (NMIB) established by the PRG. As Wallace Joefield-Napier points out in his chapter on the functioning of the Grenadian economy under the PRG, all of this does not mean that there weren't problems or that the PRG's economic policy didn't create difficulties of its own. What it does mean is that, during a particularly difficult period in the international economy, a small, extremely open (and therefore very vulnerable) economy like Grenada's was able to do quite well even as it pressed forth with major changes.

What was the key behind the considerable economic achievements of the PRG? As Frederic Pryor argues in his chapter in this book, foreign aid was undoubtedly a vital tool to achieve the government's objectives, but this still begs the question as to what was done to obtain such a considerable amount of external assistance in the first place and, no less important, what lay behind the extremely effective and efficient utilization of such resources.

Three aspects are particularly worth underscoring in this regard. The first is the ability shown by the PRG leadership to identify the main bottleneck hampering the development of the Grenadian economy and to act to remove it with great determination and boldness. The "can do" attitude that permeated the PRG was nowhere as evident as in its relentless determination to construct the international airport and thus overcome what the World Bank described in 1979 as "the most limiting single factor in achieving the island's growth possibilities."[21] Revealingly, the World Bank itself opposed the immediate construction of the airport, arguing that further studies were needed and that construction of the airport had to go hand in hand with expansion of Grenada's hotel capacity. Various international agencies also sought to limit the length of the runway, offering support if it was kept to 7,000 feet—insufficient to receive jumbo jets. None of this sidetracked the PRG's determination to build a full-length international airport.[22]

The second aspect relates to the very tight control that was exercised over public spending. Government agencies had to submit monthly expenditure reports to the Ministry of Finance, where they were checked as to whether they were in line with projected spending. No purchases could be made without a voucher countersigned by the Ministry of Finance. It was this tight fiscal management that allowed the PRG to increase social services and capital expenditures considerably and to get inflation under control. By not giving in to the populist temptation of untrammeled government spending that has been a hallmark of socialist transitions elsewhere, the PRG showed that efficient and successful economic management is by no means incompatible with a commitment to socialism. In fact, as the cases of Chile and Jamaica clearly demonstrate, such management may be becoming more and more a prerequisite for avoiding the failure of such transitions. With slogans such as "You can only take out what you put in," its emphasis on matters like productivity and output, and its involvement of the people in the discussion of the national budget, the PRG effectively linked the Grenadian people's heightened expectations with their own abilities to make possible a higher standard of living for all.

The third element of the PRG's economic policy that stands out is the acute consciousness among the leadership about the very real limits of the regulatory capacities of the state in peripheral societies. As Maurice Bishop put it in November 1979,

> We are not in the least bit interested as a government in attempting to run all sectors of the economy. That would be an impossibility. The massive problems we already have with storage space, with qualified personnel, and that kind of thing in the few areas we have moved into, like the National Commercial Bank and the National Importing Board, shows very clearly to us that it would be a massive nightmare for us if, for example, we were to go and try to sell cloth or rice and saltfish or even operate a Coke factory.[23]

This pragmatism was come by not by a painful trial and error method but as a result of an examination of the experience of other developing societies undergoing socialist transitions; and it was applied from the very beginning of the PRG. It resulted in a policy that paid handsome dividends in many areas. Contrary to the advice of visiting Bank of Guyana officers, for example, the PRG never established foreign exchange controls. As a result, hard currency remittances from abroad into Grenada not only never dried up but tripled from E.C. $16 million in 1978 to E.C. $42 million in 1980 and stayed in that range for the duration of the revolution.[24]

INTERNATIONAL AFFAIRS

Much more radical than the controlled and incremental changes brought about in domestic economic policy by the PRG were those implemented in Grenada's foreign relations. Diplomatic relations with Cuba were quickly established, and a movement toward a relatively close alignment with the Soviet Union as well as with militant Third Worldism in a variety of international fora also took place. This was part of the reason for Washington's unremitting hostility toward the revolution. This seeming mismatch between domestic policies marked, in general, by pragmatism and accommodation and a foreign policy so daring in its defiance of the United States is one of the puzzles about the Grenadian Revolution.

As Anthony Payne discusses in his chapter on Grenadian foreign policy, the basis for this approach can be found in the theory of the noncapitalist path, predicated as it is on antiimperialist solidarity in ever closer connection with the world socialist system. The strong antiimperialist posture adopted by the PRG ever since Maurice Bishop's 13 April 1979, "In nobody's backyard" speech—far from being a mere exercise in rhetoric seemingly divorced from Bishop's conciliatory approach to domestic politics—performed two important functions. On the one hand, it was a tool to mobilize support for the PRG, tapping again into that reservoir of nationalist appeal that had for long been one of the NJM's strong suits. "I have never felt as much a Grenadian as I do today," was the way noted Grenadian journalist Alister Hughes put it in May 1981, two years into the revolution.[25] On the other hand, the PRG's antiimperialist foreign policy allowed it to gain access to the sort of international funding for its projects it was interested in, not only from Cuba, but also from countries such as North Korea, Libya, and Iraq, not to mention the Soviet Union itself.

There is little doubt that, in terms of both objectives, the policy paid handsome dividends for quite some time. As Robert Pastor underscores in his chapter on U.S.-Grenadian relations, though, it also contributed to a steady deterioration in relations between Washington and St.

George's, a deterioration that culminated in the October 1983 invasion of Grenada by U.S. troops.

In the end, perhaps the most striking thing about Grenada's foreign relations was the high price the PRG paid for its strong support for the Soviet Union and how little it got in return from the Soviets (as opposed to the Cubans and other foreign donors). The Soviet Union took almost four years to establish a fully manned embassy in St. George's and provided no major economic aid, although treaties for substantial amounts of military aid were signed in 1983.

CHARISMA, CLASS, AND CRISIS

As Grenadian political scientist Patrick Emmanuel has observed, most West Indian political parties have been "one-man shows." But the essential condition for such domination has been the overwhelming personal popularity of the leader, who could use this resource to deal with the threat of "independent-minded men" within his organization.[26] This is valid from Alexander Bustamante's Jamaican Labor Party to Eric Williams's People's National Movement, from Vere Bird's Antigua Labor Party to Eric Gairy's GULP. Such leaders have fallen into one of two categories: they have been either trade union organizers who have risen up through the ranks, using their trade union base to build up their political following (and their political party), or middle-class professionals (often lawyers or scholars) trained abroad who at some point return to their homeland and are able to translate their educational credentials and eloquence into considerable political capital—"middle-class heroes," as Singham put it. Eric Gairy and Maurice Bishop clearly embody these two very different types of leaders. But whereas Gairy found it difficult to reach beyond his fundamentally rural trade union base and exercise a genuine national appeal, Bishop's charisma was such that it allowed him to reach Grenadians from all backgrounds and social classes. Even people who had become hostile to the revolution retained their faith in Bishop's leadership.

Although much ink has been spilled on the internal crisis of the revolution and the increasingly personalized conflict between Bernard Coard and Maurice Bishop, most of it has tended to focus on the ideological dimensions of this conflict rather than on its psychological roots. Using psychoanalytic tools, and going beyond the relatively static analysis that has emerged from the reductionist casting of Coard and Bishop as two different political "types" bound to come into conflict with each other, Jorge Heine explores in some depth the personal and political background of the dramatis personae in the revolution's final crisis. From his interweaving of Bishop's and Coard's psychological profiles with a detailed examination of their behavior during the crisis emerges a new interpretation of the revolution's abortion.

GRENADA IN PERSPECTIVE

Inevitably, then, the Grenadian experience raises questions that transcend the confines of that small island.

What does the Grenadian experience tell us about the problems and prospects faced by Caribbean socialism? Carl Stone's chapter examines the Grenadian experience in a comparative perspective, analyzing both the political capacities inherent in the socialist development model and the capabilities for economic management and transformation. In examining socialist initiatives in Grenada, Jamaica, and Guyana, Stone concludes that in none of these three cases were these attempts at socialist transformation anchored in strong, reliable, and progressive working class support. Whereas the Guyanese regime built socialism on black ethnic support, in Jamaica it was the subproletariat rather than the working class that gave fullest support to the socialist agenda, and the Grenadian revolution was based mainly on younger generation enthusiasm. Ironically, while Grenada avoided many of the economic mistakes of both Jamaica and Guyana, it ultimately revealed a limited capability for political management. For Stone, the Grenadian Revolution thus reinforced the fragility and vulnerability of Marxist regimes in a region within the U.S. sphere of influence, where the Eastern bloc is unwilling to risk confrontation with the United States to secure the defense of such regimes.

Laurence Whitehead, in turn, provides in his chapter a thorough analysis of the rationale behind the reluctance of so many Third World revolutionary regimes to submit themselves to the will of the electorate. And though he finds impeccable the instrumental logic behind this reluctance, he also contends that it betrays a fundamental lack of respect for the people whom socialism is being built for.

How should the PRG be characterized, to place it within a comparative perspective? Perhaps unsurprisingly, the various labels used by commentators tell us more about their own biases than about the PRG. Can writers who variously refer to the PRG as a "peaceful revolution," as "Leninist in conception and Stalinist in practice," as akin to the welfare states of northern Europe, and as Communist all be referring to the same process?[27] Moreover, what explains the penchant among some observers to attribute to the PRG a rather schizoid character, as embodying a "conflation of revolutionary and neocolonial principles" or a "new Grenadian Bonapartism . . . of the petty bourgeoisie, i.e., a mediated form of oligarchic rule?"[28]

The fact is that, as the inadequacy of these various categories to encompass the richness of the Grenadian Revolution clearly shows, the process that took place in Grenada from 1979 to 1983 defies easy categorization. It should also be apparent that, perhaps to the chagrin of academic taxonomists, the single best classification of the PRG remains the one used by the theorists and leaders of the revolution themselves, that is, that of a regime of "socialist orientation" embarked on a noncapitalist path of development. A government that, until its final crisis, did not execute its opponents (including convicted terrorists), that developed extensive grass roots political participation mechanisms, and under which the luggage of incoming visitors from abroad was not even searched at the airport can hardly be classified as Stalinist. Any parallels with the welfare states of northern Europe, on the other hand, seems inappropriate for a country in which, in four years of revolution, central government expenditures reached a mere 29 percent of GDP, one of the lowest of all members of the Organization of Eastern Caribbean States and of the English-speaking Caribbean.

Many of the most distinguishing features of the PRG—the nonantagonistic relationship it developed with the private sector, its reluctance to engage in widespread expropriation of landholdings, the determinedly pro-Soviet stance it took in foreign policy matters, the priority given to the island's infrastructural development—all flow from a diagnosis that identified the national-democratic stage of development as the one Grenada was undergoing. It also showed a remarkable ability to learn from other experiences of socialist transition, through direct consultation with government officials in the case of Jamaica and Guyana and, though less directly, from the failure of the Unidad Popular in Chile.

Was the theory of the noncapitalist path appropriate for Grenada? Given the capitalist nature of relations of production throughout the Commonwealth Caribbean, the argument has been made that the noncapitalist path is quite inadequate for the region.[29] Such sweeping statements fail to take into account the specificities of the Grenadian social formation. By 1979 Grenada was among the least developed territories in the Caribbean. With 2.7 percent of value added in manufacturing as percentage of GDP, it had the lowest level of industrial development of any territory in the Caribbean Community. The fragmentation of landholdings has also led to the emergence of an extensive peasantry and a rural petty bourgeoisie, with subsistence agriculture coexisting with the traditional cash crops like nutmeg, mace, and cocoa. The almost total absence of foreign corporate landowners and the decline of the locally owned estates also meant that agricultural capitalism in Grenada was present only in its most primitive and underdeveloped form.

In this context, critiques of the Grenadian Revolution as "petty bourgeois" or as attempting to bring to Grenada the "Puerto Rican

model"[30] miss the point and show a thorough misunderstanding of what
the revolution was all about. Whether the noncapitalist path is applicable
to all of the Commonwealth Caribbean is an open question; it is likely
that it would not be for several of the more developed countries in the
region. But as far as Grenada is concerned, given the almost total absence
of an industrial working class, the revolutionary potential of the petty
bourgeosie and the intelligentsia, and the numerical importance of an
extensive peasantry, the noncapitalist path provided the revolutionary
leadership with a most appropriate theoretical tool kit to chart the course
of the revolution.

Yet, is it not the case that the ultimate failure of the Grenadian
Revolution is conclusive proof of the inadequacy of the noncapitalist
path for the Caribbean? Not necessarily. If we accept Heine's assessment
of the revolution's final crisis as fundamentally rooted in the compulsive
behavior of Bernard Coard and the inadequacy of Maurice Bishop's
response to it, a rather different response emerges. A cross-section of
social and economic indicators as well as any evaluation of the political
situation in Grenada in the summer of 1983 show a revolution about
the consolidate itself. If that is the case, the PRG's application of the
noncapitalist path would have to be considered as quite successful, only
having been derailed by a failure of political leadership of the highest
order.[31]

Ironically for a theory originated in the Soviet Union, the one aspect
of the noncapitalist path that in the Grenadian experience proved to be
extremely inadequate was the one postulating, as leit motif, an ever
closer alignment to the Soviet Union. Given Grenada's geopolitical
context, this was one of the main sources of the implacable hostility of
the United States to the revolution. It also led Grenadian revolutionaries
to place high expectations in the Soviets' willingness to help the PRG,
expectations that were ultimately disappointed.

Our understanding of the processes of social, economic, and political
change unleashed in Grenada by the PRG and their implications for the
rest of the Caribbean and the developing world is only beginning to
emerge. The ensuing chapters of this book should provide us with the
sort of foundation any such beginning demands.

NOTES

1. Among the very few books dealing with the subject systematically is
Richard R. Fagen, Carmen Diana Deere, and Jose Luis Coraggio, eds., *Transition and Development: Problems of Third World Socialism* (New York: Monthly
Review Press, 1986).

2. Leading Soviet sources on the theory of the noncapitalist path are R. A.

Ulyanovsky, *Socialism and the Newly Independent Nations* (Moscow: Progress Publishers, 1974); V. Soladerikov and V. Bogaslovsky, *Non-Capitalist Development: A Historical Outline* (Moscow: Progress Publishers, 1975); and K. N. Brutents, *National Liberation Revolutions Today* (Moscow: Progress Publishers, 1977).

3. See I. I. Potekhin, "African Socialism. A Soviet View," in William H. Fordland and Carl G. Rosberg, Jr., eds., *African Socialism* (Stanford: Stanford University Press, 1964), pp. 97–112.

4. See Michael Fleet, *The Rise and Fall of Chilean Christian Democracy* (Princeton: Princeton University Press, 1985), p. 10.

5. See particularly Clive Y. Thomas, "The Non-Capitalist Path as Theory and Practice of Decolonization and Socialist Transformation," in *Latin American Perspectives* 5 (Spring 1978), pp. 10–28; and Ralph E. Gonsalves, *The Non-Capitalist Path of Development: Africa and the Caribbean* (London: One Caribbean Publishers, 1981); for a critical discussion of it, see Patrick Emmanuel, "Revolutionary Theory and Political Reality in the Eastern Caribbean," *Journal of Interamerican and World Affairs* 25 (1983), pp. 193–227.

6. The semiofficial book on the revolution and the history of the New Jewel Movement, Richard Jacobs and Ian Jacobs, *Grenada: The Route to Revolution* (Havana: Casa de las Americas, 1980), makes repeated references to the noncapitalist path as theoretical guide for the revolution. Both Maurice Bishop and Bernard Coard in speeches and interviews characterize the Grenadian Revolution as being in the national-democratic stage. See particularly Bishop's Line of March speech to the general meeting of the party, 13 Sept. 1982, in which he explicitly discusses the political and the economic essence of the national-democratic path. For text of speech, see Michael Ledeen and Herbert Romerstein, eds., *Grenada Documents: An Overview and Selection*, vol. 1 (Washington, D.C.: Depts. of State and Defense, 1984), document 1.

7. See M. G. Smith, *Social Stratification in Grenada* (Berkeley: University of California Press, 1965).

8. See George I. Brizan, *The Grenadian Peasantry and Social Revolution 1931–1951*, ISER Working Paper 21 (Mona, Jamaica: University of the West Indies, 1974); and John Brierly, *Small Farming in Grenada, W.I.* (Manitoba: University of Manitoba Press, 1974).

9. See Archie W. Singham, *The Hero and the Crowd in a Colonial Polity* (New Haven: Yale University Press, 1968).

10. The New Jewel Movement Manifesto, in 1973, used this epithet.

11. For a thorough discussion of Grenadian politics leading up to 1951, see Patrick Emmanuel, *Crown Colony Politics in Grenada, 1917–1951*, ISER Occasional Paper 7, (Cave Hill, Barbados: University of the West Indies, 1978).

12. The only person quoted by name in the long New Jewel Movement Manifesto is Julius Nyerere.

13. Whereas in 1946 there were only 75 secondary school students in Grenada, this number had reached 4,967 by 1970. The Jacobses estimate that in the late sixties there were 500 Grenadians enrolled at universities abroad. Tourism expanded steadily through the sixties and early seventies; tourist arrivals peaked at 37,933 in 1973 and dropped sharply after independence. See Jacobs and Jacobs, *Grenada*, p. 94.

14. The three NJM candidates elected on the ticket of the Popular Alliance

in 1976 were elected in the St. George's area—Bernard Coard, Unison White-man, and Maurice Bishop. For the 1984 survey data, see Patrick Emmanuel, Farley Brathwaite, and Eudine Barriteau, *Political Change and Public Opinion in Grenada 1979–1984*, ISER Occasional Paper 19 (Cave Hill, Barbados: University of the West Indies, 1986).

15. Personal interview with Lyden Ramdhanny, PRG deputy minister of finance and minister of tourism, Grenville, 30 Aug. 1987.

16. Ibid.

17. Allan Harris, "The Road to Coup D'Etat," *Trinidad Guardian*, 8 Apr. 1979.

18. Harold Hoyte, "The Popular Revolutionary Government," the *Nation* (Barbados), 19 Mar. 1980.

19. World Bank, "Current Economic Position and Prospects of Grenada," Report 2439-GRD, 19 Apr. 1979.

20. Paget Henry, "Grenada and the Theory of Peripheral Transformation," paper delivered at the Ninth Annual Conference of the Caribbean Studies Association, St. Kitts, 30 May–2 June 1984.

21. World Bank, "Current Economic Position."

22. Interview with Ramdhanny.

23. Maurice Bishop, the *Nation* (Barbados), 21 Nov. 1979.

24. Bernard Coard, statement from the dock, in Friends for Jamaica, "The Side You Haven't Heard: The Maurice Bishop Murder Trial" (New York: mimeo, 1987), p. 11.

25. Comments made to the author, May 1981, Barbados.

26. Emmanuel, *Crown Colony Politics,* p. 102.

27. See, respectively, Ecumenical Program for Inter-American Communication and Action, *Grenada: The Peaceful Revolution* (Washington, D.C.: EPICA, 1982); Anthony P. Maingot, "Grenada and the Caribbean: Mutual Linkages and Influences," in Jiri Valenta and Herbert J. Ellison, eds., *Grenada and Soviet/ Cuban Policy: Internal Crisis and U.S./OECS Intervention* (Boulder: Westview, 1986), p. 144; Gordon K. Lewis, *Grenada: The Jewel Despoiled* (Baltimore: Johns Hopkins University Press, 1987); and Gregory Sandford, *The New Jewel Movement: Grenada's Revolution, 1979–1983* (Washington, D.C.: Foreign Service Institute, U.S. Department of State, 1985).

28. See Hilbourne Watson, "Grenada: Noncapitalist Path and the Derailment of a Populist Revolution," paper delivered at the Ninth Annual Meeting of the Caribbean Studies Association, St. Kitts, 29 May–2 June 1984; and Fitzroy Ambursley, "Grenada: The New Jewel Revolution," in Fitzroy Ambursley and Robin Cohen, eds., *Crisis in the Caribbean* (New York: Monthly Review Press, 1983).

29. See Watson, "Grenada."

30. Ibid.

31. In fact, Ulyanovsky has been explicit in stressing the considerable importance of "farsighted and realistic political leadership" for the "successful affirmation of the socialist orientation and its firm consolidation in all aspects of national life." See Ulyanovsky, *Socialism,* p. 56.

Part I

THE DOMESTIC RECORD

1. People's Power in Theory and Practice

Tony Thorndike

T HE NEW JEWEL MOVEMENT (NJM) could have remained in the political wilderness like all its contemporaries in the Commonwealth Caribbean. That it didn't was entirely attributable to the unique political circumstances of the miniscule Grenadian polity, dominated as it was by the bizarre and corrupt dictatorship of Sir Eric Gairy. Popular reaction against his rule was skillfully exploited; coupled with effective mobilization programs and well-thought-out and expressed reformist policies, the NJM gained widespread public support, the essential ingredient that enabled it to seize and maintain power.

HISTORICAL ORIGINS

The critical role of public support for reform in what is possibly the most colonized of societies was an issue addressed at the Rat Island (St. Lucia) meeting in June 1970. Progressive activists and intellectuals from several parts of the Commonwealth Caribbean gathered on that occasion to discuss agendas and strategies for change. They were for the most part reformists rather than revolutionaries. Maurice Bishop was no exception; of those present only Trevor Munroe of Jamaica made his Marxist-Leninist credentials clear. All, however, had been radicalized by their educational experience overseas at a time of resurgent racism, widespread anti-Vietnam protests, and student dissatisfaction. Furthermore, they had all been galvanized into action by the populist black power movement then sweeping the region. Collectively and individually, they were determined to raise the political consciousness of the West Indian masses and to mobilize them to challenge the deep-seated dependency—economic, structural, and psychological—that shaped their destinies. In their idealist innocence, the Rat Island participants decided that political parties were neither desirable nor necessary.[1] Instead, a series of discussion groups (FORUMs) would be established in each territory, through which progressives could map out a new future. This represented, they believed, a new politics: a break from the colonial mold toward the formation of new representational and popular institutions.

But the concrete circumstances of West Indian political culture, heavily influenced by the party-based Westminster system, made political organization essential. Gradually, following a pattern established elsewhere, the informal, numerically tiny, and urban-professional-dominated FORUM in Grenada gave way in early 1972 to a more structured group, the Movement for the Advancement of Community Effort (MACE)—which by October was rechristened the Movement for the Assemblies of the People (MAP). The need for more formal structures was acknowledged at a further gathering of progressives. Meeting in Martinique in February 1972, their vision was of a new Caribbean society based upon people's ownership and equal distribution of all Caribbean resources, the destruction of the traditional class structure in which skin color played such a significant role, and equal access to welfare facilities. To achieve this, it was necessary to analyze the nature and effectiveness of existing political parties and other organizations, such as trade unions, in the respective territories. Challenges to them could not be mounted by discussion groups but only by similar structures and, where opportunities presented themselves, by infiltration. The need for organization and popular identity was made all the more imperative by the experience of the general election in Grenada in the same month. A few youthful progressives fought under the banner of the middle-class-dominated opposition Grenada National Party (GNP), led by Herbert Blaize. A bland, rather ineffective organization representing local professionals and commercial interests, the GNP couldn't have been more different from the group of young radicals arguing for a major overhaul of Grenadian society. Not surprisingly, given this mismatch, they lost disastrously and, disillusioned with parliamentary politics, decided to link up with some self-educated farmers to build a base in the rolling hills of St. David's parish. Led by Unison Whiteman, they organized a month later as the Joint Endeavor for Welfare, Education, and Liberation (JEWEL).

The hallmark of the JEWEL was its advocacy of agricultural cooperatives and the instilling of national consciousness and pride through history lessons and a library. It sought to promote Grenadian traditions of community action by such initiatives and, almost unconsciously, advocated forms of primitive socialism. Its links with the peasantry were on a personal basis, and mushroomed through mobilization around popular grievances. Regional attention was finally arrested by a mass demonstration against an unpopular British landlord, Lord Brownlow, who blocked off access to the sea through his La Sagesse estate. Although the MAP and the JEWEL had already begun discussions on cooperation before this incident, its success prompted a merger. On 11

March 1973, the New Jewel Movement was born. At the inaugural congress on the day, the MAP delegates made clear that only a mass uprising led by an organized mass movement could seize political power; the basis of that uprising was to be JEWEL's mass support.

The nature, characteristics, and to an extent, the structure of what was to be labeled people's power, as developed by the NJM and proclaimed by it to be the cornerstone of its identification with the people—the "masses"—and they with it, had much to do with the differing philosophies and priorities of the party's two progenitors. The MAP was until the merger continuing to evolve a political philosophy and strategy, but one principle was clear: the parliamentary system was both corrupt and undemocratic. Inspired by President Julius Nyerere's *ujamaa* experiment in Tanzania, the coterie of London-trained lawyers and their followers resolved on a system of village and workers' assemblies controlled by, and answerable to, the masses. This participatory democracy would, in effect, put an end to a system by which the masses were consulted only at election time, and thereafter ignored.

Self-governance through decentralization was the goal, but this required widespread political education and mobilization, particularly in the rural heartland. For its part, the JEWEL had rediscovered and breathed new life into what had been a revolutionary force in the countryside. Long ignored by government, the black peasantry had suffered deprivation largely in silence. The fact that some 9,000 were landowners made little difference, as few farms exceeded five acres in area; they were joined by another 25,000 or so who were part-time farmers or tenants.[2] They, and the urban dispossessed, had undergone a traumatic experience when, in 1951–1952, the then young union leader Eric Gairy scored a spectacular success in organizing them and articulating their demands and frustrations. The JEWEL leadership counselled self-reliance on a cooperative basis and a determination to challenge the existing order.

The revolutionary potency of working class Grenadian society was just below the surface and ready to be exploited, so long as it was recognized that working class demands for recognition, reform, and representation had to be within the accepted constitutional and judicial order. Gairy recognized this but, craving for recognition by the lighter-skinned merchant and bureaucratic elite, he gradually distanced himself from his peasant base. The peasantry and the working class slowly lost their leadership and sense of direction. As the cancer of corruption spread to the produce marketing boards and to land titles, if the unfortunate owner was perceived to be working against the Gairyite interest, the potential for mass support was obvious.

But there it might have ended if it had not been for the independence crisis of 1973–1974. By effectively tapping the distrust with which most

Grenadians viewed a Gairy-led independence, the NJM managed to emerge as the leading opposition force in the island. Arguing that the first priority ought to be ensuring Grenada's economic viability, the NJM convened a People's Convention that met on 4 November in Seamoon and was an enormous success, attracting a crowd of 10,000 (in marked contrast to the mere 2,000 who attended a GULP rally held on the same day in St. Andrews). The convention approved a People's Indictment, which formulated twenty-seven charges against the Gairy government and called for its resignation no later than November 18.

Not surprisingly, Gairy responded in kind. During a visit to Grenville on 18 November, six members of the NJM leadership—including Maurice Bishop, Selwyn Strachan, and Hudson Austin—were arrested and brutally beaten by the police, in what later came to be known as Bloody Sunday. This was in many ways the catalyst for a nationwide repudiation of Gairy's regime, on the one hand, and for the ensuing radicalization of the NJM on the other. A broad-based group of civic organizations, the Committee of Twenty-two, was formed to protest against government repression and to demand an investigation of the whole Grenville incident. Although not a member of the committee—which included such disparate bodies as the Chamber of Commerce and the Teachers Union—the NJM became, in effect, the driving force behind a growing coalition of anti-Gairy forces.[3]

But the whole experience, and the extent of Gairy's violent reaction, pushed the NJM to far more radical positions and, two months after independence in February 1974, finally to decide that it was a Marxist-Leninist vanguard. Although the implications of this in terms of party organization, structure, and policy took some time to materialize, they represented a fundamental break from its idealist and reformist period. This break, however, was not made public, although several governments overseas suspected the motives behind the constant favorable references to Cuba. Neither did it cause any change of tactic in the struggle against Gairyism. Effective leadership, tactical skill, and, above all, popular programs enabled the NJM to assume a position denied similar parties elsewhere: that of representational participation, following the 1976 general election, as the senior partner in an opposition alliance in the House of Assembly.

By the time of the insurrection on 13 March 1979, the NJM's erstwhile partners in the People's Alliance had been outmaneuvered, the government largely discredited, and public support secured. This support had been nurtured not only by effective campaigning against Gairyism: the NJM also publicized principled positions on human rights, welfare, health, and education, all of which were under increasing threat, and set forth its policies regarding the nature and direction of future economic progress and "people's power." But it was in the latter area, perhaps the most critical for the regime's survival, that problems surfaced. The blueprint, drawn up in the idealist-reformist period, could not be carried out, as it ran against Leninist principles of organization, leadership, and control.

THE BLUEPRINT

Of all the People's Revolutionary Government's (PRG) internal policies, people's power was clearly the most visible. That the NJM's commitment to the principle was genuine cannot be doubted. It took three main forms: mass organizations, participatory democracy, and industrial democracy.

The participatory element was the most developed in the NJM's thinking before the insurrection—indeed, well before its shift to the revolutionary stage. Its conception of village-based assemblies attracted widespread interest and fired the imagination of socialists and nonsocialists alike. By comparison, industrial democracy, essentially the repeal of antiworker ordinances, was not particularly innovative; neither was the concept of mass organizations.

For socialists, the appeal of participatory democracy lay in its challenge to bourgeois conceptions of representational democracy. Popular involvement in the decisionmaking process offered a breakthrough in the struggle against corporatism, whether public or private. It also fitted the requirements of the theory of the noncapitalist path (NCP), which had been specially formulated by Marxist theoreticians to meet the conditions of developing countries. A gradualist approach toward socialism, the hallmark of the theory, was only sustainable if there was popular mobilization, political education, and public awareness in support of the revolution.

To nonsocialist idealists and libertarians, as well as to sympathetic liberals in the region and elsewhere, participatory democracy in Grenada represented a unique sociopolitical experiment. Some saw in it a resurrection of sorts of Aristotelian principles, atavistically recalling the much eulogized "supreme human association" of the lost Greek polis. Others had reservations about the full applicability of the Westminster model and its constituent myths and presumptions to little Grenada. Its small size (115 square miles) and village and smallholding population (only about 15 percent of the 90,000 population can be reasonably classified as urban) suggested that new and imaginative constitutional structures could be built. And, after the dark years of Gairyism, they, in common with the great majority of Grenadians, fully expected that once the revolution had been consolidated, participatory democracy would incorporate the legal assumptions of the Westminster model, namely a commitment to constitutionalism, judicial rights, and the rule of law.

They were encouraged in these expectations by Bishop and his associates soon after the NJM's formation. After all, the very name of Bishop's Movement for the Assemblies of the People expressed a clear and highly suggestive commitment. As Bishop explained,

> MAP was right from the start a political organization in the sense that it decided that what was required in Grenada was a political organization which could deal with the realities of seizing power from out of the hands of the Gairy regime. . . . The name . . . Assemblies of the People, relates to the political form which the movement was recommending. . . . MAP's initial position . . . was to spend a great deal of time criticizing very severely the present electoral party political system we operate. We saw the possibility of power being transferred in fact without necessarily the need for holding an election. . . . Electoral politics represents one form of politics . . . another form you can call people's politics, whereby for example people can take the road, can take to street marches and demonstrations, advocate civil disobedience, call on the Government to resign and in that way in fact make a Government dissolve. . . . Our position, based on Assemblies of the People, is that elections in the sense we now know would be replaced. . . . We envisage a system which would have village assemblies and worker's assemblies. In other words, politics where you live and politics where you work. The village assemblies would in turn elect parish assemblies and . . . also elect representatives to a National Assembly. . . . The Assembly would appoint or elect from its own members a National Assembly Council, which would in effect be the present Cabinet you have.[4]

During this extensive press interview, the scope and extent of which was never to be repeated, Bishop went on to insist that this method of participation "is much more rooted to our people than, say, going to the House and listening to Gairy talking there or going to the Senate and listening to the others talk there," citing the rural cooperative tradition in particular.

Furthermore, the 1973 manifesto ("We'll be Free in '73") had expressed much the same sentiments. People's assemblies expressed "pure democracy," involving "all the people all the time." Each assembly, and assemblies representing occupational groups, would send representatives to a National Coordinating Council of Delegates, charged with the task of replacing the present "pappy show" constitution by one reflecting "genuine aspirations and ideas about justice." Only by this, it stressed, could the fundamental rights and freedoms of the people be enforced. It made the position crystal clear:

> Let us state that we are rejecting the party system for many reasons. Firstly, parties divide the people into warring camps. Secondly, the system places power in the hands of a small ruling clique. That clique victimises and terrorizes members of the other party. Thirdly, the ruling

elite seizes control of all avenues of public information, for example the radio station, and uses them for its own ends. Finally, and most importantly, it fails to involve the people except for a few seconds once in every five years when they make an "X" on a ballot paper.[5]

Interestingly, the manifesto eschewed any ascription of political label. That was entirely consistent with its position at that time: vaguely radical and idealist-reformist.

THEORETICAL FOUNDATIONS

By the time of Bishop's interview in March 1974, he and his fellow activists had gone through an ordeal by fire, both physically and intellectually. Imprisonment, beatings, arson, and even murder was visited upon them by a vengeful Gairy. To this was added the gradual conversion to revolutionary socialism. Not surprisingly, the sterility and limitations of much of black power philosophy had become painfully obvious. Walter Rodney signaled the way out: the dispossessed, he argued, were almost invariably black. Therefore, the real holy grail was not assertiveness of racial pride but socialism. Rodney defined black power as "a movement and an ideology springing from the reality of oppression of black peoples by whites within the imperialist world as a whole."[6] His prescription—a break with "historically racist imperialism" and the assumption to power by the black masses for whom socialism was the only effective guarantee of self-determination and economic and social advance—found a ready audience in NJM meetings.

A critical factor in their incrementalist intellectual and ideological development was the return to the Caribbean of Marxist-Leninism in the guise of the theory of the noncapitalist path. Marxism had been lost to the region with the voluntary exile of such thinkers as C. L. R. James and Richard Hart, while socialists such as Gordon Lewis in Puerto Rico, let alone the more Soviet-oriented theorists in Cuba, were isolated by the continuing division imposed by colonial history. The 1975 Havana Conference of Communist Workers' Parties put the NCP at the center of the debate within the Caribbean left. It was taken up and developed with alacrity by such regional activists as Trevor Munroe, Ralph Gonsalves, and Clive Thomas—and by the New Jewel Movement leadership. Here at last was not only a logical ideological framework but also a concrete strategy.

In essence, the theory sought to justify and map out a path for Third World political elites wanting to disengage their economies from the international capitalist system by bypassing the capitalist stage on the road to socialism. It urged an incrementalist approach to revolutionary transformation, to take account of the numerical weakness of the proletariat in international capitalist-dominated economies. Central to this process, argued its Soviet progenitors, was the necessity to establish a "national democratic" regime as soon as possible after the grant of formal independence. Its primary aim would be to nip the development of capitalism in the bud and,in doing so, to establish an era of "socialist orientation." This stage would act as a springboard for the realization of the next, that of "socialist construction," when the pace of socialization of the economy would be quickened. Obviously, firm and popular leadership was necessary to weaken the bonds of capitalist dependency and to develop nationally controlled economic and political institutions, while retaining public support. The name of the regime defined this leadership: it had to be the national democratic bourgeoisie, or the progressive bourgeois elements in the intelligentsia, military, trade unions, and the economy generally. They would be nationalistic, challenging imperial penetrations and combating the *comprador* bourgeoisie, which it spawned. They would also be democratic in their clear identification with the struggles of the working class and peasantry, not only in their own society but also in the international capitalist system as a whole. In short, they would be committed socialists and would look toward the socialist world for aid and succor.

But, echoing Lenin, the Soviet theorists stressed three caveats. First, that the national democratic bourgeoisie had to lead the struggle for socialism within a multiclass alliance. Through mobilization, education, and emulation, progressive elements in other strata, notably the peasantry and the nascent proletariat, would join them. As the economy and society became more socialistic, these formerly disadvantaged strata would gradually assume dominance and, ultimately, dictatorship. The second caveat counselled against possible corruption and private accumulation. The national bourgeoisie may by definition be progressive, but they were bourgeois all the same and open to all the lures of capitalism. Coming from a life of manual ease with, in all probability, secure incomes and widespread connections with the commercial elite, the bourgeoisie carried with it a real risk of degeneration. Moreover, nobody enjoyed actively working for their own extinction, and the national democratic leadership would be no exception. Their sincerity and resoluteness of purpose, therefore, had to be absolute. But therein lay the third caveat and possibly the most important.

Overzealousness could easily lead to deviationism and "ultraleft adventurism." Gradualism was essential. There had to be a slow process of political education, while socialist policies should be implemented only at a pace that the masses could follow and support. Sudden nationalization of foreign assets could result in economic chaos, undermining the national democratic regime. Likewise with foreign relations; while the rights of sovereignty had to be upheld, an overenthusiastic embrace of socialist countries could bring retaliation and economic disruption. In short, those who, in their enthusiastic zeal, mistook the national democratic revolution for a socialist revolution and hence insisted on pressing ahead immediately with the process of socialist construction should be ignored. Ultimately, although the multiclass alliance was to continue in the stage of socialist construction, the leadership by that time would have decisively switched to the working class.[7]

The NJM constantly stressed that, within the confines of the theory, the PRG regime was wholly national democratic. Although socialist, its leaders never argued that socialism was to be established from the start: only the groundwork was to be laid. Indeed, there was scant nationalization (mostly of Gairy's assets and of public utilities), even less land reform, and practically no attempt at rural collectivization. The objective difficulties were backbreaking: the enormous social importance of property ownership to the average Grenadian stood in sharp contrast to the collectivist heritage of tribal Africa, for which the theory of noncapitalist development was originally designed. Worse was the already firm establishment of capitalism, both petty and institutional. Ultimately, socialist orientation only really became manifest in foreign policy. Within a few months of the insurrection, a "nonnegotiable" alliance was forged with Cuba, soon to be followed by a steadily increasing eulogy of all things Soviet. But even here, indelible family links and critically important trading links with centers of international capitalism—Britain, the United States, Canada, and Trinidad—could not be threatened, let alone replaced.

There was no argument, of course, that socialism meant an unambiguous commitment to the principle of human rights to work, welfare, health, education, and leisure, and, in Thomas's words, to the "wider participation of the masses in administration, defense, public order [and] justice."[8] Further, this process of democratization had to go hand in hand with a resolute fight against all dictatorial and antipopular methods of government. But in the pursuit of these worthy hallmarks of socialist democracy, the PRG found itself impaled on the horns of a dilemma.

THE CONTRADICTIONS EMERGE

In a nutshell, the idealist-reformist postures and beliefs of an earlier era had to face the reality of Leninist organization and leadership. The result was that the blueprint of people's power in general, and of participatory democracy in particular, continually changed. The decision in favor of a vanguard structure in April 1974 in many ways formalized an existing situation. Given the need for secrecy and democratic centralism as a defense against the constant harassment by Gairy's police aides, the notorious Mongoose Gang, the NJM was, in effect, a vanguard type of party. The implication, however, was that the scope for decisionmaking implied in people's power had to be severely restricted. Power had to lay unambiguously with the central party apparatus: first, the Political Bureau and, on its establishment in September 1979, the Central Committee, both successively backed up by the Organizing Committee, which monitored party discipline and oversaw the work of lower level organs. Leninist orthodoxy dictated strict control. The NJM reinforced that by an ever stricter selectivity of membership, which resulted in a small proportion of an already limited list of full members (which hovered around seventy in the last two years of the PRG regime) having to assume all the burdens of leadership and guidance. Meetings could be authorized only by the party and discussions directed only by its most dedicated cadres. Concurrent with this was an intensification of Leninism in its organization and principles.

Not surprisingly, while the institutions of people's power largely followed the blueprint, their actual operation reflected self-imposed contradictions. The "new democracy" was a commitment to an indigenous political system where, as the 1973 manifesto put it, "power . . . will be rooted in our villages and at our places of work." In other words, through a strategy of cooperative self-reliance, the masses—"our most important resource"—would realize their full potential. It is clear, then, that the manifesto projected a system whereby power flowed from the bottom up. But Leninist insistence on control by an elite cadre of revolutionaries dictated otherwise. Their leadership would ensure that the "backward" Grenadian people would gradually free themselves from imperialist dependency and move toward a new socialist society. The backwardness of Grenadian society was, not surprisingly in this vanguard context, a constantly reiterated theme. The low political consciousness of the Grenadian working classes, their poverty, and their strong adherence to religious belief—often of the messianic kind, where salvation often lay in the next world rather than this—dictated such a strategy, particularly after state power had been seized. The same backwardness also demanded that secrecy be maintained and, indeed, intensified. But not all party members were happy with this. For instance, Richard Jacobs, PRG ambassador to Cuba at the time, advised Bishop in 1980 that

> We must tell the people the *whole truth*. This involves an analysis of where we were, and are, coming from. . . . It involves a public discussion of our tactics for the ultimate victory. . . . Such an approach I know means sacrificing certain not so well kept secrets about the ideological

orientation of the leadership before, and after, our revolution. . . . But the preoccupation with secrecy of our ultimate political goal is a characteristic of opposition clandestineness which could well be considered to have outlived its usefulness.[9]

MASS ORGANIZATIONS AND INDUSTRIAL DEMOCRACY

The establishment of a monopoly of power began almost immediately after the insurrection. A memorandum to Political Bureau members in May 1979 urged the necessity "to get key members and supporters systematically into key positions . . . to watch events and enable better control by leadership."[10] The first of the mass organizations, the National Youth Organization (NYO), reflected this process. Formed out of two small youth groups in 1974, its initial links with the NJM were only at leadership level. It stressed national pride, physical fitness, and political awareness: sports events were effective in meeting all three objectives. By 1978 it came under tighter party control with the formation of the NJM Youth Committee. A year later, alleged "lumpen" elements were removed and greater emphasis was put upon political education. NYO leaders were appointed by, and reported to, the NJM Organizing Committee. As "an antiimperialist organization," according to a NYO publication, its duty was to teach youth "how imperialism as a system of exploitation is responsible for high unemployment, how it prevents them from having adequate facilities for sport and culture, how it is responsible for the poverty of our nation."[11] The creation of branches in every secondary school and village was strongly encouraged. By mid-1981, membership topped 8,000, in some 100 groups. What began as a nationalist organization aiming at instilling virtues of self-reliance among the large number of mainly unemployed youths became a Leninist style "drive belt" by which the vanguard's ideological imperatives and directions could be transmitted. But, despite a massive membership drive, membership fell to less than 4,000 two years later. Poor administration, lack of money, overrapid expansion with limited leadership, resentment against authoritarian control by zealots, anger at the detention without trial of young Rastas and "lumpen elements," and erratic political education campaigns were all factors contributing to the decline.

Much the same experience characterized the National Women's Organization. Formed in December 1977, it had a restricted membership but, three years later, assumed a mass character. However, central control was even more pronounced than with the NYO, with the same small leadership that headed the newly formed Ministry for Women's Affairs. Membership peaked at 6,500 in 155 branches in mid-1982, but actual activity was decidedly patchy. In its earlier days it was especially valuable in identifying need, distributing cooking oil and flour to the needy, supporting primary schools, and organizing nutrition and child-care lessons; also, with the NYO, it was active in the National House Repair program and the Center for Popular Education, whose adult literacy campaigns attracted international attention and critical praise. The other mass organizations—the Productive Farmer's Union, National Students' Council, and the very small Young Pioneers—were far less important and effective. The militia was in a different category of mass organization, and through its auspices over 3,500 received military instruction. But that too declined in appeal. Organization was lacking, despite officer training sessions by Cuban civil defense experts, and constant sentry duty held little interest.

On the industrial front, the repeal of anti-trade-union legislation led to a 50 percent jump in union membership by October 1979. Recalcitrant employers found a determined government, and in general wages and conditions did not suffer as the world recession deepened. By 1981, this proworker philosophy was highlighted by proposals for institutionalized industrial democracy. Production committees with joint management and union representation were to be established in every workplace. Deputy Prime Minister Bernard Coard was especially keen on this, viewing it as a "viable alternative to public ownership in the short to medium term."[12] Responsible for drafting, discussing, and operationalizing work plans and monitoring management to prevent "abuse of power," these committees were to be paralleled by disciplinary, education, and emulation committees. The latter, said Coard, would set productivity targets "and devise and organize brotherly and sisterly competition," rewarding the efforts of "exemplary workers."[13] But very few were in any form of existence by October 1983, particularly because of the relatively small size of most Grenadian enterprises, which are often family operated. Discussions took place within the Ministry of National Mobilization—formed in August 1981—on the possibility of establishing networks of committees over several similar workplaces, but nothing was done. In the public sector, the principle was used to justify work plans (which non-NJM section heads heartily endorsed for their subordinates) and compulsory political education periods (which they did not). Resentment at the latter by many civil servants led to a threat of dismissal. Attempts at similar education by trade unions were equally unsuccessful. "The emphasis on the ideological development of the workers has not shown any improvement," complained one Central Committee member, and "a lot of people fall asleep."

Another problem in implementing industrial democracy was that trade unions, even when led by NJM members, rigorously pursued their members' interests in the tradition of West Indian unionism. They complained about the pay and conditions of the many non-Grenadian "internationalist" workers who worked for the PRG. Strikes for higher pay in the public sector also took place.

PEOPLE'S POWER IN THE PARISHES

The most significant manifestation of people's power, though, was the parish and rural councils. And although in the early part of PRG rule the institutions were established and initially enjoyed wide support, the ultimate failure of participatory democracy was the most dramatic. It experienced most of the same problems that undermined the mass organizations, but there was one central underlying reason for failure: they had no power and no direct role in the decisionmaking system. What, nonetheless, was the structure?

Previous to, and immediately after, the insurrection, the NJM relied upon mass rallies and on regional work conducted by parish-based NJM branches. By mid-1979, the PRG decided to revive the long-defunct parish councils, to be led by the party branches. Parish councils were established, exclusive to members and supporters. By the end of the year, however, participation was open to all. Each of the seven councils was headed by a Central Committee member or nominee. The meetings were to enable local people to discuss policy with the PRG leadership and civil servants. Such was their popularity that, by late 1980, each was subdivided into village-based zonal councils. Each zonal council reported to its parish council, which channeled opinions to the national level via the NJM party branch. In practice, due to the relatively small number of activists involved, often the same people filled leadership posts at zonal, parish, and party branch levels. Parish councils had residual duties, announced as discussion forums for local workers and women, but this only duplicated the work of local trade union and NWO branches. Thirty-six zonal councils eventually emerged; like the parish councils, none had any legal standing.

In fact, both parish and zonal councils became significantly less important by mid-1982. Coordination of their work with the mass organizations, the militia and, the trade unions, was through village coordinating bureaus (VCBs). The VCBs became the most important link between party and countryside. Its delegates, together with those from the councils and the mass organizations, came together regularly as a National Conference of Delegates. But this only happened twice, each time to discuss the annual budget. Although heavily publicized, these only lasted one day, since all prior discussion on the draft was deemed to have taken place. As an "internationalist" worker enthusiastically recorded, "Today in Grenada, Parliament has moved out of towns into the communities. Government has escaped . . . and spread into community centers, school buildings, street corners, marketplaces, factories, farms and workplaces around the country. Political power has been taken out of the hands of a few privileged people and turned over to thousands of men, women and youth . . . in every nook and cranny of Grenada, Carriacou and Petit Martinique."[14]

Popular enthusiasm for the councils was strong; that the structure had to be dramatically expanded is proof enough. In the early days, meetings were relatively informal, with a high degree of spontaneity. True to West Indian tradition, most would start late but then could last for several hours. Formality, in the form of agendas and time limits for discussion, crept in by mid-1980. Senior officials often offered themselves voluntarily for questioning in the early days of the experiment, but as time wore on, it became up to the councils to request attendance, which became progressively less forthcoming. By late-1981, this aspect of the councils' proceedings became relatively uncommon, except when there was a particular issue that the PRG wanted to explain and discuss, notably the budget. It was left to party members to explain policy.

Meetings sometimes split up into "workshops," to enable detailed discussion on a number of issues and to encourage local residents to speak up. Some of these meetings were recorded by the PRG in a publication, *To Construct from Morning*, detailing how the "people's budget" was determined. The zonal council of St. George's South East was attended by 250 people, who were divided into three groups: women, youth, and trade unionists and other workers, each to discuss items of specific interest; forty resolutions emerged. Another at the birch Grove Roman Catholic school attracted 100 people, and twenty-nine resolutions were passed, including one calling for a reduction of food for prisoners and detainees. Some resolutions were vague: "cut out waste and corruption," "make use of local herbs" (but higher fines for *ganja* smoking), and organize "seminars for road workers." The meeting at Concord had thirty-six resolutions; the one at St. Patrick's, thirty-five, including "produce more food" and "serious road drivers to manners slack road workers."[15] Personal attendance at five council meetings in mid-1981 and mid-1982 confirmed the impression conveyed by the official commentary: that sessions were lively and earnest but that there was considerable difficulty in focusing discussion on specific issues and to any depth. At Grand Bay in May 1981, for instance, over forty issues were raised by some seventy participants, in addition to those officially introduced. While some were, as noted, vague, others were specific and reflected local experience and common sense. There were many useful suggestions on how to improve agricultural production, the marketing of locally produced goods, such as those from the new agroindustrial plant, and the growing of import substitutes. In his March 1982 budget presentation, Coard happily reported that "we have tried to deliberately scoop the ideas and opinions of literally every section of the economy, leaving nothing to chance or guesswork. What we found as a result of all these sessions was an amazing commonality of opinion being expressed in all the villages of our country. People in Tivoli were making the same basic points as those in St. George's, Gouyave was echoing St. David's."[16]

The party and government did note popular preferences and priorities. As Coard explained,

> The positive benefit of the council meetings is twofold. First, we have been able to utilize local knowledge to see where improvements can be made and where our development should be directed, and that is worth more than any of the highly profitable investment surveys operated by the capitalist development agencies as a substitute for action. Second, we have a feedback regarding policy implementation which allows us to fine-tune. A benefit of a different kind is that many of our slogans come from the councils. Our people love slogans.[17]

The meetings were also important for political education purposes. The formation of the Ministry of National Mobilization, self-proclaimed the "people's ministry," encouraged and accelerated the process. A particular feature by 1982 was the role of "internationalist" workers and foreign sympathizers. They were invited to speak and, although their contributions were mainly limited to fraternal greetings, they often backed party members in explaining what they saw as the nature of imperialism and in urging vigilance against counterrevolution. By 1983, the emphasis in political education generally appeared to be biased toward this. No doubt it reflected the fears of U.S. destabilization and invasion, with well-publicized naval maneuvers being conducted around Grenada and occasionally in sight of the island. Central to such discussions were both denunciations of the Reagan Doctrine, which undermined progressive regimes, and support for socialist allies, notably Cuba and the Soviet Union, and progressive movements overseas fighting imperialism and racism, as in Nicaragua and Angola. By contrast, socialist theory generally took second place, the exception being a constant stress on the need for cooperative agriculture. But communalization was rarely touched upon; the sensitivity of this and associated goals was rationalized by "a lack of suitable texts" or that it was "inappropriate to discuss at this stage."

It would be true to say that the emphasis upon imperialism in political education partly explained declining popular enthusiasm, which by mid-1983 turned to outright hostility. Several party members and participants reported sharp exchanges over the harm being done by the PRG's anti-American policy. Declining U.S. tourist numbers and denial of U.S. aid could not be made up by the tiny number of Eastern bloc visitors permitted to visit Grenada, while Soviet and Cuban trade involved barter and aid, often in the form of unreliable equipment. The aloofness of the strictly segregated Soviet technicians and teachers was unfavorably commented upon, as was the shooting down by the Soviet Air Force of a South Korean jumbo jet. But the fundamental issue was Leninism.

Party power and control manifested itself in the councils' operations in two ways. First, however useful their suggestions, their output remained at that level. The system was for explanation of policy, mobilization of support, political education, and the defense of the revolution in general terms. At no point could, or was, policy challenged, let alone changed; neither could council delegates to higher organs debate priorities. They were there to ask questions and to approve. In other words, the councils were excluded from the decisionmaking process. To a postrevolution commentator, the deliberation of the councils "in fact resulted only in the compilation of a wish list." As regards the budget,

> What these meetings represented was only the first step in the process of budget revision. It is only after the desires of the population are articulated that the real process of politics—self-governance—gets under way. In any society it is easy enough to provide an inventory of needs and good ideas. Politics begins when priorities among these needs and good ideas must be established. . . . Politics, like economics, is concerned with how much of one thing a community is willing to give up in order to gain something else.[18]

In fact, most of the meetings specifically concerned with the budget were called only a month or so before presentation through a detailed publication to the National Conference of Delegates. So, while earlier meetings might have been the first step (although they were not directed specifically at the budget process), the ones called for the purpose had proposals already decided upon explained by officials, who put them into more readily understood language.

The second manifestation of Leninism was the stress, after 1981 in particular, on selectivity of membership. This effectively prevented the emergence of leadership at all levels below the Central Committee. In July 1979, the membership structure of the Communist Party of the Soviet Union was introduced. Three categories were formally established: full member, candidate, and applicant. A fourth was informally added later, that of potential applicant. There was among some zealots even a suggestion for a fifth, prospective potential applicant. Devotion to duty had to be absolute, and apprenticeships became virtually indefinite. During 1983, only five candidates became full members. At the time of the revolution's collapse, there were but 72 full members, 94 candidates, and 180 applicants.[19] There were, in other words, simply not enough people to provide the leadership of the kind of state the PRG actually wanted. Furthermore, neither the participatory democracy system nor any other aspects of "people's power" could challenge the membership of the Central Committee. In that respect, the NJM was indeed undemocratic. The leaders were, in a real sense, self-appointed, although it was insisted that they had been confirmed in their role by popular acclaim at the Seamoon Congress in 1973. The first congress was planned for 1985 to ratify a party constitution; some drafting of this had begun in 1978, but work was suspended until late 1982 as events overtook it the following year. It was planned that party policy and Central Committee membership would be reconfirmed on that occasion.

Self-governance through debate, dialogue, and discussion in the decisionmaking process was further blocked by the PRG's persistent refusal to hold elections. Although they were promised immediately after Gairy's overthrow, the position of the PRG was summarized in the words of PRG minister and cofounder of MAP, Kendrick Radix: "elections are not an issue . . . people now see a lot of change, bases on the roads, the airport, free education. Whenever the masses want elections, they'll get them."[20] For some time, regional opinion was appeased by the lack of an electoral list. But offers to help construct one were rebuffed and, in any event, People's Law No. 20 (1979), which was drafted as the legal basis for enumeration, was withdrawn and never gazetted. Ironically, if an election had been held, especially in the first few months of the regime, the NJM would have won a very handsome victory. But, as a vanguard party, the NJM had eschewed "the dysfunctional elitist and alienated structures that were inherited from British colonialism . . . (and other) crippling undemocratic institutions of the decrepit and exploitative structures of the past."[21] It followed that elections could only take place once a new constitution for Grenada had been drafted and approved by a referendum. Notes in Bishop's handwriting suggest this would be in December 1986, the constitution to take effect the following March, presidential elections (Grenada was throughout PRG rule a monarchy) by about December 1989, and elections to a National Assembly by December 1990, in time for the Second Party Congress.[22]

THE ATTEMPT AT REVIVAL

The strengthening of the village coordinating bureaus was a tacit admission of the difficulties of the partycentric strategy and the lack of leadership through the selectivity process. When Coard assumed the chairmanship of the Central Committee during Bishop's absence in September 1983, he characteristically got to the point. He urged decentralization and an emphasis more upon workplace and class interest than territorial activism. The shortage of committed activists at the local level stemmed, he judged, from an "insufficient confidence in the masses" by members. The result was multiple membership by a few of all the various constituents of "people's power," which begged the question of "how many leaders a village has." He proposed, to widespread approval, a two-tier structure pending the creation of new institutions, as and when "scientifically and materially" justified. The first was a strengthening of the seven parish councils, which would become party institutions, headed by a Central Committee member living in the parish. In short, he echoed Munroe's advice to the Workers Party of Jamaica, namely that members "should merge, but not submerge, with the masses."[23]

The second tier was to ensure a greater and more real public involvement through the VCBs. Their functions would be broadened, although no thought was given to how these would either overlap or duplicate those of the constituent bodies—the zonal councils and the local branches of the mass organization—that they were meant to coordinate. Nonetheless, Phyllis Coard looked forward to their having a positive role.

> The Bureaus should be bodies that the entire population should relate to, whether they support the Party or not, and anyone who wanted to can become a member. This will help incorporate the stronger elements in the village into the nucleus of local government. [They] will have no party function. The village council will also evolve into a state body to monitor, supervise, control and ensure the implementation of the revolution and state on how it affects the village and the community. They must have no party function but the Party should function inside them, to supervise and guide them.[24]

As before, she added, the village (zonal) councils could "manners bureaucrats" and undertake "house-to-house" mobilization. Ultimately, it was forecast that the bureaus would evolve into executive bodies "with committees and commissions to do the work in all areas, for example, water, health and housing." There was a note of caution, however. The party had to ensure that "the bourgeois be kept from these bodies because they will seek control." Phyllis Coard said that this would be handled by invitations issued by the parish chairman (i.e., Central Committee member), based upon a percentage, "giving the majority to the working class." By that method, both party and class interest would have been satisfied: but the seed of further contradiction would have been sown if the revolution had been allowed to continue.

CONCLUSION

It is ironic that Bernard Coard, widely denigrated as the arch-Leninist who galvanized opposition against the allegedly more pragmatic Maurice Bishop, was the one most clearly conscious of the need for meaning-ful popular participation. He and his supporters realized, too late, that the blueprint had become unworkable.Not only had the rules of the game changed once state power was achieved, but the strict application of Leninist doctrine ensured constant movement of the goalposts. The revised blueprint discussed just a month before the invasion tried to address seriously the problem of reconciling participation and party control and direction.

But although the massacre of Bishop and his supporters, and the subsequent invasion, ensured that nobody would ever know whether the "new democracy" would ever become a reality, it can safely be assumed that it would have not. Democracy in the original MAP sense meant self-governance and popular involvement in a decentralized deci-sionmaking system. But the MAP had been elitist, and its leadership had to rely upon another group, JEWEL, for linkages to the masses. As centralization grew apace, so a paternalistic socialism emerged, capped by an authoritarian and undemocratic core, where dissent could, and was, met with severe punishment, as Bishop himself was to experience. Paternalism, as Jay Mandle points out, rules out a dialogue among equals. "The leading party acts as if it were a signatory to a social contract [where] mutual responsibilities and benefits are implicitly defined. In exchange for the people ceding to the party the responsibility to govern, the party promises to implement policies which would be benevolent and supportive of the welfare of the population."[25]

In other words, the party embodied the people's aspirations and interests, which it contracted to advance, especially in the welfare field. To pursue these interests and social goals, mobilization and education by a firm leadership was necessary. And as this leadership's priorities and aspirations were of the people, there could be no questioning of basic policy. In any case, as Bishop's Line of March speech made clear, the leadership was "way, way ahead" and "much more politically and ideologically developed" than the masses, who had to be led to a new life and consciousness. Further, the mandate derived from the dialectic forces of history, which only correct class analysis revealed. The forces were predetermined and, once understood, could be operationalized. In this momentous unfolding, the party had to be in strict control.

But, ultimately, any regime depends upon a modicum of public support. Secrecy had hidden the true nature of the regime's goals from the people, and support was based on tangible benefits and Bishop's magnetism and charisma. When the economy soured in 1983 and wel-fare benefits were cut, attempts to mobilize support by more sloganizing by activists became embarrassingly less successful. True to established pattern, the public at large were kept resolutely in ignorance of the one issue that ultimately overwhelmed the party and the leadership, that of joint leadership. No wonder, then, the outburst of emotion when it was known that the people's folk hero, Bishop—who few thought of as a Marxist—was under arrest. His rescue by thousands was, in essence, the only exercise in genuine people's power, albeit one that ended in tragedy. Perhaps the last word should go to Fidel Castro, who all in the NJM leadership admired without hesitation. "We will be the vanguard, not because of what we think of ourselves, but because of what the people think of us."[26]

NOTES

1. Tony Thorndike, *Grenada: Politics, Economics, and Society* (Boulder: Lynne Rienner, 1985), pp. 23–24.

2. George Brizan, *The Grenadian Peasantry and Social Revolution, 1931–1951,* ISER Working Paper 21 (Mona, Jamaica: University of the West Indies, 1979), p. 6.

3. For a more detailed discussion of this period, see David Lewis, *Reform and Revolution in Grenada, 1950 to 1981* (Havana: Casa de las Américas, 1984).

4. "Interview with Maurice Bishop," *Trinidad Express,* 10 Mar. 1974. An extended version appeared in the *Caribbean Monthly Bulletin* (Puerto Rico) 8 (Mar. 1974).

5. New Jewel Movement Manifesto, Mar. 1973, p. 9.

6. Walter Rodney, *The Groundings with My Brothers* (London: Bogle D'Ouverture, 1969), p. 28.

7. R. A. Ulyanovsky, *Socialism and the Newly Independent Nations* (Moscow: Progress Publishers, 1974), pp. 440–49.

8. C. Y. Thomas, " 'The Non-Capitalist Path' as Theory and Practice of Decolonization and Social Transformation," *Latin American Perspectives* 5 (1978), p. 19.

9. Maurice Bishop, *Line of March for the Party* speech, in Michael Ledeen and Herbert Romerstein, eds., *Grenada Documents: An Overview and Selection,* vol. 1 (Washington, D.C.: Depts. of State and Defense, 1984), pp. 1–17; 1–48. Hereafter, this volume is referred to as *Grenada Documents.*

10. Quoted in Gregory Sandford, *The New Jewel Movement: Grenada's Revolution, 1979–1983* (Washington, D.C.: Foreign Service Institute, U.S. Department of State, 1985), p. 197.

11. *Grenada Documents:* Document GD 002378, Memorandum: Some Proposals Arising from Today's Meeting (handwritten), May 1979.

12. Basic Training Course for NYO Recruitment, undated, quoted in Sandford, *New Jewel Movement,* p. 98.

13. Personal interview, June 1982.

14. *To Construct from Morning: Making the People's Budget in Grenada* (St. George's, Grenada: People's Revolutionary Government, 1982), p. 30.

15. *Is Freedom We Making* (St. George's, Grenada: People's Revolutionary Government, 1981), p. 30.

16. *To Construct from Morning,* pp. 36–51.

17. Ibid., p. 10.

18. Personal interview, June 1982.

19. Jay Mandle, *Big Revolution, Small Country: The Rise and Fall of the Grenada Revolution* (Lanham, Md.: North-South, 1985), pp. 61–62.

20. Quoted in Michael Massing, "Grenada Before and After," *Atlantic Monthly,* Feb. 1984, p. 79.

21. *To Construct from Morning,* p. 10.

22. Document GD 001899, quoted in Sandford, *New Jewel Movement,* p. 102.

23. Trevor Munroe, *The Working Class Party: Principles and Standards* (Kingston, Jamaica: Vanguard, 1981), p. 48.

24. *Grenada Documents:* Central Committee Minutes, 28 Sept. 1983, p. 6.

25. Mandle, *Big Revolution, Small Country,* p. 53.

26. Fidel Castro, *Second Congress of the Communist Party of Cuba, December 1980* (Havana: Government of Cuba, 1980), p. 16.

2. Socialism and Cultural Transformation in Grenada

Paget Henry

G RENADA'S EXPERIMENT with socialism, though brief, has posed a number of important challenges to the theories often used to explain the institutions of the English-speaking Caribbean. Kept within the capitalist orbit by centuries of colonial domination, regional theorists have only recently begun to confront socialist realities. Consequently, the rather sudden appearance of a revolutionary socialist regime in Grenada was a development that took political practice several steps beyond regional academic theorizing. The inability of old theories to deal with the new reality has been apparent in economics, in politics, in culture—in short, in every major institutional area.

This chapter is an attempt to assess the significance of this socialist experience for theories of Caribbean cultural systems. The assessment begins with the claim that the experience of decolonization had already made existing theories of regional cultural systems obsolete. Thus, the second step in the argument is a brief outline of a more appropriate model. The third is a brief analysis of the nationalist period, while the fourth provides a detailed analysis of the cultural changes of the socialist period, including the new forms of cultural organization, the new patterns of legitimating state authority, and the changes in collective identity that this socialist experiment produced. At the same time, I attempt to situate these changes within the broader framework of cultural change in socialist societies. This comparative perspective will allow us to see the trends and conditions that were peculiar to Grenada and those that were shared with other socialist countries.

In the concluding section, I suggest that the changes described and analyzed here took place within an overall framework that was shaped by two opposing tendencies. The first was the determined effort to end bourgeois domination of the cultural system and to make the culture of the masses more central to the system. The second was the equally strong effort to increase state control over the system. This I argue is a characteristic that Grenada shared with other socialist countries and was related to the special conditions of legitimating socialist states. The tension between these two opposing tendencies, along with a persistent attachment to prerevolutionary traditions, became the sources of new crisis tendencies. These were all phenomena that previous theories of Caribbean cultural systems did not have to confront.

CARIBBEAN CULTURAL SYSTEMS:
A THEORETICAL ANALYSIS

Existing theories of Caribbean cultural systems fall into three broad categories: The Africanist theories, such as those of Herskovits and Jahn; pluralist theories, such as those of M. G. Smith and Nettleford; and the reticulated theories, such as those of R. T. Smith and Despres.[1] Unlike current theories of Caribbean economic and political systems, these theories were originally formulated prior to the decolonization of the region. Thus many of the political, social, and economic assumptions upon which they rest are more reflective of the late colonial period than of the postcolonial situation. The impact of processes such as unionization, political enfranchisement, the decline of ritual, the decreases in classism and racism, which were characteristic of the postcolonial period, have continued to accentuate this gap. Consequently, the study of Caribbean cultural systems is undergoing a paradigmatic crisis, as the major theories all rest on assumptions that are in need of radical revision or replacement. The tension that this crisis has created with the newer paradigms in economics and political science can be seen in the more recent works of Nettleford and M. G. Smith.[2]

It is therefore necessary to recast the conceptual framework in which regional cultural systems have been studied. Both as a preface to our analysis of the Grenadian case and as a step toward this conceptual shift, the remainder of this section will be devoted to three theoretical exercises. The first is an attempt to redefine the cultural system so that it is more reflective of the contemporary situation. The second is a respecification of the culture-society problematic, which will provide us with a common framework for analyzing the various periods of the Grenadian case. And the third introduces the notion of cultural crisis tendencies.

Among anthropologists, culture has often been defined as the total way of life of a people. Not surprisingly, this view has influenced regional theorists, many of whom have been anthropologists. However, from a sociological standpoint, the level of institutional differentiation characteristic of modern societies makes this definition somewhat inappropriate. Given the clearly differentiated concepts of the state and the economy found in the social science literature of the region, an equally differentiated concept of the cultural system is called for. Toward this end, I suggest that we define the cultural system as the set of signifying systems through which the symbolic resources of a society (meaning and information) are produced, stored, and communicated. In other words, the differentiating criterion here is the production in sign systems (science, music, religion, philosophy, etc.) of meaning or information as opposed to the production of goods. On this basis, the cultural system can be identified by its primary concern with signifying and the developing of new signs systems. Economic and political systems also make use of signs; but the production of signs is not their central objective. The same, I would argue, is true of the family, which should be considered in a category by itself. Table 2.1 summarizes the very components of the cultural system emerging from this approach.

Specified in this way, we now have a limited area of society to examine, an area that has its own institutions, patterns of internal organization, and means of production. But, as we have analytically separated it from the larger society, the relations between the two must be examined.

At the level of particular signifying systems such as literature, music, religion, and philosophy, it is customary to establish a figural or symbolic relationship between culture and society. Thus works in these areas are often viewed as interpretations, reflections, symptoms, and symbolic resolutions of societal tensions. But, in addition to these symbolic relationships, there are a number of more functional relationships that derive from societal demands on the cultural system as a whole. For our purposes, it will be sufficient to identify three crucial external constraints, to which cultural systems must respond as they pursue internal goals: (1) the legitimacy demands of the dominant classes and the state; (2) the information needs of the production system; and (3) the identity-maintaining needs of the population. In other words, while cultural systems are engaged in pedagogic, creative, and self- reproductive activities, they must also aid in the reproduction of the social order.

For the purposes of this chapter, the most important of these relations is the first one. The importance of this relationship lies in the fact that legitimacy constitutes "the ultimate grounds for the 'validity' of a domination."[3] The need for validity in this context raises the issue of justification, which in turn raises the issue of legitimating arguments

Table 2.1
A Model of Grenada's Cultural System

Languages	*Beliefs*	*Knowledge Production*	*Arts*
English	Religion	Education	Mass communications
Grenadian Creole	Ideology	Research	Fine arts

supplied by the cultural system. In other words, the exercise of power or the institutionalization of privilege rest in part on social norms, beliefs, or claims that are in need of justification. These arguments are usually supplied by the cultural system and have the ability to ground the authority of dominant elites. Because of this ability, legitimacy may be viewed as a form of symbolic power and, thus, as a strategic resource in the accumulation of power by elites. The power of legitimacy is symbolic in that the consent to authority it generates is not the product of coercion but results from the demonstration in language of the rational bases for the acceptance of authority and social inequality.

This concept of legitimacy as symbolic power has to be distinguished from and supplemented by the concept of symbolic violence. Bourieu and Passeron define the latter as the imposing of a meaning while at the same time "concealing the power relations which are the bases of its force."[4] Here, acceptance is affected through the systematic distortion of accepted patterns of discourse and argumentation, in the effort to justify the claim to privilege or authority. Like physical violence, symbolic violence is an unstable instrument in that it tends to generate resistance. But it does have the ability to aid the grounding of authority and, consequently, is also an important resource in the accumulation strategies of elites.

In sum, the demands for symbolic power and symbolic violence generated by the class structure and the political system establish an extremely important link between the cultural system and the larger society. Maintaining adequate supplies of the appropriate arguments and discouraging or containing the growth of inappropriate ones thus become important aspects of relations between the state and the cultural system. In the language of modernization theory, this entire process can be viewed as the creating of a relevant and supportive political culture, through appropriating and reworking the signifying activities of the cultural system.

Implicit in all this is the relative autonomy of the cultural system. This autonomy rests upon the institutionally differentiated nature of the system and on the signifying or semiotic aspects of cultural production. As a result, cultural systems have internal dynamics that may be sources of crisis tendencies. Thus, such tendencies may arise at the level of particular signifying systems, such as the current crisis of the anthropologically oriented studies of Caribbean cultural systems, because of widening gaps between established formulations in these systems and actual reality. Similarly, crisis tendencies can arise as a result of conflicts between sectors or subsectors of the cultural system: one language against another, one religion against another, science against religion, religion against art—all conflicts with significant crisis potential.

But our primary concern will be with the crises that derive from the external relations that involve the cultural system in the reproduction of the larger society. We noted above that the semiotic aspects of cultural production give it a degree of autonomy, making it thus not completely reducible to the more instrumental logics of the state and the economy. However, in spite of this relative autonomy, our discussion of the relationship between culture and society indicated that there were areas of cultural production that have been instrumentally appropriated and subjected to the needs of economic and political reproduction.

Crises in these areas are the result of interruptions in the exchange of resources between the cultural system and the larger society. As Habermas puts it, crises in these areas arise when "normative structures change, according to their inherent logic, in such a way that the complementarity between the requirements of the state apparatus and the occupation system, on the one hand, and the interpreted needs and legitimate expectations of members of the society, on the other, is disturbed."[5]

This general principle can be illustrated with regard to the state. The interruption of needed supplies of legitimacy often occurs when the delivery of expected resources from the state has either been unsatisfactory or simply not forthcoming. This interruption may take the form of a decrease in support for justifying arguments or an increase in the production of delegitimating arguments. Both can erode the power of a regime and initiate a crisis of political accumulation.

Crisis tendencies of a different nature can develop as a result of imbalances between culturally shaped expectations and the demands of the occupational system. Crises of this type have been endemic to Caribbean societies. If the demand for trained personnel is not being adequately met, interruptions will occur in the process of economic accumulation, which may in turn generate demands for educational reform. Similarly, if the economic rewards to trained labor do not meet culturally shaped expectations, both legitimacy and labor may be withdrawn. Thus, the educational subsector must meet both the reproductive needs of capital accumulation and the professional aspirations of the people. In short, because of the instrumentalized and exchange-oriented nature of the links that define the relationship between culture and society, interruptions in any of these can be the source of important crisis tendencies.

Using this framework, the pluralist and postpluralist phases of the Grenadian cultural system will be analyzed. To do this, we will conceptualize the latter in terms of the sectoral model diagramed earlier. What political formations did this cultural system have to supply with legitimacy? There were basically three such formations: the colonial, the liberal nationalist, and the socialist. Each of these had their own special set of cultural and symbolic requirements and their own impact on the

Grenadian cultural system. In the following sections, we will attempt to show that the pluralist phase was largely a response to the legitimacy needs of the colonial state, while the current phase of formal dominance by a dependent Afro-Caribbean cultural system has emerged in part as a response to the legitimacy demands of the liberal-nationalist and socialist states.

CULTURE, COLONIZATION, AND PERIPHERAL CAPITALISM

The transition to a modern society via capitalist reorganization is often a violent and socially disruptive process. Barrington Moore divides these transition processes into two groups: those that were a part of revolutions from above and those that were a part of bourgeois revolutions.[6] Examples of the former are Germany, Turkey, and Japan, while England, France, and the United States are examples of the latter. Countries such as Grenada, which came to modernity via peripheral capitalism, are closer to the first group. That is, although the transition was carried out by bourgeois elements, it was an external imposition from above.

In spite of these differences, capitalist revolutions from above share a number of features. First, they are undertaken by relatively independent fractions of the dominant class. Second, they usually involve a reorganization of the state and the class structure to facilitate new forms of surplus extraction and international competition. In this reorganization, not only are the balances of power between the classes reset, but some classes may be eliminated. For example, in the case of Japan, the Meiji Revolution centralized the Japanese state, reorganized the economic foundations of the dominant landed classes (the *diamyo*), eliminated the *samurai* class, created a new class of landlords, and contained peasant rebellions.[7] In other words, capitalist modernization via elite revolutions involves the institutionalization of new political structures as well as new patterns of class inclusion and class exclusion, which will more firmly secure the economic and political positions of the revolutionary elite in the modern period.

In Grenada, a similar pattern of elite-oriented reorganization marked the early phases of the transition to peripheral capitalism. Thus a centralized authoritarian political system was set up, and attempts were made to convert the indigenous population into the labor force of the new agricultural economy. Because the latter project was not successful, Africans were imported to meet the demand for labor. Thus the social revolution that gave birth to peripheral capitalism in Grenada established a colonial state, created a European landed elite, a supportive middle class of bureaucrats and merchants, a class of African workers, and eliminated the noncooperative indigenous population.

Whether we are speaking of Japan or Grenada, such major shifts in the patterns of political and social organization must be accompanied by equally dramatic changes in the relation between culture and society. The cultural system has to make available new sets of legitimating arguments if it is to play an active role in the ongoing reproduction of the new order. This relationship between social inequality and the use of cultural symbolism is a well-established one, and the Hindu caste system of India is a prime example of it.

In particular, colonial Grenada needed a cultural system that would legitimate external authority, external control of the economy, the enslavement of Africans, the elimination of the indigenous population, and the position of the middle class. But, as their actions derived little justification from the cultural systems of colonized groups, the colonial state started with major legitimacy deficits. To compensate for these, it had to substitute both physical and symbolic violence. The latter took the form of interpretations of sociopolitical reality, which relied on a supposed European superiority, Britain's civilizing mission, and racism and classism more generally—all crucial elements of the political culture needed by the colonial state.

This attempt to force legitimating responses from the cultural systems of the colonized resulted in two broad policy strategies by the colonial elites. As Fanon points out, the first was a policy of violent suppression that prevailed throughout the slavery period.[8] Its primary aims were to silence delegitimating responses and to unify the system under colonial control. This policy provided the basic framework in which African and European cultures were brought together in a hierarchical system that reflected the new class arrangements. At the conclusion of this period of suppression, several subsectors of the African cultural system had been eliminated, leaving in place only a poor replica of the original.

The second policy strategy, reaching well into the postslavery period, was that of limited assimilation. Its primary aim was to inculcate the new interpretation of sociopolitical reality and their justifications. Earlier experiences had shown that such a shift could further stabilize the social order. By this time a mulatto middle class had emerged between the European upper class and the African working class. Thus the plural features that were to be the basis of M. G. Smith's theory were now very much in evidence. The effects of the new policy were most evident in the religious and educational subsectors of what was now an Afro-Caribbean cultural system. The former subsector was subjected to a new round of systematic Christianization, while the latter was reorganized around a system of primary education. Through the firm administrative control of these two subsectors, the dominant sociopolitical and religious interpretations were inculcated, eventually becoming institutionalized parts of the Afro-Caribbean cultural system. This eased but did not eliminate the legitimacy problems of the colonial state.

In other words, the centralized but ethnically stratified cultural system of postslavery Grenada was the product of a long period of imposed meanings and forced reorganization by colonizing elites. The latter made these changes as they established a peripheral form of capitalism in Grenada. As Smith points out, the cultural system that emerged from this reorganization was a multilayered one, which bore all the marks of the context of its birth and the new systems of privilege and authority that it would have to legitimate.[9]

It consisted of three basic strata. At the top was a Euro-Caribbean stratum, primarily English and French in orientation. At the bottom was an Afro-Caribbean layer, which was primarily African in orientation but was increasingly absorbing European views. Finally, in the middle there was a mulatto stratum, which was a mixture of the other two. Cultural differences reinforced race and class hierarchies, helping to provide the social order with needed symbolic support.

The linguistic sector of the Afro-Caribbean layer included Grenadian Creole and standard English. The former is a pidgin language spoken by the majority of Grenadians. Its vocabulary is now largely English with some French, African, and Indian words; its syntax is a unique blend of African and European rules of speech. Standard English was systematically introduced with the establishing of primary education after slavery. It is spoken competently by only a small proportion of Afro-Grenadians. However, it is the language with the higher social status and the important social functions, such as those of administration and formal instruction. This sector is thus bilingual in structure, with a hierarchy between the languages that both reflects and reinforces the hierarchical patterns of the society.

As far as the belief sector is concerned, the religious subsector is bicultural in makeup—a mixture of African and European religions, in which the latter is now predominant. Grenada was originally a French colony, and the imposition of Christianity began comparatively early as mandated by the terms of the Code Noir of 1685. Similar policies were later pursued by the British without being able to dislodge the predominance of Catholicism established by the French.

In spite of these efforts to replace African religions, however, they continued to exist and recreate themselves. So, in addition to Christianity, this subsector was also characterized by the worship of Shango, and the practice of African magic (*obeah*). Shango was of course the Yoruba god of Thunder and War. He was a primary symbol of the tragic hero who brought troubles on himself through his own somewhat rash actions. Other gods in the African pantheon did not survive the policies of Christianization. Colonial reorganization thus radically transformed the religious subsector of the Afro-Caribbean layer, making it predominantly Christian.

Similar transformations occurred in the ideological subsector. African traditions of kings, courts, chiefs, subchiefs, and the ideologies that legitimated them had to be eliminated. Their place had to be taken by the colonial state and the imperial monarch, along with the racist ideologies that supported them. Thus even more than African religions, African ideologies were victims of high levels of symbolic violence as they represented more direct threats to the illegitimate domination upon which the colonial state rested.

However, these attempts to monopolize the production of ideologies were not completely successful. Just as they reinterpreted Christianity, Afro-Grenadians reinterpreted elements of the colonial ideologies that they had internalized to reflect their own interests. Thus in the late colonial period, the most important of these counterideologies were the ideas of the movement for representative government and Garveyism.

Similar analyses can be made of the knowledge-producing and arts sectors. In the former, the crucial changes introduced by the capitalist revolution were the linking of the colonial economy to the knowledge-producing sector of the imperial cultural system and the introduction of primary education. These changes made local knowledge production redundant and established new patterns of formal instruction and ideological indoctrination. In the arts sector, the big changes resulted from the suppression of drumming and of African religions. In African cultural systems, artistic production was largely determined by the religious demand for symbolic objects, drumming, songs, ritual dances, and so forth. With the conversion of Christianity, this religious basis for artistic production declined sharply. The result was a dramatic transformation of the arts sector, which was rather poorly reconstituted around the artistic demands of the annual Christmas festival.

The symbolic requirements of the transition to peripheral capitalism in Grenada thus resulted in the creation of a plural cultural system, made up of African and European elements. To stabilize the system, it was not only necessary to impose an administration center, but also to make a number of changes in the Afro-Caribbean layer of the system. Along with these changes, rigid barriers were maintained between the various strata of the system. These barriers helped to contain the spread of Afro-Grenadian influence throughout the system. The result was a rigid hierarchical system in which processes of interculturation and Creolization were artificially arrested. But in spite of this centralization and the subsectoral changes, the Grenadian cultural system was never able to overcome the illegitimate roots of the colonial state. This legitimacy deficit was a permanent source of crisis and symbolic violence for the Grenadian cultural system throughout the colonial period.

CULTURE AND THE RISE OF THE LIBERAL
NATION-STATE IN GRENADA

The emergence of peripheral capitalism in Grenada was accompanied by particular patterns of class exclusion, class inclusion, and distributions of authority and privilege—all of which had to be legitimated. The symbols through which these elements of the new order were justified became crucial in the colonial political culture and, hence, also a part of the larger cultural system. Although not as dramatic, the transition from colony to nation was also a period marked by changes in the existing patterns of class relations, thus also demanding the generation of new symbols.

Despite these similarities, it is necessary to take note of two important differences between the capitalist and the nationalist revolutions in Grenada. First, the latter was not an attempt to introduce a new mode of production. Rather, it was an attempt to finally resolve the illegitimate foundations of the colonial state; second, as the nationalist revolution was essentially an anticolonial movement, it pitted the colonized Afro-Grenadian population against the Euro-Grenadian elements. In class terms, it produced an alliance of the lower-middle and working classes against the landed and upper-middle classes. Thus, its success would reset the balance of power between the classes, but there would be no change in the mode of production.

The decolonization of the Grenadian state took place in the context of its gradual democratization through constitutional changes and the formation of mass political parties and labor unions. Through elections based on universal suffrage, this new mobilization resulted in increasing control over the state by Afro-Grenadians. This terminated the monopoly that the landed and upper-middle classes had over the state and led to a sharing of its control with the lower-middle and working classes. Also, these changes in the political position of the working class made possible a substantial penetration of the middle stratum of the society, which now ceased to be predominantly mulatto. As the movement toward a legitimate nation-state approached completion, the above shifts in the colonial class structure continued. The result was a substantial, but by no means complete, weakening of the political base of the upper classes; the elimination of the mulatto middle class; and an increase in the power and degree of inclusion of the lower classes. In short, it reduced the inequality between the classes created by the capitalist revolution.

Given these political and social changes, it became evident that the cultural infrastructure that supported the colonial state would no longer be adequate. Ideologies of external rule, upper-class democracy, racism, and so forth, would only delegitimate the new independent state and its control by Afro-Grenadians. Consequently, a new political culture would have to be introduced to give this political system the symbolic support it needed.

The new symbols included nationalism, mass liberal democracy, Pan-Africanism, and developmentalism. This new political culture was largely the result of the strategic reinterpretation of European political ideologies to legitimate decolonization and independence.

The gradual creation of this legitimate nation-state, the emergence of these new supportive ideologies, and the shifts in the class structure had very significant consequences for the cultural systems. First, the changes in the class structure led to a loosening of the stratification patterns of the cultural system, a positive reevaluation of the African heritage, and a devaluation of the European heritage.

Second, decolonization gave control of the administrative centers of the system to Afro-Grenadians, through their control of the state. Thus control of the more bureaucratized subsectors, such as those of religion and education, were now in local hands.

Third, these changes in patterns of administrative control and stratification resulted in the addition of a middle layer to the Afro-Grenadian cultural system. This layer was characterized by higher levels of education than the working class layer and was therefore oriented to cultural forms and products that reflected this level of education. This stratum was the carrier of the regional revolution in high- and middle-brow culture that accompanied and sustained the nationalist movement.

Fourth, these changes severely rocked the plural structure of the system and established the conditions for the formal dominance of the Afro-Caribbean layers. This dominance, by releasing the artificially suppressed tendencies toward interculturation, opened up the possibilities for a more uniform Creole system based largely on the Afro-Caribbean experience, a major development of the postpluralist period. However, the power of old elites to resist these trends and the dependent nature of the Afro-Caribbean cultural system also have to be considered.

Fifth, and finally, there were the organizational changes that had to be made in the cultural system if the old political culture was to be removed and a new one put in its place. This brings us to some of the specific policies of the Gairy regime.

The new political culture that the Gairy regime needed to institutionalize found two challenges: (1) legitimating the overthrow of colonial authority; and (2) legitimating the exercise of local national authority and the specific compromises that had to be reached with both old and new imperial powers. Overthrowing colonial political culture was not very difficult. Neither was the inculcating of a new political culture. Hence, there was no need for policies of silencing or suppression. The easiness of this process of political reeducation was the result of three crucial factors. The first was the high level of complementarity between the anticolonial sentiments of the mass of the population and the symbolism of a legitimate nation-state. This complementarity supplied the early years of the Gairy regime with its legitimacy surpluses. The second was the already extended exposure of the population to European liberal ideologies that were now being appropriated and reinterpreted by local political elites. Third, there was the Africanist element in the new political culture that had long been a part of the suppressed popular culture. Because of these and other factors, neither special schools of instruction nor imposed interpretations of reality were necessary for gaining needed symbolic support. The informal political education undertaken by political parties and labor unions more than sufficed. Thus the Grenadian nation-state began its career with a legitimacy surplus and low levels of symbolic violence.

However, even before independence this situation reversed itself. The reversal was related to the second set of challenges faced by the new political culture: the exercise of local national authority and its compromises with elites at home and abroad. In most postcolonial societies, the nature of the compromises made with old and new imperial powers will greatly affect the legitimacy of the new local elites. Very often, the justifying of these compromises leads to splits in the unity of the preindependence period. Positions with varying degrees of closeness to the central capitalist countries are taken and justified. At one extreme are economic elites whose nationalism takes second place to their economic concerns; at the other are nationalist and socialist groups that will seek to increase the distance or make a radical break. Compromises with the central capitalist countries often lead to ideological divisions and polarizations that affect the very legitimacy of a regime.

The emergence of these conflicts in the second half of Gairy's rule led to tensions with the old plantocracy and the radical forces that would become the New Jewel Movement (NJM). Gairy's response was a Bonapartist one. Through violence, intimidation, clientelism, and "mesmeratic leadership,"[10] he attempted to make himself more powerful than any of the above groups. The result was a dramatic increase in the level of repression, which soon produced legitimacy deficits and an increasing need to resort to symbolic violence—that is, to the imposition of a Gairyist interpretation of sociopolitical reality. The increased resistance generated by this authoritarianism (both physical and symbolic) was a crucial factor in his overthrow in 1979. In sum, the basic policies of the Gairy regime that mediated the culture-state relationship went through two basic phases. The first was shaped by the problems of legitimating decolonization, the second by the compromises that had to be made with elites and imperial powers.

As in the colonial period, the consequences of these policies were evident in many aspects of the Grenadian cultural system. At the most general level, they had the effect of reinforcing the broader tendency toward lessening the social distance between the African and European elements of the system. In the linguistic sector, the policies had only minor effects. The hierarchy between the languages continued even though there was a noticeable improvement in the appreciation of Grenadian Creole. In the religious subsector, the changes were largely formal. The organizational structures of the major Christian churches were separated from administrative centers overseas and replaced by local ones. However, this reorganization was not accompanied by any major changes in doctrine or in relations with Afro-Caribbean religions.

The ideological subsector very quickly came to mirror the ideology of the state in the early years. Thus it soon lost its colonial heritage and began producing some of its own justifications for a modern, independent Grenada. However, with the passage of time this unity was replaced by a polarization around the capitalism-socialism alternative, which led to attempts to control ideological output. The educational subsector also changed quite significantly during the nationalist periods. In 1930, after one hundred years of colonial schooling, 56 percent of the population was illiterate.[11] At the primary level there were sixty-six schools with a total enrollment of 13,343 and an average attendance of 62 percent.[12] At the secondary level, there were four schools with a total enrollment of 478, which was drawn primarily from the middle class. At the tertiary level, there was one island scholarship to a British university that was awarded every two years. Teachers at the first two levels were very poorly trained, while the curriculum is still best remembered for its irrelevance to local needs. Except for some minor reforms in the late forties, this was the educational system that the nationalist period inherited.

Between 1952 and 1979, both the Blaize and Gairy regimes significantly expanded the system. The number of secondary schools increased from four to fourteen, with an enrollment of 4,295 in the 1979/80 academic year. But in spite of these substantial increases, there were many who were still unable to get an education. At the primary level, the number of schools declined slightly, to fifty-nine, although enrollment increased to 30,522 in 1970/71, and then declined to 22,861 in 1978/79.[13]

Unfortunately, these quantitative increases were not matched by qualitative increases. At both levels, the problems of teacher training and inappropriate curricula persisted. In 1957, only 8 percent of teachers at the primary level had been trained.[14] In 1962, Grenada opened a teacher training college, but this only very partially remedied teacher deficiencies. In sum, the educational subsector experienced significant expansions throughout the nationalist period, but these expansions were not enough to meet the educational demands of the society.

The mass communications subsector is small but of considerable strategic importance. It consists primarily of radio, newspapers, and systems of public address and has been an important barometer of trends in state-culture relations. Expansions and contractions in the use of the above media have tended to reflect major social conflicts and the state's response to them. Thus the early decolonization period was marked by the opening up of this subsector to Afro-Grenadian views. This opening up was reflected in the editorials and articles of newspapers such as the *West Indian* and the *Star*. In the second half of the Gairy administration, the tensions of this subsector no longer reflected the anticolonial struggle but the increasing ideological polarization around development issues and the struggle for state power. Newspapers were now largely controlled by political parties, while the only radio station was government owned. As the polarization and competition between parties increased, Gairy sought to establish a tighter control of this subsector. First, he closed off the access of opposition groups to radio. Second, he passed the Newspaper Amendment Act, which required the payment of $20,000 before a paper could publish. Third, he passed the Public Order Amendment Act, which controlled the use of public address systems. Consequently, opportunities for communicating via mass media declined sharply in the second half of this period.

Last but by no means least are the fine arts. This subsector experienced two important developments. First was the already mentioned regional revolution in high- and middle-brow art. This gave rise to a regional literature of the highest quality. Second was a significant increase in the appreciation of the art of the masses. Here the major developments were in music. These developments in the arts not only helped to shape this period but were themselves shaped by it.[15]

To summarize, these subsectoral changes during the nationalist period all reflected patterns of limited growth, of slow movement toward a more uniform national culture, as well as of ideological polarization. Together with the overall weakening of colonial stratification patterns, these trends took the system into a distinct postpluralist phase. Here, the long-term problems facing the system are postcolonial interculturation and institutional expansion, so that the system can meet more of Grenada's cultural needs. In the short run, the most disruptive source of crisis appears once again to be the level of symbolic violence required by a state experiencing severe legitimacy deficits. We will now turn to our examination of the socialist period in Grenada.

CULTURE AND SOCIALISM IN THE PERIPHERY

Unlike the bourgeois revolutions that gave rise to capitalism, socialist revolutions have been revolutions from below. That is, they have been based largely on peasant and worker uprisings. As Moore points out, "the process of modernization begins with peasant revolutions that fail. It culminates during the twentieth century with peasant revolutions that succeed."[16] The classic examples here are, or course, China and Russia, and in the Caribbean region, Cuba.

Like capitalist revolutions, socialist revolutions have attempted to modernize society and to introduce new modes of production. Consequently, socialist revolutions have also been accompanied by dramatic changes in economic and political organization and in patterns of class exclusion and inclusion. As these changes are introduced, they reverse a number of tendencies in capitalist revolutions by making the bourgeois and landed upper classes their primary targets.

Because of the consolidation of capitalism in North America and Western Europe, and of socialism in the Soviet Union and Eastern Europe, it is primarily in the underdeveloped capitalist societies of the Third World that socialism continues to be an appealing alternative. However, this relationship between capitalism and socialism in the periphery is a complex one. On the one hand, because socialism is perceived as a threat, it has consistently forced reforms in capitalist societies that contribute to their stabilization. The role of the Cuban Revolution in stimulating the Alliance for Progress remains a classic example. On the other hand, because of the existence of other socialist societies, socialist revolutions can do more than force reforms in capitalism. They can now offer concrete alternatives to capitalism.

However, it is important to point out that this existence of real socialist societies has introduced elements of caution in regard to this alternative. This caution has followed from the realization that the social order of socialist societies is subject to new contradictions; they are not the utopias they were once believed to be. These contradictions derive from the fact that the abolition of private ownership of the means of production has not resulted in popular ownership, but in state ownership. This state ownership, which provided a framework for rapid industrialization, has also been the basis for new forms of mass domination by state and party elites. The 1968 crisis in Czechoslovakia, the worker self-management movement in Yugoslavia, and the Solidarity Movement in Poland, all reflected the crisis tendencies within existing socialist societies.

Using the Czechoslovakian case, Rudolf Bahro describes the nature of these crisis tendencies rather succinctly: "What the Czechoslovak transformations brought to light was simply the real structure of the society emerging from the East European revolutions and ultimately from the October revolution. And the pace of the transformations . . . showed how pressingly this new structure is waiting, at least in the industrially developed countries, to throw off the armour that protected it in its larval stage, but now threatens to choke it."[17] Thus, unless socialist states are able to move quickly toward genuine forms of mass ownership and participation, they very soon experience legitimacy deficits for which symbolic violence must be substituted. It is the emergence of authoritarian features such as these that have lessened the appeal of socialism in the peripheral countries.

However, assuming that one of these countries embarks upon a socialist course, the above-mentioned features of socialist revolutions will be extremely important in determining the kind of symbolic and organizational requirements that will be made of the cultural system. At the organizational level, there will be the structural changes required by the collectivist principles of the new order. Thus, the system will have to adjust to a greater degree of state control and regulation. Crucial centers of cultural production—such as publishing companies, academies, newspapers, journals, and educational systems—will cease to be privately owned and will fall under state control. The major exception will, of course, be the church.

At the symbolic level, the new political elites must secure the ongoing reproduction of a Marxist-Leninist political culture that will support the new socialist state, its economic reforms, and patterns of class exclusion. However, given existing levels of transformation of political culture, literacy, and the dominant role of religion in peripheral societies, this is a major undertaking. These types of cultural changes are often quite resistant to administrative manipulation or coercion. It took centuries of capitalist domination and inculcation to detach Afro-Grenadians from their precapitalist cultural orientations.

The introduction of a Marxist-Leninist political culture will be successful if there is a readiness on the part of masses to abandon old orientations for the new ones. Without such a predisposition, old orientations will persist, in spite of administrative attempts to eliminate them. The persistence of these prerevolutionary orientations often places significant restrictions on accumulation of legitimacy for radical changes. Consequently, the extent to which disaffection from the old order, through dissatisfaction and revolutionary struggle, weakens prerevolutionary attachments will be important for a solution to this problem. If attachments are severely weakened, the new political culture can be introduced without high levels of coercion. If they are not, the regime faces an uphill battle. In this case, the casting of Marxism in the language of religion or the dominant signifying system may be the only real option.

Finally, how the new socialist state justifies its monopoly over resources and its delays in the transition to popular control will also be important factors affecting levels of legitimacy and relations with the cultural system. Given the wide recognition of the crisis tendencies of existing socialist societies, the contradictions that follow from their highly centralized forms of political rule cannot be ignored. If they are not addressed, other models of socialism are sure to emerge.

SOCIALISM AND TRANSFORMATION IN GRENADA

Socialist revolutions seek to substitute the principle of collective ownership for the more private orientations of capitalism. Consequently, in the transition period, attempts are made to mobilize the basic resources of the society through suspending their use as means of private accumulation. This process of mobilization should in theory be followed by the reallocation of these collectively owned resources so that everyone shares equitably in the benefits of their productive use. However, actually existing socialist societies vary widely in the extent to which these basic principles are actualized. Grenada's experiment represents a case in which they were far from being realized.

Instead of the extensive collectivization of resources, Grenada's experiment was based upon a limited mobilization that made possible a number of shifts in the balance of power between the classes established under Gairy. The compromises of this period were not eliminated, but their terms were reset in ways that favored the socialist countries and the working classes.

Grenadian mobilization was not equally extensive across the society's institutions. It was greatest in the political arena and least in the cultural. In the former area, a revolutionary government was established. The reorganization that accompanied this development suspended many of the liberal features of the nationalist state. Replacing most of these were Cuban-style organs of popular democracy, a Leninist vanguard party, and a foreign policy that was openly antiimperialist and prosocialist. Thus the revolution separated the Grenadian state from its liberal premises.

In the economic arena, the processes of mobilization and reorganization were not as extensive as those described above. They did not produce a clear outline of a new economy based on a socialist mode of production. Rather, a three-sector (state, private, cooperative) economy in which the state sector would be dominant was established, an indication of the shift in power relations with both local and foreign capitalist classes. It was also a part of the larger strategy of building a national economy more responsive to local needs, more locally owned, and less dependent on the peripheral functions that it performed for a central country.

In the cultural arena, mobilization was even more partial. It focused upon gaining control of the ideological, educational, and mass communications subsectors of the cultural system, along with attempts to reduce the influence of its religious subsector. This slight increase in the degree of state control produced some significant changes but did not radically alter the nature of the Grenadian cultural system. The latter remained an externally dependent system, still in the process of resolving the internal conflict between its pluralist past and its more uniformly Creolized future.

SOCIALIST RESTRUCTURING OF THE GRENADIAN CULTURAL SYSTEM

As indicated before, the mobilization of cultural resources fell far short of a program of radical collectivization. As a result, the general level of state control over the cultural system was significantly lower than that found in most socialist states, and not much more than that of the Gairy period. Without this more comprehensive mobilization, the scope of the changes that the People's Revolutionary Government (PRG) could introduce was quite limited. In fact, the scope of these changes was determined by the real size of the *additional* institutional space created by the adjustments in the crucial compromises mentioned above; it is the use of much of this institutional space for working class interests that stands out.

Operating within the constraints of this limited mobilization, the PRG focused on a number of specific problems, rather than on the cultural system as a whole. The regime did not have a clear policy for the restructuring of the cultural system, as it did for the economic and political systems. The basic internal dilemmas of the cultural system were not fully recognized nor effectively addressed. General problems, such as external dependence and interrupted patterns of interculturation were not explicitly identified and linked to the program of socialist transformation. Rather, they remained implicit in the more specific problems that were addressed.

As already indicated, the primary targets were the educational, ideological, and mass communications subsectors. The PRG also sought to lessen the influence of the religious subsector and to encourage the growth of Grenadian Creole. The period of revolutionary mobilization in Grenada had a very significant impact on the linguistic sector of the cultural system. As we saw earlier, this sector was bilingual, with a hierarchy that reflected changing trends in the Grenadian class structure. By making additional changes in the balance of power between the classes, the experiment with socialism was able to take the changes of the nationalist period a few steps further. The basic problems of this sector are related to the normative and structural relations surrounding the social use of Grenadian Creole. The latter's underdevelopment has derived largely from its low social status and its restriction to domestic use. This exclusion from the schools and other public institutions has left it with very little stimuli for growth.

The linguistic policies of the PRG recognized the bilingual nature of this sector. These policies attempted to ease the hostility between standard English and Grenadian Creole, which has been so much a part of the system. In Searle's words, the regime sought "to reconcile both languages for the benefit of the people, to take the strengths of both, to exorcise the complexes within both that raised up stigmas and attitudes of inferiority and superiority, and to maximize everything that the meaning, analytical power and beauty of both could bring to the people."[18] In short, it was a policy that attempted to further decolonize the relations between the languages so that both could play their crucial roles in processes of identity formation and communication.

The concrete attempts to implement this linguistic policy were integral parts of literacy and teacher training programs of the PRG. Shortly after the revolution, a literacy campaign was undertaken. This campaign was administered by the newly formed Center for Popular Education (CPE). Thus, in addition to the teaching of specific skills, the CPE was also a mobilizing and resocializing agency. Prime Minister Bishop made this quite clear: "The Center for Popular Education is not just reading and writing, it is also about consciousness, about developing a nation that for the first time will begin to put proper values on those things that are important."[19] Among the many areas of Grenadian culture on which "proper values" had to be placed was Grenadian Creole, and one of the primary resocializing tasks of the CPE was the changing of peoples' attitudes toward this language. While it was improving popular skills in standard English, the CPE was also attempting to remove old normative regulations and prejudices about Grenadian Creole.

The big taboo that the regime broke was the nonacceptance of Grenadian Creole in the classroom. In CPE classes, there was genuine acceptance of this language by both student and teacher. These classes were bilingual in the sense that the teaching of standard English was conducted in Grenadian Creole. This penetration of the classroom was not confined to the CPE program. It reached the primary level of the educational system through the National In-Service Teacher Education Program (NISTEP). In this training program, primary school teachers were introduced to the new way of looking at the linguistic situation, and its pedagogic implications. As a result, teachers were encouraged to view Grenadian Creole as another language, to recognize that Grenadians have to be taught standard English with many of the techniques of foreign language teachings, and that the pupils' normative expectations of standard English had to be changed.

These increases in the acceptance and the social demand for Grenadian Creole were important developments that reflected the class orientation of the revolution. They gave new support to the language and stimulated a lot of writing in it. For the working classes, these changes lessened their exclusion from the key centers of the society by increasing their degree of linguistic enfranchisement.

In marked contrast to the supportive and growth-oriented approach to the linguistic sector, the PRG's policy toward the religious subsector was of a containing and confining nature. Religion was seen as an outmoded signifying system, one surpassed by science. According to one report on the church, it was to be "nothing but a fetter on our development."[20] Second, and more important, both the church and the PRG very quickly came to see each other as a threat. The explicit secularism of the latter made church leaders uneasy. They feared for the place of Christianity in the mix of scientism, anti-imperialism, and Marxism that constituted the secular outlook of the PRG. In the main, the response of the church was to step up its proselytizing activities in an effort to maintain its influence over the minds and identities of Grenadians. Church leaders felt themselves in competition with the mass organizations of the PRG for this influence. But these stepped-up activities only made the regime feel this competition more intensely.

By early 1980, relations between some church leaders and the PRG had deteriorated quite rapidly. This was clear from Bishop's speech on freedom of worship in February of that year. Bishop quoted the text of a letter written by a group of Grenadian religious leaders to a Dominican order in England. The letter expressed grave concerns about preaching the Christian gospel in a Marxist society and requested the assistance of priests familiar with Marxist ideology.[21] This group of religious leaders also published anticommunist tracts and cooperated closely with capitalist groups that were openly opposed to the revolution. The actions of these church leaders produced an overreaction on the part of the PRG. Such actions should have been expected and allowed. Given the fact that the goal of the regime was not an all-out war on religion but the diminution of its influence, the need for the above forms of religious resistance may have subsided with the passage of time and the emergence of a new balance of influence between the ideological and religious subsectors.

However, this was not the strategy pursued by the PRG. On the contrary, they continued to see the resistance of these religious leaders as a threat to the revolution. In his report on the church, Major Roberts concluded that it was "the most dangerous sector for the development of internal counter-revolution."[22] Thus he recommended such things as the strengthening of scientific and political education, increasing the efforts of the mass organizations, continued church surveillance, and closer contact with the liberation theology movement.

In short, the socialist period in Grenada initiated a period of conflict and competition between the ideological and religious subsectors that was not very productive. It prevented the PRG from making use of opportunities for further developing local skills in the use of this signifying system, as it did in the case of language. Rather, the production of religious discourses was viewed primarily in ideological terms. As a result, opportunities for gaining legitimacy from supporting Afro-Caribbean religions, nationalist elements in the Christian churches, and the starting of a genuine Christian-Marxist dialogue were left largely unexplored. Such a strategy might have produced changes in the religious subsector that advanced working class interests and a positive appraisal of the Afro-Caribbean heritage.

In the area of education, PRG policies were much more forward looking. Control of this subsector brought with it an attack on many of the problems of the education system: illiteracy, teacher training, irrelevant curricula, and the limited opportunities at the secondary and tertiary levels of the system. This restructuring of the educational system was clearly intended to advance working class interests. It was an integral part of the cultural revolution, which Bishop described as "the spreading of the socialist ideology, the wiping out of illiteracy, and the building of a new patriotic and revolutionary-democratic intelligentsia."[23]

As we know from our analysis of the Gairy period, the expansions that had taken place in education were not enough to meet the demands of the population. Fees still kept many from entering secondary schools, while there was a need for more schools and more teachers. The PRG's educational strategy was essentially fourfold: (1) to reach those that the existing system had failed to reach; (2) to improve the performance of the system; (3) to increase opportunities at the secondary and tertiary levels; and (4) to raise consciousness about inherited attitudes toward education.

At the time of the revolution, it was estimated that approximately 7 percent of the population was illiterate. To deal with this problem, the PRG embarked upon a literacy campaign. This campaign attempted to provide the illiterate with basic skills in reading and writing. Although there are no final statistics of this campaign, its successes have been acknowledged even by critics of the regime.[24] Building on this initial success, the program was expanded to include a system of night schools. The goal of this new program was to provide six-month courses for

CPE graduates and others who had no educational certification. Forty-eight centers, in which a variety of skills were taught, were established across the island. Upon completing these courses, individuals were given CPE adult education certificates.

In short, the CPE was a new layer of educational system, servicing those left behind by the primary and secondary layers. It was an extremely popular program, strongly identified with the working class. Among this group one often heard the expression "CPE is we." Educational restructuring thus produced results similar to those following the restructuring of the linguistic sector. It furthered the educational enfranchisement of the working class and the positive reappraisal of their Afro-Caribbean heritage.

While adding this new layer, the PRG also tried to improve the educational system's overall performance. At the primary level, a basic problem was that of teacher training. To address it, the PRG established its in-service program, NISTEP. In-service programs were not new to the region. What was new was the attempt to train *all* teachers who needed training. It was a bold, imaginative, and ambitious undertaking, which trained teachers for three years. Under this program, teachers would conduct classes for four days a week and be trained on the fifth. On the latter day, the students would go on field trips supervised by the Community School Day Program. NISTEP is difficult to evaluate, as the time was too short for the production of a significant number of graduates and for these graduates to have had an impact on the primary layer of the system.

At the secondary level, a similar training program was envisioned but not implemented. The basic changes introduced here were of a different sort. School fees were first reduced and then eliminated, making this layer more accessible to all. Also, the PRG expanded the number of places available by building a new school, with a capacity of 500 students. This layer now had the capacity for servicing 5,230 students.

The tertiary level of the educational system still remained abroad: university training had to be acquired outside of Grenada. Although this fact did not change, the PRG significantly increased the number of university scholarships available to qualified graduates of the secondary schools. Many of these scholarships were tenable at universities in socialist countries, a new departure for Grenada and the Eastern Caribbean.

As in the case of other long-term programs of the PRG, an assessment of its educational policies is made difficult by the premature collapse of the regime. How well these educational reforms would have worked out is impossible to say. But they clearly amounted to the most comprehensive attack ever made on Grenada's educational problems. During the period they were in operation, two important advances were made: the inclusion of a larger segment of the working class within the reach of the system; and the raising of consciousness about the role of education in postcolonial Grenada.

This leaves us with the ideological and mass communications subsectors to examine. Because the control of these subsectors was more explicitly involved in the legitimation of the regime, the changes in these areas were more than just organizational or reallocative. They were integral parts of the PRG's strategy for accumulating symbolic power and establishing a monopoly of the means of symbolic violence. Unlike the previous set of changes, the immediate objective was not the advancement of working class interests but the creation of cultural conditions for the legitimation of the socialist state. Over and above the making of particular structural changes, there would still be the problem of getting these two subsectors to produce symbolic outputs of a Marxist-Leninist nature. Because of these differences, the discussion of changes in these subsectors will be taken up in the next section.

In sum, the conditions under which the PRG came to power increased slightly the state's control over the cultural system. With this limited control, the PRG attempted to make changes in the linguistic, educational, and religious subsectors. Except for the religious subsector, the changes furthered many of the prematurely arrested tendencies of the nationalist period. This pattern of change supported the growth of Afro-Caribbean culture. The CPE and NISTEP are good examples of this. The momentum of change in these two subsectors encouraged similar trends in other areas of the system that were less directly controlled. Thus, in the fine arts, particularly music and poetry, the impact of the revolution and its changes were very clearly reflected. A House of Culture, similar to Cuba's, was planned but never established.

Except for the attempts to contain religion, the overall thrust of the PRG's attempts at cultural restructuring was the expansion of the working class base of the Afro-Caribbean cultural system. As a result, the postpluralist phase of the national cultural system was further consolidated.

LEGITIMATING STATE POWER

With these changes in the cultural system, the PRG attempted to secure the legitimacy it needed. Legitimating this revolutionary socialist state required, among other things, the introduction of a Marxist-Leninist political culture in the place of the liberal-Gairyist one. As noted earlier, changes of this type require a readiness on the part of the masses to abandon the old culture and to embrace the new one. If the "temperature" achieved by the period of revolutionary mobilization is high enough to melt prerevolutionary attachments, the task will be that much easier.

In Grenada, the temperature achieved by the process of revolutionary mobilization was comparatively low. Consequently, there was substantial resistance to the new political culture. This resistance had two sources. First, the continuing existence of a capitalist class still strong enough to put together an organized resistance to socialism. Second, the fact that the popular sentiments that legitimated the PRG were not so much prosocialist as anti-Gairy and antineocolonial. Whether this anti-Gairy and antineocolonial consciousness could be translated into socialist ideology became thus a key question for the PRG. Would it be intense enough to burn away popular attachment not only to the Gairyist but also the liberal aspects of the old political culture? The evidence seems to indicate that it was intense enough to easily undermine the former but not the latter. Attachments to this and other aspects of the political culture persisted. Such patterns of cultural continuity are to be expected. Thus in Cuba, where the revolutionary period was much more intense, Castro was also forced to recognize the inertia of the past: "It is well known that to build communism we must confront . . . in the ideological sphere, the extraordinary weight of the ideas, habits and concepts that society has accumulated for centuries. The past has it claws into the present."[25]

The new regime could count on a pool of anti-Gairy and antineocolonial sentiments (which, however, still had to be linked to a socialist alternative). But the PRG also had to overcome important obstacles. The first was the organized resistance of the church and capitalist groups. The second was the more explicitly secular nature of socialist political culture. This is important, as the period of revolutionary mobilization left popular religious attachments very much intact. This is not unusual, as the experiences of other countries suggest that the institutionalization of science and technology are the forces with the greatest power to dissolve religious orientations. Given the level of scientific development in Grenada, detachment from religion to a more secular ideology was bound to meet resistance.

For all of these reasons, the PRG had to engage in more extensive programs of political education than the nationalist leaders. They had to go beyond established styles of political education within Grenadian parties. In addition to these, they adopted Cuban methods of political education and resocialization through participation in mass organizations. Thus the National Women's Organization, the Young Pioneers, the CPE, and the zonal councils were all important instruments of political education and resocialization. Their roles were similar to mass organizations of the Cuban Revolution, such as the committees for the defense of the revolution, or the schools of revolutionary instruction.[26] In addition to these mass organizations, the emulation and education committees for workers also devoted time and resources to political education. It is in the context of this attempt to legitimate the state and the revolution through the development of a new political culture that the changes in the ideological and mass communications subsectors must be analyzed.

In its redirecting of the ideological subsector, the PRG had little choice but to try to forge a strong link between the anti-Gairy and antineocolonial sentiments of the population and socialism. To do this, the PRG was able to use the revolution itself to establish the sense of a new beginning. Using this divide, it was possible to delegitimate Gairy-ism and capitalism in much the same way that the nationalist leaders had been able to delegitimate colonialism. Between this new beginning and the socialist future was "our process," that is the revolutionary process. Historical time now came to be experienced in terms of this dynamic process leading to a new future. The process was of course the process of struggle. It was the living record of the struggle against Gairy, against neocolonialism, the struggle to build the airport, and so forth. In short, it was by making "the revo"—this crucial subjective link between a declining capitalist present and socialist future—that meaningful attachments began to form around the new political culture.

Although elements of this social ontology spread quite widely, there is little evidence to suggest that the same can be said for the more specific and technical aspects of Marxism-Leninism. The time was by far too short, given the level of literacy, the religious orientation of the masses, and the novelty of the ideas. The particular brand of Marxism-Leninism that came to dominate the ideological subsector under the PRG was a contradictory mixture of indigenous radical thought, with elements of Cuban and Soviet Marxism. The tensions in this mixture were primarily with the Soviet elements. Regional notions of popular democracy fitted easily with Cuban views and institutions of popular power. In contrast, the building of a vanguard party, with its monopoly on state power was in definite tension with regional traditions of popular and liberal democracy. But in spite of these competing strains, the official designation of the PRG's ideological position was that of noncapitalist development. This designation reflected more the eagerness of the PRG to be accepted into the socialist bloc than the realities of its ideological situation.[27]

In its effort to introduce the socialist ideology, it was not the theory of noncapitalist development that was pushed, but the above mixture. These ideas were introduced through the mass organizations, with the goal of establishing rational arguments between the capitalist organization of Grenadian society and the poverty of the masses on one hand, and the transition to socialism on the other. But this protoscientific interpretation of sociopolitical reality remained beyond the grasp of the masses. Among young people, the antiimperialist fragments were partially understood, but the grasp of the whole remained a long way off.

Consequently, the complementarity of sentiments and symbols that legitimated the regime were largely anti-Gairy and antineocolonial in nature. Legitimacy was also derived from the organs of popular democracy, as well as from the boldness and success of many of the regime's programs. It is arguable that additional legitimacy also came from the attempts to create prosocialist sentiments and views of reality. But it is equally arguable that these attempts also generated much resistance—that many experienced them as uncomfortable impositions. Given the strength of prerevolutionary attachments, the only symbolically nonviolent solution to this problem would have been more open dialogues between Marxists, liberals, Christians, and other representatives from the old political culture. In the absence of such exchanges, the introduction of socialism into the ideological subsector was only partially supported by the available anti-Gairy and antineocolonial sentiments. Hence the forced and state-directed nature of changes in the subsector.

Finally, we come to the mass communications subsector. Even more than its religious and ideological counterparts, this subsector revealed the resistance that the PRG had to overcome in legitimating itself. This resistance sprang from groups with newspapers who were openly opposed to the revolution and to socialism. The result was an extended conflict between sections of the church leadership and fractions of the capitalist class, on the one hand, and the revolutionary government on the other. If the educational and linguistic subsectors reflected the new patterns of class inclusion, the mass communications subsector more than any other mirrored the new patterns of class exclusion.

The seizure of power, the suspension of liberal politics, the setting up of a revolutionary government, and the commitment to socialism were actions resisted by those committed to liberal capitalism. The adjustment in class relations caused by the revolution clearly favored the working classes. This proworking class and antibourgeois orientation was widely proclaimed: "The point," Bishop said, "is that all rights are not for them [the bourgeoisie], all freedoms are not for them, but all rights and freedoms are now for the majority who are no longer oppressed and repressed by a tiny minority. That is very important to understand, because that is what dictatorship or rule means."[28] By interpreting its role in terms of the Marxist "dictatorship of the proletariat," the PRG assumed the right to a limited repression of bourgeois opposition to the revolution. It was in the midst of this smoldering war that the mass communications subsector was caught.

This war began with acts of "destabilization" on the part of those opposed to the regime. These acts were cause for concern from the very first days of the revolution. Just one month (13 April) after the seizure of power, Bishop addressed the nation on this issue, which was to be the start of an escalating pattern. Thus his next address, less that a month later, followed two fires. In November, the Wilton de Raveniere plot was uncovered. But of all the attempts to overthrow the regime, it was the Queen's Park bombing of June 1980 that led to the government's offensive against its enemies. This and the other attacks were seen by the PRG as counterrevolutionary attempts organized by groups both inside and outside of Grenada. It was in its moves against the local elements involved in these activities that the PRG's policies toward the mass communications subsector emerged.

As the only radio station on the island was government owned, state control of radio was already a reality when the PRG came to power. The exclusion of opposition groups from access to this medium was a well-established practice of the Gairy period. The PRG continued this monopolistic practice. However, broadcasts from other islands could be heard in Grenada, so the government's station was not the only one available.

With regard to newspapers and public address systems, the situation was quite different. The state had to share these fields with private owners. Through these privately owned media, groups opposed to the revolution attempted to mobilize mass support.

In the first months of the revolution, the PRG's policy toward newspapers and public address systems was to relax the restrictions of the Gairy period, abolishing the Newspaper Amendment and Public Order acts. However, as counterrevolutionary activities increased and the newspapers were perceived as playing strategic roles, this changed. In his second national address on destabilization, Bishop singled out the *Torchlight* as "a local agent of international reaction."[29] He pointed to a number of articles in the paper and to its failure to carry his 13 April address to the nation, while giving front-page treatment to a response by the U. S. Embassy in Barbados. This tension only increased with the passage of time. By the sixth month of the revolution, relations with opposition newspapers had grown considerably worse. In his address of 18 September, Bishop accused several regional newspapers of engaging in "conscious destabilization."[30] These included the *Daily Gleaner,* the *Torchlight,* and the *Trinidad Express.*

To counter this growing resistance, two laws were passed that gave the PRG a de facto monopoly in newspaper publishing. The first was People's Law No. 81, which forbade the publishing of a newspaper if there were individuals in the company who owned more that 4 percent of its shares. This law was clearly aimed at the capitalist organization of newspaper ownership, and the *Torchlight* in particular, which subsequently became illegal. At the same time, it represented the first signs of a new but as yet unformulated media policy. The second law came after two attempts by the same opposition groups to publish papers in violation of People's Law No. 81. It was passed in June 1981, and forbade the publication of any newspapers for a whole year, until the government had formulated its new media policy.

By early 1982, the outlines of this new policy began to take shape. It was centered around People's Law No. 81. If papers in which individuals owned more that 4 percent of the shares could not be published, then papers had to be collectively or group owned. The policy operated on the principle that the positions affirmed in a paper reflected the interest of the owners. Thus collectively owned newspapers should result in a more accurate representation of the opinions and interests of the masses than papers owned by a small number of people. To further this line of thinking, a concerted effort was made to collectivize the ownership and production of newspapers. This drive resulted in the publishing of newspapers by a number of mass organizations. The goal was to establish a form of state-sponsored working class control over the production of newspapers in the place of private and often bourgeois control. As Bishop summarized it: "We uphold the freedom of the majority of the working people . . . to express their views and their right to have access to the mass media, which serves their interests, which reflects their struggles and aspirations, their perceptions and opinions."[31] At the same time that these changes were made in the production of local newspapers, there were no changes in the regulations governing the entry of foreign newspapers and magazines.

As in the case of the ideological subsector, these attempts to restructure the mass communications subsector, in the context of intense resistance, were not too successful. The problem was not that the policy was a bad one, as in the case of the religious subsector. On the contrary, it shared many of the progressive and working class orientations of the changes in the linguistic and educational subsectors. Rather, the policy was the victim of the ability of local newspaper owners to mobilize resistance. The closing of the *Torchlight* was given global coverage; the new policies hardly any. It is doubtful if the image of the regime ever recovered from this imbalance in coverage. Also, the new policy gave no timetable for the state-sponsored period of transition to collective ownership. As a result, there was always the concern that the new policy was simply a mask for continued state control of the press. Thus because of their role in legitimating the PRG, restructuring of the ideological mass communications subsectors did not have the same effects as the restructuring of the linguistic and educational subsectors. But together, these changes constituted the core of cultural transformations of the socialist period.

CONCLUSION

From our analysis of the cultural changes produced by Grenada's experiment with socialism, two sets of results emerge: findings affecting directional trends in the Grenadian cultural system as a whole, and findings related to the difficulties this system created for the socialist transformation of the society.

With regard to the first of these, our analysis of the various subsectors suggest that PRG policies had four primary effects on the overall structure of the cultural system. The first was a slight increase in the level of state control of the system. The second was a further reduction of the influence of the upper classes on the system. The third was the strengthening of several areas of Afro-Caribbean layers of the system through increased institutional support, more positive official evaluations, and greater degrees of involvement in the day-to-day reproduction of the society. Fourth and finally, the above three sets of changes further weakened the stratification patterns of the system. This weakening restarted the trends toward a more uniformly Creolized cultural system, which the nationalist period had initiated.

These findings in regard to changes in the overall structure of the Grenadian cultural system are significant for several reasons. The most important is that they point to some of the special problems that socialist regimes in peripheral countries are likely to inherit from the prerevolutionary period. The difficulties derive less from the imperatives of socialist transformation that from the cultural deformations produced by the legitimacy demands of the colonial state. The long-term affects of these demands has been the maintaining of distinct national and ethnic identities through hierarchical divisions and the arresting of trends toward interculturation. Consequently, the often unfinished task of creating a genuinely national cultural system in the postcolonial period is a problem that socialist regimes in the periphery are likely to inherit.

With regard to the difficulties arising from the imperatives of the transition to socialism, our analysis of the Grenadian case suggests that they are likely to emerge from the introduction of the Marxist-Leninist political culture, which is necessary for legitimating the state and programs of radical change. These difficulties can be divided into two broad categories: (1) those that arise from sharp discontinuities between the old and the new political cultures, and (2) difficulties that arise from the contradiction between state power and popular power, which usually characterizes the transitional period.

Because of its short life and abrupt end, the Grenadian case sheds useful light on only the first of these two sets of problems. It shows the many ways in which low levels of literacy, a limited degree of revolutionary mobilization, strong attachments to prerevolutionary cultural orientations, and organized opposition from capitalist groups all combined to create resistance to the new political culture. Consequently, the PRG was forced to develop strategies to overcome this resistance. The result was a period characterized by an initial drop and then a rise in the level of symbolic violence. The latter was concentrated primarily in the ideological and mass communications subsectors.

Finally, the tragic end of Grenada's experiment demonstrated very clearly the potentially explosive nature of the contradiction between state power and popular power. Most dramatically reflected in the struggle to establish the absolute hegemony of the Central Committee, this contradiction was a part of the set of forces that consumed the revolution. Had the revolution survived, at some later date the regime would have been faced with the problem of legitimating high levels of state control in what was supposed to be a people's democracy. In cultural terms, this contradiction gives rise to ideological debates between various models of socialism. The Grenadian case did not get to the cultural translation of this contradiction. But for those countries that survive its initial political manifestations, the resolution of the tensions it creates will not be complete without addressing these cultural implications.

These findings on patterns of cultural resistance and levels of symbolic violence are also important for their broader significance. They suggest that introducing the new political culture will be a difficult task, one likely to raise the level of symbolic violence. This will be evident in a number of subsectors, depending on the particular policies being used. In the case of the PRG, the size of this increase was comparatively small because of the role of the zonal councils and the existence of strong anti-Gairy and antineocolonial sentiments. However, it could have been lower had the regime adopted a more imaginative policy toward the religious subsector.[32]

NOTES

The author would like to thank Julie Franks (SUNY, Stony Brook) and Leigh Walter (University of Virginia) for their assistance in the gathering of the data on which this chapter is based.

1. Melville Herskovits, *The Myth of the Negro Past* (Boston: Beacon Press,

1970); Janheinz Jahn, *Mantu* (New York: Grove Press, 1961); M. G. Smith, *The Plural Society in the British West Indies* (Berkeley: University of California Press, 1974); Rex Nettleford, *Caribbean Cultural Identity* (Kingston: Institute of Jamaica, 1978); R. T. Smith, *British Guiana* (London: Oxford University Press); Leo Despres, *Cultural Pluralism and Nationalist Politics in British Guiana* (New York: Rand McNally, 1967).

2. Nettleford, *Caribbean Cultural Identity*; M. G. Smith, *Culture, Race and Class in the Commonwealth Caribbean* (Mona, Jamaica: Department of Extra-Mural Studies, University of the West Indies, 1984).

3. Max Weber, *Economy and Society*, vol. 2 (Berkeley: University of California Press, 1978), p. 953.

4. P. Bourdieu and J. Passeron, *Reproduction* (Beverley Hills: Sage, 1977), p. 4.

5. Jürgen Habermas, *Legitimation Crisis* (Boston: Beacon, 1975), p. 48.

6. Barrington Moore, *Social Origins of Dictatorship and Democracy* (Boston: Beacon, 1967).

7. Ibid., pp. 247–55.

8. Frantz Fanon, *The Wretched of the Earth* (New York: Grove, 1968), p. 236.

9. Smith, *Plural Society*, pp. 276–80.

10. George Danns, *Domination and Power in Guyana* (New Brunswick: Transaction Books, 1982), pp. 68–72.

11. George Brizan, *Grenada; Island of Conflict: From Amerindians to People's Revolution, 1498–1979* (London: Zed Books, 1984), p. 286.

12. Ibid., p. 289.

13. *Annual Report* (St. George's, Grenada: People's Revolutionary Government, Dept. of Statistics, 1982), p.5.

14. A. S. Phillips, "Teacher Education in the British Caribbean," *Caribbean Quarterly* 12 (Mar. 1966).

15. For a more detailed application of this model to the nationalist period in Antigua, see my *Peripheral Capitalism and Underdevelopment in Antigua* (New Brunswick: Transaction Books, 1985), pp. 169–200.

16. Moore, *Social Origins of Dictatorship and Democracy*, p. 453.

17. Rudolf Bahro, *The Alternative in Eastern Europe* (London: NLB, 1978), p. 10.

18. Chris Searle, *Words Unchained* (London: Zed Books, 1984), p. 24.

19. Ibid., p. 44.

20. Paul Seabury and Walter A. McDougall, eds., *The Grenada Papers* (San Francisco: Institute for Contemporary Studies, 1984), p. 144.

21. Maurice Bishop, *Selected Speeches* (Havana: Casas de Las Americas, 1983), pp. 81–86.

22. Seabury and McDougall, *Grenada Papers*, p. 147.

23. Ibid., pp. 77–78.

24. Gregory Sanford and Richard Vigilante, *Grenada: The Untold Story* (Lanham, Md.: Madison Books, 1984), p. 71.

25. Richard Fagen, *The Transformation of Political Culture in Cuba* (Stanford: Stanford University Press, 1969), p. 147.

26. Ibid., pp. 84–109.

27. Tony Thorndike, *Grenada: Politics, Economics and Society* (Boulder: Lynne Rienner, 1985), p. 82.

28. Seabury and McDougall, *Grenada Papers*, p. 72.

29. Bishop, *Speeches*, p. 20.

30. Ibid.

31. Chris Searle, *Grenada: The Struggle Against Destabilization* (London: Zed Books, 1983), p. 156.

32. The virtual absence of references to the research subsector stems from the fact that there was little or no increase in the output and storage of scientific knowledge. This stagnation in scientific output was related to the predominantly agricultural nature of the economy and to the weak ties between the knowledge-producing sector and the production system.

3. Macroeconomic Growth Under the People's Revolutionary Government: An Assessment

Wallace Joefield-Napier

THE ECONOMIC policy of the People's Revolutionary Government was a partial, but unsuccessful, break with the past. Since the early 1950s, the management of Grenada's economy had relied heavily on the use of the market as an allocative tool which opened up the economy to private investment, both domestic and foreign. The PRG's policies reflected an abandonment of the market approach in some areas of the economy in favor of one that relied on a "material balance" approach, patterned along the lines practiced in socialist countries.[1] As applied in segments of the Grenadian economy, the planning process made little use of market prices as allocative instruments. State ownership and operation of most public utilities, commerce, and other nonagricultural activities increased sharply. Extensive controls were applied to export agriculture through the appointment of government representatives to commodity boards.

The new policy was adopted at a time when the economy was in considerable disarray due to a number of factors, some of which were beyond the country's control (Hurricane Allen, falling export prices). In general, however, it seems that the talent required to make central planning effective was simply unavailable, even with the help of advisors from other Caribbean and socialist countries. Because of a greater reliance on central planning, prices in many spheres of economic activity simply did not reflect (and were actually misleading as to) the real supply and demand situation. As subsequent events amply demonstrated, a transition from primary reliance on a market mechanism to central planning entailed severe short-run dislocations.

It is therefore useful to think of Grenada's economic system as being in a dysfunctional state during the period from 1979 to 1983. In other words, in the dysfunctional state, the market mechanism was less effective than it was before, and government-owned and -operated parastatals became dominant. Moreover, the persistent inability of the PRG to implement a satisfactory central planning mechanism to replace the market mechanism seriously impaired the functioning of the economic system. In addition to the economic damage created by the use of state controls under the ideological mystification of socialism, Grenada, of course, experienced a wide range of conventional economic problems facing developing economies—unproductive technologies, short supply of skilled labor, low domestic saving rate, heavy defense burden, limited resource endowment, the dearth of manufacturing enterprises, and so forth.[2] These issues, in turn, were all affected by the delicate international position that the PRG faced in its efforts to transform the economy.

However, not all of the conditions under which the Grenadian economy operated were unfortunate ones. Although receipts from traditional exports fluctuated sharply, the PRG had greater access to foreign exchange, as these receipts were supplemented by remittances from Grenadians living abroad as well as by grants and loans from multilateral lending organizations. To some extent, these "outside" resources pushed back some of the constraints imposed by shortages in foreign exchange supplies. Some macroeconomic indicators thus began to improve, the economy as a whole grew, and the balance of payments position, in particular, was strengthened considerably. At the same time, problems created by dysfunctional economic management continued, leading to low growth rates in key sectors of the domestic economy (tourism and manufacturing), misallocation of investable resources with consequent underutilization and low productivity growth, and an increase in social and political tension. The favorable macroeconomic indicators therefore hid important problems, the solution of which was essential for building an economy that could increase the social and economic welfare of the populace during the transition toward "the successful construction of socialism."[3]

The general milieu within which economic policy was made under the PRG can be summarized as follows:

1. The mixed economy, state sector dominant model of development was the primary political directive. The aim was to facilitate as quickly as possible the transition toward socialism, rather than to recreate the market-oriented approach of the Gairy years. A primary concern of the PRG with a free-market approach to economic development was that it would "have tremendous dangers for the successful construction of socialism and leave the PRG without the effective possibility of guiding and regulating economic development through the imposition of taxes, the granting of credits and concessions, and the use of all arms of the state apparatus."

2. The availability of very large amounts of outside funds was expected to be of short duration. In any event, it was felt that it would have

been inappropriate and risky for a country of Grenada's size and position in the socialist camp to be dependent on foreign resources over which it had no control.

3. Management and organizational skills were scarce relative to foreign exchange availability. Many projects, especially in productive sectors, took considerable time to be developed and implemented, and in the medium term they turned out to be less productive than expected.

4. Grenada's government bureaucracy constituted a major barrier to change. A bureaucracy is rarely an effective agent of change, but in the case of Grenada it seemed to have become an effective barrier to it.

5. Grenada, with the forces of traditional society still exercising a far stronger influence than those of modernity, like most Third World countries was itself in a transitional state. Thus a high rate of investment in nonagricultural activities during the period 1979–1983, even if managed efficiently, would necessarily have enhanced social tension by imposing on the community much that was new and alien.

6. Finally, the international environment, combined with social and political objectives, dictated against socialist policies that were uncertain and, hence, risky. A very high premium was placed on social and political stability; economic measures whose impact would have contributed to political instability were to be eschewed.

Such an environment clearly limited the options available to PRG policymakers. The development strategy pursued by the PRG was based on the development of a mixed economy whose cornerstone was the dominance of the state sector over the private and cooperative sectors.[4] But this essentially meant an emasculation of the role of the private sector in the development process. In fact, under the PRG, there was a progressive growth in the state sector in major areas of economic activity (such as commerce, agriculture, banking, and public utilities) at the expense of the private sector. In addition, several major infrastructural projects were started and other new projects were announced on a regular basis. The problem is that this "strategy" depended critically on very substantial capital inflows from outside the system, whose future availability was by no means assured. More important, the approach did not improve economic management and hence did very little to influence real economic growth. Indeed, the strategy allowed the PRG to avoid difficult (risky and, hence, politically unpalatable) decisions that were necessary to raise the productivity of domestic resources. While investment projects were of course necessary to carry them out, without fundamental changes in economic management and organization, they only worsened other problems. In fact, geographical disparities in prices and incomes persisted; so did social tensions and inequalities of various kinds, and these detracted from much of the economic welfare gains produced by increased output.

LEGACIES OF THE PAST

The PRG inherited an economy that had undergone international economic upheavals, domestic economic mismanagement, and civil disturbances during the seventies. Although by 1983 the economy had made some headway, many deep-rooted structural economic and social problems persisted. Unemployment and underemployment were endemic, and balance of payments deficits constant. Even in the labor intensive tourism sector, import content continued to be high. Entrepreneurial talent also remained scarce, and the supply of skilled labor limited.

The Sixties

Although detailed official national accounts are unavailable, data published by various international agencies suggest that in the ten-year period 1960–1970, GDP grew at an average annual rate of 8.5 percent in nominal terms and 5 percent in real terms—a more than satisfactory performance for a small country such as Grenada. In the main, growth was confined to two major export sectors, agriculture and tourism. In the former, the growth originated in the sustained efforts to reestablish the production of traditional export crops, which had been devastated by Hurricane Janet in 1955, thus recovering previous production levels rather than attaining new ones. On the other hand, the growth in tourism during the same period showed a genuine increase, with visitor arrivals increasing from a negligible number in 1960 to over 30,000 in 1970. Similarly, the public sector showed strong growth during the 1960s, with a value added increasing from 14 percent of GDP in 1960 to nearly 20 percent of GDP in 1970.

However, structural imbalances within the balance of payments and fiscal accounts emerged, becoming the major source of economic difficulties during the 1970s. Table 3.1 shows that imports grew rapidly, but since a part of this was related to the growth of tourism, tourism receipts dampened the full impact of capital outflows on the country's balance of payments. Inasmuch as the rate of growth of the country's exports fell below that of imports, the deficit of Grenada's balance of trade account grew from U.S. $3.9 million in 1960 to U.S. $16 million in 1970. Yet, the country was able to finance the substantial deficits on its current account. This was accomplished mainly through grants and concessionary financing to the public sector and through private capital inflows.

The expansion of the public sector during the sixties occurred at a time when tax revenues were increasing rapidly, although from a very

Table 3.1
Grenada's Balance of Trade, 1960–1970
(millions of current U.S. dollars)

Item	1960	1965	1966	1967	1968	1969	1970
Merchandise imports	7.4	9.5	10.8	12.1	13.2	17.1	22.1
Merchandise exports							
(including re-exports)	3.5	5.5	5.1	4.3	5.1	7.7	6.1
Balance of trade	−3.9	4.0	5.7	7.8	8.1	9.4	16.0

Source: Government of Grenada and Caribbean Development Bank. Unless otherwise indicated, data in all other tables in this chapter are from the same sources.

low tax base. Nonetheless, the rate of growth of the government's current expenditures was in excess of the country's revenue generation capability, and the central government had to cope with a persistent deficit in the public sector's current account. Despite persistently negative public sector savings, however, the continued expansion of current expenditure was made possible by budgetary assistance in the form of external grants. Correspondingly, the capital budget was financed, initially, through grant assistance and external borrowings, but toward the end of the decade borrowings from the domestic money market increased in importance.

The Immediate Preindependence Period

During 1970–1974, GDP stagnated in nominal terms and declined in real terms, as structural weaknesses persisted and a series of unfortunate events ensued. In particular, adverse weather conditions in 1973 led to a substantial reduction in agricultural output and, in turn, export receipts. This was followed by a serious economic recession in 1974. Political unrest and civil disturbances, which accompanied independence early in that year, had a devastating effect on tourism, and the number of long-stay arrivals dropped by more than 50 percent below the 1973 level. Other sectors of the economy were also affected by the 1974 crisis. In fact, the complete closure of the port of St. George's by strike action during the first three months of that year led to a virtual suspension of foreign trade, totally disrupting commerce and industry. Political instability also had negative repercussions upon the public sector revenues, which, as in most export-propelled economies, were heavily dependent on export sector taxes.

The problems that Grenada faced in the early years of the 1970s were also due to structural deficiencies in three major sectors—agriculture, tourism, and government. In agriculture, a steady decline in all major export crops took place during 1970–1973. Although unit values did show some increases, the fact that volume figures fell sharply pointed to fundamental weaknesses in the sector. Visitor arrivals peaked in 1972, and the subsequent decline in 1973 and 1974 reflected not only a general slackening of demand for Caribbean tourism but also the lack of an effective tourism development strategy. The problems that the public sector faced can be traced back to the structural imbalances in the fiscal system that were evidenced during the 1960s. In 1970, the United Kingdom ceased to provide budgetary support, and this led to a serious contraction in public sector operations.

All of this led to severe foreign exchange pressures. Given the nature of the country's monetary arrangements, however, the foreign exchange squeeze that it faced during the period 1970–1973 manifested itself in a fall in real incomes rather than in a balance of payments deficit. As expected, therefore, the foreign exchange crunch led to a substantial fall in import volumes in 1974; this was further aggravated by the virtual collapse of the tourism industry in that year as well as by the sharp increase in international prices.

To summarize, the rapid compression of imports significantly squeezed the national economy and, so, perversely accelerated price increases during the first few years of the 1970s. Moreover, as a result of the poor performance of the productive sectors and the high propensity to consume of the economy as a whole, the pattern of public sector savings established in the 1960s continued throughout the early years of the 1970s. With the end of British grant-in-aid in 1970, the financing of the deficit on the public sector's current account became problematic, thus terminating the rapid expansion in the public sector's current expenditures that began in the 1960s. Furthermore, tax revenues declined substantially because of the contraction in the economy. In 1974, fiscal problems became particularly acute when, with the suspension of international trade, current revenues fell by almost 25 percent. Once begun, fiscal insolvency was avoided by external financial assistance.

Overall, the performance of the economy in mobilizing domestic savings during the period of economic decline (1970–1974) was dismal. Domestic savings were virtually zero throughout most of the period; for some years they were even negative. The shortfall in gross domestic savings was largely met by foreign capital inflows, mainly in the form of grant assistance for public sector projects and direct capital inflows. Foreign private capital inflows slackened in 1970 and 1971, however, with the completion of a number of hotels. In view of the decline in foreign capital inflows, and as a result of the slow rate of growth of national savings, the country faced no other choice but to put a break on its overall investment effort.

The Pre-PRG Years

During 1975–1978, a number of events helped to avert total economic and fiscal collapse. First, world market prices for the country's major export crops increased dramatically, leading to a sharp increase in export earnings: 1978 export earnings increased by almost 76 percent over the 1974 level. Cocoa earnings rose particularly sharply, followed by those of bananas. Second, both overnight and cruise ship arrivals increased markedly from their low 1974 levels. Third, a medical school was established near St. George's in 1977, and the influx of foreign students boosted domestic demand for housing and other goods and services. Gross domestic product thus grew by 15 percent in real terms during this period.

However, the rapid growth of foreign exchange receipts from export earnings did not contribute much to the transformation of the economy; the absence of a consistent import substitution policy made it impossible to create backward linkages from exports to the production of domestic inputs. Consequently, import growth increased in tandem with the growth in foreign exchange receipts, and much of the former was in the area of consumer goods.

Consumer prices increased significantly during this period. The main reasons for this were the depreciation of the pound (to which the Eastern Caribbean dollar was pegged in 1975 and 1976), the introduction of stamp duties on imports, foreign exchange taxes in 1977–1978, and relatively high inflation rates experienced in countries supplying goods and services to Grenada.

Because comprehensive wage statistics are unavailable, it is difficult to assess the welfare effects of price increases on the working population. Nevertheless, rough estimates indicate that wage increases in the private sector kept pace with the increase in inflation. However, this was not the case with civil servants' wages, since they did not receive any salary increases between 1971 and 1975. In 1976 civil servants received an interim wage increase averaging 18 percent retroactive to 1975; a final settlement was reached in 1978. This latter settlement entailed a 27 percent wage increase to civil servants on average and, besides being retroactive to 1977, was valid to the end of 1980.

Despite the introduction of new revenue-generating tax measures—including a stamp duty, a tax on interest paid by commercial banks, and a telecommunication tax—the fiscal performance of the government continued to remain weak. The major source of fiscal weakness was the rapid growth of current expenditures because of increased spending in public sector wages and salaries. In 1978, the government wage bill was almost two and a half times that of 1975, in nominal terms. Other factors that contributed to the deterioration in government finances were inadequacies in public expenditure controls and a high level of subsidies to state enterprises. In 1977, the government instituted expenditure monitoring procedures in order to bring expenditure in line with revenues; however, unbudgeted expenditures persisted. And with current expenditures exceeding revenues, the government continued to rely heavily on external grants and loans to cover its current accounts deficits.

As for capital expenditures, it might also be noted that budgetary allocations of funds exceeded actual expenditures, but this was mainly due to shortcomings in project preparation, implementation, and monitoring. More important, because public sector savings were negative for most years, the financing of capital projects continued to rely heavily on foreign capital inflows. In particular, net foreign capital inflows financed nearly four-fifths of the overall deficit between 1975 and 1978, and only one-fifth of development expenditures funding was obtained from domestic sources.

Gross domestic saving remained relatively low during this period, averaging about 5 percent of GDP. To a large extent, this low savings rate can be attributed to the high level of real consumption and consistently high negative public sector savings. Because of high levels of remittances from abroad, however, national savings rose to progressively higher levels when compared with the level attained during the period 1970–1974, averaging 10 percent of GDP.

The external environment was conducive to a rapid revival in Grenada's external sector, and both merchandise exports and tourism receipts showed strong gains. Moreover, these gains enabled the country to partially offset a rapid increase in imports, and this, in turn, led to some improvements in the current account of the balance of payments. The current account deficit, which averaged U.S. $6.3 million in 1971–1974 and was equal to 18.4 percent of GDP, dropped to an average of U.S. $1 million in 1975–1978, or 2.1 percent of GDP. Further cuts in public sector deficits during 1975–1978 seemed to have been difficult. In fact, any attempt to curb imports without being able to adjust the country's exchange rates would undoubtedly have led to civil discontent and a reduction in the momentum of economic growth within the country. Such an outcome would have had severe consequences for Grenada's long-term development. Thus the essence of the government's policy during the period 1975–1978 was the enhancement of private sector confidence and the laying down of general principles and procedures to govern foreign investment.

The Balance of the Gairy Era

As can be seen from the foregoing analysis, the PRG leadership inherited an economy that was plagued by many constraints to rapid economic growth, which tended to minimize the welfare gains of all sections of the community. A major growth constraint was an over-emphasis on a few traditional export crops—cocoa, bananas, nutmeg, and mace. In fact, the government made very little use of policy instruments to offset instability in farmers' earnings from export agriculture, to enhance labor productivity in agriculture, and to improve the rural living environment.

Another constraint was the shallowness of the industrial sector. Up to 1979, the industrial sector in Grenada was small, contributing less that 1 percent to GDP. Much of industrial production was for the domestic market and depended to a rather high degree on imported raw materials and intermediate goods. Grenada also imported all of the machinery and equipment required for investments in productive sectors.

A third major area of weakness was the inability of the government to develop a stock of skills to meet the needs of the country's development process. Up to 1979, Grenada was in dire need of a diverse array of training mechanisms—private and public, formal and informal, institutional and on the job—to meet a growing need for skills. Furthermore, although there were several academic high schools in existence, trade schools were rare, and emphasis was placed on academic rather than on vocational training.

In addition to the preceding problems, institutional rigidities and economic inefficiencies resulted in the retardation of economic growth, leading to a structure of demand that contributed little to enhancing the standard of living. Among the institutional constraints was the lack of resolve and commitment by policymakers to pursue a sound development strategy. A striking example of the lack of resolve and commitment was evidenced by deficiencies in tax administration, particularly during the 1960s and 1970s, when the elasticity of the country's tax system was extremely low. Among the factors responsible for the inefficiency and ineffectiveness of tax administration were (1) strong reliance on traditional methods and procedures, which impeded the efforts that were made to attract and retain competent staff; and (2) lack of a compliance program.

To some extent, the first problem was compounded by the shortage of trained staff and material resources. The second problem was due mainly to the fact that records of taxpayers were incomplete and inadequate. Tax avoidance and evasion were widespread, which directly affected the ability of the state to finance social and productive sector programs. Some argue that, at the microlevel, political involvement in the day-to-day operations of the public service was excessive and public sector managers had no incentive to increase efficiency because their primary concern was to please the political directorate. Substantial wage increases to workers have also been criticized for making the economy vulnerable to external shocks outside its control. The massive increase in wages to public sector workers in the period 1970–1978, while narrowing the income differentials between farm and nonfarm workers, seemed to have reduced the incentive of the former group to improve the efficiency of the agricultural sector.

To be sure, there were positive developments during the period, not the least of which was the reduction in the birth rate, which fell from 44.5 per thousand in 1960 to 27.8 per thousand in 1978. In addition, the country's tourism industry developed rapidly. However, structural problems seemed to outweigh much of the beneficial developments. It is against this background that the PRG tried to implement a new development strategy and so lay the foundation for a radical change in the structure of the Grenadian economy.

THE PATTERN OF GROWTH UNDER THE PRG

Table 3.2 shows the development of Grenada's national account over the period 1980–1983.[5] Several observations about this development are of particular relevance in assessing the country's economic performance under the PRG.

First, the rate of growth of GDP in real terms shows an upward, but fluctuating, trend between 1980 and 1983; the rate of growth increased by 9.4 percentage points in 1980–81 and 2.7 percentage points in 1981–82, but fell by 2.2 percentage points in 1982–83. At the same time, the data show a growth rate of 1.7 percent over the entire 1980–

Table 3.2
Grenada's Gross Domestic Product by Industrial Origin, 1980–1983
(millions of 1980 U.S. dollars)

Item	1980	1981	1982	1983	Growth Rate (%)
Agriculture	14.8	16.5	14.4	16.2	2.3
Crops	12.5	15.2	12.8	14.5	3.8
Livestock, forestry, and fishing	2.3	1.3	1.6	1.7	−7.3
Quarrying	0.7	0.8	0.9	0.7	
Manufacturing	2.0	2.1	2.4	1.9	−1.3
Utilities	1.5	1.5	1.5	1.5	
Construction	3.7	6.6	9.7	7.7	20.0
Transportation and communications	5.2	5.3	5.8	5.5	1.4
Hotels and restaurants	3.1	3.1	3.0	3.1	
Retail and wholesale trade	12.8	12.5	13.3	12.8	
Financing and housing	4.5	4.5	4.9	4.9	2.2
Government services	14.8	14.9	15.0	15.0	0.3
Other services	4.0	4.3	4.5	4.4	2.4
GDP at factor cost	67.1	73.4	75.4	73.7	2.4
GDP per capita	74.5	83.2	82.5	79.8	1.7

1983 period. This, of course, is a fair showing in the Grenadian situation, especially given that both output and prices of major export crops were affected by bad weather, outbreaks of disease, and shrinking markets resulting from a worldwide recession at the beginning of the 1980s.

Second, during the period 1980–1983, the agricultural sector grew by almost 4 percent. However, the increase in growth evidenced by this sector seemed to have been due mainly to a change in the composition of agricultural output rather than increased output across the board. In particular, banana and cocoa output fell sharply, and yields of nutmeg and mace were constant or declined. At the same time, production and yield of fruits and vegetables seemed to have increased sharply, and this probably reflected the buoyant demand for fruits and vegetables on the Trinidad and Tobago market during the early 1980s. More important, the growth of livestock, forestry, and fishing clearly lagged behind the output of export agriculture, and the 1983 output of this subsector was markedly below that of 1980.

Third, growth in the manufacturing sector showed slight increases in both 1981 and 1982, but a substantial drop in 1983. Indeed, the slow growth in the manufacturing sector probably reflected a lack of entrepreneurial expertise, the high price of energy and capital, and an unreliability in the supply of inputs in productive processes, among other factors.

Fourth, government services, one of the major sectors within the economy, showed a very small increase in terms of its contributions to GDP, moving up from U.S. $14.8 million in 1980 (at constant 1980 prices) to U.S. $15 million in 1983. In any case, the rate of growth recorded by this sector was only 0.3 percent over the four years. Other sectors that recorded negligible rates of growth were transport and communication, hotels and restaurants, and retail and wholesale trade.

Fifth, the rate of growth of the construction sector accelerated after 1980, and by 1983 construction ranked as the fastest growing sector within the Grenadian economy. The bulk of capital formation within the sector was undertaken by government, with investments concentrated in a few projects, including the Point Salines Airport, feeder roads, and water projects. At least in the short term, this high concentration of investments in a few areas did not have the positive impact on the economy that was generally expected, as critical investments in growth-generating, short-maturation, productive sector projects were neglected.

Sixth, private sector investment fell rapidly, dropping from U.S. $5.8 million in 1980 to U.S. $3.5 million in 1983 (see table 3.3). Much of this investment was concentrated in the service and construction sectors. In view of the attempts made by the PRG to attract private sector investment, an analysis of the factors that led to a retardation in the rate of growth of private sector investment is especially relevant for

Table 3.3
Grenada's Gross Domestic Product by Expenditure, 1980–1983
(millions of 1980 U.S. dollars)

Item	1980	1981	1982	1983
Consumption expenditures	65.3	65.4	68.2	68.7
Public	17.3	17.4	17.4	17.3
Private	48.0	47.0	50.8	51.3
Gross domestic investment	20.7	32.1	37.4	31.7
Public	13.7	25.7	32.9	29.5
Private	5.8	5.0	3.9	3.5
Change in stocks	1.2	1.4	0.6	−1.2
Net exports of GNFS	−21.0	−27.0	−37.7	−36.3
Exports	39.6	39.3	38.4	39.1
Imports	60.6	66.3	76.1	75.4
Statistical discrepancies	5.5	5.6	1.0	−1.6
GDP at market prices	59.5	64.0	67.0	65.6

understanding the problems of economic management under the PRG. This issue will be addressed later on.

Finally, the growth of public sector consumption expenditure (in constant 1980 prices) remained virtually constant over the period 1980–1983. On the other hand, private sector consumption expenditure increased from U.S. $48 million in 1980 to U.S. $51.3 million in 1983. As will be discussed later, the increase in private consumption expenditure seemed to reflect a response of consumers to uncertainty in terms of both real and nominal income.

THE BALANCE OF PAYMENTS UNDER THE PRG

The pattern of visible trade traced by the current account of the balance of payments during the PRG years did not differ significantly from that observed in earlier years. For instance, after increasing sharply between 1975 and 1978, the acceleration in import growth continued moving up from U.S. $47.3 million in 1979 to reach U.S. $64.6 million in 1983.

The growth in export earnings rose at a much slower rate during the PRG years when compared with the rate of growth during the 1975–1978 period. After increasing sharply between 1978 and 1979, export earnings fell sharply in 1980, and then recovered slowly and haltingly during the period 1981–1983. Overall, the visible trade deficit widened from U.S. $25.9 million in 1979 to U.S. $45.7 million in 1983.

The sharp increase in the visible trade deficit during the PRG years was accompanied by a decline in net factor service receipts, with net receipts falling from U.S. $0.3 million in 1979 to negative U.S. $4.5

million in 1983. While tourist receipts provided a positive balance on the country's foreign travel account during the same period, total receipts from the tourist sector dropped sharply, from U.S. $19.5 million in 1979 to U.S. $14.7 million in 1983. Major factors underlying the erosion in foreign trade balance, however, were outflows in income payments to Cuban labor working on the international airport and payments that were made for miscellaneous transactions.

Developments relating to current transfers seem to cast some doubt on the popular view that uncertainty played a major role in the economic fortunes of Grenada under the PRG. As shown in table 3.4, although net current transfers stood at only U.S. $1.3 million in 1979, by 1983 the figure rose to U.S. $10.8 million. In addition, since remittances represented a major component of net current transfers, the upward trend in net transfers seems to suggest that the inflow of remittances increased during the PRG years.

While foreign capital inflows, especially in the form of aid, surged during the PRG years, the positive balance on the country's capital account was able to offset the deficit on the country's current account during only two years, 1979 and 1982. As shown in table 3.4, net capital movements increased from U.S. $14.9 million in 1979 to U.S. $26.7 million in 1983. Almost all capital inflows went to the public sector (private capital inflows remained small and, indeed, were negative in 1979). Since private capital failed to complement public sector capital inflows, the country's external public debt began to gain importance as aid began to diminish after 1982. This may explain why the country's total debt to GDP ratio rose from 13.2 percent in 1979 to 58.3 percent in 1983.

Table 3.4
Grenada's Balance of Payments, 1979–1983
(millions of U.S. dollars)

Item	1979	1980	1981	1982	1983
Export of goods NFS	40.3	39.6	39.3	38.2	39.0
Imports of goods NFS	56.9	60.3	68.2	77.6	74.3
Factor services (net)	0.3	−2.2	−4.9	−5.3	−4.5
Interest payments	−0.3	−0.5	−0.6	−0.9	−1.2
Current transfers (net)	1.3	9.6	10.4	11.0	10.8
Current account balance	−15.0	−13.3	−23.4	−33.7	−29.0
Capital account	14.9	12.9	15.4	34.0	26.7
Official grants	12.7	12.7	12.9	16.7	12.8
Public borrowing (net)	2.2	1.3	7.5	9.5	14.7
Other		−1.1	−5.0	7.8	−0.8
SDR allocation		0.5	0.4		
Overall balance financing	0.1	−0.1	7.6	−0.3	2.3

MAJOR PROBLEM AREAS UNDER THE PRG

Our overview of the Grenadian economy under the PRG, then, indicates considerable successes in a number of areas. However, the available evidence also suggests that, beneath the favorable picture, the economy was still beset by numerous economic problems. The prevailing favorable trend in prices for traditional export crops in the period 1975–1978, which stimulated domestic savings, was expected to carry over to the PRG years. However, this was not the case, and major difficulties appeared in the traditional export sector and in the mobilization of domestic resources, in general.

The problems faced by the traditional export crops are illustrated by the figures in table 3.5. The volume of banana exports declined steadily after 1979, and although there were some increases in prices, this was inadequate to compensate farmers for the fall in output. In contrast, the volume of nutmeg exports showed an increase in 1981–1983, after

Table 3.5
Grenada's Major Exports, 1979–1983

Item	1979	1980	1981	1982	1983
Re-exports (value)	0.78	0.54	0.40	0.75	0.49
Domestic exports (value)	20.63	16.85	18.62	17.82	18.43
Bananas					
Value	3.74	4.11	3.71	3.39	3.24
Volume	31.03	27.46	22.41	21.17	19.53
Unit value	0.12	0.15	0.17	0.16	0.17
Cocoa					
Value	10.03	6.76	7.06	4.62	4.06
Volume	5.34	4.11	5.90	4.62	4.92
Unit value	1.88	1.64	1.20	1.00	0.83
Nutmeg					
Value	4.60	3.16	3.02	3.02	3.25
Volume	5.07	3.35	3.79	4.50	5.34
Unit value	0.91	0.94	0.80	0.67	0.61
Mace					
Value	0.89	0.68	0.63	0.93	0.76
Volume	0.74	0.55	0.46	0.72	0.75
Unit value	1.20	1.24	1.37	1.29	1.02
Fresh fruits					
Value	0.36	0.28	0.49	1.67	4.14
Volume	1.43	0.85	1.73	5.69	15.17
Unit value	0.25	0.33	0.28	0.29	0.27
Clothing (value)	0.37	0.88	2.17	2.43	1.77
Other (value)	0.64	0.98	1.54	1.76	1.21
Total exports (value)	21.41	17.39	19.02	18.57	18.92

Note: Value is in millions of current U.S. dollars; volume is in millions of pounds; unit value is in U.S. dollars per pound.

falling sharply in 1980—but even so, earnings fell because of a sharp reduction in prices. Fluctuations in export volumes and a declining trend in export earnings were experienced by cocoa: the volume of cocoa exports peaked in 1981, fell sharply in 1982, and recovered slightly in 1983. Cocoa earnings reached a high in 1979, but declined substantially thereafter. Overall, the combined export earnings from Grenada's three major export crops fell from U.S. $18.4 million in 1979 to U.S. $10.5 million in 1983. The shortfalls in export earnings, together with the contraction in production experienced in the other areas of the economy (tourism and manufacturing), clearly reflected the persistence of a number of structural rigidities in the economy, including a low savings rate, low investment and productivity in both agriculture and manufacturing, the vulnerability of the economy to imported inflation, and a lack of general employment and management policies that could have effectively created incentives in the economy at large. More generally, the failure of the export sector under the PRG reflected to a large extent an inability to design and implement meaningful economic policies, which were imperative if the large inflow of foreign capital were to be used effectively.

It should not be concluded that exogenous factors (falling export prices, shrinking markets, etc.) were unimportant influences on Grenada's growth performance under the PRG. The point, rather is that the failure of the export sector was partly due to half-hearted attempts to introduce major policy initiatives. As was mentioned previously, one of the most significant developments in the Grenadian economy under the PRG was the large influx of foreign aid. Yet, given the substantial amount of foreign assistance the country received, PRG policymakers were unable to formulate and implement policies leading to a more effective utilization of aid funds. Consequently, because of the inadequacies in the PRG's policymaking mechanism, many of the country's economic and social problems remained unresolved; as these problems persisted, their correction became increasingly more complex.

Several pieces of evidence suggest that after 1980 problems of economic management within Grenada were mounting. Although the available data are sketchy, several of these problems, including skewed investment and low productivity, the tight labor market, a high level of unemployment, and maldistribution of income, are noted below.

Investment and Productivity

Data on the allocation of gross fixed investment indicate that the share of public sector investment in GDP rose from 3.9 percent in 1978 to 44.9 percent in 1983, but these figures hide problems in three major policy areas.

In the first place, there was a gross shortage of personnel with managerial and organizational skills within the public sector, and this impeded efforts to utilize foreign aid effectively. Second, it would seem that the interventionist policies pursued by the PRG produced a set of ambiguous price signals and policies that led, in the manufacturing and agricultural sectors, to a misallocation of resources. Furthermore, these policies seemed to have provided disincentives to individual economic agents in their search for ways to use available resources more effectively. In other words, it would seem that not only was Grenada getting less output for every investment dollar that flowed into the country (excluding the PRG's investment on the Point Salines Airport) but, even more important, new investments were contributing little to a substantial reduction in the structural rigidities that fostered low productivity.

Third, production bottlenecks within the country persisted and these were caused in the main by the country's high capacity to import. In turn, the country's high capacity to import was attributable to a high level of nonearned foreign exchange—that is, foreign exchange unrelated to productivity in the real economy.

Evidently, Grenada's high reliance on imports, which continued during the PRG years, would not have been an issue if investments outside of the Point Salines Airport project were in productive sector projects and the output from such projects were internationally competitive. Evidently this was not the case, and consequently, nonearned foreign exchange was used, not as a means of providing special financial relief to productive sector projects in the short to medium term, but to offset problems created by the inability of the system to use foreign exchange efficiently.

The slow growth of the manufacturing sector has already been mentioned. There were several factors accounting for the slow pace at which the sector grew during the PRG years; included among these were a lack of clear regulations on pricing policy, wage setting and dismissals, custom relief for intermediate and capital goods, foreigners' access to land, and the repatriation of profits. These various factors were, of course, not mutually exclusive. Nevertheless, policy issues relating to these factors revealed the dilemma that the PRG faced during the national democratic phase.[6] The PRG found it inadvisable to move completely and unambiguously to state control of the means of production, yet the incentives that it provided to promote higher levels of private sector investments discouraged capital accumulation by the private sector.[7] Thus for the most part, private investors adopted a wait and see attitude during the PRG years.

The Labor Market and Employment Creation

Although the available employment data are open to numerous questions, some generalizations about the operations of Grenada's labor market during the PRG years are possible.

First, during the PRG years the government continued to be one of the largest employers of labor, but for the most part, wage increases within the public sector were marginal, being constrained by the tight economic situation and a virtual wage freeze for a number of years. The slow rate of wage rate increases and the low wage levels of career civil servants were, however, offset by advantages, such as readier access to bank credit and security of tenure. Juxtaposed against the marginal improvement in the material well-being of career civil servants, however, were the substantial benefits that accrued to noncivil-service technical staff recruited from outside of Grenada. This category of workers were paid salaries well in excess of those paid to career civil servants. In addition, they obtained substantial perquisites. Despite the low wages, however, employment within the public service was relatively attractive when compared to employment in agriculture, and the PRG's attempt to control the "commanding weights of the economy" resulted in a sharp increase in the number of people employed by the state during 1979–1983.

A second major aspect of the operation of the labor market was the politicizing of the civil service. Over time—beginning in the colonial period—Grenada's civil servants had been oriented, in the main, toward a nonideological style. However, in 1983 the PRG decreed that virtually all public servants who work in government ministries and state agencies must attend political education classes as an essential part of their work routine. The penalties for nonattendance at political education classes were severe and threatened the civil servants' very livelihood. Among the penalties were the elimination of annual salary increments and a loss of pay.

A third aspect of the operation of the domestic labor market that became more pronounced during the PRG when compared to the Gairy years was the large-scale migration of skilled and unskilled labor, especially to Trinidad and Tobago and to North America. Of course, much migration of skilled and unskilled labor from Grenada had occurred prior to the PRG assuming power, but political pressures under the PRG regime seemed to have provided an added impetus to the outward flow of labor during the period 1979–1983. Net migration during 1975–1978 averaged 1,408 persons per annum, compared with 1,584 during 1979–1984. Although remittances from Grenadian workers overseas represented an important source of foreign exchange inflows, the exodus of skilled workers led to important problems within the domestic labor market. It particularly exacerbated production bottle-necks in the construction and agricultural sectors. In other words, the ready availability of jobs in foreign countries imposed on the domestic labor market distortions in domestic productivity and wage rates, and this, in part, confused the internal labor market's allocative mechanisms.

A fourth aspect of analytic interest was the reluctance of the government to use wage rates as an allocative mechanism. Rather than enacting labor laws that gave employers some independence in adjusting wages and employment practices in order to restore growth in tradable goods and services, the government sought to subordinate the role of the private sector to that of the state by strengthening its ties with major segments of organized labor. This was done by a "combined program of infiltration, activism and intimidation."[8] By the end of 1983, therefore, the labor policies adopted by the PRG were decidedly in favor of the unions that supported it, leading to indiscipline among workers and the alienation of the business community. Consequently, the adjustments and adaptation to changes in labor demand that occurred during the PRG years were slow and, in some cases, painful to workers.

In combinations, the preceding factors created the appearance of a tight labor market situation in the period 1979–1983. For some skills and in some sectors within the economy, money wages were increasing faster than the rate of inflation, and so real wages rose. At the same time, in other sectors available labor was utilized ineffectively. In overall terms, however, the rate at which productive sector jobs were created lagged behind the number of new entrants to the labor force.

In sum, the creation of productive sector jobs in Grenada during the PRG years was a difficult task, although labor market policies (hiring, wage, and dismissal policies, etc.) aimed at easing the pain of inadequate employment were formulated and implemented. However, many of these policies were based on political opportunism rather than being geared toward bolstering economic growth. The net effect of the PRG's labor policies was that it made it extremely difficult for the country to create new employment opportunities. Furthermore, the huge influx of unearned foreign exchange facilitated a sharp growth in the country's import bill, without a concomitant growth in exports. At the same time, the encroachment of government into the import-export trade increased, leading to a collapse in business confidence as well as to further distortions in the domestic labor market.

Distribution of Income

Although the data are incomplete, it is possible to come to some broad tentative conclusions about income changes over the period 1979–1983.

1. There was a definite, though mild, trend of improvement in the distribution of aggregate income, associated with higher levels of employment in the public sector, including the military.
2. Some large income disparities between landless laborers and small farm owners persisted throughout the period, despite the adoption of land reform measures by the PRG.

3. The relative scale of income differential between unskilled urban workers and agricultural laborers remained much the same.
4. The biggest gain in aggregate income accrued to top functionaries within the PRG.
5. Voluntary redistribution through kinship bonds increased, ensuring that relatively better off urban income earners passed some of their earnings to poor relatives in rural areas.

Prices and Wages

It seems unnecessary to stress the need for some knowledge of the trend in the development in real wages in Grenada during the period under investigation. Such knowledge would provide valuable insights into the question of the direction and extent of changes in the standards of living or workers under the PRG.[9]

Grenada's first consumer price index was compiled in 1979. In that year, the rate of inflation averaged 12.4 percent. In 1980, price inflation rose to 21.2 percent, but in subsequent years the rate of increases slowed appreciably (see table 3.6). The overall rate of inflation was determined principally by the behavior of food prices, since spending on food accounted for over 50 percent of total consumer expenditures between 1979 and 1983. Hence, the intensification in the price inflation, especially between 1979 and 1981, mainly reflected an acceleration in the rate of increase of household supplies, transport, and food prices; the latter was promoted by growing demand and a poor food crop harvest in 1980. Imports did play an important role in alleviating domestic food supply shortages, but unfortunately, the price of goods supplied mainly or entirely from abroad rose even faster than the price of domestically produced goods during the period.

In fact, during 1979–1981, the price levels of fuel and light and of transportation rose by 30.9 percent and 32.3 percent, respectively, while those of clothing and footwear and of household supplies increased by 28.2 percent and 22.7 percent, respectively. Overall, it is clear that the economy was inflation prone during the 1979–1983 period, and this to a large extent was due to the underutilization or misallocation or labor and physical resources and to the unavailability of instruments to correct the existing situation.

The PRG viewed the sharp increase in prices as being due to the "antisocial behavior of sellers." Consequently, the condemnation of "profiteers" became popular, and tighter price control measures were introduced. Adjustments in relative prices were avoided, because it was felt that such adjustments would raise prices in critical areas. In certain critical areas, prices were thus kept fixed at a level that perpetuated market distortions, retarded the responsiveness of supply, and added to the inflationary pressures inherent in the system. Furthermore, in order

Table 3.6
Grenada's Retail Price Index, 1979–1983
(January 1979=100)

Item	Weight	1979	1980	1981	1982	1983
Period average index						
Food and beverages	0.590	113.3	134.8	163.9	172.4	182.2
Tobacco and alcohol	0.025	104.1	125.6	149.6	168.0	181.0
Clothing and footwear	0.080	116.3	140.8	172.7	187.6	198.3
Housing	0.065	101.7	111.4	115.4	128.0	149.3
Fuel and light	0.060	124.5	170.6	186.4	186.5	182.1
Furniture and appliances	0.030	100.2	104.3	163.1	261.9	274.8
Household supplies	0.035	119.7	154.1	165.1	193.5	219.8
Transport	0.040	118.5	162.4	183.1	202.5	217.7
Other services	0.075	102.4	128.5	144.7	150.2	158.4
All items	1.000	112.4	136.2	161.8	174.4	185.1
Percentage change						
Food and beverages			19.0	21.6	5.2	5.7
Tobacco and alcohol			20.7	19.1	12.3	7.7
Clothing and footwear			21.1	22.7	8.6	5.7
Housing			9.5	3.6	10.9	16.6
Fuel and light			37.0	9.3	0.5	−2.4
Furniture and appliances			9.1	49.2	60.6	4.9
Household supplies			28.7	7.1	17.2	13.6
Transport			37.0	12.7	10.6	7.5
Other services			25.5	12.6	3.8	5.5
All items			21.2	18.2	7.8	6.1
End of period index						
Food and beverages		128.1	150.7	170.8	177.2	186.5
Tobacco and alcohol		107.9	139.7	153.2	174.6	187.4
Clothing and footwear		124.9	166.2	181.2	188.7	212.0
Housing		105.4	116.4	114.1	145.7	146.1
Fuel and light		135.9	179.2	189.2	184.7	184.8
Furniture and appliances		100.6	156.4	171.3	264.2	310.2
Household supplies		144.3	161.1	164.8	211.3	225.8
Transport		134.4	170.6	195.6	205.1	216.2
Other services		103.9	140.5	146.5	151.5	172.4
All items		124.5	151.7	167.8	179.4	191.1
Percentage change						
Food and beverages			17.6	13.3	3.7	5.2
Tobacco and alcohol			29.4	9.7	14.0	7.3
Clothing and footwear			33.1	9.0	4.1	12.3
Housing			10.4	−2.0	27.7	0.3
Fuel and light			31.9	5.5	−2.3	0.1
Furniture and appliances			55.5	9.5	54.2	17.4
Household supplies			11.6	5.4	24.4	6.9
Transport			26.9	14.7	4.9	5.4
Other services			35.2	4.3	3.4	13.8
All items			21.8	10.6	6.9	6.5

to subsidize the role of the state in providing larger and larger quantities of low-cost goods and services to the general public, the government found it necessary to increase its borrowings from commercial banks, thus putting further pressure on the system.

MACROECONOMIC MANAGEMENT UNDER THE PRG

In light of the preceding discussion, let us summarize briefly some of the insights arising from our examination of the PRG's macroeconomic policies.

First, the data clearly indicate that there were improvements in the balance of payments and real GDP in specific years after 1979. However, both of these developments were mainly due to factors exogenous to the real economy.

Second, despite a substantial inflow of aid funding, the investment allocation problem remained largely unresolved. Consequently, many of the social welfare objectives of the PRG (high levels of employment outside of agriculture, reduction in income inequality, stable prices, etc.) were impaired.

Third, although the PRG was committed to the principles of scientific socialism, it was reluctant to move resolutely in the direction that would "eliminate all the vestiges of capitalism by means of socialist structural revolution."[10] More specifically, it would seem that this reluctance on the part of the PRG to reorient social and material technology in order to enhance the capability of the system to meet the demands of a democratic-socialist development strategy was strongly influenced by compelling social and political forces, including interclass divisions with the country, external political pressures, and ideological differences within the PRG itself. In fact, the PRG felt that the continuation of the capitalist mode of production during the transformation process was necessary in order to avoid social and economic disintegration in the short term.[11]

Finally, the reluctant action in the economic sphere by the PRG carried within itself a strong dose of inertia, which seemed to have had negative side effects on the general socioeconomic equilibrium of the system as a whole and economic management in particular—an obstacle that has received less attention in the assessment of the economic performance of Grenada under the PRG than it deserves.

As indicated earlier, modes of production and employment have a substantial influence on the use of production opportunities. This applies particularly to labor mobilization but also to the utilization of capital resources. Terms-of-trade and development obstacles arising from foreign exchange shortages are also related to the economic system in operation, as is the ability of government policy to lead to an efficient allocation of resources. Among the economic management problems faced by the PRG were the influence of economic and political forces that imposed feasibility constraints on government policy, such as foreign exchange considerations or demands created by subsidy decisions, government employment, defense, and the nationalization of private sector enterprises. Given the constraints faced by the export sector, it is not difficult to see that the availability of foreign exchange was of key importance to the PRG's public investment decisions. Even so, domestically generated funds were used to finance some elements of the government's investment program.

The PRG's efforts to diversify the agricultural and manufacturing sectors were partially financed through the domestic banking system. In view of the critical role that the availability of domestic funds played within the Grenadian economy, it seems appropriate to examine money supply and demand developments during those years.

Total liquidity in Grenada during the PRG period developed as indicated in table 3.7. Annual increases during the period were as fol-

Table 3.7
Monetary Survey of Grenada, 1979–1983

Item	1979	1980	1981	1982	1983
Assets	*Millions of current U.S. dollars*				
Foreign assets (net)	3.8	2.8	3.7	−5.8	−3.5
Domestic assets (net)	33.5	35.6	36.8	47.8	44.9
Net credit to central government	7.2	5.5	6.0	16.7	18.1
National Insurance Board deposits					−0.4
Net credit to other public sector	−0.4	−0.3	0.6	1.3	2.2
Net credit to nonbank financial intermediaries	−0.5	−0.7	−0.9	−1.7	−1.9
Credit to the private sector	26.8	31.2	32.3	33.2	33.0
Interbank float	1.1	1.6	1.8	2.7	2.0
Net unclassified assets	−0.7	−1.7	−3.0	−4.4	−8.1
Liabilities					
Narrow money (M1)	21.5	24.0	24.3	23.4	23.4
Currency in circulation	10.5	11.9	13.6	14.6	15.1
Demand deposits	11.0	12.1	10.7	8.8	8.3
Broad money (M3)	53.7	57.3	62.0	64.6	64.9
Liquidity ratio	57.6	62.5	60.1	55.7	36.6
	Percentage change				
Narrow money (M1)		11.6	1.0	−3.7	
Currency in circulation		13.3	14.8	7.4	3.4
Demand deposits		10.0	−11.6	−17.8	−5.7
Broad money (M3)		6.7	8.2	4.2	0.5
Time deposits		−11.4	24.6	22.8	0.8
Savings deposits		9.5	9.4	4.0	1.3

lows for the different categories: money supply (M1), of which currency and demand deposits were 1.4 percent; time deposits, 6.2 percent; and savings deposits, 4 percent. Inasmuch as real balance and the ratio of real balances to GDP showed sharp increases during the period, the logical questions that must be asked are, what factors were responsible for the increase in liquidity and how did the economy absorb the increases in liquidity?

The rapid increase in central government borrowing from the domestic banking system was partly responsible for the rapid growth in liquidity. When faced with liquidity problems, the government and state-controlled enterprises exercised overdraft privileges and borrowed extensively from commercial banks. This increased the money supply and had a direct impact on the spending stream of consumers. As already indicated, a substantial part of government's capital inflows was in the form of aid funds, but there are strong a priori reasons that suggest that the government deficit understated the extent to which the country's money supply was affected by government financing. For instance, to the extent that only a part of aid funding went toward meeting the foreign costs of projects, the residue would have been converted to domestic currency, and this, in turn, would have boosted the money supply through government spending.

For all these reasons, the economy was relatively more liquid than in previous years, although price increases were below what one would have expected given the high level of liquidity. Given the strong negative effect of government borrowing (through the crowding out of private borrowing), the private sector response appeared to have been extremely cautious, particularly between 1979 and 1981. For example, currency outside of commercial banks went up by nearly 30 percent between 1979 and 1981, reflecting a strong precautionary holding of cash by the public during the three years. At the same time, despite efforts to restore confidence and stimulate the economy, the liquidity rates of commercial banks became excessively high, with the ratios moving up from 57.6 percent in 1979 to 62.5 percent in 1981. Starting in the latter year, however, the situation changed somewhat, with the ratio falling to 55.7 percent in 1982 and to 36.6 percent by 1983. Clearly, the preference of precautionary holding of liquid assets on the part of the public appeared to be dissipating by the end of 1983, as confidence was being restored.

What about the role of foreign exchange in demand, time, and savings deposits? Data on these variables are presented in table 3.8; the foreign exchange referred to in this table pertains to foreign exchange in commercial banks. To be sure, there was foreign exchange circulating in the country that did not enter commercial banks, and consequently, actual liquidity may have exceeded the amount shown in table 3.7. Even

Table 3.8
Foreign Exchange Operations of Grenada's Commercial Banks, 1979–1983
(millions of current U.S. dollars)

Item	1979	1980	1981	1982	1983
Assets					
Foreign assets (net)	3.8	2.8	3.7	−5.8	−3.5
Foreign assets	15.0	13.8	16.2	7.7	7.1
Foreign currency holdings	−0.7	−0.9	−0.6	−0.6	−0.8
Claims on ECCA	−4.1	−3.7	−6.0	−2.0	−2.4
Currency holdings	1.8	2.1	2.1	1.7	2.1
Claims on ECCB area banks	−6.2	−3.8	−2.8	−2.2	−0.9
Claims on banks abroad	−3.9	−5.4	−4.0	−2.9	−2.2
Other			−2.7		−0.7
Liabilities					
Balance due to ECCA				0.9	1.1
Balance due to ECCA area banks	1.5	1.6	1.5	2.7	
Balance due to banks abroad	3.6	2.6	3.1	1.8	
Nonresident deposits	5.9	6.9	7.9	0.8	8.5
Demand deposits	0.6	1.0	0.9	1.1	1.2
Savings deposits	4.1	4.9	5.8	5.7	5.9
Time deposits	1.2	1.0	1.2	1.2	1.4

so, available information suggests that between 1979 and 1983 over 30 percent of the increase in total savings deposits was in the form of foreign exchange, while 4 percent of the increase in total time deposits was in the form of foreign exchange. Although total demand deposits fell by 7.3 percent between 1979 and 1983, nonresidents' demand deposits rose by almost 2 percent. It must be mentioned that part of the new increment in foreign exchange was not a new increase, but evidently, part was due to a shift from demand to time deposits. In fact, the latter shift was probably due to an increasing trend in the movement of funds between demand and time deposits as well as to interest rate developments among members the Organization of Eastern Caribbean States.

The data in table 3.8 show that by the end of 1982 a substantial part of total assets held by Grenadian banks was in the form of "claims on ECCB and other banks abroad." This seems to suggest that foreign exchange deposits with Grenada's banking system were redeployed abroad either because earning rates were higher in those markets or because foreign deposits offered domestic banks some protection against future contingencies. In other words, deposits outside of Grenada seem to have been used by commercial banks as hedges against any diminution of their earnings. Quite naturally, for commercial banks the precautionary motive prevailed, and this dampened the increase in liquidity, and in turn, inflationary pressures were held in check.

In sum, there were two major flaws in the mechanism for absorbing liquidity within the Grenadian economy during the PRG years. First, since a large part of total liquidity was remitted through the commercial banking system, it meant that part of the foreign exchange inflows that occurred during the PRG years was unavailable for domestic investment and so unable to contribute to growth. Moreover, there was a dire shortage of mechanisms that could have contributed to the optimal use of foreign exchange. In particular, during the PRG years domestic investment opportunities were insufficiently attractive to induce businessmen to invest; among the disincentives to investment were the PRG fiscal programs.

A second flaw was that, because the country was a member of the Eastern Caribbean Currency Authority, the government found itself unable to influence directly the disposition of the increased liquidity through standard instruments of monetary policy. In other words, increases in domestic savings and lending rates would have provided some relief in stemming the outflow of capital, but it appears that the retention of a statutory rate of interest under the Money Lending Ordinance accentuated the imperfections in the domestic money market. Moreover, during the PRG years commercial banks, being traditionally risk averters, hardened their security requirements, repayment terms, and so forth.

Together, the preceding instruments led to a situation wherein the loan menu of commercial banks consisted mainly of self-liquidating, low-risk, and low-return commercial loans rather than of high-risk, high-return loans to productive sectors within the economy. Consequently, the distortions in the loan market produced by both government and commercial bank policies facilitated the outflow of capital.

The main conclusion from the foregoing analysis is that macroeconomic management under the PRG left much to be desired. A cursory examination of government fiscal measures seems to indicate that direct forces were not aimed at controlling direct spending and reducing distortions in the economy but rather at raising revenues. In other words, it would seem that the PRG's spending decisions were based primarily on the need to pay its wage, subsidy, and defense bills and to undertake some public investment. Investments in both defense and large public sector projects were limited in the main by the availability of foreign exchange, but in order to finance the overall public sector deficit the PRG pursued policies that, in effect, led to a withdrawal of part of money balances from circulation. Funds people held in their homes seemed to have offered them protection against possible confiscation. Funds held by households largely originated in remittances from Grenadians living abroad and from the proceeds of foreign aid.

Also, the kinds of investments in which the increases in liquidity were absorbed restricted the PRG's access to a substantial part of foreign exchange inflows. In turn, this resulted directly in lower productive investment than otherwise would have been possible and (indirectly) reduced the efficiency of government policy instruments for financing productive sector projects.

ECONOMIC GROWTH IN GRENADA AND OTHER OECS STATES: A COMPARISON

The belief that the weak growth performance exhibited by Grenada during the period 1980–1983 was similar to growth performances in other OECS member states has been quite strong, especially among international study groups. The major argument is that traditional agricultural exports constitute the bulk of total exports in most OECS member countries and, faced with sharp fluctuations in prices in export markets, OECS member countries experienced sharp declines in their economic rates of growth.

A completely different line of argument supporting an exceptional growth achievement of the PRG has rested on alleged high public sector expenditures on social services in Grenada relative to other OECS member states. Since these hypotheses have a bearing on the findings of the previous sections, they are looked at in some detail below.

Gross Domestic Product

In table 3.9 average annual growth rates of GDP and its components in individual OECS member countries are shown for the period 1980–1983. The first thing one observes in the data is that the overall rate of Grenada's economic growth during the review period was much slower than that of either Dominica or St. Vincent and the Grenadines but exceeded that of Antigua and Barbuda and of St. Lucia. The economy of St. Kitts and Nevis grew at the same rate as the Grenadian economy. The second point to note is that the growth rate of the agricultural sector in Dominica, St. Lucia, and St. Vincent and the Grenadines exceeded that of Grenada. On the other hand, both Antigua and Barbuda and St. Kitts and Nevis experienced slower rates of growth in their agricultural sectors than did Grenada. It must, of course, be pointed out that both Antigua and Barbuda and St. Kitts and Nevis are largely tourism-based economies, whereas the previously mentioned countries are not. Thus, contrary to the widely held view, the relative expansion of the agricultural sector in Dominica, St. Lucia, and St. Vincent and the Grenadines, compared with that of Grenada, seems to suggest that other factors beside the dampening of export prices in traditional markets were responsible for the slow growth performance of the Grenadian economy.

Table 3.9
Gross Domestic Product and Sectional Rates of Growth, Organization of Eastern
Caribbean States, 1980–1983
(percent)

Sector	Antigua and Barbuda	Dominica	Grenada	St. Kitts and Nevis	St. Lucia	St. Vincent and the Grenadines
Agriculture, forestry, and fishing	−4.4	6.0	2.3	−4.5	6.2	11.8
Mining and quarrying	−1.7	3.9			−18.0	4.7
Manufacturing	5.7	8.9	−1.3	−0.9	5.0	2.5
Electricity, gas, and water	7.4	4.0		2.7	3.9	3.6
Construction and installation	−10.9	−8.6	20.0	−9.4	−14.4	2.1
Distributive trades	1.5	0.2		7.0	−0.1	1.9
Tourism	4.4	3.6		−1.1	−1.3	−0.9
Transport, storage, and communication	6.5	9.0	1.4	8.7	1.4	8.9
Financial services	2.2	1.0	2.2	2.2	3.1	1.4
Government services	0.9	2.1	0.3	−2.3	8.5	1.0
Miscellaneous services	1.7		2.4	11.7	2.9	2.1
Less imputed banking charges				−2.3	3.5	1.0
Total at factor cost	2.2	2.7	2.4	2.4	1.7	5.5

Note: Data for Montserrat was not available.

An examination of the rates of growth for economic sectors other than agriculture indicates that Grenada, relative to most of the other OECS member countries, experienced greater diminution over time in the sizes of the following sectors: mining and quarrying, manufacturing, electricity and gas, distributive trades, and tourism. Conversely, Grenada emerges as the country with the largest construction sector among OECS member countries at the end of 1983.

The makeup of GDP in OECS member countries seems to suggest that the absence of growth within Grenada's tourism sector during the PRG years partially retarded the country's economic growth performance.

Public Sector Expenditure

An analysis of changes in the distribution of public sector expenditures in GDP over time is an important step in the evaluation of changes in the standard of living. Table 3.10 assembles relevant data on Grena-

Table 3.10
Grenada's Public Sector Expenditure, 1975–1983
(as percent of GDP)

Year	Total Public Sector Expenditure	Current Expenditure on Goods and Services	Current Transfers (including interest payments)	Capital Formation
1975	25.9	21.3	2.2	2.3
1976	28.9	25.1	2.6	1.0
1977	27.2	20.1	3.6	2.7
1978	32.2	25.6	3.9	2.3
1979	38.7	22.5	4.1	12.1
1980	40.8	21.2	4.5	15.2
1981	50.2	20.0	3.9	25.9
1982	52.7	18.5	5.6	25.5
1983	47.9	18.8	4.9	22.5

Source: Various government publications.

da's public sector expenditure share in gross output, both at the aggregate level and in terms of broad economic categories.

First, during the pre- and post-PRG years, a very high proportion of total domestic expenditure was undertaken by the central government; the share of government expenditure in GDP averaged 38.3 percent. Second, aggregated figures conceal a rather uneven pattern of public sector expenditure shares during the subperiods 1975–1978 and 1979–1983. In particular, between 1975 and 1978, public sector expenditure share in GDP increased by 6.3 percentage points, compared to an increase of 9.2 percentage points between 1979 and 1983. Moreover, if the subperiod 1979–1983 is considered in more detail, we observe that public sector expenditure share on GDP rose by 2.1 percentage points between 1979 and 1980. By 1982, however, there was a sharp upward shift of 11.9 percentage points. After 1982, there was downward deviation of 4.8 percentage points from the 1982 level. Third, in terms of sectoral allocations of public sector expenditures, the data show that 4.3 of the 6.3 percentage points increase between 1975 and 1978 was accounted for by expenditures on goods and services; current transfers accounted for 1.7 percentage points. (The contribution of the share of capital formation to the overall change in total public sector expenditure share was negligible.)

In contrast to the trends discussed above, during 1979–1983, the contribution of public sector expenditure on goods and services to the 7.1 percentage points increase in total public sector expenditure share was negative (−4.3 percentage points). However, current transfers accounted for 0.8 of a percentage point increase in the total, while capital formation accounted for 11.4 percentage points.

Clearly, the above analysis shows that, during 1975–1978, the growth in the share of public sector expenditures on goods and services in GDP was the dominant factor in the overall growth in public sector expenditures. On the other hand, the growth in the share of capital formation was the dominant factor during 1979–1983.

In view of the assertion that the PRG allocated a substantial amount of public sector income (revenues) toward the financing of social programs, it may be useful to examine more closely the average percentage share of public sector expenditures on social sectors relative to other sectors. The data assembled in table 3.11 show the following. First, Grenada's central government current expenditure ratios for defense, education, health, and economic services were much higher during 1979–1983 than during 1975–1978. Second, its current expenditure ratios for general purposes, social security and welfare, housing and community amenities, and other community and social services were higher during 1975–1978 than the subsequent reference period. Third, current expenditure share of social services, combined, accounted for 0.8 of the 9.2 percentage points increase in total current expenditure share during 1979–1983. In contrast, during 1975–1978, the combined expenditure ratios accounted for 0.3 of the 6.3 percentage points increase in current expenditure share.

The preceding analysis establishes that greater welfare gains associated with increased current expenditures on health and education accrued to Grenadians during 1979–1983 than during 1975–1978. That public sector expenditures in most areas of social services were higher during 1975–1978 than after 1978 seems to suggest that welfare gains were more widely spread in the earlier period.

In order to throw light on whether the pattern of Grenada's public expenditure shares was unique among OECS member states, we can examine current expenditure shares in several OECS member states over the period 1975–1978 and compare these with Grenada's expenditure shares. From the evidence provided in tables 3.11 and 3.12, we can draw three conclusions: (1) The average percentage share of Grenada's central government on social security and welfare, housing and community amenities, and other community and social services ranked among the lowest within the OECS. (2) Even though Grenada's expenditures share on economic services show the most rapid rate of increase among OECS countries, its share was below the median for the group as a whole. (3) Grenada's expenditure shares for both health and education were above the median share for all OECS member countries. The comparison seems to suggest that, during the period 1979–1983, Grenada's public sector expenditure performance was clearly superior to those of other OECS countries only in limited areas, mainly health and education.

Table 3.11

Central Government Economic Components in Gross Domestic Product,
(average growth

Classification of Expenditure	Antigua and Barbuda		Dominica	
	1975–78	1979–83	1975–78	1979–83
General purposes	2.87	4.23	−3.55	−3.83
General administration	1.85	4.08	−3.44	−4.08
Public order and safety	1.03	0.15	−0.11	0.25
Defense	0.04	0.34	0.20	−0.72
Education	.00	0.19	−0.94	−1.03
Health	−0.69	1.52	−0.47	−0.26
Social security and welfare	0.42	0.77	−9.50	1.96
Social security	0.36	0.80	−0.49	1.78
Social assistance and welfare	0.06	−0.03	.00	0.18
Housing and community amenities	0.25	−0.54	0.04	−0.98
Housing	−0.30	.00	0.23	−1.10
Community development	0.08	0.12	−0.10	0.38
Sanitary services	0.48	−0.65	−0.08	−0.26
Other community and social services	−0.17	−0.09	0.47	−0.03
Economic services	1.53	−0.36	0.82	−8.92
General administration	0.23	0.15	0.07	−1.55
Agriculture, forestry, and fishing	−0.13	−0.61	0.84	−3.37
Mining, manufacturing, and construction	1.06	−0.15	−0.04	1.36
Electricity, gas, and water	0.24	−0.04	0.04	−0.11
Roads	−0.91	0.43	−0.42	−4.20
Transportation and communication	0.53	−0.12	0.29	−0.85
Tourism		0.66	0.03	−0.20
Other economic services	0.52	−0.67		
Other purposes	−0.08	1.33	−1.26	−1.27
Interest and commissions	0.20	1.33	−1.24	1.72
Other	−0.28		−0.01	−3.00
Total expenditures	4.18	7.39	−5.18	−15.07

SOME CONCLUSIONS

When the economic system and the basic lines of economic policy
are kept stable and the basic economic structure remains unchanged,
macroeconomic perceptions and an analysis of the overall economic
growth performance would by themselves provide reasonable insights
into the process of economic growth. However, when these conditions
are not met (as was the case of Grenada under the PRG), the economic
growth process has to be studied not simply in terms of a macroeconomic relationship, but by taking into consideration a number of additional factors, including

1. The economic system (such as ownership patterns of various
   production and management units, the system of economic control

Organization of Eastern Caribbean States, 1975–1978 and 1979–1983 in percent)

Grenada		Montserrat		St. Kitts and Nevis		St. Lucia		St. Vincent and the Grenadines	
1975–78	1979–83	1975–78	1979–83	1975–78	1979–83	1975–78	1979–83	1975–78	1979–83
4.87	−3.29	−1.93	−6.39	2.32	−0.87	−3.93	−2.83	1.14	−2.72
4.80	−3.56	−1.33	−6.65	1.58	−0.99	−1.07	−4.33	1.92	−3.35
0.07	0.27	−0.60	0.26	0.74	0.12	−2.87	1.49	−0.78	0.62
−0.72	0.61	−0.01	0.01	0.22	−0.40				
−0.79	2.99	−1.11	−1.46	8.09	−0.67	−8.45	0.69	−0.36	0.12
1.24	1.85	−5.53	0.23	1.61	0.82	−3.64	−0.01	−0.56	0.41
0.04	−0.07	−0.16	0.27	1.11	0.28	−0.54	1.10	0.10	1.59
		0.01	0.84	1.01	0.59	−0.25	1.05		1.16
0.04	−0.07	−0.17	−0.57	0.11	−0.31	−0.29	0.05	0.11	0.43
−0.05	−0.28	−1.10	−0.51	0.30	−0.27	−0.25	−0.28	−0.16	0.08
		−1.20	−0.20	0.08	−0.02	0.10	−0.71	−0.26	−0.19
0.11	−0.17	0.18	0.35	0.09	−0.18	−0.12	0.06	0.08	0.28
−0.17	−0.11	−0.08	−0.66	0.13	−0.07	−0.24	0.37	0.02	−0.01
−0.05	−0.16	−0.06	−0.10	0.05	0.20	−0.73	0.46	0.09	−0.24
0.39	0.82	−2.83	−2.52	1.82	−14.94	−7.85	−4.48	−2.56	−0.21
−0.02	0.89	0.11	−0.30	0.12	−1.08	−0.66	−0.38	0.72	−0.37
0.38	−0.22	−1.40	−0.17	2.18	−1.36	−0.82	−2.20	0.02	0.12
	1.09	0.47	−1.06	−0.07	0.53	−0.10	0.59	0.72	−0.37
−0.01		0.32	−0.19	−0.09	−0.38	−0.99	−0.44	−0.31	0.06
−0.02	−1.42	−0.66	1.52	0.13	−2.18	−3.49	−2.10	−1.92	−1.67
−0.04		−3.24	−2.02	−0.68	−11.18	−1.48	−0.08	−0.44	−0.50
0.10	0.48	0.25	−0.30	0.22	0.74	−0.32	0.27	−0.09	−0.01
				0.01	−0.03	0.02	−0.14	−0.54	−0.13
0.23	2.00	−0.14	0.28	−0.39	0.92	−1.54	0.95	−0.74	0.59
0.23	1.77	−0.14	0.28	−0.41	0.98	−1.58	0.95	−1.30	0.62
	0.23			0.02	−0.06	0.04		0.56	−0.03
5.80	4.47	−12.88	−10.18	15.14	−14.94	−26.94	−4.40	−3.06	−0.37

and planning, and the degree to which the market economy and traditional institutions are allowed to operate);

2. Basic economic policy (such as the determination of the targets of social and economic development, the speed and main course by which these targets are attained, and the principle of incentive price formation);

3. The economic structure (such as factor endowments, the structure of productive forces, and the state of interdependence of individual economic units);

4. The government's capability in economic planning and policy formulation (such as the capability to adapt the existing economic system and policy lines to changing economic conditions); and

5. The political and social variables affecting the economy.

Table 3.12
Share of Government Expenditure in Gross Domestic Product,
(percent)

Classification of Expenditure	Antigua and Barbuda		Dominica	
	1975–78	1979–83	1975–78	1979–83
General purposes	9.87	13.49	13.98	12.53
General administration	7.24	11.57	10.58	7.99
Public order and safety	2.62	1.92	3.40	4.54
Defenses	0.11	0.27	0.50	0.28
Education	3.60	2.89	6.37	5.93
Health	2.78	2.83	4.21	4.65
Social security and welfare	0.57	1.46	0.57	2.11
Social security	0.44	1.36	0.21	1.54
Social assistance and welfare	0.14	0.10	0.36	0.57
Housing and community amenities	1.52	0.51	0.65	0.91
Housing	0.42		0.30	0.39
Community development	0.08	0.12	0.15	0.36
Sanitary services	1.02	0.38	0.20	0.16
Other community and social services	0.27	0.17	0.77	0.45
Economic services	7.41	2.98	7.25	6.28
General administration	0.69	0.40	0.85	1.27
Agriculture, forestry, and fishing	1.51	1.01	2.93	2.28
Mining, manufacturing, and construction	1.53	0.36	0.08	0.94
Electricity, gas, and water	0.29	0.01	0.16	0.15
Roads	1.34	0.61	2.77	1.38
Transportation and communication	0.38	0.02	0.33	0.22
Tourism		0.45	0.14	0.04
Other economic services	1.69	0.13		
Other purposes	1.65	3.32	1.64	3.15
Interest and commissions	1.57	3.32	1.63	2.41
Other	0.07		0.01	0.73
Total expenditures	27.77	27.92	35.94	36.28

An additional complication in the case of Grenada is that both economic growth performance and the underlying factors in these different dimensions underwent substantial changes both before and after the PRG years. The assessment of overall growth performance must therefore be accompanied by an explanation of these changes. In the remainder of this section, we will thus examine the interrelationship between the individual performance of the main sectors and aspects of the macroeconomic dimensions and the interaction of the multidimensional factors behind the overall growth performance, focusing particularly on why the economy in general performed better during 1979–1983 than in the earlier years.

Organization of Eastern Caribbean States, 1975–1978 and 1979–1983

Grenada		Montserrat		St. Kitts and Nevis		St. Lucia		St. Vincent and the Grenadines	
1975–78	1979–83	1975–78	1979–83	1975–78	1979–83	1975–78	1979–83	1975–78	1979–83
12.31	10.34	12.83	10.92	12.17	10.92	13.81	11.78	10.40	8.72
8.79	7.78	9.98	8.75	9.24	7.95	10.44	8.54	6.79	5.36
3.52	2.55	2.85	2.17	2.94	2.97	3.36	3.24	3.61	3.36
0.47	2.06	0.08	0.07	0.41	0.27				
4.94	6.21	6.79	3.21	7.69	6.19	7.30	5.85	5.37	6.22
3.89	4.36	7.71	3.16	3.97	4.25	4.58	2.89	4.08	3.58
0.08	0.01	0.87	0.97	0.74	2.05	0.53	1.27	0.43	1.64
		0.22	0.85	0.30	1.84	0.30	1.09	0.28	1.13
0.08	0.01	0.65	0.11	0.44	0.20	0.23	0.18	0.16	0.50
0.24	0.06	0.99	0.65	0.63	0.62	0.45	0.79	0.74	0.63
		0.31	0.04	0.13	0.15	0.03	0.14	0.20	0.04
0.04	0.03	0.25	0.48	0.08	0.05	0.10	0.06	0.08	0.11
0.20	0.02	0.43	0.13	0.42	0.42	0.32	0.58	0.46	0.48
0.37	0.03	0.13	0.14	0.46	0.22	0.75	0.75	0.32	0.25
2.67	4.50	10.86	5.72	8.18	5.39	8.82	5.87	10.79	7.18
0.02	0.28	0.66	0.45	0.66	0.56	0.76	0.33	0.47	1.69
1.30	1.45	2.66	1.05	4.72	1.09	1.74	2.03	1.88	1.22
	2.16	1.53	0.21	0.13	0.26	0.05	0.46	0.21	1.06
0.01		0.24	0.26	0.45	0.08	0.88	0.23	0.31	0.07
1.15	0.28	2.77	2.29	0.83	0.62	4.31	2.38	5.15	2.67
0.08		2.66	1.04	0.83	2.24	0.62	0.05	1.90	0.20
0.12	0.32	0.34	0.42	0.56	0.55	0.44	0.36	0.45	0.24
					0.01	0.01	0.03	0.41	0.03
1.15	2.42	0.25	0.27	2.39	1.86	1.58	1.23	1.55	1.24
1.15	2.32	0.25	0.27	2.37	1.85	1.60	1.23	1.40	1.23
	0.10			0.02	0.01	−0.02		0.15	0.01
26.12	29.98	40.52	25.12	36.65	31.77	37.82	30.42	36.67	29.45

The Centralized Public Sector

In this sector, the Point Salines Airport project received an extremely high proportion of investment funds, constituting a high proportion of national income. The funds were mobilized through the centralized planning mechanism, which aimed in the immediate and long run at bringing about both a high rate of growth of national income and a steady improvement in the living standard of Grenadians. However, because of long gestation periods, the marginal output-capital ratios in the public sector investments did not show a considerable increase over the five years (1979–1983); hence, the expected rise in national income and living standards did not materialize. For the same reasons, the expected increase in the allocation of investment to other sectors, particularly agriculture, did not materialize.

The Domestic Industrial Sector

This sector was successful to some extent in producing and supplying locally an increased amount of agriculture-based products. However, only a small amount of central government resources were used in inducing increased output in the privately owned segment of the manufacturing sector. Consequently, by the end of 1983 the manufacturing sector was still unable to meet a large part of the total requirements of the dominant agricultural sector, which during the 1960s and 1970s became heavily dependent on ever increasing supplies of modern inputs. It also appears that the slow rate at which the privately owned segment of the industrial sector expanded was partly influenced by intensive competition with state enterprises for loanable funds from the banking system.

The Agricultural Sector

The mobilization of domestic resources (in particular, labor) influenced increases in agricultural output more profoundly than increases in the domestic industrial sector. However, climatic factors, such as Hurricane Allen in 1979, and unfavorable export prices for traditional crops (nutmeg and bananas) also influenced output growth.

Foreign Trade

Progress with import substitution was not as successful as had been expected by the PRG's planners, due to internal factors. First, in view of the dire shortage of entrepreneurial talent, the expertise for setting up and managing manufacturing enterprises was lacking. Consequently, a considerable amount of the foreign exchange earned by traditional export crops was diverted toward the importation of consumer durable and nondurable goods. Second, because of the low level of technological capability during 1979–1983, Grenada continued to import a substantial amount of parts and components for maintenance and repairs, and these became additional claimants upon foreign currency.

Intersectoral Flows of Factors and Products

Most of these flows were controlled by planning or administrative rules or by discretion. These controls and regulations were to some extent ineffective in the sense that they led, formally and informally, to very little movement in factors between sectors. To be sure, there was an overall improvement in economic planning, since this was much more orderly than it was in previous years. However, the controls and regulations adopted discriminated strongly in favor of what the PRG considered to be priority sectors and—under the severe constraints coming from an extreme shortage of domestic resources for investment, foreign exchange, and vital inputs—it is unlikely that the policies adopted could have achieved speedier economic development.

Overall Growth of Income and Consumption

Given the effects of the preceding factors, the per capita rate of growth achieved during 1979–1983 was very bad. However, if different policies had been adopted, it is possible that per capita income could have improved significantly. As such, economic performance was far poorer than what might be expected under the development strategy of the PRG. It should be noted that the interrelationships between the main sectors in the economy during 1975–1978 were, to some extent, at variance with those adopted during 1979–1983.

The pattern of investment funds allocated by the central government to state enterprises during 1979–1983 resulted in building up a foundation, albeit weak, for overall industrialization. However, the pattern of agricultural investment and production was essentially the same in both the pre- and post-1979 periods, although in the former, less reliance was placed on central government financing. Traditional staple exports in the main supported large-scale importation of both consumer and durable and nondurable goods in both subperiods, and the importation of machines and industrial intermediate goods was small. Thus a technological base for the industrialization of the Grenadian economy was not created even by 1983.

Interaction of Multidimensional Factors

An exploration of the above-mentioned macroeconomic growth process indicates that the interaction between multi-dimensional factors could best be attempted, first, by exploring macroeconomic growth mechanisms such as the rates of change of domestic investment, national income, fixed capital formation, and marginal output-investment ratios; and, second, by investigating the impact of other dimensional factors on the working of macroeconomic mechanism. A full examination of the macroeconomic growth mechanism underlying the growth process in Grenada under the PRG is beyond the scope of this chapter, but the mechanism may be essentially expressed as a composite model integrating (1) a socialist-type growth model that focuses on the growth of the modern industrial sector; (2) a dualistic industrial development model, with a small enterprise sector using low opportunity cost domestic resources; and (3) an agricultural development model in a densely populated, small, export-propelled economy.

The Political and Social Situation

The impact of these factors was direct and most significant, especially when they were related to changes in the international situation. For instance, the incorporation of Grenada within the socialist fold seems to have led to a huge expenditure by Cuba on the construction of the Point Salines Airport. In other cases, the impact was indirect. For example, the changes in the political influence of certain members of the PRG leadership affected the operation of mechanisms through their impact on policy determination. The situation affecting mutual trust among the PRG leadership also affected the masses; this, in turn, had an impact upon the working of the system and policy lines. Ultimately, political and ideological struggles within the leadership of the PRG affected it through their negative impact upon the nature and direction of the system and policy revisions.

Economic Structure

While the economic structure was transformed after 1979, in particular through the greater involvement of the state in the industrial and financial sectors, the available evidence seems to suggest that the Grenadian economy remained rather underdeveloped. The impact of underdevelopment on the economic structure of the country was evidenced by the severe constraints put on savings, foreign currency earnings (tourism), and industrial employment.

Economic System and Policy Lines

The centralized physical planning system and the high-growth and high capital accumulation policy based upon it often resulted in the interruption of a normal operation of the economic growth mechanism. This, in turn, prevented an expected rise in per capita income and consumption. However, some of the policy lines adopted were new and in disharmony with the economic growth mechanism that the PRG inherited. Therefore, it is understandable that the PRG would have faced problems in harmonizing the two economic growth mechanisms.

Economic Planning and Policy Formulation

The failure to achieve a reasonably appropriate allocation of capital construction investment (outside of the Point Salines Airport project) among the various sectors and the failure to recognize and correct the grossly unbalanced growth process during 1979–1983 seems to be mainly due to the inadequacy of the country's planning capability. A further shortcoming was the failure to detect and correct the utterly inappropriate pricing of services supplied by public utilities which led to a situation in which substantial subsidies had to be provided by the state for provision of services such as electricity and water. The PRG's inability to revise major economic policy lines when the necessity for it arose was even greater than the above discussion suggests.

Such incapability reduced policy implementation to a method of trial and error, thus probably inviting political or ideological intervention in determining policy lines. I wish to emphasize the importance of avoiding trial and error methods of economic development, although, under a situation such as that which existed in Grenada under the PRG, in which a rapid development of statistical and planning facilities and techniques cannot be immediately achieved, a trial and error method at the margin may be inevitable for exploring the state of proper macroeconomic balance.

NOTES

1. My discussion is confined to the economic performance of the PRG. Useful critiques of the political record of the PRG can be found in Fitzroy Ambursley, "Grenada: The New Jewel Revolution" in Fitzroy Ambursley and Robin Cohen, eds., *Crisis in the Caribbean* (New York: Monthly Review Press, 1983); E. Archer, "Garyism, Revolution and Reorganization: Three Decades of Turbulence in Grenada," in *Journal of Commonwealth and Comparative Politics* 23 (July 1985); H. O. Shaughnessy, *Grenada: Revolution, Invasion and Aftermath* (London: Sphere Books, 1984); Selwyn Ryan, "The Grenada Question: A Revolutionary Balance Sheet," *Caribbean Review* 13 (1984); and Gregory Sandford and Richard Vigilante, *Grenada: The Untold Story* (Lanham, Md.: Madison Books, 1984).

2. For a discussion of some of the economic problems that Grenada faced in the 1970s and early 1980s, see Ambursley "Grenada: The New Jewel Revolution."

3. For a discussion of the benefits that accrue to households out of the social consumption fund in a socialist-oriented economy, see J. Wilczyuski, *The Economics of Socialism* (London: Allen and Unwin, 1977), esp. chs. 6 and 15.

4. See *Report on the National Economy for 1982 and the Budget Plan for 1983 and Beyond* (St. George's, Grenada: People's Revolutionary Government, n. d.).

5. The kinds of statistical measures of the Grenadian economy issued by the PRG were related to its policy concerns and orientation. The continued determination of the PRG to maintain the soundness of the currency and to further the growth of foreign trade was reflected in an excellent published series on imports and exports, government revenues and expenditures, and money and banking. However, the government's lip service to the preservation of a free-enterprise economy in which market forces would have adequate scope to allocate resources efficiently meant that it had no need to prepare and publish reliable national product and income accounts. Recently, however, more reliable

estimates of GDP for the period 1980–83 have become available, and these will be used to assess the growth performance of the PRG.

6. For a discussion of the problems faced by technologically backward developing countries during the transitional phase to socialism, see R. A. Ulyanovsky, *Socialism and the Newly Independent Nations* (Moscow: Progress Publishers, 1974).

7. See Maurice Bishop's Line of March for the Party speech in Michael Ledeen and Herbert Romerstein, eds, *Grenada Documents: An Overview and Selection*, Vol. 1 (Washington, D. C.: Depts. of State and Defense, 1984), pp. 1–49.

8. See Sanford and Vigilante, *Grenada: The Untold Story.*

9. No index of the evolution of wages and salaries exists for Grenada. But judging on the basis of wage contracts during the period 1979–83, it may be safely assumed that real wages rose in 1979 and fell appreciably in subsequent years. The fall in real wages was felt most acutely by unemployed workers in urban areas.

10. See M. Abraham, *Perspectives on Modernization: Towards a General Theory of Third World Development* (Washington, D. C.: University Press of America, 1980), esp. pp. 118–200.

11. See Bishop, Line of March for the Party.

Part II

INTERNATIONAL AFFAIRS

4. The Foreign Policy of the People's Revolutionary Government

Anthony Payne

THE DEVELOPMENT and prosecution of a new foreign policy was always regarded as one of the central tasks of the Grenadian Revolution. All the major accounts of the revolution both before and after its collapse confirm this and give a prominent place to the international activities of the People's Revolutionary Government (PRG). Yet several years after the disintegration of the revolution no serious attempt has been made to come to grips with Grenadian foreign policy per se. Only two essays—both of them very brief—have been published directly on this theme. The first, by Henry Gill, was written after only the first two years of the revolution and so must be regarded as no more than a preliminary assessment based on partial evidence. Even so, he drew attention in 1981 to "the accentuation of the ideological line" in respect to antiimperialism, which already characterized the PRG's foreign policy, and astutely warned against the rigidity of such an approach. The revolution, he wrote, had taken up "a position that makes no concession to the concerns of others, friend or foe, and yet demands recognition of one's own concerns."[1] The second piece, by Anthony Gonzales, has the advantage of being written after the invasion and in the light of the many official documents found in Grenada and subsequently published by the Americans; it takes a very different line. "When one cuts through the rhetoric and comes to the bottom line," says Gonzales, it is evident that "the over-riding consideration" of the PRG's foreign policy was "the maximization of Grenada's national interests by the pursuit of solid pragmatism."[2] He considers too that, until the conflicts that wrought havoc among the revolutionary leadership in its last few months, this task was undertaken in a professional and dynamic way. Although neither writer fuller develops his point of view, the two commentaries are valuable because in their contrasting perspectives they pose the central analytical issue facing students of Grenadian foreign policy. It can be expressed most simply as follows: ideology versus pragmatism, revolutionary theory versus the national interest. In practice, of course, the choice is rarely perceived so starkly. Yet the two parameters compete, and the potential conflict needs to be kept in mind as we proceed with the analysis. Let us start with the so-called noncapitalist path of development, which significant elements within the PRG took as their guide.

NONCAPITALIST DEVELOPMENT AND FOREIGN POLICY

The theory of the noncapitalist path was first developed by Soviet scholars during the 1960s. Its principal exponent, Professor Ulyanovsky, was a noted Soviet academician and influential advisor on Soviet foreign policy toward the Third World.[3] As it was first formulated, the theory had a tendency to be associated exclusively with the prospects of socialist transformation in the newly independent states of Africa and Asia. In June 1975, important aspects of it were incorporated into the Declaration of Havana, the final document unanimously approved at the Conference of Communist and Workers' Parties of Latin America held in Cuba. A transition to the Caribbean was thereby affected, and the theory was taken up with particular vigor by a number of Commonwealth Caribbean intellectuals who saw in it a plausible route to power.

As explained by one of them, Ralph Gonsalves, the theory "has its roots in the science of historical materialism as creatively applied to countries where capitalism is either non-existent or underdeveloped, as in Africa and the Caribbean" and posits that "capitalism can be by-passed or interrupted on the route to the construction of socialism."[4] Critically necessary for the realization of this is "a broad class alliance involving the proletariat, the semi-proletarian masses, the revolutionary or democratic strata of the petty-bourgeoisie," governing through "a revolutionary democratic or national democratic state which links up itself increasingly with the forces of world socialism."[5] It is clear from the writings of Gonsalves and others that the decisive aspect of noncapitalist development resides in the realm of politics, deriving its force from a "relative autonomy" of the state evident in many postcolonial countries. It follows that the policies pursued by such states are crucial in determining whether or not they are following the path of noncapitalist development—or socialist orientation, as it has increasing come to be called.

Gonsalves lists nine main features of the noncapitalist path: (1) the abolition of imperialism's political domination by means of an actively antiimperialist foreign policy; (2) the reduction and eventual abolition of imperialism's economic control; (3) the consolidation of the mixed structure of the economy and its development into one in which the state and cooperative economic sectors become dominant; (4) the transformation of the political culture toward socialist values; (5) the engendering of new attitudes toward work and production; (6) the expansion of mass participation in and control of the state administration and state economic enterprises; (7) the removal of plantocratic national bourgeois and imperialist elements from the supreme command of governments and the transference of power to revolutionary democrats and scientific socialists; (8) the development of appropriate planning techniques and organizational methods to raise productive forces; and (9) a raising of the cultural, scientific, and material levels of living for the mass of the people.[6] The noncapitalist road therefore involves both analysis and program, theory and practice, of one possible path to socialism. If fully implemented, it does not constitute socialism itself but rather a political, material, social, and cultural preparation for the transition to socialism.

A grasp of these arguments is important, because from the outset some theoreticians from within Grenada argued that the revolution was guided by just such a perspective. For example, the Jacobs brothers, in a kind of semiofficial exposition of the philosophy of the revolution, claim that this commitment went back to the emergence of the New Jewel Movement (NJM) at the beginning of the 1970s. The 1973 NJM Manifesto is cited as evidence of a "non-capitalist ideological perspective," and the NJM party structure is seen as possessing "distinctly scientific socialist characteristics." Additional considerations were the preeminence within the NJM's leadership of "the progressive young middle-class intelligentsia"; the class character of the emerging political forces opposed to Gairy; "the need to maintain the neutrality, if not the support, of the middle strata"; and, finally, the frank recognition, given the circumstances in Grenada, that "to adopt an overtly Marxist-Leninist path . . . to court alienation and take a deliberately long route to national liberation."[7] Accordingly, the noncapitalist way emerged as "the most appropriate intermediate option"—a strategy that permitted "the mobilization of diverse social elements in the movement towards national liberation and revolutionary change."[8] After the revolution was made, much less was said in public about the theory of noncapitalist development. However, the released documents reveal the extent to which the tenets of the thesis had captured the minds of the most important figures in the party and government. In some quarters the adherence was nothing short of slavish. One text in particular was used and was widely regarded as the revolution's bible. It was published in Moscow and entitled *National Liberation Revolutions Today* by K. N. Brutents.

From our point of view, Brutents is of further significance because he discusses the international dimension of noncapitalist development at greater length than most other theoreticians. Among the tasks facing the national democratic state is listed the pursuit of "an active antiimperialist foreign policy" focused upon three goals: (1) the furtherance of "favorable international premises for the struggle for economic emancipation," (2) the "development of all-round cooperation with the socialist countries," and (3) "coordination of action by the national states against neocolonialism."[9] The first point is not developed, but seems to mean that young national democratic states must fully express in their inter-state relations a growing acuteness of the contradiction that exists be-tween their legitimate aspirations and the forces of imperialism. All that Brutents says is that there will inevitably take place "a *protracted* struggle" with imperialist powers over "the orientation of the young states' devel-opment."[10] The second point is, however, given much more extensive consideration. It is noted that the policy of the socialist countries and the international communist movement in supporting national liberation struggles has not changed since the days of Lenin. "This is part and parcel of proletarian internationalism."[11] What has altered is that this alliance is now being effected less by ties among equivalent social organi-zations and political parties and more and more via interstate relations between the socialist and the newly liberated countries. In particular, since the end of the colonial era the Soviet Union has been prepared both to establish diplomatic relations with appropriate national demo-cratic states in Africa, Asia, and Latin America and to offer specific forms of cooperation. The support of the socialist states is regarded as vital to the struggle for national liberation and is set out by Brutents as follows:

> *In the political sphere,* it is consolidation of the young states' independence, their rights and practical potentialities in deciding for themselves which social orientation to take; efforts to eliminate all expressions of inequality and imperialist dictates from international relations and to strengthen world peace and security of nations.
> *In the military sphere,* it is strengthening the defense capacity of the young states and helping them to defend themselves against aggressive acts and military pressure from the neo-colonialists; resistance to imperialist attempts to use areas of the former colonial and semi-colonial world as strategic and military bridgeheads against the forces of national liberation and the socialist countries.
> *In the economic sphere,* it is struggle for the economic emancipation of the developing countries from imperialism and construction of their national economy; extension of mutually advantageous economic cooperation between states, and against inequality, exploitation and discrimination in international economic relations. . . .
> *In the ideological and spiritual sphere,* it is exposure of the imperialist policy and ideology; struggle against the ideas of national and racial opposition, and against the spiritual expansion of neo-colonialism; and for a cultural revolution in the newly independent countries.[12]

Finally, in respect to the third point, national democratic states are urged to strengthen ties among themselves as a means to consolidating their political independence and winning greater economic emancipation.

In broad terms, therefore, the foreign policy of noncapitalist development could not be plainer—antiimperialist solidarity in ever closer connection with the world socialist system. But in matters of detail—at the level, one might say, of tactics rather than strategy—there are huge gaps as well as lack of clarity as to the pace at which the various aspects of policy actually delineated should be implemented. In short, within the theory a good deal of flexibility (or, more critically, guesswork) is left to the practitioners of foreign policy in the new national democratic state. Skill and subtlety are bound to be at a premium, especially as the state encounters what even Brutents and the official theorists regard as "the prime factor which tends importantly to complicate the progressive development of the young states."[13] This problem is crucial and consists of the fact that imperialism is still a mighty force, which can be expected to fight back. Hence "the impossibility for the countries which have opted for the socialist orientation not only immediately to withdraw from the world capitalist economy but also to bring about a fundamental change in the relations with it, the necessity to carry on non-capitalist development while maintaining inequitable ties with this economy which are dangerous in socio-economic and political terms for a more or less protracted period."[14] At worst, one might consider the dilemma insoluble, the contradictions impossible to reconcile; at best, one could not but admit that, in the international climate of the Western Hemisphere in particular, noncapitalist development would have "to make headway in struggle."[15]

THE PRG'S "PRINCIPLED POSITIONS"

Perhaps surprisingly in the light of the importance attached to international affairs by the PRG in Grenada, there do not exist many fully elaborated accounts of the theoretical basis of the regime's foreign policy. A short section was devoted to regional and international matters in the NJM's first manifesto, but although the thrust of the new line was obvious enough, the detailed commitments scarcely extended beyond the recitation of slogans. Thus the manifesto declared:

> We support completely the political and economic integration of the Caribbean. But . . . we believe in real and genuine integration of all the Caribbean for the benefit of all the people. . . . We stand firmly committed to a nationalist, anti-imperialist, anti-colonialist position. We fully support the Organization of non-Aligned Nations in their courageous attempts to prevent big-power domination of their economies and internal politics, and propose to join that Organization at the earliest possible opportunity. For as long as the present composition of the OAS is maintained, we will not apply for admission to that body. We condemn in the strongest possible terms the intervention of the U.S.A. in the internal affairs of the South East Asian countries and the

genocidal practices being committed on their peoples. We support in
particular the heroic struggle of the people of Vietnam and Cambodia.
We reject the right of the U.S.A. or any other big power to control the
economies and the lives of any people anywhere. We support fully the
liberation struggles being waged by our African Brothers in South
Africa, S.W. Africa, Rhodesia, Mozambique, Angola and Guinea-Bissau
for self-determination."[16]

Although Bishop's speeches frequently dealt with international questions, it was not until some two and a half years after the seizure of
power that another coherent statement of the revolution's foreign policy
direction was provided. It came in a speech delivered by the foreign
minister, Unison Whiteman, to the First International Conference in
Solidarity with Grenada held in St. George's in November 1981.[17] In
his address, Whiteman enunciated "five basic principles," which, he said,
guided the conduct of the new foreign policy of the PRG.

1. *Antiimperialism and Nonalignment,* which was declared to be the
main pillar supporting the edifice of Grenadian international relations.
It was noted that the former commitment had "quite understandably"
led Grenada to establish "strong bonds of friendship with the socialist
world and with other democratic and peace-loving nations";[18] but interestingly the main emphasis was put upon the policy of nonalignment.
It is important, though, to note the way that the regime interpreted the
concept. As illustration, Bishop's speech to the UN General Assembly
in October 1979, by which time Grenada had already joined the nonaligned movement and attended its first summit, was quoted at length.

> Non-Alignment does not imply for us that we must be neutral in the
> sterile and negative sense, nor does it imply that our country must
> regard itself as a political eunuch in the conduct of our international
> affairs. Our non-aligned policy will certainly not lead us to surrender our
> independence of judgement in world affairs, or to retreat from our right
> and duty to fully participate in international forums and discussion con-
> cerned with issues vital to our interests, concerns and principles. On the
> contrary, nonalignment for us is a positive concept characterizing a
> vigorous and principled approach to international issues.[19]

What is immediately striking is the unequivocal rejection of nonalignment defined as neutrality and the corresponding assertion of the right
to pursue a *principled* foreign policy.

2. *Achievement of a new international economic order,* which was regarded as the obligation of the foremost Western industrialized nations
given "their long history of imperialist expansion and control of Third
World economies."[20] As Bishop put it in the same speech to the United
Nations, "we desire a new system of international interdependence,
based on mutual respect for sovereignty and a collective will to put

an end to imperialist machinations designed to disrupt our unity and purpose."[21]

3. *Promotion of world peace and cooperation,* which even Whiteman conceded was one of the loftier goals of Grenada's foreign policy. Besides giving general support to the notions of détente and disarmament, what was specifically meant was the promotion of the idea of the Caribbean as a "zone of peace." This was understood to imply a prohibition on the introduction of nuclear weapons into the region, an end to all military maneuvers in the area, the dismantling of all foreign bases, and the termination of colonialism in the Caribbean once and for all.

4. *Pursuit of regional cooperation and integration,* which reflected the PRG's full acceptance that, because of geographical location and shared historical and cultural experience, Grenada was naturally linked to the Caribbean and the broader Latin American region. As such, a firm commitment was given to continue working toward the further development of the Caribbean Community and the OECS. Yet principle was not forgotten. Whiteman added tellingly that "in Grenada's relations with her Caribbean neighbors we insist on respect for the principles of legal equality of all nation states, mutual respect for sovereignty, territorial integrity, ideological pluralism, non-interference in the internal affairs of other states, and the right of every country to develop its own process in its own way free from all forms of outside dictation and pressure."[22]

5. *Support for national liberation struggles,* which included solidarity with a wide array of groups and organizations, ranging from the FDR/FMLN alliance in El Salvador to SWAPO and the ANC in Africa and the PLO in the Middle East. The only qualification proffered was that the liberation struggle be "genuine," the critical adjective being left undefined.

As was generally the case with PRG declarations of policy, all these commitments were made with intense moral fervor. Whiteman in his pejoration typically referred to the five positions as "sacred principles."[23] They certainly constitute an unequivocal reiteration of the antiimperialist character of the Grenadian regime. What is more, they also flow directly from the theory of noncapitalist development, thus providing firm a priori evidence of the existence of a heavy ideological bent to PRG foreign policy. Yet, as always, the proof of the pudding is in the eating; or to put the point another way, a speech to a solidarity conference is not necessarily the same thing as a manual of foreign policy practice.

POLICY IMPLEMENTATION

In examining the record of the international dealings of the PRG over its four and a half year life, I tried initially to see if it was possible to discern different phases, each characterized by some change of approach, into which the period could be neatly divided. I came to the conclusion that this was ultimately not a very helpful way of proceeding. Admittedly, it took a year or so for the regime to acquire confidence in its approach, and unquestionably there were fluctuations in stance and attitude to particular powers in the last few months of the revolution. However, what appeared above all to emerge from the evidence was the forging of a broad, settled, theoretically based strategy of international activity, but which left room for tactical disagreements and was certainly not pursued with the subtlety required if it was to have any chance of succeeding. I would suggest that the best way to see this is to examine in turn Grenada's major external relationships under the PRG.

Relations with Cuba

Cuba must be the starting point, because all interpretations of the Grenadian revolution agree that Cuba was the PRG's foremost external friend. In official U.S. government eyes, the relationship was essentially one in which Cuba controlled the PRG. However, no serious analysts of the situation, including those writing from a right-wing perspective, have claimed as much. Even Sandford and Vigilante, who admit that their research was made possible by the assistance offered by the U.S. Department of State and who argue (correctly enough) that Cuba's influence on Grenada was "profound," reject as a "misapprehension" the fully-fledged "surrogate" thesis.[24] So let that be dispensed with at the outset.

In fact, the evidence suggests that it was the Grenadians who first wooed the government of Cuba, not the other way round. Bishop and other NJM leaders had visited Cuba during the 1970s and can be expected to have benefited from advice and encouragement in Havana, especially as we now know that as early as 1975 the party's Political Bureau had moved to turn the NJM into a Marxist-Leninist party. Whether or not Cuba was actually involved in the 1979 coup is more debatable. Shortly afterward, Bishop himself talked of the party's army commanders having received training somewhere outside Grenada,[25] while the local journalist, Alister Hughes, has been quoted as recalling an NJM source saying that the attacking force included "forty-seven Grenadians and a few other people, of whom we're not saying anything now."[26] These fragmentary pointers—for that is all they are—are used by Sanford and Vigilante to allege that "NJM soldiers were trained in Cuba . . . prior to the 1979 *coup*." Yet they can produce no more than unspecific "hints from people in the know" that Cubans actually participated in the coup itself.[27] In the absence of firm documentary evidence on this point, continued speculation about it is not justified.

As regards the period immediately after the coup, the position is clearer. Cuba was not the first country to respond to the PRG's request for assistance and solidarity—Jamaica and Guyana had this honor, according to later remarks by Bishop[28]—but it was very quick off the mark. Within a month, Cuba had supplied the new regime with weapons, unloaded in the harbor of St. George's by dark, as well as advisors to teach the new People's Revolutionary Army (PRA) how to use them. From this beginning, the links between the two states developed quickly, promoted with equal vigor by both parties and soon extending well beyond the supply of arms. Swift mutual diplomatic recognition led to the formalization of an elaborate economic and technical agreement in June 1979. Aid at this stage consisted mostly of the supply of medical assistance and the granting of scholarships, but was extended a year later to include the encouragement of Grenadian agriculture and fishing and the improvement of the island's water supply. In time, further areas of cooperation were added, and although a further and more extensive military agreement signed in 1981[29] was kept secret, public declarations of the alliance were made by the inauguration of direct flights to Grenada by Cubana Airlines and the cancellation of visa requirements for nationals traveling to and from the two countries.

By far the most visible indication of the very close relationship between the PRG and Cuba concerned the building of the new international airport at Point Salines. Indeed, the controversy surrounding this project represents one of the nodal points in the debate about Grenadian foreign policy during the revolutionary era. In my view, there is little doubt but that the airport was conceived by the PRG as the cornerstone of an expanded tourist industry, which would provide the steady flow of foreign exchange needed to finance the remainder of its social and economic program. Bernard Coard himself indicated as much on several occasions.[30] The accepted inadequacy of the airfield at Pearls, the commitment of the former Gairy regime to a new airport, and the long history of project analyses of the Point Salines site, all confirm that there was nothing novel about the PRG's basic thinking. What aroused attention was the announcement in September 1979 that, in the spirit of fraternal cooperation within the socialist world, Cuba was prepared to supply U.S. $30 million worth of labor and machinery toward the project. This was a very considerable sum for such a country to offer, amounting at the time to over half the estimated total cost. The offer was made before the PRG had had time to seek assistance elsewhere and thus fueled the assumption, subsequently fixed in the minds of U.S. policymakers, that with the connivance of the PRG the Cubans were really building a military airfield designed not only to extend the reach of Cuban jets throughout the Caribbean region but to provide an important refueling station for Cuban transport aircraft on their way to Angola.

The allegation is critical to any perception of Grenadian foreign policy. Can it be proved? The answer is surely no. It is striking that in all the Grenada documents there was found only one notational reference for the whole argument. It was a single phrase in the rough notes made by Liam James (deputy commander of the PRA) of a party meeting held in March 1980, and read as follows: "The Revo has been able to crush Counter-Revolution internationally, airport will be used for Cuban and Soviet military."[31] According to Ledeen and Romerstein, who edited many of the documents for the State Department, "this apparently reflected a decision of the NJM leadership . . . that the airport was going to be used for military purposes."[32] Maybe so; but other interpretations are possible. The remaining notes of the meeting, for which the main agenda item was an assessment of the "present political situation," consist of evaluations of the successes and failures of the revolution to that point. It is not inconceivable, especially given the casual way in which the minutes of party and government documents were prepared in Grenada, that the passage in question was in effect trying to say: the revolution has been able to crush [the claim of] counterrevolution internationally [that the] airport will be used for the Cuban and Soviet military.

At best, the textual evidence to the contrary is flimsy. It is hard to believe that in March 1980, when bulldozers had only just arrived at Point Salines and before any military agreement of any sort had been signed with the USSR, the PRG would have taken a decision that the airport would be turned over to military use. If this had been the case, why were military facilities not secretly installed from that moment onward? The postinvasion statements of the British company responsible for the airport's electronic equipment established beyond doubt that this was not done, thus leaving the question and the whole allegation hanging uneasily in the air. In short, the hard evidence to support U.S. claims is not available. This is not to say that, if asked, the PRG would have denied Cuba military use of the airport once it was complete. Airports can accommodate all types of aircraft. But it is to assert that there are other adequate explanations for the Grenadian decision to embark upon its construction (namely, perceived economic need) and for the Cuban decision to assist in it (namely, advertisement of the strength of its own revolution throughout Latin America and the Third World).

From Grenada's angle, the point is that the airport, which became progressively the foremost symbol of the revolution, simply could not have been built without Cuban aid. There were also many other areas where the PRG could claim tangible successes, such as health, training, and housing, which were dependent on Cuban assistance. Indeed, it is not unreasonable to wonder if the PRG could have survived at all without Cuban support. As Henry Gill put it, "Cuba has become the PRG's saviour. This is why Grenada's friendship with Cuba is not negotiable."[33] Aid, therefore, was the bottom line in the Grenada-Cuba relationship, and that is worth stressing. Yet it is also the case that there would not have occurred the substantial escalation of Cuban assistance to Grenada if there had not existed such a close ideological compatibility between the two revolutions. As Bishop indicated time and again in his speeches, Cuba was the model, "the best example in the world of what a small country under socialism can achieve."[34] In his speech celebrating the first anniversary of the coup, he went so far as to declare that "if there had been no Cuban revolution in 1959, there could have been no Grenadian revolution in 1979."[35] There was thus steadily forged a strong emotional commitment to Cuba among the revolutionary leadership in Grenada, felt by nobody more intensively than Bishop himself, for whom Castro was nothing less than an avatar.

What is interesting is that the PRG obviously felt it could defend its Cuban link. In fact, the regime's rhetoric was positively flagrant in its affirmation of solidarity with Havana. It has to be remembered that Cuba was a neighboring state with which other Commonwealth Caribbean territories had previously established diplomatic and aid relations; that at the time it possessed impressive Third Worldist credentials, reflecting the fact that it was as much a leading member of the nonaligned movement as it was a minor member of COMECON; and that its achievements in the areas of health and education gave it a certain standing in the eyes of European social democrats.[36] In this context, the warmth of Grenada's relationship with Cuba does not of itself describe the essence of PRG foreign policy. In establishing close ties with Cuba, the PRG could be said to have been behaving in a way that was as consistent with the imperatives of radical nationalism as it was derivative of the theory of noncapitalist development. To see the distinction, we have to turn to the question of relations with the Soviet Union and the rest of the socialist community.

Relations with the Soviet Union

In this area of foreign policy, the private face of the Grenadian Revolution was exposed much more. Whenever it could, the PRG preferred to keep secret the extent of its developing links with the Soviet government. As a result, the public record revealed only certain points of contact and support, which did not add up in themselves to a client-patron relationship. It was obviously known, for example, that diplomatic relations were established between the PRG and the Soviet Union in December 1979, but a Soviet embassy was not set up in St. George's until nearly three years later. In May–June 1980, Bernard Coard openly visited Moscow and other Eastern European capitals but returned with only relatively minor aid and trade agreements. These early moves could reasonably be seen as the attempt of a radical Third World regime to diversify its traditional Western-oriented external relationships and thereby assert its sovereign right to establish links with whatever foreign governments it chose.

The one issue in the first two or three years of the revolution which cast doubt on this interpretation was Grenada's vote in support of the Soviet Union in the United Nations General Assembly resolution on Afghanistan in January 1980. Cuba was the only other country in the Western Hemisphere to do likewise. Jamaica, Nicaragua, and the majority of nonaligned Third World countries either voted to oppose the intervention or abstained. Although the U.S. administration took this as a definitive signal of where Grenada stood on East-West questions, its view was not necessarily immediately convincing, since there were those who tried to argue that it had all been a mistake. Grenada, it was said, must have thought that Nicaragua and other such radical governments would support the Soviet Union, perhaps only finding out to the contrary when it was too late to change its vote. On the Third Worldist line of argument then generally prevalent about the ideological direction of Grenadian foreign policy, there was no other obviously available explanation of the regime's apparent decision to anger the Americans for seemingly so little purpose.

Confidential sources now suggest that the decision on the vote was taken primarily by Coard in the absence off the island of Bishop, who later acquiesced in it apparently out of a desire to maintain unity and prove himself in the face of what he took to be a test of his radicalism.[37] Too much, however, can be made of this disagreement, assuming that it existed. It does not in any way negate the evidence, which emerges overwhelmingly from the Grenada documents, that the PRG began to court the Soviet Union ever more intensively from about the end of 1979 onward. It did so primarily by displaying for Moscow's approval its credentials as a noncapitalist regime actively engaged in the process of socialist orientation. Support for this argument is to be found in a remarkably candid analysis of the state of Grenada's relations with the Soviet Union sent back to his government in July 1983 by Richard Jacobs, the PRG's ambassador in Moscow. Jacobs reported that he was disturbed at the low level of Soviet officials detailed to cover Grenada and felt that the NJM was not being taken seriously enough, given that it was a genuine Marxist-Leninist party. He wrote:

> Grenada is regarded as being on the path of socialist orientation. There is a general acceptance among Soviet authorities that we are at the national democratic, anti-imperialist stage of socialist orientation. . . . In terms of their priorities, the countries of socialist orientation come right after the socialist community. . . . The Comrades responsible for Grenada

in the International Section, have told me that they operate on the basis that the NJM is a "communist party" [but] one is not too sure about the authoritativeness of this statement. . . . The core of the matter, however, is that they regard Grenada as a small distant country and they are only prepared to make commitments to the extent of their capacity to fulfill, and if necessary, defend their commitment.[38]

Jacobs went on wryly to observe that on one occasion he had been trying to explain the political situation in neighboring St. Vincent to Soviet party colleagues, only to be told "this is all very interesting but St. Vincent is so far away!!"[39]

Jacobs had many recommendations to make as to how this situation could be improved, of which two stand out. First, he warned that "the Soviets have been burnt quite often in the past by giving support to Governments which have either squandered that support, or turned around and become agents of imperialism,"[40] citing as examples Egypt, Ghana, and Somalia. As a result, they were very careful—"for us sometimes maddingly [sic] slow"—in making up their minds about whom to support.[41] In these circumstances, the NJM's best strategy, he thought, was to show stability and predictability in terms of policy and positions, demonstrate a clear and consistent socialist orientation, and be willing to develop relations at all levels with members of the socialist community. Second, though, Jacobs argued that Grenada could expect to win increased favor by playing more of a vanguard role in Caribbean affairs.

> By itself, Grenada's distance from the USSR, and its small size, would mean that we would figure in a very minute way in the USSR's global relationships. . . . For Grenada to assume a position of increasingly greater importance, we have to be seen as influencing at least regional events. We have to establish ourselves as the authority on events in at least the English- speaking Caribbean, and be the sponsor of revolutionary activity and progressive developments in this region at least.[42]

The tenor of this last extract is, in fact, typical of the whole memorandum. What characterized Jacobs' analysis was a desperate, almost pathetic desire to see Grenada regarded with greater priority in the socialist world. To this end, he reported to Bishop, Coard, and Whiteman that he never tired of reminding his hosts of Grenada's consistency and loyalty in supporting the Soviet position on Afghanistan and every other international issue since. In his conclusion, therefore, he was delighted to be able to tell his political superiors at home that, in his view, the Soviets were "satisfied with the degree of support that they received from Grenada."[43]

So, indeed, they should have been! It is hard to conceive how the

PRG could have been more fawning in its attitude to the USSR. The question that arises, of course, is whether the Grenadians were happy with the support they received in turn from Moscow, and it is clear that they were not. Listen to Jacobs once more, who observed at one point in his analysis that "considering the risks that we have taken on this and other matters, it might be fair to say that their support for us is actually below our support for them."[44] This disappointment needs to be recalled when the actual evidence of Soviet-Grenadian cooperation is examined and the more egregious claims of U.S. spokesmen that Grenada had become a Soviet client are subsequently considered. Having said that, it cannot be denied that ties between the two states grew considerably as the revolution progressed and were only revealed in their full extent after the U.S. invasion.

We now know that the first secret arms agreement was signed in Havana in October 1980 and provided for 4.4 million rubles worth of mortars, machine guns, antitank grenade launchers, and the like; that a second was signed, again in Havana, just over three months later, providing a further 5 million rubles worth of equipment; and that, finally, a third agreement was negotiated, this time in Moscow, in July 1982, which raised the stakes still more significantly. By 1985, the Soviets were to have provided Grenada with the basis of a substantial military force: 50 armored personnel carriers, 60 mortars, 60 antitank and other heavy guns, 50 portable rocket launchers, 50 light antitank grenade launchers, 2,000 submachine guns, and much more besides.[45] Beyond the military sphere, there was revealed in the Grenada documents the existence of party-to-party accords permitting the training of young Grenadians in the Lenin School in Moscow and in KGB counterintelligence establishments, as well as evidence of the Soviet supply to Grenada of construction materials for a new NJM party headquarters, some cars and buses, a few small generators, a light airplane, and toward the end, some science teachers.

The details could be further elaborated, but the real question must be what it all signified. Manifestly, by 1983 Grenada's relations with the USSR were quite close and would in all probability have become still closer. Yet, to my mind, the evidence does not entirely support those who, like Ledeen and Romerstein, note "how *thoroughly* Grenada was integrated into the Soviet World,"[46] and certainly not those who, like the Valentas, assert that "the Bishop regime's interest in cultivating close ties with foreign communist states was *fully* reciprocated by the Soviet Union."[47] What is more apparent is the hardheadedness with which the Soviets dealt with the PRG, reflecting a much more realistic, indeed cynical, view of international relations than that possessed by Grenada's youthful revolutionaries. In regard to economic matters, for example, the Soviet Union refused to buy 1,000 tons of nutmeg, as requested by Grenada, on the perfectly understandable grounds that it only consumed 200–300 tons a year. Nor was any money provided for the airport, despite a Grenadian request and the serious financial straits into which the PRG had got itself on this project by 1983. The Soviets knew precisely how far they were prepared to go. On one occasion, their trade officials warned that, while they were trying to give Grenada "every support possible," their assistance "must never be provocative from the point of view of the international situation." In a meeting with Bishop in April 1983 (on Bishop's last trip to Moscow), Soviet Foreign Minister Gromyko made much the same point, advising the Grenadian leader that leftist groups in the Caribbean must "exercise great care and flexibility so as not to provoke the imperialist forces to smash the progressive forces."[48] These were insightful words and a reminder that the Soviet Union fully grasped the implications of Grenada's geopolitical location in the Western Hemisphere, even if the PRG did not always fully do so. Here too, perhaps, lies the explanation of the fact that Bishop was refused an audience with President Andropov on his 1983 visit to Moscow—if nothing else, a pointed indicator of where Grenada stood in the Soviet scheme of things and an ironic prelude to the similar refusal of President Reagan to see him when he was in Washington a mere two months later.

Relations with the United States

That last point brings us to the question of the PRG's relations with Washington. Given the ideological predisposition of the Grenadian revolution and the fact that U.S. administrations have long viewed politics in the Caribbean primarily in national security terms, this was bound to be the most demanding test of Grenadian diplomacy. Some degree of conflict with the United States was unavoidable and therefore needed to be anticipated and treated carefully by the PRG, the weaker party in the relationship. In practice, as will be seen, the regime handled Washington inconsistently: it exacerbated, ultimately with fatal consequences, tensions that could have been lessened, even if not eliminated.

In the saga of U.S.-Grenada relations, the beginning is widely agreed to have been particularly important—although, unsurprisingly, interpretation of the events is still subject to controversy. Bishop was the first to place his version on the record. A month after the making of the revolution, he gave a national broadcast that came to be known as his "backyard" speech. In it he reported that the U.S. Ambassador to the Eastern Caribbean, Frank Ortiz, on a visit to the island a few days before, had gone out of his way to draw attention to the importance of tourism to Grenada's economy. According to Bishop, "the Ambassador went on to advise us that if we continue to speak about what he called 'mercenary invasion by phantom armies,' then we could lose all our tourists."[49] He was also said to have stressed the fact that his government would view with great displeasure the development of any relations between Grenada and Cuba. "The Ambassador pointed out that his country was the richest, freest, and most generous country in the world, but, as he put it, 'We have two sides'."[50]

It was at the end of this discussion that Ortiz apparently gave Bishop the typed note, which has become notorious, warning the PRG of the consequences of establishing close ties with Havana. Moreover, in response to Grenada's short-term request for aid, Bishop claimed that the ambassador offered to fund a few small projects but only up to the paltry maximum of U.S. $5,000 each, and refused outright his request for military assistance to prevent a counterattack by Gairy. The latter decision was loudly ridiculed—"we reject *entirely* the argument of the American Ambassador that we would only be entitled to call upon the Cubans to come to our assistance *after* mercenaries have landed and commenced the attack."[51] Moved to anger by the offense to Grenada's dignity, which in his view this approach entailed, Bishop made the first, and most famous, of his strong defenses of Grenada's right to pursue an independent foreign policy:

> From day one of the Revolution we have always striven to have and develop the closest and friendliest relations with the United States, as well as Canada, Britain and all our Caribbean neighbors. . . . But no one must misunderstand our friendliness as an excuse for rudeness and meddling in our affairs, and no one, no matter how mighty and powerful they are, will be permitted to dictate to the government and people of Grenada who we can have friendly relations with and what kind of relations we must have with other countries. . . . We are not in anybody's backyard, and we are definitely not for sale. Anybody who thinks they can bully us or threaten us, clearly has no understanding, idea or clue as to what material we are made of.[52]

This dramatic account of the early moves between Grenada and the U.S. government became part of the legend of the revolution and has only recently been challenged by an alternative version. This emerged, at first circuitously, as a product of the access that Sandford and Vigilante were given to an internal State Department paper on the record of U.S.-Grenada relations, prepared in late 1982 by a political officer in the U.S. embassy in Bridgetown, Barbados. The paper naturally gives a different impression of the events and adds considerably to our knowledge of them, but does not directly contradict the key parts of Bishop's account. It claims, for example, that relations between the two countries actually got off to quite a good start. Specifically, Ortiz met Bishop and White-man on 23 March 1979 and, while urging them to hold elections quickly, also indicated that the United States was not only willing to continue to provide Grenada with multilateral aid channeled through the

Caribbean Development Bank but was also ready to consider requests to draw upon the Bridgetown embassy's Special Development Activities fund for community-based projects. This was the offer of U.S. $5,000 for small projects referred to by Bishop. According to the paper, Bishop and Whiteman "seemed interested" but remained "noncommittal."[53] When Ortiz returned to Grenada on 10 April he claims to have found the Grenadian leaders obsessed with the threat of a countercoup by Gairy and desperately concerned to obtain arms, from Cuba if necessary. According to this account, Ortiz took note of their request, reminding them that it was the first time he had heard it and at the same time delivering the much-discussed warning about any tendency on Grenada's part to develop closer ties with Cuba. In the U.S. view, relations were still amicable when, in his Backyard speech, Bishop maliciously chose to distort what had taken place in an attempt to justify his long established, but hitherto secret, preference for the Communist alliance.

The substance of this version of events has since been given further credence by an account of U.S.-Grenadian relations provided by Robert Pastor, director of Latin American and Caribbean Affairs on President Carter's National Security Council between 1977 and 1981, in his chapter in this book.[54] He confirms Bishop's initial interest in U.S. aid and reports that he also expressed a willingness to see an increase in the number of American Peace Corps volunteers sent to Grenada. Nothing, however, was done to follow up these possibilities before Ortiz made his controversial second visit to the island in April. According to Pastor, the State Department sent instructions to its ambassador "to express concern as delicately but clearly as possible" that, if Grenada developed "close military ties" with Cuba, this would "complicate" relations with the United States.[55] Having talked subsequently to Bishop and Coard and listened to their perceptions of the visit, his conclusion is of the greatest importance: "Ortiz's lectures on the vulnerability of tourism and the dangers of relations with Cuba and his style of delivery confirmed all of their preconceptions of the U.S. as a destabilizing imperialist. Ortiz made a mistake in expressing displeasure with Grenada's relations with Cuba rather than just the military relationship, and his delivery of the talking points was an unprofessional error."[56]

What is to be made of these accounts? What was the PRG seeking in these early critical dealings with Washington? It is, of course, quite likely that in the flurry of events it did not clearly know and certainly possible that it was divided. We do not have evidence to this effect (as for the last months of the revolution), but we know that the decision to embark on the coup was decided on a majority basis, and there may well have existed different views about the appropriate signals to give Washington in the first instance. No matter how much the extent of their commitment to the theory of noncapitalist development was concealed or, for that matter, not yet fully developed, no one in the revolutionary leadership can have believed that the U.S. government would be anything other than hostile to the PRG's program. The tactical issue at stake was whether to buy time for the revolution by seeking to persuade Washington that it could live with Grenada in its backyard. On this matter, the regime seems to have vacillated: perhaps it should seek and accept U.S. aid as a means of constraining U.S. hostility—but not if the price to be paid was the rejection of a close relationship with Cuba, something that was ideologically prized as well as practically valuable; perhaps the best way to resolve the contradiction was to go on to the attack and try to organize a diplomatic front against the United States around the themes of nonintervention and sovereignty—that would be ideologically satisfying in itself, would allow the Soviet Union to be courted, and could indeed be the most effective constraint upon the United States. All this is to speculate, but it may be close to the sort of thinking in which the PRG engaged during these early emotionally charged weeks.

Once the Backyard speech had been made, and once the vote on Afghanistan had taken place in January 1980, the nature of Grenada's relationship with the United States is easier to grasp. From the U.S. side, there was well-documented hostility in a variety of fields; from the Grenadian side, there were repeated attempts to appear reasonable in the face of superpower bullying. Charge met countercharge in an increasingly strident and absurd exchange. There is no doubt that in this battle the PRG achieved a considerable number of propaganda successes (e.g., over the airport, aid provision, threatening military maneuvers, unanswered letters, and so on), although equally it has to be added that many were handed to it by the extraordinary clumsiness of U.S. policy. What it was not able to do, however, was to lessen the real impact of U.S. hostility. As time went on, the pressure began to tell: not only was the regime running into serious problems as a result of the squeeze imposed on the Grenadian economy, but its leaders were becoming convinced, whether rightly or wrongly, that the United States was preparing at any moment to invade the island. The combination of a rhetorical offensive by President Reagan and extensive military maneuvers just off the island in March 1983 seems to have genuinely alarmed the revolutionary leadership. Bishop cut short his stay at the nonaligned summit in India and flew home to put all of Grenada's forces on invasion alert. The panic may have been traumatic, because it led shortly afterward to a series of diplomatic exchanges with the U.S. government, which some analysts have interpreted as an attempted, although aborted, rapprochement with Washington on the part of the PRG.[57]

Ironically, given the role that the airport had played in concentrating U.S. fears, it was also one of the main triggers of this initiative. As

Bishop himself had admitted in his Line of March speech to the party six months earlier, "there is no way we can ever pay back for that International Airport in a short or medium term if we don't have tourism developed."[58] Tourism means tourists and, given Grenada's location, tourists had predominantly to be American and Canadian tourists. If they were to come to Grenada in sufficient numbers, there had to be an easing of tension between the U.S. and Grenadian governments. Thus once the furor surrounding the March 1983 alert had died down, Bishop proposed to the party's central committee that a moratorium on public denunciations of the United States would be appropriate. It is not possible to know his precise thinking, but he had in all probability come to the conclusion that the revolution would be stronger if it did not have to deal constantly with the costly effects of U.S. destabilization. At any rate, conciliatory noises were made behind the scenes and eventually generated a response. Bishop was invited to Washington by Mervyn Dymally, the Trinidad-born leader of the black caucus in Congress, and accepted. A minute of the party's political bureau set out the purpose of the visit, as conceived in Grenada, by identifying three broad objectives: (1) to convey to the U.S. press and people the image of Grenada's prime minister as a sober and responsible statesman committed to normalizing relations with the United States; (2) to develop firm unshakable links and bonds of identity with the black community in the United States; and (3) to promote tourism, primarily among the U.S. black community.[59] In short, the trip was regarded by the PRG mainly in public relations and lobbying terms.

A request from Bishop for a personal meeting with Reagan was rejected, but once he was in Washington at the beginning of June strong congressional and media pressure forced the administration to concede a thirty-minute meeting with National Security Council chief William Clark and Assistant Secretary of State Kenneth Dam. A set of handwritten minutes of this meeting was found in the Grenada documents and shows that Bishop made few real concessions. He called for dialogue and a normalization of relations, only to be told by Clark that the United States was more interested in a change in Grenada's conduct, meaning specifically a lessening of Soviet influence in St. George's. Dam reiterated this point, to which Bishop in reply admitted that "we can explore any range of subjects,"[60] including, he hoped, an end to economic destabilization. The notes are fragmentary and anonymous, but it is just about possible to interpret the last reference to imply a concession on Bishop's part. If so, the U.S. regime certainly gave him nothing to take back to his colleagues, promising, for example, only to "consider" a mild Grenadian request that a U.S. diplomatic mission be established on the island. Nevertheless, confidential sources suggest that, whether justifiably or not, some of Bishop's emerging critics on the Central Committees were alarmed that he may have given away more than was agreed. In one sense, this is a side issue, relating more to the politics of the intraparty struggle than it does to an analysis of PRG foreign policy. The point is that the committee as a whole agreed to the visit, although apparently only after a week's long and argumentative debate. It is also known that one of Richard Jacob's memoranda from Moscow that a decision was taken not to inform the Soviet Union of the meeting before it took place.[61]

From the available evidence, therefore, it looks as if the Washington visit should be interpreted, not so much as a change of strategy in any serious sense, even less an ideological compromise, but rather a tactical adjustment designed to take the heat off the revolution for a while. Support for this position is provided by an analysis of the visit prepared for the NJM political bureau. Rather than concentrating on the meeting with Clark and Dam, the writer emphasized Bishop's contacts with Congress and the media, and concluded with satisfaction: "It was clear that all these editorial personnel had one major objective; to assess . . . whether we are communists or more 'Revolutionary Nationalists.' And this is where the proof of our success in those meetings lies, for it is obvious that almost all of them went away, maybe seeing us a bit naive, in a specific context, but . . . brave little fellows who are much more nationalists than communists."[62] The problem was that such winning diplomacy had been left far too late.

Relations with the Commonwealth Caribbean

A similar pattern of policy can be seen in Grenada's dealings with its fellow Commonwealth Caribbean states. In the beginning, the PRG's line was aggressively ideological. Apart from Jamaica and Guyana, where democratic and cooperative socialist regimes, respectively, were in power, the other governments in the subregion were all of a conservative hue and already frightened by the manner of the NJM's assumption of power. In the circumstances it might have been wise for the PRG to have been a little circumspect in its approach to them. Yet its "principled" stance on foreign policy did not initially allow this. Convinced, as Bishop put it in his speech to the nonaligned summit in September 1979, that there was "being built a new Caribbean—Jamaica, Guyana, a new Grenada, Dominica, St. Lucia"[63] (the last two references reflecting left-ward changes of regime in these territories shortly after the Grenada coup), the PRG was in no mood to allay the anxieties of its neighbors and regional partners within CARICOM.

Just over a year later, however, the Commonwealth Caribbean must have looked rather different to the Grenadian leadership. A series of events combined to isolate the regime in the region. First, the anticipated further radicalization of small-island politics did not ensue, elections in

St. Vincent in December 1979 and Antigua in 1980 returning right-wing governments. Second, the potential for support that briefly appeared to exist from new reforming governments in Dominica and St. Lucia rapidly evaporated. Third, relations with Guyana were soured when in June 1980 the PRG bluntly accused the Burnham government of complicity in the murder of the well-known political activist, Dr. Walter Rodney. Last, and of critical importance, there was the defeat of the Manley government in Jamaica in October 1980. Manley had been the only Commonwealth Caribbean head of government to attend the first anniversary celebrations of the Grenadian Revolution in March 1980 and had been an invaluable supporter of Grenada within the region. To make matters worse, the Grenadian government had been unable to establish more than correct relations with oil-rich Trinidad, repeated personal letters from Bishop and other PRG ministers to their counterparts in Port of Spain going unacknowledged and unanswered.

Increasingly beleaguered within his own region, Bishop's temper finally snapped in response to criticism of his government by the then Barbadian Prime Minister Tom Adams. Speaking immediately after Reagan's election to the U.S. presidency in 1980, Adams warned that Grenada's failure to hold elections would soon begin to damage the ability of one of the most important regional institutions, the Caribbean Development Bank, to attract funds from international lending agencies. There followed an exchange quite oblivious of diplomatic niceties, in which Bishop described Adam's call for elections as "provocative and hostile" and disparagingly referred to him as "Uncle Tom Adams." "Like an expectant dog barking for his supper," Bishop went on, "he rushes in to please his new master, Reagan, like all good yard fowls, by attacking Grenada."[64]

Sharp and offensive words! In the event, however, the row marked the nadir of the PRG's relations with other Commonwealth Caribbean governments. By 1981 the latter were beginning to realize that the revolution in Grenada was not the harbinger of other similar acts throughout the region. By the same token, the PRG was concerned about its isolated position in the Commonwealth Caribbean and more ready to be conciliatory in dealings with its immediate neighbors. From the outset, it had professed a belief in Caribbean integration—a commitment made in the NJM's original 1973 manifesto—and had continued to participate in meetings within CARICOM. What it eventually realized was that CARICOM constituted a potentially useful diplomatic base from which to resist U.S. attempts to undermine the revolution. When, therefore, in 1982 Adams and the new conservative Prime Minister of Jamaica Edward Seaga voiced the idea of changing the CARICOM treaty so as to commit its members to the maintenance of parliamentary democracy and thereby expel Grenada, the PRG determined to mobilize its energies to resist the move. The Political Bureau decided, accordingly, that the delegation to attend the CARICOM heads of government meeting in Jamaica would be "high powered."[65] At the summit, Bishop and Whiteman sought to explain as calmly as possible where Grenada stood on a range of issues of concern to its regional partners. The meeting was a triumph for their personal diplomacy, for the heads of government eventually adopted a statement on human rights, called the Declaration of Ocho Rios, which not only omitted the original Barbadian call for free and fair elections but, at Grenada's instigation, specifically included a commitment on the part of CARICOM to the notion of ideological pluralism in the Caribbean and the right of all states in the region to choose their own path of development.

Commonwealth Caribbean issues were obviously of minor importance compared to dealings with Havana, Moscow, or Washington, but from this point onward they were treated with importance by the PRG. Perhaps in the light of other pressures, they were given too much attention. In a conversation in September 1983, Unison Whiteman told me that he estimated that some 80 percent of his energies during the previous twelve months had been devoted to the question of Grenada's relations with other Commonwealth Caribbean states, whom he perceived as a bastion against possible U.S. aggression. As it happened, of course, his judgment proved to be wrong, but by then the revolution had disintegrated, and the whole geopolitical situation changed as a consequence. The initial perception was sound enough and should have been grasped by the PRG earlier rather than later.

Relations with Other States

The PRG's relations with other states can sensibly be considered together because they reflected a desire to diversify both its international contacts generally and its potential sources of aid. To this end, ministers and representatives traveled to countries never previously considered to be part of the international terrain of a Caribbean state. They are too many to be itemized in full, but certain links are worthy of brief comment. In Western Europe the European Economic Community itself was courted both as a source of development assistance, especially in respect to the airport, and as a counterweight to U.S. pressure. Particularly warm ties were established with France under President Mitterrand, who received Bishop in Paris in September 1983 as the first Commonwealth Caribbean head of government ever officially to visit France. No such equivalent relationship was struck with Britain, where the Thatcher government was content to follow the lead of the Americans. In respect to Latin America, the Grenadian Revolution came too late to take advantage of the actively social democratic foreign policies pursued by Venezuela and Mexico in the first half of the 1970s. Thus no specially close links were established, in the former case because of growing suspicion of the ideological orientation of the PRG by the Christian Democratic government elected in 1979, and in the latter case because of intensifying financial stringency. Nevertheless, Grenada determinedly aligned itself with Latin America—and against its Commonwealth Caribbean neighbors—in condemning the British reinvasion of the Falkland Islands in 1982. Among African states, although good relations existed with Algeria, Nigeria, and Tanzania, the only country to establish a diplomatic mission in Grenada was Libya. The PRG's association with the Libyan "ambassador" was not always easy, but he proved to be a further useful source of funds.

In short, in some contexts the PRG was prepared to deal very pragmatically with whatever regimes would deal with it. The nature of the relationships varied, of course, but they were all regarded as valuable in some way. This policy has been viewed as hypocritical by some commentators, a point that has come up with particular reference to Grenada's role within the Socialist International (SI) during the course of the revolutionary era. The NJM had sent observers to SI meetings before coming to power and late in 1979 successfully applied for membership in the organization. This has been regarded by some as an odd decision for a Marxist-Leninist party to take, something that can only be satisfactorily explained as an attempt to subvert from within the ideological coherence of the SI. Ledeen and Romerstein state the argument directly. They suggest that some of the documents found in Grenada demonstrate that "the NJM was fundamentally opposed to the democratic ideals of the Socialist International, that the Grenadans [sic], along with others in the region, worked in lockstep with the Cubans to undermine the SI's effectiveness, and that the Grenadans' [sic] greatest objection to the SI was its insistence on democratic institutions and democratic elections."[66] The supporting evidence depends mainly on accounts of two meetings. One was a two-day SI meeting on Latin America and the Caribbean in Panama in February/March 1981 attended by Whiteman. In a subsequent memorandum to the party leadership, he reported his opposition to a Venezuelan proposal that the names of Cuba and the Soviet Union be added to a draft resolution demanding an end to the supply of arms to El Salvador. On Grenada's behalf, he argued that the SI "should not equate arms for the oppressors with weapons to defend the people in their just struggle."[67] The second meeting was the convening of a "secret regional caucus" in Managua in January 1983 of five left-wing parties affiliated with the SI, including the NJM and the Communist Party of Cuba. According to the NJM delegate, the representatives considered "initiatives to neutralize forces within SI that are against us,"[68] meaning by that the more right-wing social democratic parties in the organization. As already indicated, the conclusion to which all this supposedly points is that Grenada joined the SI primarily in order to disrupt it on behalf of the Soviet Union and Cuba.

It is difficult to accept this thesis in its entirely. That Grenada sought to push the SI to the left is beyond dispute. So are, for a host of other reasons, its alliance with Cuba and its wish to impress the Soviet Union. But, having conceded these points, it is not evident that the PRG joined the SI as a kind of Soviet "mole." Indeed, there is a report in a note to Bishop from Bernard Bourne, one of Grenada's counselors in its Moscow embassy, that the Soviets "do not understand clearly" Grenada's membership in the SI.[69] In these circumstances, there is no real reason to doubt the arguments contained in an unsigned document, apparently from the 1980–1981 period, assessing the SI from Grenada's perspective. The author began by noting that one of the major objectives of Grenada's foreign policy was "to harness moral, political, economic and other support from the international community so as to stave off and combat external aggression."[70] A potential way of achieving that was to become a part of international organizations, like the SI, "which condemn firmly, militantly, imperialism and its aggressive manoeuvers and henchmen."[71] Similarly, another general objective of PRG policy was to support the struggles of oppressed people, and again the SI was useful. Through membership, "Grenada can express organized support for the progressive struggle; in Southern Africa, the Western Sahara, Palestine, El Salvador, Nicaragua and other parts of Latin America."[72] It was readily admitted that "the Grenada revolution aspires to advance beyond democratic socialism" and that there existed "fundamental contradictions" between revolutionary and democratic socialists, but this did not mean that "the two cannot strike a working relationship under certain conditions when the objectives are sufficiently broad."[73] Membership of the SI was not a central plank of PRG foreign policy, but it had its part to play. Conceived in the terms used by the unnamed Grenadian analyst just quoted, it was not inconsistent with the broader framework of the PRG's relations with other states.

CONCLUSION

What can be said by way of conclusion? I shall not discuss what one might call the technical efficiency of Grenadian foreign policy, other than to observe that the captured documents are full of references to inadequate staffing, the absence of briefings, and late arrival at meetings. Resources were thinly stretched in all areas of the revolution, and foreign policy was no exception. Yet it would not be right to suggest that it was the level of competence with which policy was pursued which was the critical factor. Most observers concede that the PRG managed to cut quite a dash internationally, especially considering the facilities and the staffing it had available. The real question, therefore, is whether the broad program undertaken by the PRG was a feasible project in the first place. To put it at its bluntest, could a foreign policy of noncapitalist development be effected successfully within the U.S. backyard?

All the theorists of noncapitalist development, when discussing foreign policy, stress the need for flexibility in its execution. Ralph Gonsalves, for example, points out that "the pace at which the state disengages from imperialism and embraces socialism internationally depends on . . . its geopolitical position." A Caribbean country, he goes on, "is probably more circumscribed in its actions by its giant neighbor, the United States, than say a non-strategic state in Africa."[74] That may be to do no more than state the obvious, but it is still an important cautionary note. The PRG did at least recognize in principle the difficult path it had chosen to tread. Bishop showed this in his Line of March speech, when he warned party members: "Simultaneously we will be nurturing the shoots of capitalism and the shoots of socialism, and the question is which one becomes dominant and how you can control and ensure that socialism comes out and not capitalism. . . . In other words, comrades, we have a tightrope that we have to monitor very carefully as we walk it—*every single day.*"[75] The risks were thus spelled out, and the debate can move to the practicalities of tightrope walking in such conditions.

On this opinions differ. To refer again to the two perspectives counterposed in the beginning of this chapter, Anthony Gonzales, while conceding the high risk element in the PRG's foreign policy, nevertheless considered that, in the final analysis, "it was not an unreasonable political calculation."[76] In particular, as regards the airport, he suggests that the U.S. came close to facing a fait accompli, in which Western opinion would not have been greatly worried if a few Cuban planes had landed at Point Salines on their way to Southern Africa. His argument is that "while this would constitute a small strategic loss for the U.S.," it was "not enough domestically in the U.S. to justify a military intervention."[77] On this narrow point he is right. The support for Grenada generated in the Third World, in Western Europe, in the Socialist International, and in the Commonwealth Caribbean *should* have been sufficient to avoid invasion—and would in all probability have done so if the revolutionary leaders had kept their heads.

Yet this ignores the fact that the revolution was not only seen by the United States to constitute an ideological challenge to its regional hegemony, but did indeed constitute such a challenge. This was true even of the early phase of the process of noncapitalist development, when the strategy could forgivably have been mistaken for social democracy, let alone the next stage when "socialist construction" was supposed to begin. In these circumstances, any modern U.S. administration, and unquestionably one led by President Reagan, could have been expected to resort to destabilization of one sort or another. Given Grenada's small size, general economic weakness, and particular dependence on the United States for the sustenance of its tourist industry, this was a formidable, and always potentially fatal, threat. The pressure was bound to tell and to in some way undermine the achievements of the revolution. This was what Henry Gill in an opposing essay was highlighting when he wrote: "Insistence on the correctness of a position may be psychically rewarding to a country's leadership but does not necessarily redound to the advantage of a country. But the David syndrome of responding forcefully to every challenge and error by external Goliaths is a reality of Grenadian policy."[78] We all, of course, know what David achieved on one famous occasion, but most of us as betting men would continue to back Goliath. Paradoxically, therefore, Grenada's foreign policy, although buttressing the psychological security of the revolution, ended up by diminishing its real security.

The lesson is that the foreign policy of noncapitalist development undertaken in the Western Hemisphere has somehow to ward off U.S. hostility until effective transfer has been made to the protection of the internationalist socialist system. Even if the world "correlation of forces" between "imperialism" and "socialism" were moving in the latter's favor, it would be difficult to engineer; when, as in the 1980s, movement in Latin America and the Caribbean is in the other direction, it is impossible. As Thorndike graphically put it in his authoritative account of the revolution, "to believe that Grenada was not in anybody's backyard was an exhilarating experience—but it was an illusion."[79] To believe that the noncapitalist path could be trodden successfully within the international politics of the modern Caribbean was an even more fundamental illusion. At the end of the day, Grenada's revolutionaries were let down primarily by the theory to which they had so rigidly attached themselves.

NOTES

1. Henry Gill, "The Foreign Policy of the Grenada Revolution," *Bulletin of Eastern Caribbean Affairs* 7 (Mar./Apr. 1981), p. 3.

2. Anthony Gonzales, "Grenada in the Twilight Zone: Some Lessons from the External Experience," *CARICOM Perspective* (May/June 1984), p. 4.

3. See R. A. Ulyanovsky, *Socialism and the Newly Independent Nations* (Moscow: Progress Publishers, 1974).

4. Ralph Gonsalves, *The Non-Capitalist Path of Development: Africa and the Caribbean* (London: One Caribbean Publishers, 1981), p. 2.

5. Ibid., pp. 2–3.

6. Ibid., pp. 8–14.

7. W. R. Jacobs and R. I. Jacobs, *Grenada: The Route to Revolution* (Havana: Casa de las Américas, 1980), pp. 80, 78, 82, 35, and ff.

8. Ibid., pp. 35–36.

9. K. N. Brutents, *National Liberation Revolutions Today* (Moscow: Progress Publishers, 1977), p. 174.

10. Ibid., p. 293: Brutents' emphasis.

11. Ibid., p. 294.

12. Ibid., pp. 297–98: Brutents' emphasis.

13. Ibid., p. 301.

14. Ibid., p. 307.

15. Ibid., p. 306.

16. "The Manifesto of the New Jewel Movement," in *Independence for Grenada: Myth or Reality?* (St. Augustine, Trinidad: University of the West Indies, Institute of International Relations, 1974), p. 154.

17. Unison Whiteman, "Birth of a New Foreign Policy," in *Grenada Is Not Alone* (St. George's, Grenada: Fedon, 1982), p. 108.

18. Ibid., p. 114.

19. Quoted in ibid., p. 108.

20. Ibid., p. 110.

21. Quoted in ibid.

22. Ibid., p. 112.

23. Ibid., p. 123.

24. Gregory Sandford and Richard Vigilante, *Grenada: The Untold Story* (Lanham, Md.: Madison Books, 1984), p. 89.

25. D. Sinclair Da Breo, *The Grenada Revolution* (Castries, St. Lucia: Management, Advertising, and Publicity Services, 1979), p. 147.

26. Quoted in Sandford and Vigilante, *Grenada,* p. 55.

27. Ibid., p. 54.

28. Maurice Bishop, *Forward Ever! Three Years of the Grenadian Revolution* (Sydney: Pathfinder Press, 1982), pp. 111 and 129.

29. Document 16, Protocol of Military Collaboration between Grenada and Cuba, in Michael Ledeen and Herbert Romerstein, eds., *Grenada Documents: An Overview and Selection,* vol. 1 (Washington, D.C.: Depts. of State and Defense, 1984). Hereafter, this volume is referred to as *Grenada Documents.*

30. See "Proceedings of Aid Donors Meeting Held in Brussels at ACP House on 14 and 15 April 1981: International Airport Project—Grenada" (Brussels: Embassy of Grenada, mimeo).

31. *Grenada Documents:* Document 23, page of notebook of Liam James referring to military use of airport.

32. Ibid., p. 6.

33. Gill, "Foreign Policy," p. 2.

34. Bishop, *Forward Ever!,* p. 94.

35. Ibid., p. 114.

36. For a fuller discussion, see Anthony Payne, *The International Crisis in the Caribbean* (Baltimore: Johns Hopkins University Press, 1984), pp. 67–88.

37. Confidential interviews.

38. *Grenada Documents:* Document 26, Report from Grenadian Embassy in Moscow on relations with USSR, p. 1.

39. Ibid.

40. Ibid., p. 2.

41. Ibid.

42. Ibid., p. 5.

43. Ibid., p. 8.

44. Ibid.

45. For a detailed discussion of these arguments, see Jiri Valenta and Virginia Valenta, "Leninism in Grenada," *Problems of Communism* (July/Aug. 1984), pp. 11–14.

46. *Grenada Documents,* p. 7. My emphasis.

47. Valenta and Valenta, "Leninism in Grenada," p. 8. My emphasis.

48. Quoted in Sandford and Vigilante, *Grenada,* p. 92.

49. In Chris Searle, ed., *In Nobody's Backyard: Maurice Bishop's Speeches 1979–1983* (London: Zed Books, 1984), p. 10.

50. Ibid.

51. Ibid., p. 13. Bishop's emphasis.

52. Ibid., pp. 11 and 14.

53. Sandford and Vigilante, *Grenada,* p. 52.

54. Chapter 6 is based on a paper of the same title delivered to the conference Democracy, Development and Collective Security in the Eastern Caribbean: The Lessons of Grenada sponsored by the Caribbean Institute and Study Center for Latin America of the Inter American University of Puerto Rico, San Germán, Puerto Rico, 17–19 Oct. 1985.

55. Ibid., p. 22.

56. Ibid., p. 53.

57. See Tony Thorndike, *Grenada: Politics, Economics and Society* (Boulder: Lynne Rienner), p. 130.

58. *Grenada Documents:* Document 1, Line of March for the Party, p. 30.

59. Ibid.: Document 93, Minutes of Political Bureau, 4 May 1983.

60. Ibid.: Document 32, Notes on Bishop's meeting in Washington with Judge Clark et al.

61. Ibid.: Document 26.

62. Quoted in Sandford and Vigilante, *Grenada,* p. 106.

63. Bishop, *Forward Ever!,* p. 97.

64. *Latin America Regional Report: Caribbean* (London: Latin American Newsletters), RC–80–10, 5 Dec. 1980.

65. *Grenada Documents:* Document 84, Minutes of Political Bureau, 3 Nov. 1982.

66. Ibid., p. 14.

67. Ibid.: Document 41, Report on SI meeting in Panama, Mar. 1981.

68. Ibid.: Document 39, Report on Secret Regional Caucus of the Socialist International, Jan. 1983.

69. Ibid.: Document 29, Report to Bishop from Moscow Embassy, June 1982, p. 2.

70. Ibid.: Document 38, Grenadian analysis of the Socialist International, p. 8.

71. Ibid.

72. Ibid.

73. Ibid.

74. Gonsalves, *Non-Capitalist Path,* p. 9.

75. *Grenada Documents:* Document 1, Line of March for the Party speech, p. 32. Bishop's emphasis.

76. Gonzales, "Grenada in the Twilight Zone," p. 22.

77. Ibid.

78. Gill, "Foreign Policy," p. 3.

79. Thorndike, *Grenada,* p. 118.

5. Socialism via Foreign Aid: The PRG's Economic Policies with the Soviet Bloc

Frederic L. Pryor

T HE PEOPLE'S Revolutionary Government of Grenada faced three difficult economic problems. First, the government was trying to take an economy that had grown rapidly during the 1960s but that had stagnated in the 1970s and restart the engine of economic development. Such a daunting task was made more difficult by the fact that few of the New Jewel Movement's leadership had very much practical experience in administering an economy. Second, they were trying to carry this task out within a socialist framework, a goal that raised particular difficulties because of the reluctance of either domestic or foreign capitalists to risk their investment funds in a nation moving along a "socialist path." Finally, they were trying to reorient their foreign economic relations away from the island's traditional partners and toward other socialist nations, an aim that was also difficult, because the nations of the socialist bloc in Eastern Europe generally conduct little trade and give little foreign aid to Third World countries with a socialist orientation.

The materials captured in the military intervention in October 1983 permit a unique insight into the way in which the PRG and NJM handled these problems.[1] Additional details were obtained from interviews conducted with Grenadian officials involved in transactions with the Soviet bloc. Although the available materials are still not as explicit on many issues as we might wish and although we are left in many cases only with evidence from a set of separate incidents, we can nevertheless draw some useful conclusions.

This chapter is organized in a straightforward manner. The first section presents some background materials on the economy. The following three sections deal, respectively, with economic aid, technical aid, and trade. In the economic discussion, I direct almost all of my attention to Grenada's economic dealings with the Soviet bloc, since these economic relations were critical to the building of socialism in

Grenada. Other aspects of Grenada's foreign economic relations, especially its trade with the West, are analyzed elsewhere.[2] Certain general conclusions are drawn in the final section.

THE ECONOMIC CONTEXT

Grenada is a small nation with a population of about 90,000 in 1981. Of the Caribbean islands, it has one of the lowest levels of per capita income and one of the highest population densities. In the 1970s, unemployment was roughly 20 percent and the emigration rate averaged about 2.5 percent per year over the decade. The GNP appears to have increased only slowly during the 1970s. Unfortunately, the statistical base to analyze the Grenadian economy is not only inadequate but also extremely difficult to locate.

The major sources of Grenada's foreign currency—and of employment—were tourism and agriculture. However, during the 1970s, the level of tourism did not increase, in part because of political instabilities experienced on the island, in part because the island was difficult to reach since the airport was inadequate and could not take large planes flying directly from Europe or the United States (so that tourists had to change planes on another Caribbean island).

The island is extremely hilly, which makes agricultural mechanization difficult: almost all exports of goods have consisted of tree products (nutmeg, cocoa, and bananas). During the entire period after World War II, flight from the land was an important phenomenon, as manifested by reductions in planted area and in the agricultural labor force. During the 1970s agricultural production focused increasingly on the major export crops—nutmeg, bananas, and cocoa; and, for the first time, the island became a net importer of agricultural products, not only to feed itself but also the tourists who visited the island. In short, it appears that the island was losing its comparative advantage in agriculture.

When the NJM took power, the public sector was relatively large. Gairy had nationalized a number of large estates producing the export crops, so that 10 percent of the land was already in the public sector. The state also owned roughly half of the public utilities. Although statistics are quite inadequate, the share of public expenditures in the GNP appeared to be somewhat higher than Third World countries in general, but somewhat lower than the average of the Caribbean nations.

The PRG took rapid steps to gain control of the "commanding heights" of the economy. It bought—or forced the sale at low prices—of all of the shares of the major public utilities and two out of the four major banks. It was in the process of increasing the state share of agricultural land from 10 to 25 percent. Direct expropriations were rare, except in the agricultural and housing sectors. It also founded or bought out a number of small industries, almost all of which were quite unprofitable. Although the government did put partly in order the island's tangled public finances, it had not yet introduced any significant type of central planning and had not sufficiently tampered with the market mechanism to prevent most prices on the island from following world market prices. Other institutional changes (e.g., various profit sharing arrangements, agricultural cooperatives, and so forth) were only in the beginning stages.

The single largest development project of the PRG was the construction of a new international airport, a project that had been under discussion on the island for several decades. This project absorbed about half of the foreign aid that Grenada received. The evidence I have been able to locate suggests that its primary usage was for civilian purposes—primarily tourism. Of course, the airport did have a military potential, to which the PRG gave some attention, but this seems to have been a secondary consideration.[3]

The PRG's strategy for development had three phases, according to Maurice Bishop's Line of March speech delivered to the party cadre in 1982. In the first five years, attention would be focused on the development of tourism (of which the airport was the key project) and agriculture; during the next five years, primary weight would be placed on agriculture and agroindustries; and in the third five-year period, development efforts would be focused on manufacturing industries that would not be agriculturally based. Like many of the PRG's plans, this had not been worked out in very much detail.

The PRG might be characterized as "foreign aid socialism," that is, the attempt to introduce socialism by a government completely dependent on foreign grants and concessionary loans of like-minded nations to achieve its economic aims. In the discussion below, I devote considerable attention to the way in which Grenada obtained foreign aid, for this was not only the key phenomenon for understanding events in that nation but also its greatest economic success.

THE QUEST FOR FOREIGN AID[4]

Background

In Grenada, the origins of the emphasis on using foreign aid for development purposes can be found in the ideas of Eric Gairy. In 1974 Bernard Coard cited the following statement, which Gairy had made two years before, to justify the severing of Grenada's colonial bonds with the United Kingdom: "it is only when we attain full independence that our independent brothers and sisters, numbering over 150 prosperous, progressive countries, can come directly to our aid."[5] Apparently,

Gairy had in mind two considerations: colonies seem able to obtain significant economic aid only from the mother country, while independent nations can ask and receive aid from all; moreover, Grenada's small size would give it a comparative advantage in obtaining aid, because a relatively minor loan in terms of the resources of the donor nation could have a very large impact on the economy of the receiver—and all aid givers like to have something important to show for their money. Unfortunately, the Gairy government proved quite inept in such efforts to obtain aid.

Successful aid begging has several prerequisites. First, the nation must be widely and favorably known, at least if the donor government is responsive to domestic political pressures. Aid programs targeted at a country almost totally unknown to most of the population in a democratic donor nation are open to strong domestic attack in the aid-giving nation. Second, the aid request must be attractively packaged. Such a package could be political, for example, the strengthening of a government intensely loyal to the donor nation; or it could represent some engineering achievement that the citizens of the donor nation can proudly point out, for example, a stadium, a steel mill, or an airport. Third, the receiving country must be expected to use such external funds in an appropriate fashion and, if a loan, to make timely repayments.

Without any doubt, the PRG's greatest economic success was in obtaining loans and grants from other governments and from international organizations. Table 5.1 reveals this accomplishment by presenting summary data on the most important foreign aid received. The data are, unfortunately, rather rough and have offsetting biases: they understate the true volume of such outside assistance, because a number of small grants are not included. For instance, Grenada had about 350 students abroad and, since they were studying primarily on the basis of scholarships and other aids from the host nation, this assistance represents an aggregate yearly grant of about U.S. $1.5 million not shown in the table. On the other hand, the nature of the sources makes it difficult in some cases to distinguish planned and actual aid, and for this reason, certain loans (especially from Libya) may be overstated.

It should be clear that Cuba was the most important patron to the island, giving about 30 percent of the total economic and military aid. It is noteworthy that most of the aid from other Marxist nations came in the form of grants and, moreover, that the Soviets contributed much more military than economic aid. Aid from Western nations was quite small and, in the case of British and Finnish loans, was tied to the purchase of equipment from these countries; U.S. aid came primarily through the Caribbean Development Bank, a multilateral lending agency, which did not accede to U.S. requests to limit aid to Grenada, even though the United States was the bank's principal donor.

Table 5.1
Major Grants and Loans to the People's Revolutionary Government by Source,
1979–October 1983
(millions of current U.S. dollars)

Source	Economic Grant	Military Grant	Loans
Socialist nations			
Cuba	36.6	3.1	
Czechoslovakia		0.7	
German Democratic Republic	1.5	0.1	2.1
North Korea		1.3	
USSR	2.6	10.4	
Radical Third World Nations			
Algeria	2.3		
Iraq	7.2		
Libya	0.3		10.4
Syria	2.4		
Other Nations Plus Government			
Guaranteed Private Loans			
Canada	2.9		
Finland (Metex)			7.3
Nigeria	0.1		
U.K. government	0.4		
U.K. (Plessy Ltd.)			1.9
Venezuela	0.6		
International and Intergovernmental			
Agencies and Banks			
Caribbean Development Bank	1.1		7.4
Eastern Caribbean Currency Authority			1.9
European Development Fund	2.7		2.1
European Economic Community Emergency Fund	0.3		
International Monetary Fund			6.6
Organization of American States	0.4		
Organization of Petroleum Exporting Countries			2.0
UN Development Program	0.4		
UNICEF/FAO	0.1		
Other and nonspecified	0.7		5.7
Total	62.3	15.5	47.3

Note: The data do not include any loans from commercial banks. Some of the estimates (e.g., for the Caribbean Development Bank) are very rough. In a number of cases, the underlying source materials conflicted with each other. Full details of estimation are given in Frederic L. Pryor, *Revolutionary Grenada: A Study in Political Economy* (New York: Praeger, 1986).

About half of the funds received came from economic grants; another eighth, in the form of military grants; and the final three-eights, in the form of loans, which were primarily given on very generous terms. Of the total amount of this foreign aid, investment in the new international airport accounted for slightly less than half.

To place these data on foreign aid in perspective, it is worth noting that average annual grants and loans were about U.S. $25 million. For a nation with roughly 90,000 population, that is quite significant—for the ratio of such aid to the average gross domestic product was roughly 30 percent for the five-year period.[6] Since it really took the PRG almost a year to get the flow started, the actual ratio of foreign aid received to GDP was much higher than 30 percent in the later years of the regime.

The Diplomatic Offensive

According to Kendrick Radix (interview), a former law partner of Bishop's and a member of the NJM Political Bureau, the coup was a hurried affair, and the NJM did not take over the government with many definite economic plans. However, within a few weeks of taking over, they reversed the position in their 1973 manifesto against the building of a new international airport at Point Salines and started to work on the project. As Radix explained, "it was the easiest way to get aid." In brief, the PRG had found an attractive package, one of the three prerequisites for obtaining foreign aid. Once started along this path, the government proceeded with great vigor and ingenuity.

A key ingredient of foreign aid socialism was Grenada's relations with the United States. Although everything started off quite smoothly, relations between the two nations rapidly degenerated, and Bishop's speech on 13 April 1979, In Nobody's Backyard, set the tone for Grenada's diplomatic offensive—incessant denunciations of the United States, combined with considerable resourcefulness in seeking aid from Eastern Europe and radical Third World nations by playing the role of a beleaguered David facing a truculent American Goliath.

Without doubt the NJM wanted to establish closer economic and political relationships with Soviet bloc nations, but this did not necessarily imply denunciations of the West. However, I believe that the strident rhetoric on the part of Bishop was absolutely necessary in order to establish the proper radical credentials to implement the strategy of maximizing foreign aid receipts and that the verbal fist shaking in the face of the United States was an important component in the exercise. In this manner, Grenada made itself favorably known to the world, which it wished to impress—another of the three prerequisites for obtaining foreign aid.

The Cuban aid, which arrived on 14 April 1979, came about because of the personal friendship between Maurice Bishop and Fidel Castro and the trust that Castro placed in the PRG. Further, in the ensuing months Cuba was enlisted in the airport project and soon sent technicians to Grenada to assist in the planning of the project. By December 1979 the first Cuban machines and contingent of construction workers arrived, and the project began in earnest. Grenada's first hesitant steps farther afield among other Soviet bloc nations were less successful. For instance, Bernard Coard's first trip to the Soviet Union in 1980 resulted in very little economic help—not even a serious trade agreement—although the Soviets did make a small grant of 4.4 million rubles (at the 1980 exchange rate, about U.S. $6.6 million) for military equipment later in the year. Forays into the radical Third World yielded more fruit.

In its fateful first year of power, the PRG had to finance its various projects primarily from internal sources, since relatively little foreign aid arrived. They were trying to get the economy in order and actually ended the year by bringing government revenues and expenses roughly in balance and reducing Grenada's international short-term indebtedness. They were also cultivating potential aid donors in order to achieve the final prerequisite for successful aid begging. In the next year, this diligence paid off and led to a flow of foreign aid, which never ebbed thereafter.

The crucial aspects of this diplomatic work were shown in an updated (apparently 1981) report to the NJM Central Committee, where the twelve most important PRG foreign policy goals are outlined, of which seven concerned the necessity of obtaining external economic aid of one type or another. Bishop continually lectured his ambassadors about how they were the key of the economic success of the nation.

The Strategy of the Quest

During its first few months, the PRG developed quite different strategies for obtaining foreign loans and grants from the socialist nations, the Western nations, and the international organizations. For the first group of nations, Grenada had prepared a shopping list of projects by May 1980 and had targeted potential donors: Bulgaria, Cuba, Czechoslovakia, Hungary, Poland, and the USSR. Interestingly, the German Democratic Republic, Romania, Yugoslavia, and the Asian socialist nations were omitted, although East Germany and North Korea later became relatively important donors. In an undated "list of countries with which Grenada does not wish to develop close relations," one finds China sandwiched in among Chile, Haiti, Israel, Taiwan, and South Africa (as well as the Comoro Islands and Egypt): clearly Grenada very carefully picked sides in the Sino-Soviet split.

THE USSR

In 1980 the Soviet Union signed an agreement to send arms to Grenada during the 1980–1983 period. However, they did not prove very forthcoming with regard to economic aid. In a meeting of the Political Bureau in June 1981, Maurice Bishop suggested that the best way to "get to" the Soviets might be through Bulgaria or the GDR. But other means were tried as well, and in a memorandum dated July 1983 Richard Jacobs, the Grenadian ambassador to the USSR, made some extremely acute observations (I have corrected punctuation and spelling):

> The Soviets have been burnt quite often in the past by giving support to Governments which have either squandered that support, or turned around and become agents of imperialism, or lost power. One is reminded of Egypt, Somalia, Ghana, and Peru. They are, therefore, very careful, and for us sometimes maddingly slow in making up their minds about whom to support. They have decided to support us for two main reasons: (a) Cuba has strongly championed our case; (b) they are genuinely impressed with our management of the economy and state affairs in general. . . .
>
> I have not formed the impression that there is any such generalized view within the [Soviet bloc] community . . . about Grenada. . . . The Soviets assess the level of state to state relations by, among other things, the extent to which we are willing to share our experiences with them and to learn from their experiences. . . .
>
> I have formed the view that the USSR is satisfied with the degree of support that they receive from Grenada. Indeed, I would say that they have every reason to be satisfied, especially if our vote on Afghanistan, for example, is recognized as one of two Latin American votes (the other being Cuba) in their favor. Considering the risks that we have taken on this and other matters, it might be fair to say that their support for us is actually below our support for them. We must therefore work to establish a balance of interest. This might best be done by gentle reminders at critical stages by members of our leadership. . . .
>
> On 27th. June, I had a very frank and friendly discussion with Boyko Demitrov—the former Bulgarian ambassador to Grenada who is now director of International Relations in the Party. He told me that . . . Grenada has to face the reality that [to the Soviet Union] it is a question of size, distance, and priorities. I think that he is correct. But we have to deal with these realities. In order to elevate our priority in the socialist scheme of things . . . we have to raise and discuss with the highest authorities *global and regional* issues rather than parochial or national issues. In other words, our legitimate begging operations have to be cast in the larger world context. We have in fact done this in the past quite successfully, linking our national requests to a global analysis. What we need to do now, it seems to me, is to become the spokesman for a broader constituency—perhaps the countries of socialist orientation.[7]

In an undated memorandum, Jacobs also wrote: "The Caribbean . . . is, frankly, not of their priority areas and this is reinforced by their interest in reducing the areas of conflict with the USA. Furthermore, the CPSU

[Communist Party of the Soviet Union] has been historically very cautious in developing relations with parties which are new to them."[8]

Although scholarships and military grants were forthcoming, it was difficult for Grenada to obtain much economic aid from the USSR. With regard to agriculture, the Soviets noted that their aid efforts in mechanized tropical agriculture had not been very successful and had resulted in a loss of prestige; therefore, they recommended that the Grenadians try the Bulgarians and Hungarians for such assistance. They also refused to help with the design of buildings, noting that the USSR generally built much larger buildings than those requested by the PRG; and they also recommended the Bulgarians for this task. They said that it was not their practice to give free technical assistance and that they didn't want to set any precedents with Grenada. In Coard's 1980 trip to the USSR, they insisted on paying world market prices, rather than subsidized prices, which might benefit Grenada. They further stressed that the Soviet bureaucracy needed a great deal of time to study various aid requests. Still later in a visit to Grenada in December 1982 the Soviet deputy chair of Gosplan, Nikolai Lebedinskiy, emphasized the importance of trade, not aid, and that such trade should be carried on "without any grant element." He appeared well aware of Grenada's realization that the major source of Soviet aid to Cuba was through subsidized sugar prices. Other aspects of this visit are discussed below.

In 1981, 1982, and 1983 the Soviet Union did make several small grants for economic purposes, but these amounted to only E.C. $7 million (U.S. $2.5 million). The Soviets did not appear interested in helping to finance the airport, and they seemed to respond slowly to the PRG's perceived economic needs; for instance, in July 1983 they turned down a Grenadian emergency request for a U.S. $6 million loan or grant on the bizarre grounds that they heard France was going to make such a grant, a claim which appeared totally baseless. Moreover, they seemed unmoved by Grenada's suggestion in 1983 for a COMECON counterpart to the IMF, which would make loans to countries with a "socialist orientation." In an internal memorandum, Richard Jacobs noted dryly that, since such a bank would probably cost the Soviets about U.S. $20 billion, it might be best to approach the matter through other socialist countries.

Nevertheless, the Soviet Union did send a series of missions to Grenada (e.g., in late 1979 and again in 1982), and they also established an embassy on the island. By 1983 Soviet interest had finally been seriously aroused: at the time of the intervention, forty-nine Soviet diplomats and advisors, headed by a three-star general, were on the island.[9] In sum, Grenada was a political plum that unexpectedly fell in the lap of the Soviet Union, and it took them considerable time to appraise its worth.

EUROPEAN SOCIALIST NATIONS

According to a high-ranking member of the PRG's Foreign Ministry (interview), the government was quite surprised to find itself being wooed by the German Democratic Republic. Both before and after the coup, Grenada may well have been the focus of a certain amount of GDR intelligence-gathering efforts, which served as a prelude to such aid.[10] The GDR's motives for giving Grenada such attention are not clear, but GDR interest started with Coard's 1980 trip to Eastern Europe. We can conjecture that Grenada provided the GDR with a relatively inexpensive means of creating a diplomatic and political presence in the Caribbean and Latin America outside of Cuba, although the purpose of such an exercise in unclear. Nevertheless, such a maneuver, if it resulted in gains for the socialist bloc, might also yield the GDR certain advantages in its dealings with the USSR. In any case, the GDR provided Grenada with a series of grants, concessionary loans, and some technical assistance.

Nevertheless, relations between the GDR and Grenada gave rise to certain difficulties. Certain aid requests for consumer goods were turned down because the East Germans refused to give any kind of grants for such purposes. A major grant of printing equipment for the PRG newspaper turned out to be a burden: an unidentified printer at the newspaper told me that servicing requires a GDR technician flying in from Europe, since facilities for such repairs do not exist in the Western Hemisphere; further, many of the manuals supplied with the equipment were written in German or Czech, which the printers could not read. More important, as I detail below, the GDR trade and aid policies were not well coordinated, and its foreign trade enterprises took great advantage of Grenadian incompetency or ignorance to obtain highly advantageous import prices from the PRG and, at the same time, to sell obsolete equipment to them.

Aid from the other European socialist nations was miniscule and is not included separately in table 5.1; for the most part it consisted of scholarships and small gifts. The obvious target for aid giving was Poland, since that country was the largest East European buyer of Grenadian products in the last years of the Gairy regime. However, exports to Poland tapered off after 1978 and stopped completely in 1981; and no aid was forthcoming. As Kendrick Radix (interview) pointed out to me, in 1979 Poland's internal political problems increased and the country came to be in no financial position to serve either as a buyer of Grenadian exports or a giver of aid. Czechoslovakia and Hungary were also natural targets for aid, but little was forthcoming until some years had passed, except for the sending of occasional technicians. Indeed, Bishop's trip to those two countries in September 1983 shortly before he was ousted and killed was to negotiate some more substantial foreign aid agreements for 1984 and 1985. Hungary, for instance, offered an electric power station and Czechoslovakia promised to send a small cement mill. I have found no evidence why the GDR created much stronger economic ties to Grenada than Hungary or Czechoslovakia did.

Bulgaria seemed to offer Grenada considerable diplomatic advice, even though no significant aid was forthcoming. In a rather imaginative swap, the two countries agreed to exchange Grenadian nutmeg for a Bulgarian ice plant (for fish processing). According to a highly placed PRG Foreign Ministry official (interview), the Grenadians considered Romania as too much of a maverick to be worth cultivating and exercised caution with Yugoslavia since it was viewed as "neither fish nor fowl." In 1983 Coard did make some preliminary attempts to obtain aid from Yugoslavia, but the major result was merely an agreement for further discussions at a later date. Apparently, Albania was totally avoided; in any case, that nation was in no position to offer extensive economic aid.

ASIAN SOCIALIST NATIONS

After 1981 Grenada went fishing for grants in the Asian socialist world that supported the Soviet Union, including Kampuchea, Laos, Mongolia, North Korea, and Vietnam. North Korea actively wooed Grenada from the very beginning; and in the PRG's first foray abroad for foreign aid in the summer of 1979, Kim Il-Sung received the group in person. The purpose of this interest is puzzling. A highly placed PRG Foreign Ministry official suggested to me that perhaps this divided nation (similar to the GDR) also saw an inexpensive opportunity to overcome its diplomatic isolation in the Western Hemisphere. It is also possible that, since Gairy was so friendly to the South Korean government, the North Koreans felt a natural affinity to the PRG. North Korea also seems to pay particular attention to small nations in which other countries are not interested, for example, its significant presence in Madagascar. In any case, three members of the Political Bureau— Hudson Austin, Selwyn Strachan, and Maurice Bishop—made separate visits to North Korea and obtained not only a U.S. $12 million grant of military equipment but also their promise to build a stadium in St. George's and assistance on a number of other projects as well.

The Grenadians appeared quite ignorant about conditions in North Korea. When Hudson Austin, the head of the army, returned home in September 1983 from a trip to North Korea, we smile in reading the Central Committee minutes that he "was surprised to see how deep the personality cult was in Korea, where the leader is worshiped almost as a God." However, the North Koreans apparently invested considerable emotional energy in Grenada: after the U.S. intervention, Western reporters in Havana greeted the plane bringing expelled foreign diplomats to Cuba and noted not only the Cuban diplomats with their clenched fists raised defiantly in the air but also the fifteen North Koreans (apparently mostly engineers) weeping into their handkerchiefs.

Grenadian relations with the other Asian socialist nations were not very significant: Vietnam gave a symbolic gift of military equipment; Mongolia and Grenada exchanged delegates to conferences held in the two countries; and the PRG planned to send a delegate to the Laos party congress. As noted above, Grenada avoided China diplomatically; and it is noteworthy that the small amount of Grenadian exports between the two countries ceased after 1979. Curiously, the small amount of imports Grenada received from China continued.

CUBA

Cuba's major support of Grenada consisted of the E.C. $82 million (U.S. $30 million) for the airport, given in the form of both manpower and equipment. But Cuba also gave E.C. $17.0 million (U.S. $6.3 million) for other projects. At the time of the intervention there were about 784 Cubans on the island, of which about 636 were working on the airport, 22 served as military advisors, 17 worked as physicians and dentists, and others worked as teachers and as advisors to the Ministry of Interior and other government bureaus.

Cuban aid was said to be given without strings and was particularly helpful to the PRG since it was continuous, responsive to the PRG's needs of the moment, directed at a variety of problems, and given as grants. In reading the minutes of the NJM Political Bureau or Central Committee, I was impressed at how the preferred solution to many small technical problems was to call on the Cuban comrades in the same manner as a hesitant child calls upon his parents to help at every moment of unforeseen difficulties. The 1982–1983 aid agreement detailed 196 different projects, including piano tuning training and instruction in table tennis. A particularly bizarre instance of Grenada's dependency on Cuba occurred in mid-1983 at the time the Cubans cut off the telephones and electricity of the Grenadian embassy in Havana when it had not paid its bills to the utility company, an event which raised anger in the Grenadian Political Bureau. This rather pointed message by the Cubans did not prevent the Political Bureau at the same time from asking Cuba for grants for construction of a power plant, bridge repairs, thirty miles of roads, farm and feeder roads, water resource development and a hydroelectricity plant, civil engineering work for a satellite dish (donated by the Soviets), civil engineering work for the Bulgarian ice plant, a national convention center, construction of a quarry, and an aquarium. Very often it seemed that the Cubans responded affirmatively to such heterogeneous requests.

As far as I can determine, the Cubans had made few extraordinary counterdemands on the Grenadians. In the early years of the revolution, the Cuban ambassador is alleged to have attended cabinet meetings, so the Cubans kept a close eye on events.[11] They also had technicians working in several of the key ministries, for example, the planning office. The Grenadians appeared most willing to coordinate their foreign policy efforts with the Cubans, which must have been quite helpful. Although the Cubans occasionally manifested displeasure with the course of Grenadian events (e.g., especially during the summer of 1983), for the most part they tried hard to maintain their role as a wise and generous uncle with considerable tolerance for an occasionally unruly nephew.

THE WEST

To complete the picture, a brief glance needs to be paid to Grenada's aid fishing in the West. Among the industrialized Western nations, the largest donor was, curiously, the United States, which saw some of its donations to the Caribbean Development Bank funneled to Grenada. In several maladroit diplomatic maneuvers, the United States tried without success to restrict such transfers. The United States was apparently more successful in making it difficult for the PRG to obtain loans or grants from international organizations such as the World Bank and International Monetary Fund, although it received considerable assistance from the ineptitude of the PRG in its lobbying for these loans. Grenada also received a series of small grants and loans from a variety of other Western sources.

An IMF emergency loan to Grenada in the summer of 1983 was apparently not opposed by the U.S. government; however, the conditions placed on this loan were sufficiently rigorous that the PRG began discussing a unique strategy in dealing with this organization: according to the minutes of a meeting of the Political/Economic Bureau, "Comrade Maurice Bishop suggested that we use the Suriname and Cuban experience in keeping two sets of records in the bank for this purpose [of reporting to the IMF]. . . . Comrades again highlighted the urgent importance of training comrades to adjust the banking figures. Someone should be sent to Cuba or to the Soviet Union."

The PRG was much more successful in obtaining grants from rich but radical Third World countries, and it worked tirelessly on these matters. The government's first great success occurred as a result of a meeting between Saddem Hussein of Iraq and Bishop at the Conference of Non-Aligned Nations in Havana in September 1979. According to a high PRG official in the Foreign Ministry, Bishop exercised his charm on Hussein, the chemistry between the two men was perfect, and as a result Iraq gave Grenada a grant of U.S. $2 million in the same year.

Other Arab nations might have also been impressed at Bishop's forth-right stand against the Camp David Agreement, his comparison of "Zionist Israel" with Pol Pot's Kampuchea, and his support for the Polisario Front. In succeeding years, Grenada received a number of grants and loans from the Arab world.

Some early grants—especially from Algeria, Iraq, and Syria in 1980—and later grants were vital not only for the completion of the airport but also for overcoming short-term balance of payment prob-lems. However, in some cases this foreign aid was not easy to obtain. Perhaps the most troubled relationship was with Libya, which the PRG had originally targeted for aid amounting to U.S. $75 million. The Libyans replied with a loan of about U.S. $4 million, some boats, and a promised grant of U.S. $4 million. Unfortunately, only a part of this aid was actually sent, because the Libyans apparently had a cash flow problem after the softening of oil prices. I was told that dealing with Qadhafi was an ordeal; the Grenadian delegation would arrive in Tripoli with a definite appointment, only to spend several days in a hotel room waiting for a phone call that the colonel was ready to see them. Although the two countries exchanged ambassadors, the Libyan ambassador be-came bored in Grenada and in April 1983 wrote Bishop that he was going to leave the island because very few people had visited him. It is unclear what happened, but seventeen Libyans were on the island until October 1983.

Not all Arab nations contributed to Grenada. Conservative nations such as Saudi Arabia, Jordan, the United Arab Emirates, and Morocco gave nothing. The radical Arab nations apparently received three gains from the relatively small amount of foreign aid they supplied: an auto-matic vote in various international organizations for their side, a strong and clear articulation of their position in the Western Hemisphere, and an inexpensive opportunity to tweak the nose of the United States.

The degree to which these friendships would have persisted if the intervention had not occurred cannot easily be gauged. The affairs with the Libyan ambassador might have been a warning. In 1983, Grenada was running into extreme financial difficulties, in good part because the U.S. $13 million aid promised by Algeria, Iran, Iraq, and Libya had not arrived.

A Perspective

Grenada's search for foreign aid in the West was straightforward. However, several aspects of foreign aid from other socialist nations to Grenada deserve brief mention, for they provide perspective on some unique aspects of Grenada's aid begging.

First, such aid appeared to be loosely coordinated among the various countries, at least from 1982 onward. The Grenadian ambassador to

Moscow sent a coded message home in January 1982 saying that the GDR ambassador and "some Cubans" told him some very good news: in the recent meeting of all general secretaries of socialist nations (apparently only those nations allied with the USSR attended), Leonid Brezhnev announced that the Soviets were going to give Grenada a "generous package" and that what the Soviets didn't supply, the other nations would when Grenadian aid teams visited them. Even more interesting is the fact that the Soviets did *not* supply Grenada with a "generous" package when Bishop visited the USSR later in the year and that aid from the other socialist nations appeared to be on the same hit-or-miss basis as before. This can be interpreted in three ways: either (1) that the mechanisms for following up decisions made at this high-level meeting were not effective, or (2) that the Soviets changed their mind after the meeting, or (3) that they decided to postpone any decision until a high-ranking official such as Lebedinskiy made a careful study of the island. Unfortunately, we have no evidence on which explanation is closer to the truth. In any case, from the archival materials available, the relations of the Soviet bloc nations with Grenada appeared quite separate, and no evidence is available that particular nations such as the GDR were "assigned" to help Grenada; indeed, Cuba's intercession with Moscow on Grenada's behalf, especially before 1982, suggests that these nations were acting quite independently.

Second, with the major exception of a loan for East German telephone equipment, these nations gave their aid in the form of tied grants or short-term trade credits. It could not be used for balance of payment purposes. The provision of technicians and of scholarships were particularly preferred.

Third, a number of technical problems in such aid arose. Some of the equipment was outmoded (e.g., some of the military equipment, and the East German telephone system). Some equipment arrived without sufficient spare parts (in April 1983 Bishop complained to Gromyko that only one-tenth of the Soviet military vehicles were in operation because of lack of spare parts). Some equipment rapidly broke down and became useless (e.g., Cuba donated ten ferroconcrete fishing boats; their engines were too weak to power the boats and had to be replaced; several sank; only one remained in operation after several years).

It is also worth noting that such aid did not come without certain costs to Grenada. The entire aid program severely overtaxed the Grenadian administrative bureaucracy. Many grants were incorrectly specified, so that Grenada received equipment it could not use or did not need. Further, when aid was not forthcoming at the expected time, the PRG found itself in severe financial straits, especially in the summer of 1983. There were also certain political costs of clientism: for instance, Grenada's vote with the Soviet Union on the Afghanistan issue was received quite negatively from many potential supporters in the Caribbean area. Finally, the constant focus on foreign affairs led to a considerable neglect of domestic economic problems. Foreign affairs seemed a much more interesting occupation than more mundane aspects of economic management. The top party leaders were quite aware of this neglect and registered their concern from time to time, but nothing was done about it. They appeared quite willing to leave most such economic matters to Bernard Coard, who was able to consolidate his political power in this fashion.

TECHNICAL ASSISTANCE[12]

Planning

The PRG had close contacts with a number of socialist nations and, in 1983, both Cuban and Soviet technicians were aiding the PRG's economic planning process. In a number of interviews with PRG officials (including Bernard Coard, the minister of Planning, as well as several of his subordinates), I asked about the type of economic advice that the PRG received, and in all cases I was informed that with one exception (discussed below) the advice was of a technical, rather than a strategic, nature. For instance, I was told that the Cuban economist working in the Ministry of Planning, Fernando Díaz, spent most of his time developing information systems for the introduction of a material balance type of planning system. All of this information about foreign advice and advisors was, however, quite vague. However, the available documentary evidence allows us only a glimpse of the type of advice given to the Grenadians, and only by the Soviets and the Czechoslovaks.

In December 1982 the Lebedinskiy mission of Soviet economists arrived for a series of meetings with PRG officials. According to the minutes of these meetings, the Soviets responded cautiously to the enthusiastic plans of the Grenadians and spent most of their time asking intelligent and sober questions, primarily about details. For instance, they questioned the advisability of Grenada's planned expansion into citrus fruits because of possible competition with Cuba and suggested coffee as a substitute product; the Grenadians replied that they had cleared their plans with the Cubans. They also advised the Grenadians to continue their exports to capitalist countries as much as possible. The Soviets replied to the PRG's boast that they would practically eliminate unemployment in the next few years with a little lecture about the mechanism underlying what bourgeois economists call the Phillips curve and how such a policy might increase the inflation potential! (It is also noteworthy that they seemed to accept exaggerated PRG claims about unemployment reduction.) They also emphasized strongly the necessity of keeping rigorous financial and statistical records. In sum, in this series of meetings the Soviets seemed to offer practical, not strategic advice, although at one point in the conversation they did suggest it was unwise to stress industry too strongly "because of the marketing problem."

In contrast, the Czechoslovaks gave very explicit advice for the long term. In 1982 Jiri Cerhonek, an economist from the Czechoslovak Ministry of Planning on loan to the Macro Planning Unit of the Grenadian Ministry of Planning, wrote a fascinating memorandum outlining a strategy of development for the next three years. Although it ostensibly covered only the immediate future, it had important longer range implications.

Cerhonek's approach was to diversify the economy and to implement an import substitution policy primarily in manufacturing. He focused almost completely on industrialization and urged investment in manufacture of goods with the following characteristics: high labor intensivity of production; not produced in the surrounding island states; high income elasticities; low material consumption; and short payout times, so that the initial investment could be rapidly recovered. He specified electronic components, agroindustry, plastics processing, wood and wastepaper processing (including furniture), woven carpets, shoe industry, garment production, and construction materials. With regard to agriculture, he suggested only the introduction of tobacco, and for other sectors his remarks focused more on the necessity of proper maintenance of existing productive facilities rather than on radical changes in investment policy. Although some of his import substitution ideas paralleled those of the PRG, Cerhonek's approach was very different from the strategy outlined by Bishop; in many important respects, it made an almost full circle to the advice given by Arthur Lewis (the West Indian economist and future Nobel Laureate) to the Caribbean nations as a whole in 1950, when he told them that labor intensive light industry was their only hope for economic development.[13]

One Grenadian official (interview) made the interesting suggestion that the Cerhonek memorandum was essentially Coard's Trojan horse to reverse the development strategy set by Bishop in the Line of March speech. This appears unlikely, because Coard's political weight was preponderantly on economic matters and, in his capacity as minister of Planning, he was undoubtedly the major architect of the Line of March approach. When I discussed the memorandum with Coard (interview February 1985) and pointed out that it ran contrary to Bishop's approach, Coard denied it. He said that the memorandum was merely useful input for the NJM's thinking about the long term. In other words, he rejected the short-term thrust of the memorandum, which downgraded the PRG's emphasis on tourism and agriculture, and took Cerhonek's advice as a set of guidelines for the third phase of the fifteen-year plan, when the island would begin to industrialize.

These two instances suggest that the PRG had clearly set its own course and, although it listened to the advice of others, it did not feel obliged to follow such guidelines. Although Grenada's relations with Cuba were much closer than with the USSR or Czechoslovakia, it seems likely to me that they maintained the same independence.

Specialists

Quite early after the coup, Cuba gave Grenada the services of about a dozen doctors and dentists, which increased the number of such medical specialists almost by half. Of particular importance, they were sent to parts of Grenada lacking in medical personnel (e.g., the islands of Carriacou and Petite Martinique, two small islands belonging to Grenada that had no permanent physicians). This increase in health inputs was perhaps the most important move in the field of health that the PRG made, for although they declared health care to be of primary importance, budgetary resources devoted to this purpose did not seem to increase during the Bishop government.[14] Proof of the popularity of this program is seen in a public opinion poll taken shortly after the military intervention, which showed that about one of seven Grenadians believed that health was the area in which the PRG did most for the nation (it followed education and the building of the airport).

For a wide number of specific projects, Cuba sent specialists to make surveys, give advice, or implement particular policies. This was part of a much larger effort by Cuba, which is said to maintain about 16,000 teachers, doctors, construction engineers, and other aid workers in twenty-two Third World nations, a program roughly three times larger than the U.S. Peace Corps.[15] The Soviets, in contrast, did not seem to send many individual specialists until 1983, when two planning specialists and twelve military advisors were posted in Grenada.

Other

A number of Soviet bloc countries gave scholarships to Grenada, and PRG officials frequently mentioned that 350 Grenadians were studying abroad in these programs. For the most part, these seemed to have been short specialized courses, although the USSR did give a number of multiyear scholarships for studying at Soviet universities. In fact, Grenada had more scholarship offers than they could fill and, as far as I was able to find out, the offers from Bulgaria and several other countries were not filled at all.

TRADING WITH THE SOVIET BLOC[16]

Grenada's trade with the West provides little of interest, since little changed from the time before the PRG. Bananas, cocoa, nutmeg, and mace provided the main exports, although private farmers were responding to market incentives and increasing the exports of citrus fruits and vegetables. Trade with the Soviet bloc, on the other hand, was quite a new experience.

Trading relations between Grenada and the Soviet bloc can be seen most easily in table 5.2, which presents data on the geographical distribution of exports and imports. During the period from 1978 through 1983 Grenada experienced considerable difficulties in its trade with the West for two reasons: its currency was tied to the dollar, which was

Table 5.2
The Foreign Trade of Grenada with Socialist Nations, 1977–1983
(millions of current E.C. dollars)

	1977	1978	1979	1980	1981	1982	1983
Exports							
China	1.29	0.31	0.67	0.00	0.00	0.00	0.00
Cuba	0.00	0.00	0.00	0.22	0.19	0.11	0.42
Czechoslovakia	0.00	0.00	0.00	0.00	0.00	0.09	0.00
German Democratic Republic	0.00	0.00	0.00	0.00	0.00	0.02	0.00
Poland	0.79	1.22	1.07	0.48	0.00	0.00	0.00
USSR	0.00	0.00	0.00	0.00	0.00	1.73	2.49
Total	2.08	1.53	1.74	0.70	0.19	1.95	2.91
All nations	36.90	44.34	55.61	45.51	50.2	˙75	48.46
Imports							
Bulgaria	0.00	0.00	0 00	0.00			
China	0.47	0.47	0.62	0.66			
Cuba	0.23	0.72	1.39	2.74			
Czechoslovakia	0.30	0.21	0.21	0.2			
German Democratic Republic	0.13	0.07	0.07	0			
Hungary	0.18	0.11	0.09	ʹ			
North Korea	0.00	0.00	0.00				
Poland	0.13	0.33	0.20				
Romania	0.00	0.00	0.0ᶜ				
USSR	0.09	0.04	0.ᶜ				
Yugoslavia	0.00	0.00	0				
Unspecified	0.07	0.10					
Total	1.60	2.05					
All nations	87.29	96.45					

Source: *Annual Digest of Trade Statistics 1982* (St.
plus data supplied by the CSO; 1983 data are pₓ
Note: E.C. (Eastern Caribbean) dollars are issued by thₑ
$2.7 = U.S. $1 during this period. Data do not include ₜₑ
million imports from Cuba for, respectively, 1982 and 1983 for ₜₑ

rising vis-à-vis the European nations with which Grenada had the greatest amount of trade; further, the terms of trade were falling about 25 percent, a set of circumstances due not only to the oil price rise in 1979 but the relative decline in prices of some of Grenada's most important exports, such as nutmeg.

As can be seen from the table, Grenadian exports to the Soviet bloc did not greatly increase. Although imports did rise, these reflected the tied grants that Grenada had received from these nations. The materials from the captured archives reveal some interesting strains in Grenada's attempts to increase its trade with its new socialist allies.

Areas of Contention

SALES

As noted above, Bernard Coard's 1980 mission to the USSR to obtain a trade agreement was unsuccessful. In 1981 the PRG announced in its newspaper that a trade agreement with the Soviet Union had been signed and that the USSR would henceforth purchase Grenadian nutmeg; however, this agreement later turned out to be a relatively meaningless "trade protocol" and covered only some short-term trading deals.[17]

In preparation for more serious trade negotiations in late 1982, the PRG position papers reveal that they wanted to sign five-year agreements to export yearly 500 tons of nutmeg (about one-fifth of Grenada's annual crop), 1,000 tons of cocoa, and 10,000 tons of bananas. However, only the five-year nutmeg contract was signed, although the Soviets also bought some Grenadian cocoa on a short-term basis. At that time Nikolai Lebedinskiy, the deputy chairman of Gosplan, told the Grenadians that he didn't have enough information on Grenada to make any more decisions. The minutes also record that "he would see what possibilities [for trade] were available. He however noted that these things were not decided upon [as] quickly as they should." Czechoslovakia also agreed to start importing eighty tons a year of Grenadian nutmeg for five years. (After the intervention, the Soviets and the Czechoslovaks quietly stopped honoring their nutmeg agreement with the Grenadian government.)[18] More disappointments to the PRG occurred because the other socialist nations also proved unwilling to import any large quantities of Grenada's agricultural exports.

Import relations with other socialist nations also raised some new problems. In certain cases, spare parts were difficult to obtain for equipment already imported. In other cases the PRG imported goods that were not suitable for Grenadian conditions, and the large order for telephone equipment that Grenada placed with the GDR illustrates some of these problems.

The Grenada telephone company (Grentel) had been discussing

plans in the late 1970s to buy some new digital (i.e., all-electronic) switching equipment from Continental Telephone Company in the United States (which was part owner of Grentel). After Grentel was nationalized, the Grenadians started negotiating with the GDR, originally to buy a digital system and later to buy a crossbar (i.e., mechanical) switching system instead. A Grentel engineer (interview) said that the digital system costs about 35 percent more; however, the equipment is much smaller and, therefore, the building costs for housing the equipment—which are significant—are less. He further noted that a digital system requires less maintenance and, in addition, is much more flexible when the system is expanded. According to Lyden Ramdhanny (interview), a former PRG cabinet minister, there was considerable dispute in PRG policy circles about what system to buy. However, Bernard Coard doggedly argued that the crossbar system should be purchased because Grenada could obtain very advantageous credit terms; and he finally had his way. Since Coard knew enough economics to recognize the fallacy of this type of argument, it is possible that other factors were involved, which he did not want to discuss, for example, that the GDR tied certain political agreements to the purchase of such obsolete equipment. In any case, the incident created considerable ill will.

José L. Mestrar, a foreign trade consultant (apparently Cuban) to the PRG read the various trade contracts the Grenadians had signed with various Soviet bloc countries and suggested that Grenada stop importing on short-term credits various products from Eastern Europe and, instead, exchange their agricultural produce for these goods. Like all good advice, it was easier said than done.

Prices

The pricing of goods in Grenadian trade with other socialist countries raised considerable difficulties. The most curious misunderstanding occurred in December 1982 when a Soviet trade mission visited the island. According to an undated memo by Coard, they "quietly" approached the nutmeg cooperative, rather than the state; further, they offered U.S. $1,500 a ton, when the world market price was supposed to be U.S. $1,950. In his memo, Coard appeared to be extremely angry at such underhanded maneuvers; however, the real story can be interpreted in a somewhat different and more interesting way.

From 1980 onward, the price Grenada received for its nutmeg had been falling and by the arrival of the Soviet trade mission the Nutmeg Cooperative had considerable unsold inventories. According to Veda Gittens (interview), executive secretary of the Grenada Cooperative Nutmeg Association, the Grenadians charged the Soviets the world market price and, further, agreed to renegotiate the price every year so that the price would follow the world market price. In actuality, according to Grenadian trade statistics, the Soviets paid a premium over the price, which nonsocialist buyers paid, of 51 percent in 1982 and 58 percent in 1983.[19] Similarly, the Cubans paid a 32 percent premium for nutmeg in 1982 and a 42 percent premium in 1983; and the GDR paid a premium of 59 percent in 1983. No nutmeg was purchased by socialist nations in 1981; in 1980 Cuba had paid a premium of 15 percent and Poland, 3 percent.

Given the fact that the Soviets wanted to pay world market prices, how could this have arisen? A certain part of the premium can be traced to the fact that in these later years Cuba, the GDR and the USSR apparently negotiated nutmeg prices a considerable time in advance of actual delivery, when the general world market price was lower.[20] However, it also seems likely that a discrepancy existed between the nutmeg cooperatives's stated belief about the level of the "world market price" of nutmeg and the "actual" price. It is worth noting that the international nutmeg market is very thin and specialized, since there are only two major world exporters and most countries such as the USSR generally buy their nutmeg semiprocessed from middlemen in the Netherlands and, as a result, are not completely aware of the world market price. Price premia for other Grenadian exports, which were for products with a well-defined world market price, were very much smaller. In any case, I suspect that Coard's anger about Soviet buying tactics may have been due either to his misunderstanding about the world market price of nutmeg or to a tactical maneuver to change the institutional structure of Grenadian foreign trade so that more trade, particularly with the Soviet bloc, would be carried out through the state foreign trade enterprise, the National Marketing and Importing Board.

More illumination about Grenadian pricing practices can be gained from a brief glance at cocoa sales. In 1983 Grenada delivered to the Soviet Union some cocoa at a 12 percent premium over the price they received from other buyers. Since the world market price of cocoa is well known, this appears surprising. However, according to Norbert Arnold (interview), the former secretary of the Grenada Cocoa Association, the GCA asked this higher price because "we felt that as an ally, they would be willing to pay more"; surprisingly, the Soviets did not appear to bargain very hard.

Grenada had a much different experience in negotiating a price for bananas with the GDR. The Germans had been talking with the PRG for some time about buying bananas, but they wanted to purchase a different kind of banana than Grenada grew, which—it should be noted—cost less but was much more difficult to ship. According to Norbert Baptiste (interview), secretary of the Banana Cooperative Society (BCS), in 1982 Grenada was selling bananas at forty-eight cents a pound. While on a visit to the GDR, George Louison, a member of the Political Bureau and the PRG minister of Agriculture, negotiated an arrangement whereby the GDR would buy these bananas at nineteen cents a pound! After learning about this agreement, the BCS registered its dismay, and the PRG obtained a new offer of twenty-four cents a pound, an amount that was about equal to the board's handling cost and that would leave the banana farmers with nothing. At this point, the BCS rejected the entire deal.

This incident has several curious aspects. First, Louison was the only member of the NJM leadership with any experience in agriculture, but he was apparently thinking in terms of the farm gate price of bananas and did not take into account the cost of their delivery to the port, which about equals the farm gate price; or else he got confused about which type of banana was to be sold. In any case, it does not appear that his staff preparation for these negotiations was adequate. Second, the BCS generally sold its own bananas, and it appears peculiar that Louison would take it upon himself to negotiate such an agreement, especially since some technical matters such as shipping arrangements are so important for bananas. Third, the GDR's offer was so insulting that one wonders why it was made in the first place, since it was bound to cause friction. Finally, the GDR did not permit Grenada to back out of the contract, since they were going to pay for the bananas in part with agricultural inputs such as fertilizer. At the time of the military intervention, Louison was engaged in working out a program to nationalize a number of estates in order to produce the bananas to meet this contract, which the private producers had refused to do.

Grenada seems to have paid reasonable prices for its imports from the other socialist countries. From a computer printout of Grenada's 1983 trade on a very detailed basis, I selected fifteen homogeneous items and computed average unit prices for socialist and nonsocialist nations. For the items I chose, there was not sufficient difference to warrant a more thorough investigation.

SOME CONCLUSIONS

Before the Grenadian experience can be placed in context, it is useful to review on an aggregative level the experience of other Third World Marxist nations in their economic relations with the Soviet bloc.

On a per capita basis, Grenada received considerably more foreign aid from various Soviet bloc nations than any other Third World nations with a "socialist orientation."[21] This was due, as I have indicated, to the generosity of Cuba. Thus Grenada's particular strategy of foreign aid socialism paid off. An examination of foreign aid receipts by all nations in the world reveals that almost all of the top ten aid receivers (on a per capita basis) are nations with very small populations, so Grenada's success in this regard is not unique in the world.

Although Soviet military aid (which was kept a secret) was forthcoming in 1980 and in the following years, Soviet economic aid was merely a trickle; two reasons for such stinginess can be conjectured. First, they did not want to rile the United States by developing unnecessarily close relations with a nation close to its shores. Second, they preferred to let Cuba carry the brunt of the aid, especially since Cuba had more experience in dealing with Caribbean conditions.

Nevertheless, I find it curious that the Soviets did not send more technicians at an earlier date, especially to help set up statistical and accounting systems, which would have permitted the Grenadians to organize their economy more efficiently; the sending of sixteen science teachers in the fall of 1983 may have been an experiment to establish a Soviet "peace corps"; however, technicians trained in fields more oriented toward production might have been considerably more useful to the Grenadians, and there is no evidence that they would have been unwelcomed. I also find it strange that the Soviet Union did not give Grenada the emergency loan it needed in the summer of 1983; from this action, it appears that at least one segment of the Soviet bureaucracy did not think Grenada of sufficient strategic advantage to spend a few paltry million rubles.

Although world data on direction of trade with the Soviet bloc leave something to be desired, it appears that Third World nations with a "socialist orientation" carry out no more trade with the Soviet bloc than other Third World nations.[22] Thus Grenada's difficulties in trading with the Soviet bloc were not unique. With regard to the pricing of Grenada's exports to the Soviet bloc, two lessons can be learned from these various incidents. First, as many (including the philosopher Hegel) have pointed out, a client can have power over his patron. The premiums the Grenadians extracted for their exports to the other socialist nations is an interesting example, especially since the Soviet Union explicitly claimed they wanted to trade at the world market price. Second, it is possible that trade and aid policies are not necessarily well coordinated in the socialist bloc, and the GDR's treatment of Grenada with regard to bananas and telephone systems illustrates this point. A more cynical interpretation of the difficulties between the GDR and Grenada is that the Germans had no real interest in trying to help Grenada but rather, in the guise of giving Grenada certain grants, was actually trying to realize a considerable net profit by selling obsolete equipment and obtaining particularly low import prices.

Grenada's confrontational stance vis-à-vis the United States and its diligence in various international arenas in furthering Soviet bloc aims was important in deepening its relations with Soviet bloc countries and radical Third World nations. However, a basic contradiction existed in Grenada's growth strategy in that the policies that yielded the most foreign aid fruits were also those that frightened away tourists, especially from the United States, which provided by far most visitors to the island. One cannot help suspecting that, once it became clear that Grenada was not developing economically, once the novelty of the new ally had worn off, and once the Soviet bloc nations saw that Grenada had scared away tourists, its major source of revenue, disillusionment would have occurred, and foreign aid receipts from the Soviet bloc and the radical Third World would have tapered off.

NOTES

Research for this chapter was financed by grants from the National Council for Soviet and East European Research and from the Swarthmore College Faculty Research Fund. To both I would like to express my gratitude and to absolve them from any responsibility for my interpretations or errors. Materials for this essay are drawn in large part from a book-length study entitled *Revolutionary Grenada, A Study in Political Economy* (New York: Praeger, 1986).

1. A microfiche version of these captured files is available to the public at the U.S. National Archives, Modern Military Headquarters Branch. As of Sept. 1985, only about three-quarters of this archives had been indexed. I cite these microfiche with the designation MF-*xxxx*, where the *x*'s stand for the last four digits of the microfiche number (thus omitting the "DIS–83-C," which preceeds each four-digit number in the archives). Some of the documents in this file have also been reproduced in Michael Ledeen and Herbert Romerstein, eds., *Grenada Documents: An Overview and Selection*, vol. 1 (Washington, D.C.: Depts. of State and Defense, 1984). Hereafter, *Grenada Documents*.

2. Frederic Pryor, *Revolutionary Grenada: A Study in Political Economy* (New York: Praeger, 1986).

3. The evidence is summarized in ibid., ch. 5.

4. Underlying documents for this section: an account of Coard's 1980 visit to the USSR, MF–4094, MF–4583, and MF–5177. PRG foreign policy goals, *Grenada Documents:* Document 106; countries to avoid close relations, Document 107; Political Bureau meeting in June 1981, Document 54. Shopping list for potential aid donors, MF–6885; the Soviet 1982 loan, MF–5178 and MF–5177; Bishop's talking points to Gromyko in his visit in Apr. 1983, MF–4708; Lebedinskiy statement, MF–4094; Soviet rejection of an emergency loan in 1983, MF–8751; the proposal for an IMF-type bank of CMEA nations, MF–8342; report on aid conditions by the GDR, MF–4741; Coard's 1983 visit to Yugoslavia, MF–5179; Kim Il-Sung's reception of the Grenadian delegation in July 1979, MF–4668; Grenada's 1982/83 request to Cuba, MF–3267; problems of payment of utility bills in Grenada's

Havana embassy and request for more Cuban foreign aid, MF–2292; the decoded version of Jacob's message about the conference of first secretaries, MF–12596; NJM discussions about cheating the International Monetary Fund, MF–2292.

5. Bernard Coard, "The Meaning of Political Independence in the Commonwealth Caribbean," in *Independence for Grenada: Myth or Reality?* (St Augustine, Trinidad: Institute of International Relations, University of the West Indies, 1974).

6. The annual GDP data (factor-cost basis) are estimates based on data (and extrapolations) from the World Bank, *World Tables,* 3d ed. (Washington, D.C.: World Bank, 1983).

7. *Grenada Documents,* Document 26.

8. MF–4673. Jacobs also wrote this report of his difficulties in finding out which part of the International Section of the Central Committee would deal with Grenada—the Latin American bureau or the Canada-Guyana bureau. "When I enquired as to what section has responsibility for Suriname, the amused response was that 'no one wants to take responsibility for Suriname'." He noted that they had little respect for the communist party in Guyana (People's Progressive Party), especially since they believed that Janet Jagan (an American) controlled Cheddi Jagan. One of Jacob's memoranda provides a unique view of the Soviet military aid bureaucracy, while in another report (MF–4840), he detailed a discussion with a diplomat from Somalia about the nation's fall from grace from the Soviet Union and analyzed other aspects of the Soviet aid program. In still another memo (MF–4888), he focused on the results of Bishop's trip to the USSR in July 1982 and why certain requests were and were not met. Jacobs was an acute observer, and these documents provide invaluable source materials about Soviet diplomatic procedures and policies. They were also extremely useful to Bishop, who crafted a brilliant appeal for aid to Gromyko during a visit in Apr. 1983 (MF–4708). The arguments in Bishop's notes are so convincing that it is difficult to remain unmoved when reading this speech; however, according to Grenadian notes of the conversation (MF–4845), Gromyko maintained his cool.

9. U.S. Department of State and Department of Defense, *Grenada: A Preliminary Report* (Washington, D.C.: GPO, 1983). According to Kai Schoenhals (interview), who met the ambassador several times, he was a long-time Latin American specialist whose abilities in English were limited and whose knowledge of Grenada was even less. His behavior was in sharp contrast to that of the Cuban ambassador (whose wife was American): the former rode around in splendid isolation in a chauffer-driven Mercedes (the only one on the island); the latter drove his own Lada, often giving rides to children walking to or from school.

10. A summary of the evidence on East German espionage is presented in Pryor, *Revolutionary Grenada,* app. A–2.

11. Timothy Ashby, "Grenada: Soviet Stepping Stone," *U.S. Naval Institute Proceedings* 109 (Dec. 1983), pp. 30–36. He relies on interview material with Lloyd Noel, who was a member of the PRG cabinet before he resigned and was subsequently arrested.

12. Supporting documents used in this section: minutes of the 1982 meeting

with the Soviet technical mission, MF–4094 and MF–6826; Cerhonek memorandum, MF–5189.

13. Arthur Lewis, "The Industrialization of the British West Indies," *Caribbean Economic Review* 2 (May 1950), pp. 1–61.

14. By 1983, government budgetary expenditures on health and housing rose 68 percent over the 1978 level, but the retail price index rose 86 percent. No better deflator for the budgetary series is available. The data come from Pryor, *Revolutionary Grenada*, table 6–4. The public opinion polling data come from Selwyn Ryan, "Grenada: Balance Sheet of the Revolution," paper presented to the Conference on Grenada, Institute of International Relations, University of the West Indies, St. Augustine, 24 May 1984.

15. The data on the Cuban and American aid programs come from James Brooke, "The Cubans in Angola: They're Not All Soldiers," *New York Times,* 22 Jan. 1985.

16. Supporting documents used in this section: PRG position papers on exports to the USSR, MF–7473; Czechoslovak contract, MF–4705; Lebedinskiy statement, MF–4094; Coard memorandum on the Soviet mission, MF–7130; other aspects of Soviet trade, MF–4845; GDR banana negotiations, MF–4405 and MF–4733; Louison's banana plantation scheme, MF–4618; identification of possible state monopolies, MF–4263; MNIB imports and exports, MF–7473; alternatives for the organization of foreign trade, *Grenada Documents,* Document 94 and SM-III-11; political background on the organization of foreign trade, MF–3498; Mestra memorandum, MF–5178.

17. The announcement of the 1981 Soviet trade agreement (and also similar "agreements" with Czechoslovakia and the GDR) came in the *Free West Indian,* 6 Sept. 1981; and the information that it was a mere trade protocol came from Lyden Ramdhanny (interview), who was the PRG minister of Tourism. It is quite unclear to me why the PRG misrepresented the nature of the trade agreement to its citizens, especially since the lack of long-run sales to the Soviet Union would become so quickly known (although the Soviets did make some short-run purchases for 1982).

18. According to some Grenadians with whom I spoke, the United States forced Grenada to cut its relations with the Soviet Union and to cancel the five-year nutmeg contract. *New York Times,* 22 Jan. 1984 placed all of the blame for the contract rupture on American pressures to break diplomatic relations. However, the American chargé d'affaires Roy Haverkamp, (interview) denied that U.S. pressures for this diplomatic rupture had ever been made.

Why, then, were the exports stopped? The executive secretary of the Grenadian Cooperative Nutmeg Association told me that, since the contract was a government-to-government agreement, they were not involved in its enforcement and they did not understand the reasons. A high official in the current (1985) Grenadian government expressed a viewpoint that appears quite believable: that the breaking of the trade contracts by the Soviet Union and Czechoslovakia was a violation of commonly accepted commercial practices but that the Foreign Ministry has been so overburdened with work that they didn't have the personnel to pursue the matter and to take the appropriate legal measures for enforcing the contract. This is another sad instance of inadequate staff work by the Grenadian government bureaucracy, which, in this case, resulted in a considerable loss of revenue to the agricultural sector. Certain domestic consider-ations might also have weighed against such an attempt to enforce the contract, e.g., if it would have required the presence of Soviet officials on the island.

19. The price data cited here and below came either from Grenada, CSO, *op. cit.*, or from a computer printout of the 1983 trade results. The latter must, however, be considered only as preliminary estimates.

20. This procedure was different from the custom among the European socialist nations of negotiating prices often many months after trade quantities have been agreed upon. Such practices are discussed by Frederic L. Pryor, *The Communist Foreign Trade System* (London: Allen and Unwin, 1963), ch. 5. This granting of such premiums for exports of unessential agricultural goods was not a usual practice between socialist countries unless a high-level political decision to grant aid in this fashion (e.g., for Cuban sugar) had been made.

21. Data on Soviet bloc aid to all countries with a socialist orientation are presented in ibid., table 3–2.

22. This generalization is based on calculations made from trade direction statistics of the United Nations. This phenomenon is discussed in greater detail by various authors in Peter Wiles, ed., *The New Communist Third World* (New York: St. Martin's, 1982); and by David Ottaway and Marina Ottaway, *Afrocom-munism* (New York: Holmes & Meier, 1981).

6. The United States and the Grenada Revolution: Who Pushed First and Why?

Robert Pastor

> Look, often things cannot be understood unless they are analyzed as a process. Nobody can say that he reaches certain political conclusions except through a process. Nobody reaches these convictions . . . in a year. A lot of time has to pass before one reaches reliable political conclusions.
>
> —Fidel Castro

TO BE PUSHED OR TO LEAP: THAT IS THE QUESTION

A LMOST FROM THE beginning of the Grenada Revolution on 13 March 1979 to its demise on 25 October 1983, the only point on which the United States and the People's Revolutionary Government (PRG) agreed was that relations between them were, at best, strained, and usually hostile. The two governments disagreed, however, on the cause of the tension and the effects U.S. policy had on the course of the revolution. In an address in June 1983, Grenadian Prime Minister Maurice Bishop blamed the United States for the poor relationship:

> From the first days of coming to power, the United States pursued a policy which showed no respect for our national pride and aspirations, and sought constantly to bring the Revolution to its knees. . . . On reflection and analysis, we conclude that such an attitude [by the U.S.] exists principally because Grenada has taken a very decisive and firm step on the road to genuine national independence, non-alignment, and self-determination.[1]

Many reporters and analysts of the events in Grenada agree with Bishop that the United States caused the tension in the relationship, but unlike Bishop, they argue that U.S. policy pushed the revolution to the left. A report by a church group stated this view most crisply: "Through its attempts to dictate policy to the Grenada government [on its relations with Cuba], the United States had provoked the very development it sought to avoid."[2] In his study of the Grenada Revolution, Hugh

181

O'Shaughnessy also agrees that U.S. policy was counterproductive: "It is ironic that the Cuban-Grenadian relationship should have been fostered by Washington, whose constant harping on the supposed strategic threat from a tiny Eastern Caribbean island caused by New Jewel Movement to militarize their society more than they might otherwise have done."[3]

The U.S. government attributed the tension in the relationship to Grenada's attitude of "hostility and suspicion" to the United States. In testimony before Congress in June 1982, Deputy Assistant Secretary of State Stephen Bosworth criticized the PRG for breaking its promises of early elections as well as for its repression, but he left no doubt that the major cause of the strained relationship was because the PRG "adopted a militant foreign policy harshly critical of the U.S. and openly aligned with Cuba and the Soviet Union."[4]

In other words, according to the U.S. government, the behavior of the PRG provoked the U.S. policy response rather than the other way around. With regard to the question of whether the United States pushed the PRG to the left and to Cuba, former U.S. Ambassador to Grenada (1977–1979) Frank Ortiz explained "a Marxist-Leninist like Bishop is not 'driven' into the Communist camp; that is where he started out to go."[5] Several others who have sifted through the roughly 35,000 pounds of internal and classified documents of the New Jewel Movement (NJM) and the PRG, captured by U.S. troops during the intervention, tend to agree with Ortiz that the revolution started as a Marxist-Leninist one.[6]

Which is it? Was Grenada pushed into the waiting arms of the Soviet Union and Cuba by insensitive and counterproductive U.S. policies? Did Grenada become dependent on the Soviet Union and Cuba because U.S. hostility left it with no other choice? Or did the Grenadian government leap onto the unsuspecting shoulders of the Russian bear because of the ideological predisposition of its leadership? Did the PRG deliberately try to provoke the United States in order to disguise and justify its international preference to ally with the Soviet Union and Cuba? Did the PRG invite U.S. belligerence in order to use it as a strategic pretext to maintain political control by ceaselessly mobilizing and militarizing the masses? This chapter will seek to answer these questions as it assesses the foreign policies of the United States and Grenada between March 1979 and October 1983.

The Grenada Revolution, of course, is hardly the first occasion for asking the above questions. They have been posed by every revolution in the Caribbean Basin. In 1959 and 1960, Fidel Castro's militant rhetoric, his actions to nationalize various U.S. business interests, and his flirtation with the Soviet Union were perceived in the United States as provocative and requiring a harsh response. Three years later, Zeitlin and Scheer reexamined the collision and concluded that, by cutting the sugar quota and trying to undermine the revolution, the United States only succeeded in pushing Castro into the arms of the Soviets:

> Had we [the U.S.] sought to understand the social revolution occurring in Cuba, to sympathize with the aspirations of the Cuban people which Fidel Castro articulated so fiercely—with their demands for economic, political, and social changes, changes that challenged our long dominance in Cuban affairs—we might have succeeded in cementing cordial relations with the new Cuban government.[7]

In arguing their thesis, the two authors borrowed the concept of the self-fulfilling prophecy, which was defined by Robert Merton as "a false definition of the situation evoking a new behavior which makes the originally false conception come true."[8] By calling Castro a Communist and developing policies as if he were one, according to this argument, the United States eventually contributed to his becoming a Communist, and his revolution becoming anti-American.

An alternative interpretation is offered by former U.S. Ambassador to Cuba Phillip Bonsal, who concludes his analysis of the cause and the consequence of the confrontation as follows: "We did not force [Castro] into the arms of the Communists, but we were, in my judgment, un-wisely cooperative in removing the obstacles to his chosen path."[9] With a similar reluctance to apportion blame and an interest in understanding the process of interaction, Cole Blasier notes that "almost from the beginning, Castro and the United States expected the worst from each other, and neither was disappointed."[10]

Jorge Domínguez offers an insight into the possible causes of Cas-tro's behavior in the early period in U.S.-Cuban relations. When the revolution triumphed, Castro found power dispersed in Cuba and poli-tics pluralistic. This political condition offered many opportunities for both the United States and established Cuban interests to impede his revolution. Domínguez believes that Castro concluded that "it was impossible to conduct a revolution in Cuba without a major confronta-tion with the United States." Soviet influence offered to reinforce Cas-tro's preference for centralized power, whereas the U.S. system encour-aged pluralism—that is, divided power—at home and abroad. Therefore, according to this thesis, Castro deliberately took steps that had the predicted effect of provoking the United States and justifying his rapprochement with the Soviet Union.[11]

In short, there is no consensus on the question of who pushed whom in U.S.-Cuban relations. The debate on the reasons for the deteriorating relationship between the United States and the Nicaraguan Revolution roughly parallels the debate on Cuba.[12] Anthony Lake finds the same pattern in other cases, not only with regard to U.S. policy but also with regard to the debate in the United States on U.S. policy.[13] Blasier systematically examines how the United States has historically addressed the issue of what to do with Latin American revolutions. He concludes that the United States has been more effective when it has been patient, but he also recognizes the importance of the response of revolutionary governments and movements to U.S. policy.[14]

The one case that neither Blasier nor Lake examine is the Grenada Revolution. It offers a particularly good case to address the questions above, for three reasons. First, the case is closed. Second, rather than just rely on the regime's public statements, the documents that have been captured from the New Jewel Movement offer a window for assessing the real views of the leadership at particular moments.[15] And third, the case neatly spans two very different administrations—Carter and the Reagan administrations. Therefore, a close assessment of the case provides an opportunity to identify the continuity in U.S. foreign policy as it approaches revolutionary governments and the perceived options for change.

GRENADA AND U.S. POLICY BEFORE THE REVOLUTION

Although Grenada has become known to the world, its politics and its problems are those of a very small island. Like many of its Eastern Caribbean neighbors, Grenada has a population of less than 100,000 on an island of 133 square miles—about twice the size and one-sixth the population of Washington, D.C. Grenada's economy is small (GDP of less than $100 million), open (the sum of exports and imports exceeds GDP), and extremely dependent (tourism earns one-half of its foreign exchange).[16]

Since universal suffrage was introduced into Grenada by Great Britain in 1951, Grenada's politics have been dominated by two charismatic, quasi-religious leaders, Eric Gairy, 1951–1979, and Maurice Bishop, 1979–1983. Both organized and led political parties but were actually "heroes" amid the "crowd."[17] Upon returning to Grenada from Trinidad's oil fields in 1949, at the age of twenty-seven, Gairy began organizing the poor estate workers. He successfully confronted the planters and the British bureaucracy and won significant concessions for workers and small farmers—and as a result, a devoted following among the poor "folk." Between 1951 and 1979, Gairy was the dominant political force on the island, although as he aged, Gairy "developed into a feared and somewhat eccentric Negro shepherd-king."[18] By the 1970s, Gairy was regularly extorting money from business, irregularly terrorizing people who disagreed with him, and periodically lecturing before conferences on unidentified flying objects (UFOs). He was an embarrassment to the newly educated Grenadians, whose path to power was blocked by his continued popularity among the poor.

Although he would later be demonized as a repressive, fascist dictator who manipulated elections to prevent anyone else from coming to power, in point of fact, Gairy had lost two of eight elections during the previous twenty-five years, and in an election on 7 December 1976, a coalition of three opposition parties, which included the New Jewel Movement, won 48.6 percent of the vote and six of fifteen seats in the Legislative Assembly.

One month later, a new administration in the United States took office, eager to formulate a forward-looking policy toward the Caribbean.[19] Since the early 1960s, the Caribbean had been transformed by the emergence of ten new nations from the English-speaking Caribbean. With the exception of Guyana, these states were democratic. All were very small in size and population, with vulnerable economies and virtually no defense forces. After failing to unify or federate the new states, the British assisted them to reach independence and then departed, hoping that the United States would soon retrieve the economic and security burden. But the United States was preoccupied with other more pressing issues—Vietnam, SALT and Soviet relations, the Middle East, and then Watergate.

The Carter administration was the first in U.S. history to focus on the Caribbean in the absence of a security threat, or as it turned out, before rather than after such a threat. This was due to the recognition that the region had changed, but also for personal and policy reasons. The administration wanted to demonstrate that it was willing to accept socialists provided they were democratic, like Michael Manley in Jamaica, and that it was capable of approaching the developing world with a North-South rather than an East-West focus. In addition, Andrew Young, U.S. ambassador to the United Nations, had personal ties to the region and was almost as popular in certain sectors of the Caribbean as he was among the American black population. Terence Todman, the administration's first assistant secretary of state for Inter-American Affairs, was born in the Virgin Islands and also had a deep personal interest in the region. The administration embarked on an unprecedented number of high-level trips to the area and consultations on developing a new approach.

In September 1977, President Carter invited all the heads of state of the Americas to Washington to witness the signing of the Panama Canal Treaties, and by doing so, to demonstrate to the American people the hemisphere's support for the treaties. In preparation for his meetings with Caribbean leaders, the National Security Council staff prepared a proposal for a new U.S. approach to economic development in the Caribbean. Instead of assisting each small nation on a bilateral basis, and thereby exacerbate the region's dependence, the proposal called for the establishment of an international group, chaired by the World Bank, and including all Caribbean recipients and as many international donors—both banks and nations—as would join. Carter approved the idea and, after consulting with several leaders and the international banks, the Caribbean Group for Cooperation in Economic Development, with thirty-one nations and fifteen international institutions, was established. Between 1977 and 1980, the group promoted regional projects and rationalized and quadrupled aid. Among the Caribbean leaders who attended the Canal signing ceremony was Sir Eric Gairy. However, Carter did not consult with Gairy on his multilateral development plan for the Caribbean, as Gairy's concerns were more celestial.

Unbeknown to U.S. policymakers charged with responsibility for U.S. relations with Latin America, the locus for policymaking toward Grenada had quietly shifted to the Bureau of Alcohol, Tobacco, and Firearms (ATF), an agency in the Department of Treasury, which investigated the illegal shipment of arms across state lines. In February 1979, the bureau arrested two Grenadians, James Wardally and Chester Humphrey, in Baltimore and charged them with six counts of crossing state lines with weapons to be transhipped to the New Jewel Movement in Grenada.

The next month, two ATF officials followed the investigation to Grenada and collaborated with the Grenadian police. According to Bernard Coard, Vincent Noel was arrested on Saturday, 10 March, and the police interrogated people in other houses belonging to other leaders in the New Jewel Movement (NJM). The NJM leadership went into hiding. When they heard that Gairy was leaving on 12 March—to attend a conference on the International Year of the Child in New York—they feared that he had left instructions for the police to liquidate them.

In the early morning hours of 13 March, four leaders of the NJM — Maurice Bishop, Bernard Coard, Hudson Austin, and one other— voted on whether or not to seize power. They divided equally, with Coard and Austin voting to do it, and Bishop and the other person voting against the coup. The four therefore decided to add a fifth member—George Louison—and he voted with Coard and Austin to attack.[20]

At 4 A.M., forty-six members of the New Jewel Movement attacked the True Blue police barracks and then seized the radio station. Two policemen were killed, and the third casualty was Patrick Mitchell, an NJM member, who in Bishop's words, "was shot while handling his own gun." The people of Grenada woke up the next morning to learn that Radio Grenada had become Radio Free Grenada, and that they had been liberated.

From the day of the coup until the intervention, U.S. policy toward

Grenada evolved through three phases. In the first crucial month of the revolution, there was an *empty embrace* by the United States. The second phase—a more *distant and cooler relationship*—began after Bishop's public condemnation of the United States on 13 April 1979 and continued with some variations through the Carter administration. The third phase of U.S. policy—one characterized by *confrontation and attempts at intimidation*—coincided with the Reagan administration.

THE EMPTY EMBRACE

The coup caught everyone by surprise. When Eric Gairy learned of it, he urgently phoned Brandon Grove, a deputy assistant secretary of state in the Bureau of Inter-American Affairs. Gairy warned that the Communists had taken over his island, and requested parachutes, helicopters, anything. Grove, a career foreign service officer, promised Gairy that he would report the conversation to his principals.

The State Department was inclined to defer to the British, who quietly sent a naval frigate that was off Puerto Rico to Grenada. Prime Minister James Callaghan phoned Barbadian Prime Minister Tom Adams for his views. Adams informed Callaghan that Gairy was indefensible, and that he had already spoken with Bishop, who sought to reassure Adams of his commitment to early elections. Nonetheless, Adams told Callaghan that he decided to call together the leaders from five of the neighboring states to discuss what to do.[21]

Bishop and other members of the NJM phoned leaders throughout the region, reassuring everyone of their moderate and constitutional intentions. He called U.S. Ambassador Frank Ortiz immediately, and as Ortiz later recalled, "solemnly assured me that U.S. lives and property would be protected, that good relations with the United States were a basic aim of his government, and that there would be prompt and free elections of a legally constituted government."[22]

The leaders of six Eastern Caribbean countries met in Barbados on 14–15 March 1979 and discussed the coup and how to respond. All were deeply concerned about the implications of the first violent, unconstitutional change of government in the area. Most knew Bishop, Coard, and some of the other leaders of the NJM either personally or through reputation as men of the "left"; the questions they asked themselves were how far left, and what were their intentions. In the communiqué issued at the end of the meetings on the first day, the Caribbean leaders reported that they had "discussed the security implications of the situation for the region as a whole." They affirmed their support for the principle of "noninterference" in the internal affairs of Grenada, but at the same time asserted "that the wider interests and unity of the area and of Grenada in particular require a return to constitutionality as soon as possible." The key point of the communiqué, however, was their taking note of "the stated declaration of the leaders of the regime in Grenada to hold free and fair elections and . . . the hope that this would be done without delay. In this regard, the Ministers pledged their help if requested."[23]

During the second day of discussions, the leaders met with George Louison, who was sent by Bishop as a representative of the new regime in Grenada. Louison repeated the assurances of elections and also promised "that steps will be taken immediately for the establishment of the machinery necessary for the early implementation of that objective." The leaders pressed him to promise to maintain the governor general, return to constitutionality, and not harrass political opponents. Louison accepted all of these points, and they were published in the communiqué issued at the end of the day on 15 March. Still uncertain, the leaders decided to withhold recognition.

A subcommittee of the National Security Council in the United States (A mini-Special Coordinating Committee or mini-SCC) met the same day—15 March. It was the first—and one of the few—National Security Council meetings on Grenada. Like the Caribbean leaders, the United States was suspicious and uncertain of the NJM. The discussion reflected some rather predictable differences between the bureaucracies—with the Pentagon and the CIA taking a more anxious view of the potential threat, and the State Department more relaxed. Nonetheless, the meeting reached a relatively quick consensus. Like Great Britain and Barbados, the United States agreed that a return by Eric Gairy was untenable, and as there were no other obvious alternatives, the subcommittee recommended to the president that the United States support Great Britain and the Eastern Caribbean nations in their efforts to influence the new regime to make good on its promise of early and free elections.

Bishop redoubled his efforts to secure recognition from his neighbors and to assure the people of Grenada that "everything is normal at home" and "a bright new dawn" had arrived. Bishop's major channels for trying to influence his Caribbean neighbors were the governments of Jamaica and Guyana. Viewing Bishop as a potential protégé, both Forbes Burnham of Guyana and Michael Manley of Jamaica tried to compete for his friendship; both soon recognized the new regime and lobbied their Caribbean Community (CARICOM) colleagues to do the same. They finally did so. As Barbadian Prime Minister Adams later recalled: "Many of us were so glad to be rid of Eric Gairy that we [the English-speaking Caribbean] were prepared to overlook the means by which this regime was ended."[24]

Despite the continuous flow of assurances, there were other signs in Grenada that were viewed by the U.S. government as unsettling. The broadcasts from Radio Free Grenada sounded more like the propaganda of a Communist regime than the newscasts of the open, democratic countries of the Caribbean. The regime's effort to portray Gairy as a Hitler and "a criminal dictator" (rather than a Charlie Chaplin trying to imitate Hitler) appeared as, at best, an overzealous exaggeration.[25] More troubling was the dismissal of the entire police force and army, a professional force, and their replacement with a political People's Revolutionary Army.

Nonetheless, after the Eastern Caribbean nations recognized the new regime, the State Department followed with a statement on 22 March that the United States "strongly supports and endorses the views expressed in these [Caribbean] communiqués, which stress the need for prompt return to constitutional norms; the necessity to respect the fundamental principles of self-determination and non-intervention . . . [and therefore the U.S.] decided to continue friendly and cooperative relations." The new Grenadian ambassador to the United States, Kendrick Radix, arrived in Washington at about the same time, and said that voter registration lists were already being compiled and that elections would be held within one year, if not sooner. He also said that the new government "had no plans to interfere with the ownership of private property on the island."[26]

On the day of the official U.S. statement recognizing the new regime—22 March—Ambassador Ortiz was instructed to travel to Grenada to meet with the new leaders and to communicate the U.S. interest in good and cooperative relations. A week before Ortiz's trip, Bishop told the U.S. consul that his government would look to the United States, the United Kingdom, and Canada for assistance to help Grenada recover from Gairy's destruction of the economy. Ortiz arrived with several embassy officials to describe to Bishop the various aid programs already available to Grenada. Bishop and the other members of the NJM were totally unaware of the five aid projects, which were regional and channeled through the Caribbean Development Bank—reflecting the emphasis of the Carter administration on assisting the Eastern Caribbean as a region.

Ortiz also informed him that the United States would be prepared to increase the number of Peace Corps volunteers on the island rapidly. When Bishop expressed interest in the volunteers, Ortiz indicated that a new group could arrive within one or two weeks. As regards other assistance, Ortiz urged Bishop to send representatives to discuss specific projects with AID personnel in Barbados. Ortiz explained that the U.S. aid program was project related and largely administered through the CDB, but the U.S. ambassador did have a very small fund that it could use quickly and at his discretion; it was called the Special Development Activities (SDA) fund, and the ambassador could immediately disburse grants of $5,000 for community-related projects. While the amount was small, these grants had proven very popular in the Eastern Caribbean. Bishop declared his interest in obtaining as much funding as possible both by drawing down CDB funds and by using the SDA fund. The United States had not made any decision on whether it could provide additional funding but instead decided to wait and see how the situation evolved and what the NJM specifically requested.

Two days later, on 25 March, Bishop held another rally and announced the suspension of the constitution—breaking one of his pledges—and decreed a package of "ten fundamental People's Laws," which included the retention of emergency arrest powers for the People's Revolutionary Army. At the same time, however, he announced that Grenada would remain in the Commonwealth and retain the governor general.

On 28 March, Bishop called the U.S. embassy and asked the United States not to send the Peace Corps volunteers. Although Bishop had appeared anxious for increased aid, he sent no one to the embassy to follow up the ambassador's suggestion.

By late March, Bishop's government seemed well entrenched. Within a week of the coup, he had arrested many of his political opponents and transferred military and police powers to his political followers. Recognized by all his neighbors, he had also had formal conversations with the ambassadors from the United States and the United Kingdom, both of whom offered assistance and reassurance that their governments wanted good relations. At this moment, when his revolution seemed more secure, the United States began to receive reports of arms shipments to Grenada from Cuba through Guyana.

Burnham had pledged to help the new government on 20 March, and a Guyanese ship landed in Grenada two days later with supplies, and possibly with arms. On 4 April, a small Cuban plane landed at Pearls airport and unloaded some small arms. Three days later, a Cubana flight from Georgetown, Guyana, to Cuba was diverted to Grenada. While the plane was supposedly being repaired, several boxes of arms were unloaded, and eight Cubans remained in Grenada. One of those Cubans was Ivor Martínez, who would be head of Cuban operations until an ambassador was appointed. On 8 April, another Cubana flight, claiming "technical difficulties," landed at the Grenada airport and left arms and people. On 9 April, the Guyanese ship *Jamaito* arrived in St. George's with arms that had been brought to Guyana by Cuban planes. The United States also learned that the Cuban ship *Matanzas* left Cuba on 6 April with a large shipment of arms; the suspicion was that it might be destined for Grenada. It arrived on 14 April.

At the same time, Bishop's speeches and his government's radio broadcasts began to warn of an imminent invasion by Gairy leading a group of mercenaries from a neighboring island. At a press conference on 9 April, Bishop said that he would request arms from the United States, the United Kingdom, Canada, and Venezuela to prevent a countercoup by Gairy. He added: "We have also asked the governments of Cuba and other Caribbean countries for assistance in military training so as to prevent an attack planned by mercenaries against our country." Since he had already received such assistance, this appeared as a trial balloon to test the atmosphere about expanding and publicizing Cuban aid.

The State Department sent instructions to Ambassador Ortiz to meet with Bishop to assure him that Gairy would not invade the island and to express concern as delicately but clearly as possible that, if Bishop developed close military ties to Cuba, that would complicate his relations with the United States. Ortiz arrived on the afternoon of 9 April and was left waiting to see Bishop for a day. While he was waiting, he witnessed the shooting by the People's Revolutionary Army of a small plane contracted by Holiday Inn to take tourist photographs of the beach and hotel.

Ortiz saw Coard first and emphasized the importance of tourism to Grenada. Then, as he later recalled, he warned Coard "that incidents such as one I had just witnessed [the shooting of the plane] and the invasion scares would frighten tourists away."[27] In his conversation later the same say with Bishop, Ortiz covered a wide range of points. He reiterated the previous offer to Bishop to send AID officials and Peace Corps volunteers, but Bishop said he wasn't ready for them. Bishop expressed interest in receiving military aid. Ortiz explained the process for requesting foreign military sales (FMS) credits and said that the Grenadian government should decide what it wanted and make a formal request. The ambassador then pressed the prime minister on his promise to hold early elections, and according to Ortiz, he showed "some annoyance" on this point.

This was in the way of introduction to the two principal points of the conversation. First, Ortiz provided proof that Gairy was in San Diego, not on a neighboring island as Bishop had repeatedly said publicly. Moreover, the United States considered any conspiracy by Gairy to invade from the United States as a violation of the U.S. Neutrality Act and would act to prevent it. He urged Bishop to try to calm the people of Grenada by conveying the information about Gairy, but according to Ortiz, Bishop declined to do so. Second, he had instructions to tell Bishop of the U.S. concern about his establishing a military relationship with Cuba, but Ortiz broadened the point: "Although my government recognizes your concerns over allegations of a possible counter-coup, it also believes that it would not be in Grenada's best interests to seek assistance from a country such as Cuba to forestall such an attack. We would view with displeasure any tendency on the part of Grenada to develop closer ties with Cuba."[28] Ortiz then gave Bishop a paper containing that talking point and the others that he made.

The same day, 10 April, Bishop met with the British ambassador, who also offered to send a development assistance team and a group of security advisors. Bishop thanked him, indicated that he would accept the security advisors, but that Britain should delay sending the development assistance team. Bishop later informed the British that they should also postpone the sending of the security advisors. He promised to let them know in about three months.[29]

Another Cubana flight arrived on 11 April, and the next day, for the first time, Radio Free Grenada announced that flight and indicated that four Cuban government officials remained for conversations. Also, on 12 April, Bishop commented that he had inspected the People's Revolutionary Army and was impressed with its "high level of readiness and revolutionary spirit."

By 13 April, Bishop felt sufficiently confident to blast the United States in his first major speech. He began by reassuring his countrymen: "there is peace, calm, and quiet in our country." Then, with the deftness of an accomplished orator, Bishop used Ortiz's demarche to demonstrate his nationalist credentials and show the United States as an insensitive bully trying to push around small Grenada. "The Ambassador," Bishop told his audience, "went on to advise us that if we continue to speak about what he called 'mercenary invasions by phantom armies' that we would lose our tourists. He also reminded us of the experience which Jamaica had had in this regard a few years ago. As some of you will undoubtedly recall, Jamaica at that time had gone through a period of intense destabilization." Striking an aggrieved posture, Bishop told his people that "we have always striven to develop the closest and friendliest relations with the United States." But when Grenada requested aid, the United States offered $5,000. "Sisters and brothers, our hospitals are without medicines. . . . Is [that] all the wealthiest country in the world can offer? . . . Let us contrast that with the immediate response of our Caribbean brothers . . . Guyana and Jamaica."

Then, after describing Gairy's imminent invasion, Bishop read from the talking points that Ortiz had left, explaining that the United States would not permit Grenada to ask for help from or have relations with Cuba. "We reject entirely the argument of the American Ambassador. . . . If the government of Cuba is willing to offer us assistance, we would be more than happy to receive it." He concluded his speech with a powerful symbol: "No country has the right to tell us what to do or how to run our country, or who to be friendly with. . . . We are not in anybody's backyard, and we are definitely not for sale. . . . Though small and poor, we are proud and determined."

The next day, as if it were a reaction—rather than the cause—of Ortiz's demarche, the Cuban ship *Matanzas* docked at St. George's and fifty Cuban technicians and many crates of arms were unloaded. The PRG then announced the establishment of diplomatic relations with Cuba. On the same day, Bishop called the U.S. chargé d'affaires in Barbados and demanded that he send the AID officials promised by the ambassador right away. The embassy, not having yet fully absorbed his speech, sent the AID official three days later to look at some projects, but no high Grenadian official would meet with him.

The speech, however, set the tone for the world's perception of the new revolution. The *Washington Post* reported that the "strong U.S. diplomatic response . . . may succeed only in pushing Grenada further to the left." While the Cubans were responsive and helpful to the revolution, the article noted, the United States only expressed "concern" and "displeasure" and regret over budgetary procedures. Moreover, public opinion on the island had turned against the United States, viewing it as "a bully and a stingy one to boot."[30]

Bishop's speech represented a turning point. The sequence of events leading up to the speech—the secret arrival of Cuban arms and advisors, the requests for help from the West without any followup—led many in the U.S. government to believe that Bishop had deliberately staged the confrontation with the United States. After promising and reassuring everyone, Bishop felt secure enough to wait for the right opportunity to denounce the United States, establish his nationalist credentials, and justify the relationship with Cuba.[31] Ortiz's demarche was the soft pitch that Bishop batted out of the park—at least this was the U.S. perception.

In October 1982, I described this perception to Bishop and Coard, and both individuals listened with what I perceived as genuine incredulity. Coard answered most candidly: "Look, this was our first revolution. We were very inexperienced." Bishop was more colorful in his response: "We are a lot like Americans. If you kick us in the shins, we will kick you in the balls." Both insisted that the Bishop speech on 13 April was not prepacked; that it was an emotional reaction to their perception of Ortiz's "lectures." Both religiously believed that the United States had consistently destabilized every independent effort in the Third World to achieve social justice. Indeed, when asked in an interview in 1983 whether he was surprised by U.S. hostility to the Grenadian Revolution, Bishop responded: "Certainly, the overall response and reaction of the U.S. frankly was no surprise to us. After all, the U.S. is the formulator of the Monroe Doctrine in 1823. The formulator of the Roosevelt corollary in 1904. The U.S. one hundred and thirty-five times invaded countries in this region over the last one hundred years."[32]

Both Coard and Bishop perceived Ortiz as an "arrogant racist," who was "condescending with blacks." Coard recalled that Ortiz "barged

into my office at 10 A.M. and didn't even knock." And then he lectured
to Coard and seemed uninterested in a response. Then he went to
Bishop's office and gave the same lecture, "the same threats." Bishop
exploded, according to Coard. Both felt that Ortiz's leaving the paper
with the talking points forced Bishop to respond. Then "the straw that
broke the camel's back," in Coard's words, was that Ortiz gave the same
lecture and "the same threats" to the head of security at the airport.
(Bishop mentioned this in his 13 April speech.) When I asked why they
didn't try to communicate their concerns to the United States in a less
public and provocative way, they confessed their inexperience and their
quick angry reaction. In Bishop's words: "Ortiz did everything possible
to arouse a black man."

Ortiz's demarche also served to reinforce their image of the United
States as an imperialist monster, bent on destroying their young revolution. And their response, in turn, confirmed the impression in Washington that these young Marxists wanted to provoke the United States to
justify their militarization and alliance with Cuba.

MOVING APART

The United States concluded that its approach had failed and decided
to reevaluate its policy toward Grenada. By mid-April, the People's
Revolutionary Army had grown from about 50 men to about 2,000
(including the militia), eclipsing all the other armies of the region
combined. There were about eighty political prisoners, and no indication that the government would release them. After Bishop's speech on
13 April, the PRG admitted receiving arms and ammunition from Cuba
and other countries. This was later estimated at about 3,400 rifles, 200
machine guns, and 100 heavy weapons.[33]

The State Department and the NSC began discussing options that
a mini-SCC meeting would address. There were four issues. First, did
Grenada's new leaders have a fixed direction toward Cuba, or was co-
optation a plausible strategy? Second, what was the best path to influence
the government to fulfill its pledges on elections, to remain closer to the
Commonwealth Caribbean than to Cuba, and to preclude any support
for radical activities in the region? Third, what were the implications of
a policy toward Grenada for the rest of the region? And fourth, what
should the United States do to preclude a repetition of another left-
wing coup in the region?

Some argued that Bishop was still co-optable, and that the United
States should give more aid to the regime and encourage the Europeans
to do more. Others argued that the 13 April speech represented a
turning point toward Cuba chosen by Bishop, and that the thrust of
U.S. policy ought to be aimed at assisting the rest of the Caribbean. To

provide bilateral aid to the one radical, nondemocratic government in the Eastern Caribbean would be to undermine the democracies and lend support to those radicals in the region who were arguing that Grenada represented the wave of the future. Moreover, it would be an invitation to other governments to seek more aid by confronting the United States.

An additional argument against the co-optation strategy was simply that the PRG showed almost no interest in being co-opted. Despite many offers by the U.S. embassy to help design aid requests, the PRG never responded, and when several AID officials traveled to Grenada on 17 April to visit SDA projects and meet Grenadian officials, the regime avoided any contact with them. Education Minister George Louison never responded to an 9 April AID offer to visit Grenada to develop education projects. And Bishop never followed up his offhand request for military aid. It appeared that he was asking for help from the United States without really wanting it. Perhaps he thought that confrontation with the United States would help them obtain more aid from other sources.[34]

Instead of calming the other regional governments and encouraging Europeans to help, as the co-optation strategy recommended, the alternative regional strategy would stimulate the regional governments to press Grenada to implement its pledges and to contain Grenada from assisting radicals in neighboring countries. Instead of providing more aid to Grenada than to the other countries, as the co-optation strategy recommended, the regional strategy would increase aid to every country except Grenada until the PRG implemented its pledges. In addition, in consultations with the countries of the region, Great Britain, and Canada, the United States would seek ways to reinforce the security of the region without jeopardizing the civilian democratic governments.

The major argument against the regional strategy was that it signified a shift toward a more indirect, distancing approach to Grenada; instead of providing direct encouragement to the regime to move toward elections and a more friendly relationship with the United States, the regional strategy provided indirect encouragement, by helping the other nations more. Those who opposed the regional strategy argued that it meant U.S. withdrawal from competition with the Cubans for Grenada's future.

At the meeting on 27 April, the mini-SCC recommended the regional strategy to the president, and he approved it. The co-optation strategy was rejected for several reasons. First, and probably most important, most felt that it would have a negative effect on those friendly democratic countries most in need; second, most thought it had already been tried and rejected by Bishop in favor of a closer relationship with Cuba; third, the regional strategy was most congruent with the administration's approach to the region; and fourth, the regional nations could probably have a more positive influence on the PRG than the United States acting directly. It appeared that the NJM was comfortable with the United States as its enemy, and perhaps the best strategy for the United States was to avoid giving it a target.[35]

The new strategy contained an irony. After two years of pushing the AID bureaucracy to accept a regional as opposed to its more bureaucratically comfortable bilateral aid approach, Grenada impelled the United States to shift toward bilateral aid programs in the region as a way to reinforce the democracies and, it was hoped, to encourage the PRG to follow in the same direction.

The regional strategy set the parameters of U.S. policy toward Grenada for the remainder of the Carter administration, although that policy itself was divided in two phases. Between April and November 1979, the United States pursued the regional strategy while continuing to seek ways to show it was interested in good relations with Grenada.

For example, Bishop insisted that his regime was threatened by Gairy and that the United States wouldn't extradite him. The U.S. ambassador explained the necessary legal procedures for extradition, and even persuaded the director of the Extradition Office of the Justice Department to visit Grenada to help the government prepare a stronger case. According to Ambassador Shelton, "Bishop agreed and said he wished to meet with him personally." When the director arrived, Bishop declined to meet him, and instead only "a middle-level functionary with no real authority" spoke with him. As Ambassador Shelton recalled, the U.S. official finally left after he and the ambassador concluded that the PRG "was not genuinely interested in resolving this issue."[36]

On 8 May, while some in the embassy were still considering ways to help Grenada design aid projects, Bishop gave a major speech, and accused the U.S. government of undertaking a massive destabilization campaign—"the pyramid plan of the CIA"—to destroy the revolution. He described in great detail how the plan would be implemented, and warned his "brothers and sisters" to be vigilant in order to "crush the enemy."[37]

The documents captured by U.S. troops show that Bishop's obsession with the CIA was not just publicly expressed to keep the masses vigilant and supportive of his government; his private thoughts and classified statements to small groups reflect the same paranoia. He received "intelligence" from Grenadians and others in the United States describing alleged CIA activities in Grenada, and he gave most, if not all, of them credence. At least until January 1981, and probably until his demise, the CIA conspiracies he "divulged" were nothing more than figments of his imagination. But obviously they had consequences for his behavior and for the relationship between the United States and Grenada.

During the remainder of the Carter administration, the United States expanded development programs for Grenada's neighbors, and after consultations, helped formulate a regional security strategy. The British took the lead in improving the region's police forces, and the United States assisted the establishment of a regional coast guard. The U.S. Coast Guard had a good reputation in the area, and it, rather than the navy, was given primary responsibility to conduct trips to the region and undertake training programs in advance of providing boats. The United States also opened a defense attaché's office in the Barbados embassy, but as it turned out, this complicated rather than facilitated the work of the Coast Guard, which was located in the Department of Transportation. The bureaucratic problems of trying to assist the unconventional security needs of the small Eastern Caribbean nations were formidable, and slowed U.S. efforts considerably. With the reassurance offered by the United States and Great Britain, the nations of the region began discussions on their own regional security needs and developed informal arrangements to help each other in times of emergency.

While Grenada tried to develop its relations with the Socialist International and a number of democratic governments, it clearly reserved its closest relationships for Cuba and the Soviet Union, and its votes in the United Nations—particularly its vote against the resolution condemning the Soviet action against Afghanistan—served as public confirmation of this closeness. On 18 November 1979, Bishop announced that Cuba would build an airport in Grenada. Though Bishop claimed it would be completed in eighteen months, the Carter administration expected that it would take much longer and questioned whether it would ever be completed. Therefore, this did not arise as an issue during the Carter administration.

Within Grenada, the New Jewel Movement adopted a hard line approach to political expression—preventing the publication of the *Torchlight,* detaining indefinitely political opponents, prohibiting other political parties to function, trying to take over the labor unions—but it proved quite flexible with regard to private business and seemed to be giving greater emphasis to the importance of tourism, a curious priority given their revolutionary rhetoric.

Though the Carter administration's policy preference was to maintain a low profile and some distance from the regime, on two occasions the United States was almost provoked toward direct confrontation. In the fall of 1979, as the two Grenadians arrested for gunrunning in February were coming to trial, the PRG intensified its efforts to get them released. The Bishop regime then arrested a U.S. citizen who was living in Grenada on grounds that she was a threat to Grenada's security. The U.S. ambassador demanded to know the evidence and the charges, and believed "we had a hostage situation on our hands." Grenada's ambassador to the Organization of American States, Dessima Williams, told a reporter from the *Washington Post* after the indictment of the two men on 1 September that her government would now have to determine how to "reciprocate" in the case of the U.S. citizen imprisoned in Grenada. The National Security Council met to consider U.S. options, but before reaching a decision, the Grenadians jumped bail, and the U.S. citizen was released.

Similarly, two months later, two other American citizens were arrested by the Grenadian regime for no apparent reason, and again the NSC met and discussed a number of serious measures, but the regime released the citizens soon after that.[38] As a result of these incidents, in the fall of 1979, the United States adopted a more formal policy of distancing itself from the regime, and restricted ambassadorial visits to the island. This phase of the "moving apart" policy remained in place for the rest of the Carter administration.

ISOLATION AND INTIMIDATION: THE REAGAN VARIATION

In a radio address in the spring of 1979, Ronald Reagan warned his listening audience that "the Caribbean is rapidly becoming a Communist lake in what should be an American pond, and the United States resembles a giant, afraid to move."[39] Few doubted that as president, Reagan would adopt a much tougher approach to the Grenada Revolution than the Carter administration, but no one was certain what that would entail. The central issue for the new administration was how to increase the pressure on the Grenadian regime.

First, it restricted any embassy contacts with the Grenadian government. While the Carter administration had refused to accredit the Grenadian ambassador because of evidence that she had been involved in illegal arms smuggling and had threatened a hostage situation, the Reagan administration refused to accredit any Grenadian ambassador and refused to seek accreditation from Grenada for its ambassador in Barbados.[40]

Second, the Reagan administration expanded and intensified efforts to stop its allies from assisting the Grenadian government.[41] In addition, in a sharp break with its predecessors' unconditional support for the Caribbean Development Bank (CDB), the Reagan administration stopped aid to the CDB unless it excluded Grenada. Although most of the Caribbean governments had grown unsympathetic to the Grenadian regime, they closed ranks behind Grenada and the CDB to block the U.S. effort.[42]

While the U.S. decision on the CDB riled the Caribbean leaders, other trends proved more powerful in uniting the region against the PRG. First, Bishop's militant denunciations were directed not just against the United States but, increasingly, at his very sensitive neighbors, especially Prime Minister Tom Adams of Barbados and Prime Minister Eugenia Charles of Dominica. Second, two of Bishop's strongest advocates in the region, Michael Manley of Jamaica and Forbes Burnham of Guyana, were, in the first instance, beaten decisively in an election in October 1980 and, in the second case, was discredited. Manley was replaced by Edward Seaga, whose view of the geopolitics in the Caribbean corresponded with that of Ronald Reagan, which in turn was a mirror image of Bishop's. All believed that the struggle in the region pitted the forces of light against the forces of darkness; they just disagreed on which was which. Seaga proved just as strong in his attacks against the Bishop regime as Manley had been in defense of it. Bishop therefore found himself increasingly on the defensive in the Caribbean Community.

On 29 October 1982, the prime ministers of Barbados, Antigua, Dominica, St. Lucia, and St. Vincent signed a Memorandum of Understanding relating to their security and military cooperation. The countries agreed "to prepare contingency plans and assist one another on request in national emergencies, prevention of smuggling, search and rescue . . . and threats to national security." They also agreed to establish a mechanism to implement the memorandum—including a central fund, a central liaison office for coordination, and a regional security coordinator. Traveling in the region at this time, I was told by several of the leaders who signed the understanding that it was the product of their increasing fear and uncertainty of the Grenadian regime. Bishop and Coard, however, saw it as part of the Reagan administration's strategy, to confront them and seek a pretext for an invasion.[43] (The PRG had already signed secret military agreements with the Soviet Union and Cuba.)

The Reagan administration also undertook military-related actions to try to intimidate the Grenadian government. In August 1981, in the largest NATO military maneuvers in the Caribbean ever, the United States led an amphibious landing on the island of Vieques in Puerto Rico. The operation was known as Amber and the Amberdines, a childishly obvious allusion to Grenada and the Grenadines. Not leaving anything to the imagination, Admiral McKenzie publicly announced that the purpose of the operation was to send a message to unfriendly countries in the region.

The Grenadian government received the message; indeed, they probably were more effective publicizing the exercises than the navy or the Reagan administration. The Grenadian ambassador to the OAS, for example, sent a memorandum to many in Washington that began: "The

People's Revolutionary Government of Grenada wishes to alert you to the fact that on the basis of documentary and circumstantial evidence and recent intelligence reports, we are absolutely convinced that our country is about to be subjected to a military invasion by the Reagan Administration." The memorandum stated that the invasion would occur before November 1981.

In July 1981, the Reagan administration was reported to have planned a covert intelligence operation against Grenada, but after meeting resistance from the Senate Intelligence Committee, the administration dropped the proposal.[44] Beginning in 1982, the rhetoric of the U.S. president began to match that of the Grenadian prime minister, for much the same reasons. Both wanted to alert the world to the evil intentions of the other in the hope that the warnings would prove disarming. In fact, the exchange of charges only served to confirm the worst suspicions each had of the other.

President Carter had avoided singling out Grenada in his statements, because his administration didn't want to exaggerate its importance. Moreover, his administration believed that the best way to strengthen its relations with the rest of the Caribbean was to leave them with an impression that U.S. interest in them was not simply a by-product of its hostility to the PRG. Therefore, in a brief speech on the Caribbean on 28 November 1979, Carter didn't even mention Grenada. In a major address inaugurating Caribbean/Central American Action on 9 April 1980, Carter's only mention of Grenada was in the context of noting both the expansion and contraction of democracy in the region: "In some [Caribbean countries], there have been temporary setbacks—in Surinam and in Grenada, for instance—but we hope that interruption will be temporary."

In contrast, the Reagan administration believed that the best way to mobilize support for a policy, and in this case to isolate a regime, was to be absolutely clear as to the moral purity of one's position and the impurity of one's rival. In announcing and describing the Caribbean Basin initiative on 24 February 1982, Reagan painted a black-and-white view of the region, with a "positive future" represented by the friends of the United States, and "the dark future" foreshadowed by the poverty and repression of Castro's Cuba, the tightening grip of the totalitarian left in Grenada and Nicaragua, and the expansion of Soviet-backed, Cuban-managed support for violent revolution in Central America.

In his annual report to the Congress on the defense budget, on 8 February 1982, Secretary of Defense Caspar Weinberger bluntly described Grenada as a "Cuban satellite." He was particularly concerned that the Cubans were building "air and naval facilities on Grenada, which far exceed the requirements of that tiny island nation."[45] Two months later, on a vacation in Barbados, Reagan said that Grenada "now bears the Soviet and Cuban trademark, which means that it will attempt to spread the virus among its neighbors." The remark offended his hosts, and ignored the fact that democracy was as strong in the other islands as ever.

The year 1983 began as a war of words and ended as a war. President Reagan's rhetorical assaults on Grenada at the beginning of the year, however, had less to do with Grenada than it had to do with Central America. To mobilize domestic support for his increased aid requests for Central America, Reagan dramatically described the Soviet-Cuban attempt to take over the Caribbean, and he used Grenada as proof of the malign intentions of the Soviet Union. Beginning on 10 March 1983, President Reagan ridiculed those who claimed that because Grenada was small and poor the United States should be relaxed. Referring to the airport, Reagan said: "It isn't nutmeg that's at stake in the Caribbean and Central America. It is the U.S. national security."

On 23 March, in his major Star Wars speech, President Reagan used satellite photographs of the airport being built by the Cubans at Point Salines to show that "the Soviet-Cuban militarization of Grenada can only be seen as power projection into the region." These statements and the publication of the report on covert actions against Grenada in the *Washington Post* on 27 February magnified the already rampant paranoia in Grenada.

Even before Reagan's major speech, Bishop delivered an address on the fourth anniversary of the revolution—13 March 1983—that blasted "U.S. imperialism" for continuing "to butcher the people of El Salvador" and all other freedom-loving peoples in the world. He condemned the administration for its "usual lies and threats." While admitting that, "yes, they could drop a bomb and wipe our country off the face of the map," he warned the United States that when the marines land: "Every last man, woman, and child in our country will fight with full resolve, until the aggressor is removed from our soil. They will feel the weight of the people of Grenada and the weight of the Grenada Revolution."[46]

Bishop followed that with a speech declaring the Westminster parliamentary system "a dead corpse," and right after Reagan's speech on 23 March, he placed the People's Revolutionary Army on alert and attacked "the war-mongering Reagan" and his "fascist clique in Washington." He told his people to get "ready for the ultimate sacrifice" because an invasion would be coming soon."[47]

The war of words between the two governments had a curious effect. U.S. correspondents—and the American public—rediscovered Grenada and found a gap between the statements of both governments and a relaxed island where tourists could leisurely take a taxi to the new airport and photograph U.S. medical students racing their motorbikes up and down the airstrips.[48] The war further alienated the region's governments from both sides. As Barbadian Foreign Minister Louis Tull put it: "I am no more enamored of the direction of the new government in Grenada than is the Reagan Administration. [But] we cannot resolve it with the more extreme position that the United States might be disposed to take."[49]

Reagan's assault impelled the NJM not to question the direction of the revolution but to try to persuade others of its correctness. Bishop accepted an invitation to address the Sixth Annual Dinner of TransAfrica in Washington, D.C., on 8 June 1983, and decided to use the trip to meet with the press and other groups and deliver his message of peace and friendship directly to the American people. Of all the documents captured, the only ones directly related to Grenada's policy toward the United States—other than those related to the NJM preoccupation with destabilization—were those few related to this trip.

In no area was the NJM's power of self-delusion more evident than in their propaganda activities in the United States. Like many Third World leftist groups, the NJM tended to mistake their friends in the United States with the American body politic. After a few meetings with Grenadian and North American sympathizers, the NJM leaders of the North American Resistance Programme filed a report to the Political Bureau in Grenada on 29 March 1983. The report began:

> Generally speaking, Grenada's fight-back campaign in North America has got off the ground. In terms of the four zones, New York is moving well; Washington has made a start; and in concrete preparations to step up their programme by Thursday, the West Coast got off the ground yesterday.
>
> Consistent with the 26 point plan, our objectives are as follows:
>
> 1. To mobilize public opinion (including in Congress) in order to restrain the U.S. government from attacking Grenada militarily;
>
> 2. To win long-term contacts and sympathy for Grenada, hence turning attacks at our advantage;
>
> 3. To solicit concrete assistance: paper, tape recorders, typewriters, etc.[50]

If one can separate the high-sounding rhetoric in this and other PRG memoranda from the real world to which it occasionally alludes, one begins to realize that, despite the "massive" support the PRG had received in the United States and the many rallies and fund-raisers, the leaders of the "resistance movement" were never able to raise enough funds to buy a word processor.

The only influential group that supported the PRG was the congressional black caucus. At their insistence, the House Foreign Affairs Committee held hearings on Grenada in June 1982 and TransAfrica invited Bishop. It appeared that many of the members of the caucus were attracted to the PRG because they too felt victimized by an arrogant

white administration. Many black leaders in the United States undoubtedly found it easy to identify with Grenada's predicament.

Bishop arrived in the United States on 31 May and told the press
that he hoped to have a "dialogue" with the administration and "personally clear up the misconceptions that exist" with the United States.[51]
The administration first stonewalled him but then accepted a meeting
for probably several reasons. First, Bishop used the press to convey his
reasonableness, moderation, and interest in just sitting down to talk.
Second, Congressman Michael Barnes, the black caucus, and the secretary general of the OAS, all encouraged the administration to speak
with him. However, probably the main reason that a meeting was
arranged was because the administration looked foolish in refusing to
talk.

Bishop met with National Security Adviser William Clark and Deputy Secretary of State Kenneth Dam on 7 June 1983 for thirty minutes.
Although much has been made of this simple encounter, it appears to
have been a pro forma exchange of positions. There is no evidence to
suggest that the meeting changed anyone's mind about anything or that
it had any effect on anyone. Some have suggested that the request for
the meeting split the more reasonable Bishop from the more pro-Soviet
Coard, but as part of its permanently aggrieved posture, the PRG always
insisted it wanted good relations with the United States and wanted to
talk. There is no evidence of any disagreement between Bishop and
Coard on this point.

In advance of the meeting, Bishop's advisors suggested he press the
United States hard to exchange ambassadors, cease economic destabilization, extradite Gairy and normalize relations. According to the notes
taken by the Grenadians, both sides agreed on the need to dialogue, but
Clark said the United States was more interested in Grenada's conduct,
and specifically with Soviet influence, which "is not acceptable" in the
region. Clark also expressed the hope that Grenada would not adopt
an Eastern European model of government, but rather return to the
parliamentary system. Clark then left, and Bishop assured Dam that
Grenada did not constitute any threat to the United States. Dam is
reported to have expressed interest in those assurances.

Compared to the exchange of insults in March, the meeting did
represent something of a toning down of the rhetoric, but nothing
positive came of the meeting. Apparently, Clark and Bishop spoke of a
possible moratorium on denunciations, which included keeping the
meeting confidential. But in a news conference the next day, Bishop
acknowledged that the talks went "reasonably well," but he also used
the opportunity to denounce again the CIA destabilization campaign.[52]

In an interview with the *Washington Post* before the meeting, Bishop
insisted that he had given "concrete assurances ad nauseum" to the

United States that the airport was strictly for commercial purposes.[53] In my conversations with Bishop and Coard in October 1982, I probed them about the possible use of the airport. Bishop told me that Grenada's airport "would not be used as a transit for Soviet or Cuban military aircraft, for example, to ferry soldiers to or from Africa, or for any other military purpose. Grenada would not even use the airport to receive weapons or armaments from the Soviet Union or Cuba." I passed this message to the State Department with my comment that he could be lying or change his mind, but that it would seem to me in the interests of the United States to obtain those assurances privately and also publicly. To the best of my knowledge, there was never any attempt to negotiate this issue seriously with the PRG. The meeting with Clark and Dam would have presented an opportunity, but there is no evidence it was discussed or pursued.

After the intervention, in response to a question about Nicaragua's statement that it would be invaded next, President Reagan said he never believed a word that the Sandinistas said. The same obviously applied to the NJM. Negotiations or even talks were viewed as a weapon in the propaganda war, but not as a tool for pursuing U.S. interests or resolving differences.

Did the administration's strategy of confrontation and noncommunication erode the NJM's coherence, leading to their division and eventual self-destruction in October 1983? The documents do not support such a conclusion. In the crucial debates in the fall of 1983 over the future organization of the government and the direction of the revolution, no one in the PRG raised the U.S. posture as a reference point, either for choosing one direction or the other.

THE CAUSES AND CONSEQUENCES OF THE COLLISION

A spokesman in the U.S. Department of State told the House Foreign Affairs Committee in June 1982, "We do not perceive that the difficulties that we have with Grenada are due to an absence of communication. Indeed, we feel that we understand very well and that Grenada understands very well the roots of our disagreement."[54]

Who pushed first? The evidence is not conclusive, but the picture is much clearer today. Those who argue that the United States pushed Grenada to the left or to Cuba are wrong. Cuban arms and support arrived covertly while the United States was pursuing a cooperative relationship with the PRG and before the Ortiz demarche of 10 April. Moreover, we now know that the New Jewel Movement privately described itself as a Marxist-Leninist party before it took power in 1979, and that it identified with the Soviet Union and Cuba in its struggle against U.S. imperialism. The first decisions of the NJM were to secretly adopt a Communist political model and seize control of the military forces,[55] while publicly assuring everyone of their moderate and democratic (including elections) intentions. There is no evidence that those pledges were ever viewed by the NJM as anything more than a temporary tactic to consolidate the revolution.

The NJM invited Cuban arms secretly and received them before it publicly requested Western military aid. Moreover, the request to the United States (and Great Britain) appears as disingenuous, as there were no follow-up with respect to the United States and an indefinite postponement with regard to British offers for aid. The relationship with Cuba grew closer not because of U.S. hostility but probably because of the deepening personal relationship between Maurice Bishop and Fidel Castro—two charismatic, nationalistic, anti-imperialistic leaders, who revelled in their defiance of the United States. In his letter to the NJM when Bishop was arrested, Castro almost sounds as if he had adopted Bishop as his protegé, and in his idolatry of Castro, Bishop more than reciprocated.

Did the PRG push first? Did it deliberately provoke the United States to justify its alliance with Cuba and establish its nationalist credentials? At the time, I believed this, but after interviews with Bishop and Coard and after reading the documents, I am inclined to accept their point that Bishop's speech on 13 April was primarily an emotional reaction to the Ortiz demarche. Ortiz's lectures on the vulnerability of tourism and the dangers of relations with Cuba and his style of delivery confirmed all of their preconceptions of the United States as a destabilizing imperialist. Ortiz made a mistake in expressing displeasure with Grenada's relations with Cuba rather than just the military relationship, and his delivery of the talking points was an unprofessional error. Bishop, for his part, not only erred in his misunderstanding of Ortiz's message but also in neglecting to calculate the costs of his emotional tirade.

Nonetheless, in the broader context of the evolution of the PRG's international relations, this meeting shrinks in importance. *Regardless of what the United States said or did, relations with the PRG were destined to be cool and distant at best, given the NJM's preconception of U.S. imperialism as the devil incarnate, and the U.S. judgement that its interests would be affected by the expansion of Soviet-Cuban influence in the Caribbean.*

However, just because relations could not be good does not mean that a collision or a confrontation was inevitable. Perceptions of each other's behavior were crucial in bringing the two governments to a collision. Each suspected the other of the worst motives and interpreted information in a way that reinforced those suspicions. From the beginning, the NJM apparently believed the United States was going to destabilize their regime, and nothing any administration could have done would have convinced them otherwise. Also from the beginning, the United States suspected that the NJM were unfriendly and undemocratic leftists, who could very well be Marxist-Leninists and more sympathetic to the Soviet bloc than to the West. Nonetheless, the Carter administration decided to give the new government the benefit of the doubt. After the first flurry of evidence confirmed its worst suspicions, however, the United States moved to distance itself from the regime. But the United States still would not have confronted the PRG if it had not been for its clear alignment with Cuba, its total disinterest in making good on its pledge for elections, and a change in administration in Washington. The Reagan administration viewed the problems of the Caribbean Basin strictly in terms of the East-West struggle, and therefore U.S. policy toward Grenada was important for what it told the world about U.S. determination to confront communism.[56]

Since the PRG apparently assumed from the beginning that the United States was a threat, the issue for them was how to respond to it. Grenada pursued several strategies, but the major instrument was propaganda. As Bishop told me, "our only means of defense [against the United States] is to warn our friends and our people of the threat." Of course, repeated condemnations of the United States served only to confirm the U.S. government's suspicions about the NJM, first creating then exacerbating a threat that did not initially exist.

Bishop's rhetoric did have one other important effect: it discouraged tourism to Grenada and thereby hurt the economy.[57] The NJM believed that the U.S. government orchestrated the adverse publicity against the revolution, but the PRG did that themselves. The U.S. government does not have the tools to manipulate the press on a story like Grenada, and indeed the two recurring themes in the U.S. press were that the U.S. government was pushing Grenada leftward and that the administration—first Carter's, then Reagan's—was behaving foolishly. If either the Carter or the Reagan administration had tried to orchestrate the news, *that* would have been the story. But no administration would choose to look bad in the U.S. press just to hurt tourism in Grenada. Indeed, the U.S. government had a simple means of discouraging U.S. tourism to Grenada—the travel advisory—but neither the Carter nor the Reagan administration used it.

Both governments were sincere in their stated interest in good relations, but on terms that were not acceptable to the other. The United States was more honest in stating its conditions, but it was also more aggressive in the sense that it was demanding that the PRG be something and do something other than what it wanted. The PRG pretended that its problem with the United States was that the United States did not respect its independence and nonalignment, when it clearly understood that the problem was that the United States would not accept its alignment with the Soviet Union and Cuba. That is why the NJM hid their aspiration of being accepted into the Communist world by the Soviet Union.

Arguments that the United States opposes revolution because it defends U.S. business interests or fears the contagion of social revolution are not supported by the Grenadian case, where no U.S. business interests were involved, and the revolution was neither social nor economic. The replacement of Gairy by well-educated, upper-class, and generally lighter-skinned leaders hardly constituted a social revolution. The NJM also went out of its way to defend its moderate domestic policy and took pride in the fact it only expropriated without compensation the property of Gairy and his deputy.[58] Ironically, as the revolution evolved, the PRG gradually discarded its dream of transforming the agricultural and agroindustrial sectors, and decided to concentrate on tourism—the sector most dependent on the United States.[59]

Why should the United States be concerned with Grenada? Its concern with the PRG was based on the implications for a democratic regime of its internal political model and its external relations with the USSR and Cuba. The expansion of Soviet-Cuban influence in the world is viewed by the United States as inimical to its central interest, which—as Dean Acheson once captured so succinctly—is "to maintain as spacious an environment as possible in which free states might exist and flourish."

This central strategic concern about the alignment of the PRG with the Soviet Union and Cuba united both the Carter and Reagan approaches. The question for the United States was what to do about the regime? When faced with a hostile regime in the Caribbean Basin, the United States had traditionally selected its policies from the following five options:

1. *Normal relations.* This option—to offer friendship and cooperation in the expectation that the other government will consider U.S. concerns seriously—can only be sustained if the recipient reciprocates, which was not the case in Grenada. Otherwise, the United States looks foolish being friendly to someone who is criticizing it.

2. *Subversion.* This option—to actively support opponents of the regime in their attempt to overthrow it—was not a viable one in Grenada, because Bishop locked up almost all his actual or potential opponents. Gairy, the only well-known political leader capable of confronting the regime, was judged indefensible and unsupportable by the other Caribbean leaders, the United States, and the United Kingdom. Moreover, in the case of an invasion by Gairy or other small groups of Grenadians, Bishop had built up a large army and probably also could

count on Cuban support. The island was so small and open that a conspiracy could probably be detected by the NJM's secret police. (Indeed, they detected many conspiracies that didn't exist.) This option can only be sustained in a darkened atmosphere of U.S.-Soviet relations, or in the few cases where the American president is willing to put the full force of his presidency behind the policy.

3. *Destabilization*. This option—to undermine the basis of a country's economy—is a variation on the subversion option and is not wisely undertaken unless one believes there is a good chance an opposition can come to power. Otherwise, it radicalizes and militarizes the regime, and really leaves them with no alternative but to rely completely on the USSR and Cuba. This option would have been easy to conduct against Grenada since nearly two-thirds of the government's foreign exchange came from tourism and the medical school. If the United States had chosen this strategy, as the NJM apparently thought it had, the United States would have declared a travel advisory and persuaded the Medical School to move to other quarters. Neither was done.

4. *Military action*. While many have asked why the intervention in October 1983 occurred, the far more interesting question is why President Reagan, who declared Grenada a national security threat on national television, waited until then. The answer is that the administration realized this option was exceptionally costly, except in the most unusual circumstances.

5. *Distancing and isolation*. This option is not chosen; it is what remains when the administration realizes that it has no other options, and that the perceived threat is still indirect and distant. This option is as close as the United States can get to ignoring the problem or hoping it will disappear. Had there been evidence that the PRG was supplying arms to radicals in the area or preparing the airfield for Soviet bombers, the United States would have reassessed this option, and perhaps traded it for one of the more militant ones above. But despite the rhetoric, such was not the case.

Both the Carter and the Reagan administrations found themselves exercising the fifth option, which still allowed for considerable variation. The Carter administration initially tried a co-optation option, and then retreated to an approach that stressed the development and security of Grenada's neighbors, rather than confronting Grenada. This strategy was aimed at stabilizing the other governments while encouraging them to take the lead in pursuing common objectives—primarily to press the PRG to fulfill its initial pledges. The Carter administration believed that these governments actually had more effective direct leverage over the PRG than the United States did. In line with that view, the administration maintained a low profile in its approach to Grenada, because it thought a more vocal approach would be counterproductive—in effect, making the PRG look heroic and the United States foolish.

Whereas the Carter administration viewed Grenada as a small, radical problem in the Eastern Caribbean, the Reagan administration approached Grenada as a small object in a larger East-West struggle. The latter apparently believed negotiations with the regime were impractical and that such a regime understands only threats, force, and propaganda. Reagan's strategy used all three. In addition, his Administration tried to isolate the PRG from the Caribbean by insisting that its contribution to the Caribbean Development Bank was contingent on excluding Grenada.

The two strategies had different effects on the region, depending on the leadership of each country. Most leaders were more comfortable with the lower profile, development-oriented, multilateral approach of the Carter administration, while a few preferred the harder line, higher profile, security approach of the Reagan administration. But the increased attention by both administrations undoubtedly assisted development, reinforced security, and contributed to stabilizing the democracies.

As to their effect on the PRG, there is simply no evidence to suggest that the different strategies made a significant difference. Perhaps the main difference in terms of effect was that the Reagan administration induced the Bishop regime to greater heights of paranoia, but U.S. policy during either administration did not seem to have any impact on either Grenada's political direction or its relations with Cuba and the USSR—the two key interests of the United States. In an interview in September 1983, Bishop seemed to suggest that the continuity in U.S. policy was more evident to him than the difference: "All United States administrations, but I would say particularly this one, is very hostile to any progressive or revolutionary regime."[60]

One can speculate about the possible impact of alternative policies. It is doubtful that even if the United States had been able to sustain a friendlier policy politically that it would have changed the PRG's political or geopolitical orientation. A more hostile, confrontational approach might have impelled the PRG to discard its tourism objectives and adopt a more radical, popular mobilization stance, which would have probably delinked Grenada from the Eastern Caribbean and forced them to become completely dependent on the USSR. In short, if U.S. policy seemed unproductive, there were worse options available.

In reading through all the documents, what seems most striking is that the United States did not seem to play as large a role in either the political, economic, or strategic thinking of the regime as their rhetoric might have suggested. Actually, it appears that the Grenadian Revolution had more of an impact on the evolution of U.S. policy than U.S. policy had on the evolution of the Grenadian Revolution.

And that may be the lesson for revolutionaries. Beware of self-fulfilling prophecy; it works both ways. Unfortunately, the NJM revolutionaries do not seem to have learned that lesson. One told Michael Massing that he was saddened that Grenada had become a "bone of contention between East and West." Massing agreed, and took the thought one step further: "The Grenadians do not have much choice. In a world divided into competing blocs and dominated by superpowers, there is little place for small nations seeking to chart a middle course."[61]

Of course, the NJM *did choose,* and their choice was not a middle course. Their choice was alignment with the Soviet bloc and confrontation with U.S. imperialism. The NJM, having claimed it was "liberated" cannot dodge responsibility for its fate. The People's Revolutionary Government of Grenada received the policy from the United States that it expected and, in a curious and unintended way, invited.

NOTES

1. Maurice Bishop, "We Proudly Share the Noble Dreams of Martin and Malcolm," address to the Sixth Annual Dinner of TransAfrica, Washington, D.C. 8 June 1983, reprinted in Chris Searle, ed., *In Nobody's Backyard: Maurice Bishop's Speeches, 1979–1983* (London: Zed Books, 1984), p. 237. Hereafter, *Bishop's Speeches.*

2. Ecumenical Program for Inter-American Communication and Action, *Grenada: The Peaceful Revolution* (Washington, D.C.: EPICA 1982), p. 61.

3. Hugh O'Shaughnessy, *Grenada: Revolution, Invasion, and Aftermath* (London: Sphere Books, 1984), p. 105.

4. Statement in U.S. Congress, House Subcommittee on Inter-American Affairs of the Committee on Foreign Affairs, *United States Policy toward Grenada,* 15 June 1982, pp. 33, 38.

5. Letter from Frank Ortiz to the editor of *Atlantic Monthly,* June 1984, p. 12.

6. See, for example, Jiri Valenta and Virginia Valenta, "Leninism in Grenada," *Problems of Communism,* July/Aug. 1984; and Paul Seabury and Walter A. McDougall, eds., *The Grenada Papers* (San Francisco: Institute for Contemporary Studies, 1984).

7. Maurice Zeitlin and Robert Scheer, *Cuba: Tragedy in Our Hemisphere* (New York: Grove, 1963), p. 9.

8. Robert Merton, *Social Theory and Social Structure,* cited in Zeitlin and Scheer, ibid., p. 6.

9. Phillip Bonsal, *Cuba, Castro, and the United States,* cited in Cole Blasier, *The Hovering Giant: U.S. Responses to Revolutionary Change in Latin America* (Pittsburgh: University of Pittsburgh Press, 1979), p. 208.

10. Blaiser, *Hovering Giant.*

11. This thesis is more useful as an ex post facto explanation of the confrontation than as a description of Castro's intentions, which, according to Lee Lockwood, *Castro's Cuba, Cuba's Fidel* (New York: Random House, 1969); and Carlos Franqui's memoirs, were more chaotic and spontaneous. See Jorge Domínguez, *Cuba: Order and Revolution* (Cambridge: Belknap Press of Harvard University Press, 1978), pp. 137–49.

12. Walter LaFeber argues that U.S. policy toward Central America—and Nicaragua, in particular—has pushed the entire region toward the revolutions it wants to avoid. See his *Inevitable Revolutions* (New York: Norton, 1983). For the argument that the Sandinistas pushed first, see Lawrence E. Harrison, "Nicaraguan Anguish and Costa Rican Progress," and Mark Falcoff, "Somoza, Sandino, and the United States: What the Past Teaches—and Doesn't," *This World* (Fall 1983). And for the thesis that both sides share the responsibility, see Arturo Cruz Sequeira, "The Origins of Sandinista Foreign Policy," in Robert Leiken, ed., *Central America: Anatomy of Conflict* (New York: Pergamon, 1984).

13. Anthony Lake, "Wrestling with Third World Radical Regimes: Theory and Practice," in John W. Sewell et al., *U.S. Foreign Policy and the Third World: Agenda 1985–86* (New Brunswick: Transaction Books, 1985), pp. 119–45.

14. Blasier, *Hovering Giant*.

15. Few of the available documents, however, were written in the pre-1982 period or specifically address Grenada-U.S. relations, and therefore, one is not on as firm terrain as one would like in drawing conclusions about the PRG's policy toward the United States at the beginning of the revolution or its subsequent evolution. I have supplemented the documents with additional sources: nearly thirteen hours in three separate interviews with Maurice Bishop and Bernard Coard on 25–27 Oct. 1982; interviews with members of the Carter and Reagan administrations; and my experiences as director of Latin American and Caribbean Affairs on the National Security Council, 1977–81, during which I participated in all of the key decisions on U.S. policy toward Grenada.

16. World Bank, *Economic Memorandum on Grenada*, Report 3825-GRD (Washington, D.C.: World Bank, 1982). Some of the background on the revolution used in this chapter is borrowed from my "Grenada, the Caribbean, and the World: The Large Impact of a Small Island," in Anthony Bryan, ed., *Caribbean Perspectives* (Boulder: Westview, 1985).

17. Archie Singham, *The Hero and the Crowd in a Colonial Polity* (New Haven: Yale University Press, 1968). That book and another by M. G. Smith, entitled *Social Stratification in Grenada* (Berkeley: University of California Press, 1965), are reviewed by Aaron Segal, "Background to Grenada: When the Social Scientists Invaded," *Caribbean Review* 12 (Fall 1983), pp. 40–44.

18. V. S. Naipaul, "An Island Betrayed," *Harper's Magazine*, Mar. 1984, p. 63.

19. For a description of the Carter administration's policy toward the Caribbean in the context of other administrations' policies, see Robert Pastor, "U.S. Policy toward the Caribbean: Continuity and Change," in Peter M. Dunn and Bruce W. Watson, eds., *American Intervention in Grenada: The Implications of Operation "Urgent Fury"* (Boulder: Westview, 1985).

20. The sequence of events is pieced together from a number of different

sources, including Timothy Robinson, "Two at Grenada Embassy Accused of Gun-Running," *Washington Post,* 1 Sept. 1979. Although the desk officer in the State Department was informed of the trip by the two ATF officials in March, neither the assistant secretary of state not I were aware of the trip. My interviews with Maurice Bishop and Bernard Coard helped fill in their perspective on the reasons for the coup; both said they were unaware of the presence on the island of the Treasury officials. In his introduction to *Bishop's Speeches,* Richard Hart disclosed the details of the vote to launch the coup (p. xxiii).

21. Adams's conversations with Callaghan and his role in the events were described in a public address that he gave at the Woodrow Wilson Center, Washington, D.C., 2 December 1981, and subsequently in an interview that day with me. In addition, he discussed these events in the Barbados House of Assembly debates (official report), 2d sess. 15 Nov. 1983.

22. Letter from Ambassador Frank Ortiz to the editor, *Atlantic Monthly,* June 1984.

23. The two communiqués issued at the end of the meetings of the leaders from the six Caribbean nations on 14 and 15 Mar. 1979 are reprinted in *Caribbean and Central America* (London: HMSO, 1982), pp. 287–88, report from the (U.K.) House of Commons Foreign Affairs Committee, sess. 1981–82.

24. Statement in Barbados House of Assembly Debates (official record), 2d sess., 15 Nov. 1983, p. 51.

25. Bernard Diederich, "Interview with Maurice Bishop," *Washington Star,* 21 Mar. 1979.

26. Karen DeYoung, "Grenada Coup Wins Cautious Acceptance," *Washington Post,* 24 Mar. 1979.

27. There are several accounts of the meetings between Ortiz and Coard and Bishop on 10 Apr. The first full account of it was in the famous speech Bishop gave three days later, on 13 Apr., called In Nobody's Backyard (reprinted in *Bishop's Speeches,* pp. 9–14). Ortiz has described his perceptions of the conversations in his letter to the editor of the *Atlantic Monthly,* June 1984, pp. 7–12. In addition, in my interviews with Coard and Bishop, I inquired with persistent skepticism as to their perceptions of that conversation and how it fit in the U.S.-Grenadian relationship.

28. After Bishop cited and criticized this point, the State Department on 16 Apr. issued a clarifying statement that Grenadian relations with Cuba was not the principal issue from the U.S. perspective: "We would be concerned [however] about the development of close military and security ties." Henry Trewhitt, "U.S. Cautions Grenada on Cuban Military Ties," *Baltimore Sun,* 17 Apr. 1979.

29. For a description of British policy toward the PRG, see *Caribbean and Central America,* pp. 280–81.

30. Karen DeYoung, "U.S. vs Cuba on Caribbean Isle of Grenada," *Washington Post,* 27 Apr. 1979.

31. In his famous, secret, Line of March speech on 13 Sept. 1982, Bishop acknowledged that the NJM undertook a number of steps, such as an alliance with the bourgeoisie, at the beginning of the revolution, to reassure everyone "so that imperialism would not get too excited, and would say 'well, they have some nice fellas in that thing; everything alright.' And as a result wouldn't think

about sending in troops." See Michael Ledeen and Herbert Romerstein, eds., *Grenada Documents: An Overview and Selection*, vol. 1 (Washington, D.C.: Depts. of State and Defense, 1984), p. 19.

32. "We Have the Right to Build Our Country After Our Own Likeness: A Last Interview with a British Journalist," Sept. 1983, in *Bishop's Speeches*, p. 255.

33. Details of this Apr. 1979 delivery are in U.S. Department of State and Department of Defense, *Grenada: A Preliminary Report* (Washington, D.C.: GPO, 1983).

34. They were right. Aid to Grenada increased from E.C. $1.6 million in 1978 to a total of $68 million in 1980–81. Government of Grenada and the Caribbean Development Bank, *Economic Memorandum on Grenada*, vol. 1 (Bridgetown: Caribbean Development Bank, 1984), p. 101.

35. For a comparison between Carter's policies toward revolutionary Grenada and those toward revolutionary Nicaragua, see Robert Pastor, "The Carter Administration and Latin America: A Test of Principle," in John D. Martz, ed., *U.S. Policy Toward Latin America: Quarter-Century of Crisis and Challenge* (Omaha: University of Nebraska Press, 1988).

36. Testimony of U.S. Ambassador Sally Shelton. See U.S. Congress, House Committee on Foreign Affairs, *U.S. Military Actions in Grenada: Implications for U.S. Policy in the Eastern Caribbean*, pp. 62–63.

37. "Organize to Fight Destabilization," 8 May 1979, reprinted in *Bishop's Speeches*, pp. 15–22.

38. See the testimony of Sally Shelton, *U.S. Military Actions in Grenada*, pp. 64–65. For Williams' remarks, see Robinson, "Two at Grenada Embassy Accused of Gun-Running."

39. Cited by Ronnie Dugger, *On Reagan: The Man and His Presidency* (New York: McGraw-Hill, 1983), p. 518.

40. For this and some other differences, see the testimony of Sally Shelton, U.S. Congress, House Subcommittee on Inter-American Affairs of the Foreign Affairs Committee, *United States Policy Toward Grenada*, 15 June 1982, p. 59.

41. Karen DeYoung, "U.S. Presses EEC to Refuse Aid for Leftist Grenada," *Washington Post*, 20 Mar. 1981.

42. John M. Goshko, "U.S. Rebuffed in Move to Bar Aid to Grenada," *Washington Post*, 23 June 1981. U.S. aid to the Caribbean through the Caribbean Development Bank had increased from U.S. $7.2 million in 1977 to U.S. $45.1 million in 1980, but in 1982, the Reagan administration refused to make any contributions to the organization. See General Accounting Office, *Report to the Administration of the Agency for International Development*, GAO/ID-83-50, 22 July 1983 (Washington, D.C.: GPO, 1983), pp. 6–19.

43. Based on my conversations in Oct. and Nov. 1982 with Foreign Ministry officials in Barbados, Prime Minister Eugenia Charles of Dominica, Foreign Minister Lester Bird of Antigua, and Prime Minister Maurice Bishop and Finance Minister Bernard Coard of Grenada.

44. Patrick Tyler, "U.S. Tracks Cuban Aid to Grenada: In '81, Senate Unit Nixed CIA Plan to Destabilize Isle," *Washington Post*, 27 Feb. 1983.

45. Report of Secretary of Defense Caspar W. Weinberger to the Congress on the FY 1983 Budget, 8 Feb. 1982, p. II–26.

46. "Bishop Denounces U.S. in Anniversary Speech," *Foreign Broadcasting Information Service,* 15 Mar. 1983.

47. His remarks about the Westminster system was reported by CANA, and republished in *Foreign Broadcasting Information Service,* 15 Mar. 1983; his speech on 23 Mar. "Every Grain of Sand Is Ours!" is published in *Bishop's Speeches,* pp. 220–27.

48. Edward Cody, "Grenadian Tempest Bemuses Tourists," and "New Fervor also Draws Smiles: Grenada, No Longer Little Noted, 'Revels' in Tweaking the U.S. Cheek," *Washington Post,* 21 Apr. 1983.

49. Edward Cody, "Grenada Unsettles Its Neighbors, but So Does U.S. Reaction," *Washington Post,* 24 Apr. 1983.

50. For this document and the others that will be cited on Grenada's approach to the United States, see Seabury and McDougall, *Grenada Papers,* pp. 151–80.

51. "Caribbean Left-wing Leader Received Coolly in Washington," *New York Times,* 1 June 1983.

52. Bernard Nossiter, "Grenada Premier Establishes 'Some Sort' of U.S. Rapport," *New York Times,* 10 June 1983.

53. John M. Goshko, "U.S. Offered Reassurance by Grenada," *Washington Post,* 1 June 1983.

54. Statement by Stephen Bosworth in U.S. Congress, *United States Policy Toward Grenada,* p. 48.

55. *Bishop's Speeches,* p. xiv.

56. For a description of the Reagan administration view of the region, see Robert Pastor, "The Reagan Administration and Latin America: The Single-Minded Pursuit of Security," in Kenneth Oye, Robert Lieber, and Donald Rothchild, eds., *Eagle Resurgent: The Reagan Era in American Foreign Policy* (Boston: Little, Brown 1987).

57. An economic report in 1984 noted that the "tourism industry was declining rapidly" during the period in which the PRG governed. Government of Grenada and the CDB, *Economic Memorandum on Grenada,* p. 22.

58. *Bishop's Speeches,* p. xix.

59. See Jay R. Mandle, *Big Revolution, Small Country: The Rise and Fall of the Grenada Revolution* (Lanham, Md.; North-South, 1985), ch. 2. The decision to give tourism the highest priority is all the more incomprehensible because the NJM already believed the United States was undermining tourism, and the PRG would have needed to negotiate a civil aviation agreement with the United States before U.S. airlines could land at Grenada's new airport.

60. "We Have the Right to Build Our Country After Our Own Likeness," *Bishop's Speeches,* p. 251.

61. Michael Massing, "Grenada Before and After," *Atlantic Monthly,* Feb. 1984, p. 87.

Part III

CRISIS AND AFTERMATH

7. The Hero and the Apparatchik: Charismatic Leadership, Political Management, and Crisis in Revolutionary Grenada

Jorge Heine

> Most West Indian political parties have . . . been one-man
> shows.   —Patrick Emmanuel
>
> [Maurice Bishop] and his contemporaries have distaste for
> one-man leadership, and he has a strong position on this.
> —New Jewel Movement General Membership Meeting

THE PRECISE SEQUENCE of events leading to the self-destruction of the Grenadian Revolution has by now been extensively described and documented.[1] What has not been done is to provide a convincing explanation as to why a revolutionary process that had so much going for it was ultimately derailed by such an improbable and unlikely chain of events: a Central Committee that approves and attempts to implement an utterly impractical and unworkable dual leadership formula; a government that then proceeds to put under house arrest the man who had come to embody the revolution; a charismatic leader that walks to his almost certain death by leading the crowd that freed him to a military installation, and then later accepts his execution with an equanimity worthy of a better cause: this is not the stuff of which "normal" revolutionary politics is made.

This chapter provides an explanation of the highly abnormal events leading to the revolution's abortion. This is done by examining the particular leadership style of Maurice Bishop, on the one hand, and of his deputy and ultimate challenger, Bernard Coard, on the other. The main argument is that, although ideology played a part in the final crisis of the revolution, the crisis itself cannot be understood without a grasp of the personalities and the particular leadership styles developed by Bishop and Coard and how they interacted in their final confrontation. The chapter is an effort to uncover the political and psychological leadership dynamic that led to the ultimate tragic ending of the Grenadian Revolution.

THE EMERGENCE OF A HERO

Maurice Bishop was born in Aruba on 29 May 1944, the son of Rupert Bishop and the former Alimenta LaGrenade.[2] The family returned to its native Grenada in 1950, where Maurice, the youngest of three children, enjoyed a carefree and sheltered middle-class childhood. As a child, he spent most of his time playing tennis, reading comics, and pitching marbles with the children from the St. Paul neighborhood he was brought up in. His friends included his future law partner and political associate Kendrick Radix, who lived only a few houses away.

Although a quick reader and gifted with an excellent memory, he was neither very bookish nor considered constant or thorough in his learning endeavors. He soon gave up on music, and he failed to get a scholarship in his first entrance examination for Presentation College, as he wrote his essay without punctuation. He did get the scholarship a year later and so attended one of Grenada's premier secondary schools. Teachers remember him as rather shy, but after he finished his "O" levels in 1960 he became active in a variety of extracurricular activities. He became president of the Student Council at Catholic Presentation College, the only high school in Grenada with a student council at the time. He was also president of the Debating Society and of the Historical Society and editor of the student newspaper. His cheery, lanky good looks made him popular with the girls in town, but he was also a good student, winning the principal's medal in 1962.

In those days, pupils from prestigious Presentation College weren't supposed to mix with those from Grenada Boys Secondary School, a public institution. But Maurice Bishop first met Bernard Coard, a GBSS student in 1962, when both got involved in the Grenada Assembly of Youth After Truth. The assembly brought together students from the various high schools in St. George's and attempted, among other things, to lift the ban on literature from the socialist countries then in force in Grenada.

Rupert Bishop, a successful businessman, wanted his only son to study medicine. Maurice played around with the idea of doing business administration instead, but after his father sold several businesses, he finally settled on doing law in London. He spent seven long years in England, following the steps of his sisters Maureen and Ann, both of whom had gone to secretarial school there.

Relatively little is known about Bishop's London sojourn, which overlapped with Bernard Coard's doctoral studies in economics at Sussex, but there is little doubt that it had a decisive impact on his political outlook and Weltanschauung. To be a West Indian student in London in the sixties meant constant exposure to the reverberations of the anticolonialist movement throughout the Third World. As in high school, the young Bishop did not confine himself to the library but became involved in the West Indian Student Union and the Standing Conference of West Indian Organizations.

The struggle for African independence had a deep impact on him.[3] The very muted response of Britain to the white minority UDI government established in Rhodesia in defiance of the Crown, in contrast to the dispatching of an invasion force to Anguilla after that island proclaimed its independence in 1967, opened his eyes to the realities of international race relations. The emergence of the black power movement in the United States at the time also raised his awareness about the need to evaluate the role of the black man in a largely white-dominated world. The writings of Fanon, Malcolm X, and Nkrumah shaped his thinking about colonialism and race relations and led also to his involvement in the Campaign Against Race Discrimination.

As with so many other West Indians, it was abroad that Bishop discovered his true national roots and identity. He wrote a forty-page paper on Julien Fedon, the man who led the rebellion against British rule in Grenada in 1795–1796. He grew a beard, which failed to hide his extremely boyish looks, and refused to wear Western-style suits.[4] He also stopped going to church, after some of his books were lost in a fire at a Catholic boarding house. It was also during his London sojourn that he married Angela Redhead, a fellow Grenadian and daughter of a St. George's lawyer.

Trinidad's 1970 "February revolution" coincided with his passing through Port of Spain on his way back to St. George's, and the recent law school graduate soon found himself leading demonstrations in solidarity with Trinidadian black power supporters. As he put it later, "In those days demonstrations were something new to Grenada, and many people thought we were crazy parading up and down with placards. In fact, a demonstration then was big when you had six people involved."[5]

He set up his law practice on Granby Street in St. George's, doing divorces, criminal law, torts—whatever came along. And being one of the less expensive lawyers in town, he soon built up a sizable clientele. He was particularly good at getting high compensation for victims of accidents, keeping only a small portion as his fee. But even then, he did not like to spend much time at the office. He preferred preparing his cases at night, at home, when he would pace up and down the house, making short notes regarding the facts of the case. Judge Archibald Nedd considered him one of the best lawyers in town, and when Bishop became prime minister, the judge said he was sorry to lose him as a lawyer, despite Bishop's disdain for formalities such as powdered wigs and other British anachronisms.[6]

As a prominent member of the highly materialistic West Indian bourgeoisie, Bishop showed an uncommon lack of interest in money or material things. After nine years of a highly successful law practice, he had not built his own home, living in the house his father gave him upon his return from England. He would always carry a wad of dollar bills in his pocket, which he would hand out liberally to those who asked him for money. And one of his first acts as prime minister was to cut ministerial salaries and allowances by 30 percent, also making it clear that everybody in the cabinet would have to pay income tax, a practice not followed under Gairy.[7]

This, in fact, was one of the sources of his appeal to the Grenadian people and his increasing aura as a hero. Being a London-educated lawyer from a well-known and respected light-skinned St. George's family, he made his own the demands and aspirations of the black rural folk. "He could live a different sort of life," people said, "but he chooses not to." He became increasingly active in the anti-Gairy struggle, first through the MAP and later the New Jewel Movement.[8]

The repression unleashed by Eric Gairy against the mounting opposition to his regime culminated in two events that were particularly significant in the early years of that struggle. One of them was the Bloody Sunday of 18 November 1973, when Bishop and several of his NJM associates, including Selwyn Strachan and Hudson Austin, upon visiting Grenville to discuss the next phase of the anti-Gairy strategy with a group of businessmen, were detained and badly beaten by the police. For years, Bishop would get headaches from the wounds suffered in Grenville.

The other event was the 1974 murder of Rupert Bishop by Gairy's police, in front of his wife and daughter Ann. According to at least one version, the police who stormed Otway House (the Seafarers and Seaworkers Union building at the Carenage), where the Bishops went after a demonstration, were actually looking for Maurice Bishop, but, unable to find him, killed his father instead.[9]

Afterward, Alimenta Bishop understandably asked her son to give up politics, but Maurice's response was that he couldn't live with himself if he did. And, although he never articulated a desire for personal revenge, he threw himself with even more vigor into the fray. Being elected to Parliament in 1976 and becoming leader of the opposition made politics an almost full-time endeavor. More and more often, clients had to return to his law office to pick up the deposits they had made, as he just couldn't find time to do the necessary legal work.[10]

His towering presence, ready smile, and easy eloquence, from the beginning made Bishop a natural leader of the New Jewel Movement, as it became the only consistent opposition to Gairyism. In contrast to other radical West Indian politicians, he was as adept at leading a demonstration across town and firing up the people at market square as he was in the more subtle games of coalition building in parliamentary politics. For example, within the Popular Alliance, he managed to out-maneuver the more senior Herbert Blaize for the position of leader of the opposition by securing three seats for the NJM (vis-à-vis only two for Blaize's Grenada National Party) in the 1976 elections, a humiliation Blaize reportedly never forgot.

As his uncle put it, however, Bishop was not so much a politician as a believer in causes: in anticolonialism and black nationalism in the sixties, in anti-Gairyism and socialism in the seventies. But above all, he was bent on improving the welfare of the Grenadian common man.[11] Whenever a decision had to be made, "for him the bottom line was: What will happen to the common man?"[12]

He was unlike other West Indian politicians of his and the earlier generation, for whom politics, particularly in its postcolonial manifesta-tion, represented an opportunity to "make it." Given his family back-ground and professional standing, being in politics represented, if any-thing, a step down for Bishop. Without the need to prove himself, imbued with an egalitarian ideology, a warm disposition, and an unwill-ingness to offend people, he led by consensus.

The charm and eloquence with which he articulated the needs of the Grenadians allowed him to establish a strong rapport with the people (see table 7.1). and made him enormously popular.[13] From the mid-seventies through the revolutionary years, organizers of public meetings had to schedule him as the last speaker, because some people wouldn't stay to listen to any speaker following him.

His attitude toward Marxism and Leninism was both ambiguous

Table 7.1
What People Liked About Bishop's Leadership

Factor	Number	Percentage
Relations with the masses	160	41.1
Development policy	123	31.6
Speeches	34	8.7
Leadership	31	8.0
Other	41	10.5
Total	387	99.9

Source: Patrick Emmanuel, Farley Brathwaite, and Eudine Barriteau, *Political Change and Public Opinion in Grenada 1979–1984*, ISER Occasional Paper 19 (Cave Hill, Barbados: University of the West Indies, 1986), p. 24.

and reverential. Speaking of it as "the science" and having great respect for people like Bernard Coard, who Bishop felt had mastered the intricacies of historical materialism, his discourse was more that of a grassroots democratic nationalist than of a hard-line Leninist. He spoke of the "masses," rather than of the "working class," of "popular revolutionary democracy" rather than of the "dictatorship of the proletariat," of a "mixed" rather than of a "planned" economy. On this island, in which the single largest factory was a brewery employing seventy-five people and the industrial working class was a miniscule part of the total labor force, such inclusionary language was needed to develop and maintain the revolutionary momentum. But this was not a perspective universally shared within the New Jewel Movement.

THE ENTRENCHING OF A FACTION

Ostensibly, Bernard Coard had much in common with Maurice Bishop. The were nearly the same age; both received a university education in England and came to socialism via black cultural nationalism; and both combined a serious interest in the world of ideas with a vocation for political action. Underlying these superficial similarities, however, were deep and profound differences in orientation toward politics and political style. These differences, which were in part due to their very different family background and upbringing, would manifest themselves time and again from the very inception of the NJM in 1973 to its final dissolution in October 1983.

Bernard Coard was born in St. George's on 10 August 1944, the seventh and last child of Frederick McDermott Coard and Flora Coard. His father, a black civil servant of uncommon intelligence and drive, served for a total of forty-seven years in the Grenadian colonial civil service. He had joined the Government Print Shop at the age of fifteen and, despite his scant formal education, rose all the way through the ranks to acting colonial treasurer and exofficio member of the executive and of the Legislative Council. These were the highest positions any Grenadian could occupy within the colonial civil service.

Obsessed with his own educational inadequacies, he expended much of his energy taking examinations designed to improve his credentials. A strict disciplinarian, he instilled in his children a highly developed need to achieve. In fact, several of the Coard children became successful professionals in Grenada and the United States.

It was in this atmosphere of pressure to achieve that young Bernard grew up. Upon graduating from Grenada Boys Secondary School (GBSS), Grenada's only existing public secondary school at the time, he received a scholarship to study at Brandeis University in Massachusetts. After receiving his baccalaureate in political science there, he went for his doctorate in development economics at the University of Sussex in England, where he reestablished contact with Maurice Bishop, then completing his law studies at Gray's Inn. In 1970 he wrote a book on how the British educational system discriminated against West Indian children.[14] Before completing his doctoral dissertation, however, he returned to the Caribbean where he took up a position as lecturer in economics at the Institute of International Relations (IIR) of the University of the West Indies in Trinidad. It was also at UWI that he had met his wife, Phyllis Evans, then a student at the Mona campus in Jamaica and heiress to the Tía María fortune.

Bernard Coard was living in Trinidad and missed the earliest and most heroic period of the NJM's anti-Gairy struggle, although from the beginning of the movement he declared himself a supporter and collaborated with its leaders in a variety of ways. Maurice Bishop asked him to help in the drafting of the party's manifesto, which they wrote in one of the Bishop family's apartments in Beverly Flats. Coard's hand is evident in the very detailed economic sections of the manifesto. Coard also went to London in 1973, representing the Grenadian opposition, to discuss the plans for Grenadian independence, and later organized a major conference on the subject at the IIR in 1974. From the start, though, Coard's relationship with the party and the anti-Gairy struggle was rather different from Bishop's.

After returning from London and starting his law practice, Bishop was naturally drawn into the anti-Gairy struggle and proceeded to earn his leadership wings on the streets of St. George's and Grenville. On the other hand, in 1974 Coard joined the NJM, though still based in Trinidad, on condition that he be made third coordinating secretary of the party. He returned permanently to Grenada in September 1976 and was appointed a member of the Political Bureau of the party. And when the slate of candidates for the 1976 elections was being assembled, Coard demanded he be put on the ticket for the city of St. George's. This was traditionally the most anti-Gairy voting district on the island, and it assured his election to Parliament only two months after having returned to Grenada.

Even before his return to the island, Coard had been closely associated with the Organization of Revolutionary Education and Liberation (OREL), a Marxist study group formed mostly by sixth formers from Presentation College and St. Joseph's Convent, Grenada's leading high schools. The group published a short-lived newspaper, *The Worker's Voice*. Though founded only in 1975, in 1976 the group joined the NJM en masse, with Bernard Coard continuing to act as their intellectual guru and mentor. It was from that younger group of party members, including Liam ("Owusu") James, Evert ("Headache") Layne, John ("Chalkie") Ventour, and Leon ("Bogo") Cornwall, that Coard started to build party cadres loyal only to him. This initial factional activity reached such a point that in 1977 Kendrick Radix, one of the founding members of the NJM and a childhood friend of Bishop, denounced it in no uncertain terms, demanding its immediate end. Coard finally acquiesced to Radix's demands, but characteristically, not without exacting a price. To appease him, in 1978 the party appointed Coard head of the Organizing Committee (widely known as the OC), a body exercising ample disciplinary powers. The OC quickly become an important power base both for Bernard Coard and his wife Phyllis, who was developing an increasingly higher profile within the party.

By 1979, Coard's unquestioned ability as an organizer and his thorough command of the Marxist-Leninist lexicon had made him the undisputed number-two man in the party. This was reflected in his immediate appointment as minister of Finance and, somewhat later, as deputy prime minister when the NJM took power in March 1979.

Much as his father had excelled at balancing the books of Grenada's Treasury Department in colonial days, Bernard Coard thrived while heading the same agency in its postcolonial incarnation, the Ministry of Finance. And while Bishop's diplomatic gifts opened the doors of many political donors, Coard's thorough follow-up work ensured that feasible project proposals were prepared and submitted, thus leading to the Eastern Caribbean's most ambitious development projects of the early eighties.

One distinctive aspect of the economic policy of the People's Revolutionary Government was the extremely tight and efficient management of government revenue and expenditure. This was a key tool to financing the diverse social programs the PRG was committed to, without leading to inflation: "Monthly limits were set on departmental expenditure, with daily summaries to be submitted to the Ministry of Finance for review. This was followed up by a monthly review to adjust the limits when necessary in order to compensate for overspending in previous months. To complement this system of expenditure controls, a daily review of aggregate cash flow records was introduced to monitor receipts."[15] Merchants were apprised of the fact that no government purchase order would be honored without a computer printout slip stamped and countersigned by the Ministry of Finance.

The economic achievements of the PRG are discussed elsewhere in this book. Suffice it to say that many of these would not have been possible without Bernard Coard's extraordinary managerial abilities. More relevent to our purpose is to understand how he applied the same long-term planning, strategic thinking, and eye for detail to the political sphere. Nurturing his own personal power base, both in the party and within the newly formed People's Revolutionary Army (PRA), became his key concern.

Leading former OREL members were sent to intensive party and military training courses in the Soviet Union and in Cuba. Even though Coard would have to do without their help for many months and sometimes years, he realized that given the veneration of educational credentials by Grenadians and the revolutionary legitimacy such training would provide them, his disciples would be of far greater value to him on their return. This systematic placing of Coard loyalists in key positions was coupled with an equally thorough effort to remove Bishop's closest allies and friends from the decisionmaking bodies of the party and the army.[16]

Coard's abilities as a first-rate organizer, the fact that most party members were not up to his own exacting standards, and his deft use of Marxist-Leninist categories to label the failings of those he wished to remove served him well in this endeavor. Trade union leader Vincent Noel, one of the Bishop loyalists killed in Fort Rupert in October 1983, was one of the first to be removed from his government post as well as from the Political Bureau and the Central Committee in 1981. Kendrick Radix, who had never gotten along with Coard, suffered a similar fate. Don Rojas, editor of the *Free West Indian,* was removed from his post in an internal coup by the paper's own staff, being replaced by a Workers Party of Jamaica member and close supporter of Coard. A continuing bone of contention was Einstein Louison's position in the PRA. As the brother of George Louison, a founding member of the NJM and a man close to Maurice Bishop, Einstein Louison's position as PRA chief of staff was clearly a source of irritation to Coard. Coard tried to remove him time and again but finally had to settle for a compromise solution, which in effect demoted Louison. At one point, Coard even suggested that Dessima Williams (the PRG's ambassador to the Organization of American States and another Bishop confidante), who had developed an effective network in Washington, D.C., where she lived for many years, be transferred to Moscow, as that "would give her experience," although nothing came of that.[17]

Coard's master stroke in the implementation of this plan took place at 12–15 October 1982 meeting of the NJM's Central Committee. Selwyn Strachan, speaking in Coard's absence, told the party leadership that Bernard Coard was resigning from the Political Bureau and the Central Committee.[18] In a revealing choice of words, Coard said he was tired of being the only "hatchet man." Everybody was relying on him for everything, and he just couldn't take it anymore. Party organs weren't operating as they should. The real issue was the chairmanship of the Central Committee (in other words, Bishop's), but he didn't want to appear as criticizing the leadership, as that had been misconstrued in the past.

Coard's refusal to appear personally to deliver his resignation should have forewarned Bishop that there was much more to this than met the eye, but it didn't. It was at the same meeting that Kendrick Radix was expelled from the Political Bureau and the Central Committee, that three former OREL members (James, Layne, and Ventour) were initiated into the Political Bureau, and the matter of Phyllis Coard joining the Political Bureau was raised and postponed for formal consideration to March 1983.

By withdrawing from the higher party organs, Coard managed to defuse suspicions that his criticism of Bishop was based on ulterior motives. But by replacing Radix with three Coard loyalists, Coard's maneuver laid the groundwork for his next step, one that would be taken without undue haste eleven months later.

Bishop's naivete at that October 1982 meeting, when he acquiesced to the removal of his childhood friend from the decisionmaking bodies of the party and accepted his replacement by the same OREL members Radix had warned about five years earlier, should not be surprising. Bishop's respect and trust in Bernard Coard knew no bounds. Many people warned him repeatedly about the Coards, including members of his own family, who "never understood why he had brought them over."[19] Upon visiting Jamaica a few months after the revolution, Bishop's uncle, Allan LaGrenade, had been told that many people in Jamaica thought Bishop was named prime minister on an interim basis, and that he would soon be replaced by Bernard Coard. When his aunt confronted him with this, Bishop angrily accused her of trying to destabilize the revolution, and told her he would have to send her "up the hill" (meaning Richmond Hill Prison) if she went on saying those things.[20] Reports of Coard's designs even surfaced in the press.[21]

Nor did Bishop object to the major political decisions Coard took as acting prime minister while Bishop was abroad. After the de facto refusal to hold elections, no other measure taken by the PRG received as heavy criticism in the international and regional press as the closing of the *Torchlight* in the fall of 1979. Yet, upon his return, Bishop failed to assert his authority by not making it clear to Coard that no major decision was to be made in his absence. In September 1981, a major reshuffling of the top PRA command took place, making Ewart Layne chief of staff, again during Bishop's absence.

THE CRISIS UNRAVELS

This is the background against which one must assess the crisis that would ultimately engulf the party and the revolution in the fall of 1983. Some commentators have seen the final crisis of the revolution as a quasi-cataclysmic event, almost as an act of nature over which the participants had no control.[22] But the evidence indicates that the key event triggering the crisis—the joint leadership proposal approved by the NJM Central Committee on 16 September 1983—was merely one additional move in Bernard Coard's long-term strategy to gain full control of the party and the state in Grenada.

The attempt to substitute the revolution's extremely popular charismatic leader with a widely disliked apparatchik was bound to end in disaster and could have been predicted by anyone with a minimal grasp of political realities. That the attempt was not nipped in the bud was largely due to Bishop's leadership style. Paradoxically, it was not "one manism" that allowed the crisis to run its full course, but the very lack of it. *It was Bishop's utter disregard for his own personal political resources and power base, so different from Coard's systematic strategic thinking, that left him in an almost indefensible position.* Examination of the dynamics of the crucial 14–16 September 1983 Central Committee meeting, which closed with the approval of the joint leadership proposal for the party, provides ample evidence for this proposition.

In the summer of 1983, the higher organs of the NJM had held several long meetings to assess the state of the party and of the revolution. The challenge posed by the increasingly vocal opposition of the churches to the PRG, the growing economic difficulties, counterrevolutionary activities in St. Andrew's, and morale problems within the party and the army were discussed. The difficulties were blamed on what the Central Committee in October 1982 had identified as the "petty-bourgeois" tendencies within the party and suggested the way out lay in strengthening Leninist discipline and by making the New Jewel Movement, already a very small organization with no more than 70 full members and some 350 total membership, even smaller and more select. This would be done by a "gradual weeding out of the worst elements within the ranks of the party" and by "a system to guarantee a more careful selection of cadres entering the party."[23] Bishop himself was blamed for the difficulties of the National Women's Organization headed by Phyllis Coard, given his "failure . . . to provide effective leadership for the period."[24] A long report was prepared as a result of the July meeting, in which the Central Committee met for fifty-four hours over six and a half days. At an emergency meeting on 26 August, Liam James, the leading member of the Coard faction, reported that "we are seeing the beginning of the disintegration of the party,"[25] a statement that was followed by heavy criticism of the functioning of the committee, particularly by Layne, Ventour, and James himself.

It was not until the 14–16 September Extraordinary Meeting of the Central Committee, however, that the Coard faction made its gambit, openly challenging Bishop. The meeting opened with Bishop's circulation of the agenda. The agenda itself was immediately challenged by Liam James, who said it "lacked in focus," and that it was "not consistent with what we agreed in the emergency meeting."[26] Ewart Layne seconded James, and John Ventour then took it upon himself to set forth what the agenda of the meeting should be—namely an analysis of the present state of the party and the revolution, an examination of the Central Committee's main problems, and the way forward. Bishop meekly responded that "he had no problem in changing the agenda, his main concern is the time limit of the analysis." But not even this quick retreat allowed Bishop to save face. Layne retorted that the "CC should take all the time necessary to do the analysis, given the state of the work. When we have exhausted the discussion of the item, we can move on," a statement supported by Phyllis Coard. The committee then proceeded to adopt Ventour's agenda.

The pattern was thus set for that and future party meetings. As if in a well-rehearsed play, with Liam James as leading actor, Layne and Ventour in supporting roles, Phyllis Coard as leading lady, and Bernard Coard as the off-stage director, the OREL group proceeded to lay the groundwork for the real purpose of "Chalkie" Ventour's agenda— the removal of Maurice Bishop from the chairmanship of the Central Committee.

The first two days of the meeting were thus spent in long and repetitive arguments, set forth mainly by the former OREL members. For them, the revolution found itself in a state of crisis due to the deficiencies of the Central Committee. Two things are most striking about this diagnosis. One of them is the extremely lopsided rhetoric-to-data ratio. For political activists supposedly so alarmed about the prospects for the almost immediate disintegration of the revolution and the party, James et al. were surprisingly short on specific examples and indicators to buttress their predictions. While there was much talk about "petty bourgeois deviationism" and the "right opportunist path," the exact reasons as to why some cash flow problems of the PRG or a few mildly critical sermons in the churches would threaten the very survival of the revolution was not specified.

The second feature of these discussions was the degree to which this extremely alarmist and, as far as can be determined from the available data, quite distorted picture of the political and economic situation in Grenada in the fall of 1983 was passively accepted by Bishop and his supporters. As he had done with the agenda and the timetable for the meeting, Bishop accepted both the diagnosis that the revolution was in crisis and attribution of responsibility for this state of affairs to the Central Committee, which he presided over.

On the third and final day of the meeting, Liam James led the discussion with a stinging attack on Bishop, himself. While acknowledging Bishop's charisma and ability to articulate the positions of the revolution, James said that "the most fundamental problem is the quality of the leadership of the Central Committee and the party exercised by Maurice Bishop," and that "the qualities he lacks is what is needed to push the revolution forward at this time: A Leninist level of organization and discipline; great depth in ideological clarity; brilliance in strategy and tactics."

Ewart Layne followed ("The salvation of the revolution calls for a mature proletarian decision"), with Chalkie Ventour taking his usual third turn, this time to use Bishop's own naive openness against him: "These criticisms were made to him in more than one occasion, which he accepted. He shows that he do not have the quality to put the party on a firm Marxist-Leninist footing." Phyllis Coard, never known for her subtleness, was especially blunt: "The Cde. Leader has not taken responsibility, not given the necessary guidance; even in areas where he is directly in charge of the guidance is not adequate. He is disorganized, very often avoids responsibilities for dealing with critical areas of work, e.g., study class."

The spectacle of the Grenadian prime minister being subjected to this sort of criticism by a group of youngsters is hard to imagine. But it is difficult to escape the conclusion that Bishop himself did nothing to discourage this sort of behavior—in fact seemed to encourage it. Bishop actually thanked those bent on unseating him from his Central Committee chairmanship, chided them for not having been more forthcoming in their criticism before, and proceeded to subject himself to a savage, and at times even demeaning, self-criticism:

> He agreed that the points are correct, especially correct application of strategy and tactics, which cannot be achieved except the other qualities are fulfill. He had had difficulties of finding a relevant material to study the question of the functioning of the P.B. and C.C., which reflects a weakness, he don't think he had given adequate leadership to bodies. . . . He also questioned his approach as regards to collective leadership, he said that there is not enough participation and discussion. . . . On the question of crisis and problems, it is correct, as the maximum leader has to take the full responsibilities.

Having accepted the questionable premises of the whole discussion about the supposed crisis of the revolution and the self-serving conclusions drawn from them (i.e., that the crisis was due to the committee's failures and was, therefore, his fault), Bishop left himself wide open for what had been the hidden purpose of the meeting all along—the dual leadership proposal. As the fifth and final point of a set of proposals to deal with the situation, Liam James "proposed a model of joint leadership, marrying the strengths of Cds. Bishop and Coard"—outlining in exact detail the areas of responsibilities of each even before this extraordinary idea had been considered.

Most commentators have failed to recognize that the joint leadership proposal was an integral part of a much broader plan, which reassigned powerful positions and responsibility within the party and the army. James's dual leadership proposal was immediately followed by a thirteen-point plan by Christopher De Riggs, another former OREL member. The plan proposed removal of George Louison from St. George's by assigning him to party work in St. Andrew's; it called for Hudson Austin's removal as head of the PRA, and his replacement by Ewart Layne;[27] put Leon Cornwall (until then ambassador to Cuba) in charge of academic and political work in the PRA; put Liam James in charge of the Ministry of the Interior, and left Phyllis Coard in charge of the St. George's Parish Coordinating Bureau of the NJM, the party's most important local body.

The idea that this was *not* a carefully orchestrated plan to leave Coard's supporters in charge of the key positions in the party and the PRG is disingenuous. And if Bishop still didn't seem to grasp the subtext of the discussion, George Louison, who had earlier joined the chorus of Bishop critics with the sharpest indictment of all ("The number one problem is the quality of leadership given the process by Cde. Bishop") finally reacted, objecting to his being farmed out to St. Andrew's instead of being appointed minister of State Enterprises, a new position he had been given to believe he would get. Louison also objected to the joint leadership proposal, as did Whiteman, possibly realizing too late they had been led down the garden path.

Bishop himself, however, seemed receptive to the idea of joint leadership: "His own idea of his role falls into what Cde. James had outlined [although] He feels that school visits should have been included under his responsibilities." And he reasonably wondered what Bernard Coard might think about all this, suggesting a meeting with him to ponder the most momentous leadership structure decision taken by the NJM in its ten-year history.

Then, suddenly, the Coard faction was in a great rush. The same people who had started the meeting by insisting they required the time that was needed to assess the state of the party and the revolution pressed for a decision on the joint leadership proposal *before* approaching Coard about it, effectively keeping Coard in the background. They further insisted the vote be taken that same afternoon. The result of the vote overwhelmingly favored the joint leadership proposal: nine votes in favor, one against (Louison), and two abstentions (Bishop and Whiteman).

BISHOP'S CRISIS MANAGEMENT

Confronted with the most serious challenge to his leadership ever, Maurice Bishop vacillated. In hindsight, almost every single step he took during the thirty-three days between 16 September and 19 October seems almost expressly designed to bring him closer to his tragic end. Perhaps most damaging of all was his almost chronic procrastination. Throughout the whole period, rather than facing the challenge head on, he kept avoiding the issue, saying he needed more time to think about it. This served only to confirm the charges of indecisiveness and irresolution made against him in the first place. This gave more powerful ammunition to his adversaries within the party, whose arguments against Bishop's position suddenly changed from a substantive criticism of his leadership of the revolution (on which they were on very weak ground) to a strictly procedural argument that a decision on dual leadership had been made and accepted by Bishop. Any attempt to prevent implemention of that decision, which is what Bishop was de facto doing, was a violation of democratic centralism and of the will of the majority ("if he wants to rule with a minority, let him go to South Africa" as Chalkie Ventour expressed it, in the spirit of "friendly" criticism that characterized the debate).

After the vote on dual leadership of 16 September had been taken, Kamau McBarnette suggested Bernard Coard be invited to attend the meeting, a proposal seconded by Layne and Cornwall. But Bishop decided he would rather not face Coard. Having difficulties with the dual-leadership model, he "proposed that the CC meet with Cde. Coard in his absence." He also opposed circulation of the minutes of the meeting to the NJM membership—for perfectly good reasons, but which again played directly into the hand of his adversaries, who waxed eloquent about "internal party democracy" and "Leninist principles."

The next day, the Central Committee met with Bernard Coard in the absence of Bishop, Louison, Whiteman (who had all gone to St. Kitt's for its independence celebration), and Bain, who was ill. *Every single member of the Central Committee who had spoken against the dual-leadership formula was thus absent at the key meeting in which Bernard Coard was officially informed of the decision* and at which the subsequent steps were mapped out. To speak of a struggle between a "Coard faction" and a "Bishop faction," therefore, is quite misleading. There was no Bishop faction to speak of. Some people on the committee were closer to Bishop than to Coard, but it was not until Bishop was arrested that they started to act, and then in a very haphazard manner.

A key component of Bernard Coard's defense at his trial, as well as that of his supporters, has been his initial refusal at that meeting to accept the dual-leadership formula ("he would like to operate as he presently is forever"), and his seemingly reluctant return to the Central Committee and the Political Bureau. But in fact such action is precisely what one would expect from a skilled practitioner of bureaucratic politics. If Coard had resigned from the committee arguing that his criticism of Bishop had been misconstrued as an attempt to unseat him, one would hardly expect him to appear (for the record) overly anxious to rejoin the committee, displacing Bishop from the chairmanship in the process.

Although he had agreed to do so, after returning from St. Kitt's Bishop stopped attending Central Committee meetings altogether. He thus missed the discussion of the report to be made on the dual-leadership formula to the general membership of the party on 25 September. The latter meeting, chaired by Liam James, started with a report by Ewart Layne on the supposed crisis faced by the revolution. It denounced the "right opportunist" path that had been followed by the Central Committee, included a list of tasks for the party to overcome the crisis, and set forth the dual-leadership formula. The formula was now portrayed as an "acknowledgement of reality existing in our party for the last ten years, and authority is now being given commensurate with responsibility."[28]

Not surprisingly, the members demanded to see Bishop himself. His standing before the membership was compromised by his refusal to attend the meeting as well as by the information conveyed that he had opposed the circulation of the committee minutes to the membership. The members then voted to send delegations to invite both Coard and Bishop to attend the meeting, with Coard arriving almost two hours before Bishop, who arrived twenty minutes later than he told the delegation he would.

Bishop had been hopelessly outvoted in the carefully rehearsed committee meetings, and this was his chance to regain the initiative. His finely honed oratorical skills and personal popularity could have easily been deployed to recapture his previously unquestioned position as the NJM's maximum leader. Sensing the potential weakness of their position, James offered the resignation of the Central Committee majority if the membership voted against the dual-leadership formula. But, as he addressed the meeting, once again Bishop was his own worst enemy. The report of his speech says that "He is now relatively confused and emotional. There are several things that concern him and thus require a lot of mature reflection. He said that he shared the basic CC conclusion on the crisis in the country and party and that the source of the crisis lies in the CC. He added that he firmly believes that the more authority and power one has, the greater responsibility for failure belongs to that person."[29] And, as if that was not enough, "He pointed out that the concept of joint leadership does not bother him because of his history of struggle, especially from 1973, which gave rise to the NJM."

After this, his only weak objection seemed to be one of image rather than of substance: "The masses have their own conception and perception that may not necessarily be like ours who study the science.

Our history shows that the masses build up a personality cult and a single individual." After such a sad performance, his attempts to question the motives of the committee majority were bound to fall on deaf ears. This no doubt was compounded by his announcement that he would withdraw from the Political Bureau and the Central Committee until he had sorted all of this out for himself. This only made him more vulnerable to the charges of "petty-bourgeois individualism," which his adversaries hurled at him with great glee.

Even close supporters of Bishop such as Einstein Louison joined the barrage of criticism to which he was subjected after this ("Cde Bishop lost touch with the reality and him").[30] And after having to endure a long string of quotations from Lenin about democratic centralism and party life, Bishop, apparently won over to dual leadership, finally embraced Coard, and the meeting ended with all members singing the Internationale. Leading party members then went to celebrate the occasion over drinks at Bishop's official residence in Mt. Wheldale.

Bishop than left for Hungary and Czechoslovakia on a trip that, according to his mother, he was reluctant to make but which Bernard Coard insisted he undertake. In Budapest, he was met by George Louison, who expressed shock at Bishop's renewed acceptance of the dual-leadership formula, and persuaded him to do something about it. After an unexpected detour through Havana, Bishop returned to St. George's on 8 October. He found he had been locked out of his official residence and went to see his mother, asking her to call a number of people to tell them that the Coards were planning to kill him. This was apparently part of the strategy Bishop developed with Louison.[31]

At the top of the agenda of the Central Committee meeting to which Bishop was taken on 12 October was the rumor about the Coards' alleged plan to kill Bishop. Although Bishop denied that he was behind it, one of his security guards, Errol George, confirmed that Bishop had instructed people to spread it. Bishop then taped a message that was played on several occasions on Radio Free Grenada denying the accuracy of such rumors, and he was placed under house arrest. The rest is history.

WHY THE COARD MOVE?

One of the crucial puzzles about the Grenadian crisis has been the motivation for the Coard coup. Why would a thirty-nine-year-old economist who had finally been given the opportunity to apply all he had ever learned in his profession as the minister of finance and deputy prime minister of Grenada risk it all for an endeavor so dubious as trying to de facto unseat the revolution's maximum leader? Why would the man whose highly effective economic management was gaining increasing respect for Grenada and for himself throughout the Eastern Caribbean and in international development circles not be content with continuing to lift the island out of underdevelopment, working together in a seemingly unbeatable team he built with Maurice Bishop? Moreover, why would he do this to a friend of twenty years, a man who had been his political mentor, had given him major responsibilities for party work even before Coard formally joined the NJM, brought him from Trinidad to run for Parliament, and who had stood up for Coard through all these years? Why did he feel compelled to devise an esoteric dual-leadership formula that was inherently unworkable, particularly in a West Indian society traditionally characterized by "doctor politics" and parties dominated by charismatic leadership?

The initial widely publicized explanation that the Coard faction was prompted into action by the implicit or explicit support of Cuba or the Soviet Union has by now been found to be baseless.[32] If the Cubans supported anyone it would have been Bishop, who had developed a strong rapport with Fidel Castro. In fact, Bishop visited Castro only days before his arrest, and also met with the Cuban Ambassador to Grenada Julián Torres Rizo, upon his return. He shared with Torres Rizo (but not with Castro) the difficulties the NJM was going through, but did not ask for help. Cuba's condemnation of Bishop's killing and its refusal to provide any support to the Revolutionary Military Council in the wake of the U.S. invasion is proof enough, if such proof is needed, that Havana had nothing to do with the Coard faction's power grab.

As for the Soviets, no evidence has surfaced that they had anything to do with the Grenadian crisis either, despite the many documents seized by the United States in the aftermath of the invasion. There is little doubt about Coard's pro-Soviet sympathies, as indicated by the active cultivation of his Soviet ties during a two-week vacation he took in the Soviet Union with his wife Phyllis and their three children in 1983, and by his presence at Brezhnev's funeral and other such occasions. But documents available on Soviet-Grenadian relations indicate the Soviets were reluctant to commit themselves too much to the PRG, and actually provided relatively little economic (as opposed to military) aid. They also relied mostly on the Cubans to guide them in the finer points of Grenadian politics. When the Soviets finally set up an embassy in St. George's, three years into the PRG, they sent as ambassador a man who spoke no English and knew little about Grenada. The notion that with such a representative the Soviet Union would engage in the Byzantine factional politics of the NJM is very unlikely.

A second explanation for the Coard coup has been the ideological one. More sophisticated than the first, it takes at face value the arguments of the Central Committee majority about the revolution being at a crossroads between the "Marxist-Leninist route" and a "petit bourgeois" or "right-opportunist" path. This is how Coard and his supporters portrayed the situation facing the NJM and the PRG in the fall of 1983; their better command of Marxist-Leninist categories coupled with the reverential awe with which Bishop and those close to him regarded Leninist analysis certainly helped Coard gain the upper hand when it came to ideological discussions. The evidence does indicate that on a number of issues the Coards took a much harsher, Stalinist line than did Bishop.[33] But what is most striking about the discussions of the Central Committee and the Political Bureau of the New Jewel Movement that are available is that *no differences existed among the party leadership as to the pace or general direction of the revolutionary process.*

In marked contrast with other processes of socialist transition, such as those in Jamaica and Chile (where issues such as the actual size of the public sector, the level and intensity of popular mobilization, and the relationship to be developed with international financial agencies such as the International Monetary Fund were the subject of heated, often public debates among leading government officials and party members), no such debate ever took place within the NJM. There seems in fact to have existed a very strong agreement among Bishop, Coard, and other party and PRG officials as to what was to be done at the state level— policies they tended to identify with the "national-democratic" stage of the revolution. Both Bernard Coard and George Louison have stated that there were no substantive policy differences, no two wings within the higher party organs.[34] Again in marked contrast with the other processes of transition to socialism in the Americas, the political opposition in Grenada had receded into the background and posed no threat to the PRG. In this context, the notion of the "imminent disintegration of the Revolution" is particularly odd and inappropriate.

This is not to say that the PRG was without difficulties in the summer and fall of 1983 or that party members did not have differing perceptions as to how to deal with them. The single most important problem confronting the NJM was that it had remained an extremely small, secretive organization, for which the burden of managing the state apparatus, setting up new programs, and developing mechanisms of popular participation and mobilization was getting to be simply too heavy a burden. "The most fundamental mistake [we made] was that we continued to run the NJM as an underground party" as one former leader put it.[35] The paradox here is that the Coard faction "solution" to this problem would only have made it worse, by calling for greater selectivity in party membership, tighter party discipline, and greater "Leninist staunchness."

Another apparent puzzle relates to the timing of the Central Committee majority decision to strip Maurice Bishop of much of his authority on the basis of the supposed crisis facing the revolution. In June 1983 Bishop had concluded a successful visit to the United States. One byproduct of this had been a toning down of rhetoric between Grenada and the United States—which had reached a high point in the spring, with President Reagan's repeated references to Grenada as a security threat to the United States. In July, after much delay, a constitutional commission, headed by Trinidadian lawyer Allan Alexander, had been appointed. Its goal was to prepare a draft constitution and consultations with the Grenadian people—a preliminary step to holding elections scheduled for 1985, two years hence. Also in July, the World Bank and the IMF had given the PRG a clean bill of health and signed new financial agreements with Grenada.

Most important, the inauguration of the Point Salines Airport, Grenada's largest public work ever, was just six months away. Timed to coincide with the fifth anniversary of the revolution on 13 March 1984, its inauguration would have brought to an end the cash flow problems some government agencies were experiencing because of the heavy drain on public resources imposed by the airport construction. It would also, of course, have been a boon to Grenada's tourism and export capabilities. Most significantly, it would have given a great boost to the PRG's popularity, effectively consolidating the NJM's rule and Maurice Bishop's own leadership.[36] Neither the domestic political situation, the international position of the revolution, nor substantive programmatic differences within the NJM can plausibly be advanced as having triggered the joint leadership proposal and the ensuing party crisis.

Arguably, somewhat different conceptions existed among the party leadership as to what the nature and character of the party should have been. Coard and his supporters stood for a "vanguardist," Leninist party structure, and Maurice Bishop embodied a more populist, mass-based, conception of what the NJM was all about. But these differences had existed since the mid-seventies, and the party had been able to live with them. Moreover, Bishop's willingness to have Coard chair the all-powerful Organizing Committee since its creation in 1978 and his well-known tendency to defer to Coard in matters of party discipline and organization (one of the reasons the NJM had remained such a small and selective cadre party even four-and-a-half years into the revolution) had led to a situation in which Coard's conception of the party was beginning to prevail. To risk it all for the sake of a dubious dual-leadership proposal makes little sense, until we factor in Coard's own personality.

Despite the obviously crucial role played by Bernard Coard in the final crisis of the revolution, a satisfactory explanation of his behavior during that period is unavailable. Reductionist portraits of a dyed-in-the-wool Stalinist lack credibility when applied to a minister of finance whose economic policy was marked by an extraordinary degree of pragmatism and accommodation to market forces. A simplistic explanation blaming the revolution's self-destruction on the uncontrolled power urge of Bernard Coard are difficult to reconcile with accounts attesting to the careful, methodical planning and strategic thinking that characterized Bernard Coard as a politician and economist, a man with a highly developed "sense of reality" and of "how things work."[37]

It is natural for people involved in politics to want to have more rather than less power. But what is striking about Bernard Coard's bid for power in revolutionary Grenada in the fall of 1983 is how irrational it was—the equivalent of a Stalin attempting to unseat Lenin in 1921, Jou En-lai challenging Mao Ze-dong in 1953, or Carlos Rafael Rodríguez trying to displace Fidel Castro in 1963. Moreover, that this should be attempted by a man so personally unpopular among his fellow Grenadians as Coard makes it even more puzzling. Wasn't Coard aware that his challenge to Bishop's leadership would meet the widespread disapproval it was met with by the Grenadian people—translating itself into slogans such as *B for Bishop and Betterment, C for Coard and Communism,* and culminating in the stoning of Coard and his wife in the bus on the way to the St. George's court, when they were put on trial for the murder of Maurice Bishop?[38]

That a trained social scientist who had written about the dynamics of small-island politics[39] would so grossly miscalculate the reaction of public opinion in his attempt to unseat the revolution's *líder máximo* requires an explanation beyond the normal urge and drive for power characterizing many political leaders. "What the party needs is not guidance but a psychiatrist," Bernard Coard told George Louison on 17 October 1983, in a revealing remark leading us to the one area of the October crisis that has remained almost unexplored—the psychology of its leading protagonists.[40]

Relying on Harold Lasswell's notion of the "power seeker" as a man who pursues power in an effort to overcome low self-esteem, as well as on Alexander George's refinement of Lasswell's concept, we will introduce Bernard Coard's personality structure as an essential link in the chain of circumstances leading to the crisis of the Grenadian Revolution and its ultimate demise.[41] It is my contention that by dissecting Coard's complex personality it will be possible to unravel the strange sequence of events of September-October 1983 in Grenada.

Bernard Coard shows the classic symptoms of a compulsive character structure: his obsession with party discipline and "heavy manners" (harsh treatment); his continuous efforts to impose his own highly demanding work habits and standards within the Ministry of Finance, the government, and the party at large; his almost total lack of humor; his permanent feeling of being overworked; and his coolly calculating manner of dealing with people, who were seen not as party comrades or citizens but simply as instruments to be used for the leader's goals and objectives. These are all features of a compulsive personality: striving for power in an effort to compensate for early childhood deprivation and feelings low self-esteem.

As Lasswell puts it, "The compulsive inclines toward carefully defined limits and the well-worked-out ordering of parts . . . [His] hallmark is the imposition of uniformity. . . . The compulsive desubjectivizes a situation, denies novelty, squeezes and compresses the dimension of human structure."[42] It is not difficult to trace to this compulsiveness the signs of Coard's frustrations and his repeated complaints about the "lack of fit" between Leninist party discipline and the behavior of his fellow New Jewel Members.

As George argues, one of the hallmarks of a power-seeking personality is the development of a "sphere of competence," an area in which his authority will be unquestioned. This allows the person to demonstrate his worth—particularly important in someone suffering from a sense of personal inadequacy. In the case of Bernard Coard, this particular sphere of competence became Marxist-Leninist doctrine and party organization. He quickly emerged as the undisputed authority on the subject within the NJM. Teaching Saturday classes on the subject, assigning reading lists to party comrades, planning socialism classes for civil servants, and providing programmatic input into major party statements such as the Line of March speech, he became firmly settled into the role of party theoretician.[43] On the other hand, he was content to leave foreign affairs in the hands of other people and would often allow his deputy, Lyden Ramdhanny, to represent him at important international meetings and negotiations.

One of the six items of behavior listed by George as possible indicators of a "striving for power gratification on the part of a compensation-seeking personality,"[44] was particularly prominent in Bernard Coard: the wish to create and impose orderly systems upon others in the political arena. From his positions on the Organizing Committee, the Political Bureau, and the Central Committee, he kept trying to build a highly centralized, hierarchical, elitist party structure in accord with his own strict interpretation of Leninist doctrine. His unilateral decisions while Bishop was abroad and his reluctance to even inform Bishop about such decisions once they were made were part of the same pattern of behavior.

Showing the existence of a strong power urge is not sufficient to provide an adequate test of Lasswell's hypothesis. One must also show that the actual exercise of power produces the sort of euphoric feelings that compensate for the subject's low self-esteem.[45] For example, feelings of unimportance should manifest themselves in a euphoric sense of uniqueness, of being indispensable. This was very much the case with Bernard Coard: "He was tired and sick of being the only hatchetman and of criticizing. The failure of CC comrades was to speak up freely, as a result he concluded that he was the main fetter to the development of the CC because everyone was depending on him for everything, especially in the area of the economy."[46]

And in the midst of the unraveling of the Grenadian Revolution (with Bishop already under house arrest), according to one account, "Coard by that time had tasted the power he always wanted and was relishing it. Both he and Strachan were in good moods, puffing cigars while the negotiations were going on."[47]

The intensity of Coard's convictions and his strength of will ("a real bulldozer" in the words of a former supervisor)[48] also confirms the compulsive nature of his character. His contempt for the Grenadian people revealed during and after the crisis also indicates that his commitment to socialism arose less from a commitment to people then out of his self-aggrandizing drives.[49]

The question remains regarding the origins of Bernard Coard's low self-esteem that propelled this extraordinary compensatory response. Bernard Coard had, by Grenadian standards, a privileged childhood as the son of a respected civil servant. What caused such feelings of personal inadequacy in such a highly intelligent man? Coard's father provides evidence regarding this in his rather candid memoirs.[50] Straying from the typically self-congratulatory tone of the genre, in *Bitter-sweet and Spice: Those Things I Remember,* Frederick McDermott Coard reveals as much about his inner self as about life in the colonial service in Grenada during the first half of the twentieth century.

"McKie," as he was affectionately called by his friends, was in many ways the ultimate colonial clerk. With a passion for order, for numbers ("I have always loved figures and was happy compiling statistics")[51] and for discipline, he was willing to go to extraordinary lengths to earn that extra bonus or to qualify for yet another promotion, however small. He served in all government departments and in all island parishes; as he put it, he had a child born in every parish.

Paradoxically, for a man who rose from the position of printer's apprentice to the top of the island's colonial civil service, his memoirs above all reflect bitterness and self-pity ("I was always the pawn in the game. I was always the sufferer").[52] He felt he was always discriminated against because of his color.

"Boys of fair complexion had a monopoly on the best jobs available, whether they were capable of filling them or not . . . boys of dark pigmentation had to make greater efforts to get anywhere."[53] He felt he was overworked and that he was constantly passed over for promotions he deserved. He felt particular resentment about having to work under people he considered to be less qualified than he was ("somehow or other I always seemed to have been in the way of certain officers who were slightly senior to me . . . it is a bad thing to be qualified and have to work under seniors who are not so qualified").[54]

F. M. Coard transmitted to his son not only a strong achievement need but also the unconscious self-hate of a talented black man who was frustrated in his career by what he considered to be racial prejudice and discrimination based on his humble origins.

What is most extraordinary is the degree to which Bernard Coard identified with his father. While it is common for a father who sets high standards for himself to enhance his children's superego as well as such character traits as self-discipline and stubbornness, it is far less common to transmit an interest in the *substance* of the activities the father engages in. Yet that is what happened in the case of Frederick and Bernard Coard. Both loved statistics and files. Both had a special interest in the economic aspect of public affairs. The Ministry of Finance under Coard was the postcolonial version of the Grenadian Department of the Treasury, in which his father served for many years, reaching the position of acting colonial treasurer.[55] Both bureaucrats to the core, the colonial civil service was to the father what the party was to the son. Their great skill as organization men reveals itself in the extent to which they mastered the "rules of the game" to rise and gain control in organizations, despite having entered them with heavy handicaps—the father's lack of formal education and the son's status as a latecomer to the NJM.

The litany of complaints by father and son about their fellow clerks or party comrades is also similar. Compare the comment by Bernard Coard in 1983 to that of his father years earlier: "For some periods of time, the PB was not functioning—no agenda, no recording of decisions; [Bernard Coard] found that he could not take those long meetings for no reason at all."[56] Frederick Coard wrote in his 1970 book, "Thus I got out of this office, which was in a miserable condition insofar as records were concerned: It was indiscipline. I found the staff a most undisciplined one."[57]

Along with this went a set of poorly developed social skills—again a common feature of compulsive personalities, which tend to dehumanize self-other relations. As F. M. Coard put it, "I have often tried to think out the reasons for my being so persistently overlooked. Sometimes I ask myself: was it because I was too outspoken (some persons have attributed this to be the reason). Was it because I was not the servile flatterer in words by words, or worse, by deeds? Was it because I had no social glands and therefore was not a social climber?"[58] And as Bernard Coard put it at his trial, "I am a very blunt person. I say things as I see them. I don't take nonsense. . . . Who vex, vex. . . . I always speak my mind. People always know where they stand with me. I'm a plain speaker. I don't *shu-shu* and I don't like gossip. I can't take *tay-bay*."[59]

It is in the context of this strong unconscious identification with his father that we must examine the impact of his father's greatest frustration—the disappointment of a lifetime—on Bernard Coard. Justifiably or not, Bernard's father felt he had given a lifetime to the colonial service but that his merits had never been properly recognized:

> My work in all Departments of the Service had always been maintained at a high standard and up-to-date. My character had been an unblemished one. As I went from parish to parish I had always played a leading role in the social and cultural life of the various communities in which I worked, whether it was in games, concerts, literary or musical pursuits. . . . Yet, on reflection I cannot say that I have reaped the reward such devoted service merited. . . . Even in the evening of my days I was denied the honor of filling the Office of Comptroller of Income Tax.[60]

Thirty years later, his seventh child found himself in a position strikingly similar to the one described by his father. He was the subordinate of Maurice Bishop, a light-skinned man from an established St. George's family, a graduate of prestigious Presentation College, and a man whom Coard regarded as his intellectual inferior. This was similar to the situation experienced by his father, who felt he had always been placed in positions below people whose main assets were lighter skin, family connections, and social graces, rather than bureaucratic skills.

It is easy to see how the length and nature of the relationship between Bishop and Coard must have been a source of deep frustration and resentment for Bernard Coard. Coard had apparently been bent on becoming prime minister of Grenada from his early twenties, an aspiration in which he was also encouraged by his wife.[61] As a medium-height, bespectacled, fat man with an unimposing presence and a cold, calculating demeanor, his appearance and personality were in direct contrast with Maurice Bishop's. Bishop was everything Coard was not: tall, handsome, popular, an inspired and inspiring public speaker, a man who had come to his leadership position in a spontaneous, natural fashion. Coard may have been respected at home and abroad because of his managerial abilities, but it was Bishop who received the accolades and the recognition. It was he who received the ovations at the public meetings.

Moreover, the possibility of anybody succeeding Bishop within the foreseeable future, be it Bernard Coard or someone else, was exceedingly slim. Once the revolution had become fully consolidated, as it clearly was on its way of doing in the summer of 1983, Maurice Bishop, at age thirty-nine, could have ruled Grenada for a generation, much as Eric Williams in Trinidad or Fidel Castro in Cuba.

The prospect of spending the rest of his professional life, as had his father, in the relative obscurity below the very top of the political structure, doing the legwork for somebody else yet never receiving proper recognition for his effort and talent, was surely unbearable to Bernard Coard. To live in the shadow of Maurice Bishop, whose father was a martyr of the anti-Gairy struggle and who had once employed Bernard's father as a clerk, was unacceptable.[62]

The increasing anxiety suffered by Bernard Coard over the last year of the revolution (an anxiety expressed in overeating and ensuing back problems) is not difficult to explain. The considerable skills with which he had applied himself to the pursuit of political power had only whetted his appetite for even more recognition and achievement; as James Mc-Gregor Burns has observed, ambition feeds on skill.[63] Yet an insurmountable obstacle stood between Bernard Coard and his goal: Maurice Bishop.

The ensuing frustration thus led to a classic conflict between Coard's superego and his ego. Unable to cope with a situation that, if left to itself, would have denied him—perhaps for decades—the full measure of political power and public recognition Coard felt he deserved, and facilitated by the relatively unstructured situation Grenada found itself in at the time, Coard's ego-defensive mechanisms came to the fore.[64] The absence of elections, of reliable public opinion polls, or even of opposition media made it easy for political actors to impute whatever they saw fit to the existing political situation and the future prospects of the PRG.

It was the emergence of these ego-defensive mechanisms—essentially rationalizations that deny, falsify, or distort reality—that allowed Bernard Coard to manage the inner conflict between his high achievement needs and the hard reality of Maurice Bishop's presence at the helm of the revolution. The public emergence of these rationalizations allow us to explain the oscillation between consummate political skill and catastrophic ineptness that characterized Bernard Coard's behavior from October 1982 to October 1983. All the subtlety and dexterity he showed in orchestrating the removal of Bishop's closest supporters in the Central Committee and the Political Bureau, and packing these party organs with former OREL members, were put in the service of an untenable proposition: the dual-leadership proposal. His successful efforts to secure the support of the party and the army against the revolution's *líder máximo* were based on the absurd assumption that the Grenadian people would willingly accept the substitution of their hero by an apparatchik. But once Grenadians had made plain they stood fully behind Bishop and began demonstrating in the streets, Coard's refusal to budge and his proposal that Bishop go off to Cuba to "cool it for a while" show a man out of touch with reality. Such wishful thinking—which is the most fitting description for Coard's actions during this period—is a classic manifestation of reality distortion produced by a frustrated superego.

Harold Lasswell has observed that one of the most disturbing facts about compulsiveness is that it occurs under the guise of apparently plausible arguments.[65] Bernard Coard's rationalization of his own inner conflicts—particularly those relating to the supposed crisis of the revolution and the presumed rationality of the dual-leadership formula—were so convincing that they even managed initially to persuade Maurice Bishop. Yet, what is most tragic about Bernard Coard's compulsiveness is that up to a point it constituted a valuable political asset of the PRG. The disciplined, thorough, and high systematic approach to economic and political management it brought about was one important reason why the PRG managed to do so much in its relatively short time in power. The role of minister of finance, never popular in any government, seemed cut out for Bernard Coard. He had the economic acumen to understand what had to be done to keep the Grenadian economy afloat while moving toward socialism, and the political will to take the necessary measures, however unpopular or unorthodox they may have seemed. The very businesslike, calculating behavior that made him such a first-rate apparatchik, however, rendered him totally unsuitable for becoming prime minister—particularly since it meant displacing one of the most charismatic leaders ever seen in the Eastern Caribbean.

It is Bernard Coard's ironic fate that, in his determination to avoid the obscurity and bitterness with which his father ended his professional life, he brought upon himself worldwide recognition as the main culprit for the abortion of the Grenadian Revolution.

WHY BISHOP'S NONRESPONSE?

If Bernard Coard's unchecked achievement needs provide us with the most coherent explanation for the onset of the Grenadian Revolution's final crisis, they do not fully account for its outcome. However Pyrrhic and short-lived his victory may have been, how did Coard manage to unseat Maurice Bishop, expel him from the party and the government, and have him put under arrest?

Many commentators have stressed the degree to which Coard and his accolytes were out of touch with Grenadian reality,[66] isolated from the sentiments of the Grenadian people, toward whom Coard ultimately revealed his contempt. Yet, if Maurice Bishop was so much more in touch with the feelings and aspirations of the Grenadian people, why was he unable to turn back the challenge to his leadership and reassert his own command of the revolutionary process? The fact is, as Kendrick Radix put it, "he did absolutely nothing to reverse the situation."[67] Why?

The answer has two parts. First, the leadership style developed by Maurice Bishop over the years left him particularly vulnerable to the attack he experienced in the fall of 1983. Contrary to the allegations of "onemanism" and the "development of a personality cult" that the Coard faction used to justify its assault on Bishop's leadership (echoed by commentators who should have known better), Bishop's approach to political management was based on consensus and accommodation rather than on the imposition of his own perspective. "His outstanding feature as a leader was his consensual leadership. He refused to proceed by enforcing his opinions. . . . He didn't develop a conceit of personal pre-eminence and unassailability," was the way a long-time associate put it.[68] And, in the words of another, "if you had one dissenting voice, he would try to obtain a consensus on the situation."[69]

The reasons for this democratic approach to leadership, so different from the West Indian tradition of "doctor politics," were expressed by Bishop himself, as reported in the minutes of the General Membership meeting: "Maybe his conception of leadership is idealistic, because of the historical abuse of power and one-man leadership. He and his contemporaries have a distaste for one-man leadership, and he has a strong position on this."[70] Such an approach meshed with Bishop's own perception of himself as a believer in causes rather than as a politician. As discussed above, he did not enter politics to obtain power and personal recognition. Given his background and professional activities, politics in fact meant sacrifice of the comfortable and socially prominent lifestyle he could have enjoyed as one of St. George's premier lawyers.

Commendable as his intentions may have been in this regard, the net result of such an approach was not always positive: "When he stood up and articulated the position of the revolution, people saw that as being a strong leader. I disagree with that. I don't think he was that strong. One shortcoming of Maurice Bishop was that he was overaccommodating as a leader. He didn't want to offend people, and therefore his own beliefs and positions were often compromised."[71]

It is this particular approach to leadership by consensus that allows us to explain Bishop's tolerance of Coard's outrageous actions in his absence (e.g, the closing of the *Torchlight*), and his acquiescence to Coard's insistence that Grenada support the Soviet position on Afghanistan in the United Nations, possibly the single most damaging step taken by Grenada in its foreign relations during the PRG. Instead of affirming his point of view and exercising authority, Bishop was chronically inclined to compromise for the sake of collective leadership, party unity, and survival of the revolution, which became the main criticism of Bishop leveled by Grenadians (see table 7.2). Ironically, it was this approach that opened the door for Bernard Coard's challenge, the party's split, and the demise of the revolution.

Bishop's disregard for his own personal political resource base is also highlighted by the extraordinary degree to which he allowed the Coard faction to displace those closest to him from the party and from key decisionmaking positions in the government, a subject discussed above. Rather than looking out for "his own men and women," he left the filling of crucial positions, such as his personal assistant, in party hands. During the last year of the revolution he had to manage without a personal assistant, as repeated calls to the Central Committee and the Political Bureau to find him one went unheeded.

Without a vacation for the duration of the PRG and with his marriage having broken up in the early years of the revolution, Maurice Bishop aged visibly from 1979 to 1983. The youthful leader of 1979 turned into a weary, gray-haired man by 1983. This leads to the second aspect of Bishop's seeming resignation in the face of the challenge by the Coard faction. Even if his leadership style opened the door to that challenge, making it difficult for Bishop to re-assert his authority after having allowed its steady erosion for so long, why at some point did he not cut his losses and fight back? Why did he procrastinate, leaving the impression that his critics were right after all? What happened to the determined and wily Maurice Bishop of the anti-Gairy struggle? What happened to the skilled coalition builder of the Popular Alliance days, or to the deft diplomat who had won over most of the skeptical Caribbean heads of government, thus developing a critical breathing space for the PRG within the Caribbean Community?

This puzzle is compounded by the resignation that gripped him once he was put under house arrest. "They had me down as one of the conspirators. They killed my father, and if they kill me it can't be helped," he told his mother in one of her two visits.[72] And even after the Grenadian people stormed his residence to release him and marched

Table 7.2
What People Disliked About Bishop's Leadership

Factor	Number	Percentage
Softness toward party rivals	59	26.2
Lack of rights	49	21.8
Communism	37	16.4
Presence of guns	29	12.9
Other	51	22.7
Total	225	100.0

Source: Emmanuel, Brathwaite, and Barriteau, *Political Change*, p. 25.

through St. George's to Fort Rupert, Bishop was less a leader determined to save the revolution than a man ready to spell out his own obituary. Merle Hodge, an eyewitness, was interviewed by a journalist of a Barbadian newspaper: "Asked if she saw a caucus in which Bishop and his supporters were trying to plan some form of action, Hodge replied: 'No, Maurice was just kinda smoking and pacing.' "[73] Bishop himself said: "My reason for coming here, you know. Radio Free Grenada is off the air, the telephone is also off, and I would like to contact my people of Grenada and the rest of the world. And when I finish speaking to them, I can die."[74] When told he would be executed, Bishop just took a deep sigh, folded his arms, turned around, and four of the PRG soldiers were used to execute the people."[75]

There is some evidence that Maurice Bishop had a strong fatalist streak in him. When he lived in London a Hungarian seer had told him he would become very famous and then die at the age of thirty-nine. When people told him not to smoke so much, for example, he would reply, "That is not what I am going to die from." And he cried upon saying goodbye to his children on their return to Canada in August 1983, perhaps a premonition he would not see them again.[76] But while such superstituous beliefs may have contributed to the detachment with which he watched the encroachment on his leadership, the ultimate cause must be sought elsewhere.

The pattern that emerges from direct interviews with friends and relatives is that of a man "fiercely loyal to his friends and political associates, putting them even above his family."[77] Bonds developed in the nine years of the anti-Gairy struggle between him and people like Selwyn Strachan, Hudson Austin, and Kendrick Radix were extremely deep; so was the loyalty Bishop believed existed between himself and Bernard Coard. In fact, he repeatedly defended Bernard Coard against the accusations voiced within the NJM of factionalism and of efforts to undermine his authority. Bishop dismissed the repeated warnings by his family about the Coards' designs; he just couldn't conceive that his own selfless commitment to the revolutionary cause was not shared equally by his party colleagues. When it finally dawned on him what was going on, "he couldn't fight people that he considered to be his fraternal friends. When these people turned on him, it destroyed part of his inner self. . . . He was destroyed by the volte face that took place."[78] His sister Ann, in fact, doubts that he would have been able to go on, had he *not* been executed, given the psychological wounds he had already suffered.

CONCLUSION

A common inference drawn from the Grenadian experience has been that it was the excessively personalized leadership of the revolution that opened the doors to the final crisis. According to this reasoning, it was the lack of established institutional structures outside the ruling party that made the revolution crumble when the internal NJM struggle erupted.[79] Although there is something to be said for this argument, it fails to address the real issue. The evidence indicates that the crisis erupted precisely at the moment when the revolution was about to consolidate. The buildup of those institutions, through the constitutional commission appointed in July 1983 and the elections to be held in the wake of the constitutional consultation process, had just started. It is difficult to escape the conclusion that the timing of the Coard faction's bid for power was to designed to avoid the institutionalization and consolidation of Maurice Bishop's rule, in which case, blaming the failure of the revolution on its lack of institutionalization is a non sequitur. In some sense, the revolution failed *because* it was about to institutionalize itself. A variant of this argument addresses the need to establish "a series of checks and balances over the charismatic leader rather than waiting until he has so completely and singly captured the loyalty of the masses that any checks on him would be viewed as a personal confrontation."[80]

At the core of this perspective lies the belief that charismatic leadership, "one-manism" in West Indian lingo, is a dangerous threat to processes of social and political change and that it has to be curtailed at any expense. Ironically, such arguments have been voiced as frequently by constitutionalists in the name of defending the Westminster system as by socialists in the name of collective leadership and "democratic centralism," by outspoken critics of the Grenadian Revolution such as V. S. Naipaul, as well as by ostensibly Leninist participants in the revolution, such as Chalkie Ventour.[81]

What I would posit is precisely the opposite. In the Caribbean, but also in other small Third World societies, where political institutions are weak to begin with, charismatic leadership can be a precious, vital resource in the transition to socialism. The process of legitimizing the revolutionary process, of having the population identify with the goals of social and economic change, of mobilizing people for the enormous task of nation building and basic economic development such a process entails are all greatly facilitated by the actions of a charismatic leader able to articulate the needs and aspirations of the common people. This is precisely what Maurice Bishop did so ably in Grenada from 1979 to 1983.

Such a leader cannot, of course, be wished or decreed into existence. But if he happens to be present at the helm of the transition process, he ought to be recognized for what he is—an extraordinary asset to the forces struggling for social change. This is not to say that mass organizations and mechanisms of popular participation ought not to be de-

veloped and institutionalized to the fullest. They remain the best guarantee against the reversal of revolutionary gains and achievements;
politically, they are what socialism is all about. But no successful
transition to socialism has been led by committee. Failure to recognize
that was the tragic mistake of Bernard Coard and his followers.

Calls for limiting a charismatic leader's powers and for otherwise
curtailing his prerogatives as the revolution's *líder máximo* in fact limit
his ability to mobilize and organize the population in situations in
which, as Samuel Huntington so cogently put it, "the problem is not
to seize power but to make power,"[82] Naive calls for the dispersal of
power in such processes of change fail to come to grips with the fact
that to bring about change in developing societies *political power has to
be created and concentrated before it can be dispersed.* The existence of a
charismatic leader *and* a well-organized political party are two vital
instruments in that endeavor.

To recognize how much of an asset for the transition process a
charismatic leader can be is imperative for party leaders and activists and
also for the charismatic leader himself; in this, Maurice Bishop ultimately
failed. Such recognition implies the leader understands the need for
constant and careful nurturing of his own personal political resources,
the protection of "his own men and women," the clamping down on
any opposition forces bent on unseating him (both outside and inside
the party), and an acutely developed early warning system to detect
impending challenges to his rule.

The nature of Grenadian political culture, which has traditionally
prized charismatic leadership, the huge size of the tasks of social and
economic development faced by the PRG, and the very real (although
by no means unsurmountable) difficulties faced by the NJM in 1983 all
put a premium on the sort of heroic leadership Bishop exercised. But
despite his enormous rapport with the people, his ability to put complicated matters in simple, straightforward terms everyone could understand, and his capacity to project a vision as to where Grenada was
headed, the *performance* of his role as revolutionary leader failed in this
crucial aspect—the ruler's imperative "to look out for number one."
His self-confidence arose from a privileged social background. It was
reinforced in the sunny halls of Presentation College, where an elite
ambiance and the majestic views of St. George's couldn't fail to instill
in its pupils the feeling that they belonged to the top of Grenadian
society. Bishop's open, friendly disposition led him to fully trust the
small circle of party comrades who had borne the brunt of the anti-
Gairy struggle. That very struggle and socialist ideology, in turn, made
him suspicious of "one-manism"—thus his leadership by consensus and
compromise rather than by principle and personal assertiveness.

But the net result of all this was that Maurice Bishop progressively became an unwitting but no less real hostage to his party rivals. He distanced himself more and more from his pre-PRG friends, even endorsing the jailing of many of them—like his former law partner Tillman Thomas. He paid no attention to his family's warnings about the Coards and brusquely dismissed the advice of visiting friendly Caribbean leaders, like Tim Hector, about the dangers of militarization.[83] His ability to acquire and process relevant information about the political and economic situation thus came to depend more and more on what was provided to him by the NJM inner circle. A political leader's crucial quality, his ability to diagnose and consequently act on a given situation was thus severely compromised. It should not be surprising, therefore, that he took at face value the self-serving depiction of the supposed "imminent disintegration of the revolution" painted by Liam James in August and September of 1983.

The maintenance and development of independence sources of advice and information are an important part of a political leader's survival strategy. Bishop's abdication of the management of his own personal political affairs is indicated by his repeated (and finally unfulfilled) requests to the party to provide him with a personal assistant. His heeding Bernard Coard's suggestion that he go to Hungary and Czechoslovakia, when it was clear he needed to stay in Grenada and reassert his leadership of the party and the government, was particularly self-defeating. Thus when it came to the final showdown triggered by the dual-leadership proposal, Maurice Bishop was totally unprepared to face Coard's challenge.

Although his crucial political asset—his enormous popularity—remained intact, his political style effectively eroded other personal political resources he could have called upon. Those closest to him were a minority in the party's ruling bodies, and his authority within the party had been diminished by his tolerance of Coard's actions in his absence. His naivete in openly admitting his shortcomings as measured against the Leninist gospel made it easy to hurl the same vague and contradictory charges against him again. All this made it very difficult for him to beat back his adversaries' challenge on their preferred terrain—the internal party bodies. And the half-hearted attempts to do so outside the party were singularly inept and self-defeating, like spreading the rumor about the Coards' supposed plan to assassinate him.

The reason for Bishop not doing the obvious thing once he was outflanked within the party's Central Committee (that is, prepare an energetic appeal to the general membership, and if need be, to the population at large) was that he lacked motivation, the other key ingredient in any power struggle. Bishop's spirit was broken by the realization that his friend of twenty years, about whom so many people had warned him, was out to get him.

In the final analysis, charismatic leaders of revolutionary processes in the Third World must realize that *no party or group of party comrades can rank higher than the process of socialist transition itself.* The survival of this process, particularly in its initial stages, may often be closely associated with the political survival of the charismatic leader himself. That Maurice Bishop understood this imperfectly sealed his fate and that of the Grenadian Revolution.

NOTES

Research for this chapter was financed by a grant from the Faculty Research Program of the University of Puerto Rico, Mayagüez. The author would particularly like to thank Dr. Juan González, who has headed that program for many years and who has done so much to facilitate faculty research. I would also like to thank Dr. Eric Phoebus, of the psychology faculty of UPR-Mayagüez, for his extensive comments on an earlier version of this chapter.

1. The most detailed narrative of the crisis can be found in Tony Thorndike, *Grenada Politics, Economics and Society* (Boulder: Lynne Rienner, 1985), pt. 3. The events are also described in Gordon K. Lewis, *Grenada: The Jewel Despoiled* (Baltimore: Johns Hopkins University Press, 1987), chs, 8, 9, and 10. For a pro-Coard interpretation, see Kai Schoenhals, "The Road to Fort Rupert: The Grenadian Revolution's Final Crisis," CISCLA Working Paper 28 (San Germán, Puerto Rico: Inter American University, 1986). For a pro-Bishop analysis, see Steve Clark, "The Second Assassination of Maurice Bishop," *New International* 6 (1987), pp. 11–98.

2. This biographical sketch is based on interviews carried out in Grenada with friends and relatives of Maurice Bishop in Dec. 1984 and Aug. 1987. It also draws on a number of interviews published in the Caribbean press, the most informative of which is the one done by Alister Hughes, "Maurice Bishop—Premier in the Spotlight," *Caribbean Life and Times Magazine*, Dec. 1979.

3. Bishop's considerable interest in Africa would manifest itself later in the active role he took in the celebration of African Liberation Day in Grenada and his membership in the Caribbean African Liberation Support Committee, his first exposure to international solidarity organizations. In fact, the first head of state to visit Grenada after the revolution was Kenneth Kaunda, president of Zambia, in Sept. 1979.

4. A picture taken of Maurice upon being sworn in as a lawyer in London shows him in an obviously rented, ill-fitting suit. According to his mother, Rupert Bishop bought his son several suits on a visit to London, but Maurice Bishop never wore them. Interview with Alimenta Bishop, St. Paul, 29 Aug. 1987.

5. Quoted in the *Nation* (Barbados), 20 Oct. 1983.

6. This paragraph is based on an interview with Maurice Bishop's sister

Ann, who worked in his office as a secretary. Interview with Ann Bishop, St. Paul, 29 Aug. 1987.

7. Maurice Bishop died a pauper, leaving only the proceeds of a small life insurance policy as his sole material legacy to his wife and children.

8. Interview with Einstein Louison, St. George's, 29 Aug. 1987.

9. One person in the crowd overheard this and later told it to Ann Bishop. Interview with Ann Bishop.

10. Ibid.

11. Interview with Allan LaGrenade, St. George's, 28 Aug. 1987.

12. Interview with Lyden Ramdhanny, former deputy minister of Finance and minister of Tourism of the PRG, Grenville, 30 Aug. 1987.

13. Although no indicators to measure Bishop's popularity during the PRG are available, a poll undertaken in Nov. 1984, with Grenada still under U.S. military occupation, showed that 86.2 percent of respondents reported being favorably disposed toward Bishop's leadership, vis-à-vis 13.8 percent who were not. See Patrick Emmanuel, Farley Brathwaite, and Eudine Barriteau, *Political Change and Public Opinion in Grenada, 1979–1984,* ISER Occasional Paper 19 (Cave Hill, Barbados: University of the West Indies, 1986), p. 24.

14. Bernard Coard, *How the West Indian Child Is Made Educationally Subnormal in the British School System* (London: New Beacon Books, 1971).

15. "Economic Memorandum on Grenada," *World Bank Report* 294P-GRD, 12 May 1980, p. 12.

16. This section draws partially on the wealth of evidence produced by Clark, "Second Assassination," in this regard.

17. Minutes of Political Bureau meeting of 17 June 1981, in Michael Ledeen and Herbert Romerstein, eds., *Grenada Documents: An Overview and Selection,* vol. 1 (Washington, D.C.: Depts of State and Defense, 1984), p. 56. Hereafter, this volume is referred to as *Grenada Documents.* Coard's position and that of his sympathizers has been that all these personnel changes were undertaken in the name of greater effectiveness and efficiency. In the case of Kendrick Radix, who allowed many of the fishing boats that Cuba had donated to sink in St. George's harbor, this may have been justified. But it didn't follow that those removed from certain government positions had also to be expelled from the Political Bureau and the Central Committee, mostly at Coard's instigation. A double standard was also at work. One of the NJM's greatest failures was its inability to develop greater support in the extremely small Grenada industrial working class. One of the key people in charge of that task was OREL member John "Chalkie" Ventour. He was ill much of the time but was handsomely rewarded for his ineffectiveness by his promotion to the NJM's Political Bureau in Oct. 1982. And the difficulties of the National Women's Organization in 1983 were not blamed on the person in charge of the NWO, Phyllis Coard, but on Maurice Bishop.

18. *Grenada Documents,* Document 105, Minutes of Central Committee meeting, October 12–15, 1982.

19. Interview with Alimenta Bishop.

20. Interview with Allan LaGrenade.

21. On 23 Aug. 1981, the Trinidad tabloid *Bomb* said "Coard is poised to replace Bishop. . . . Bishop is fighting for his political life. . . . Informed sources inside the Spice Island have told 'Bomb' that Bishop has been forced to go along with Coard with certain decisions even if he does not agree with them."

22. Gordon Lewis endorses Don Rojas's explanation of the crisis in terms of Coard allowing "an avalanche of rampaging ultra leftism within the party to grow out of control and distort his judgement." That Bishop's press secretary Rojas, himself the victim of Coard's machinations when he was ousted as editor of the *Free West Indian,* was unable even *after* the crisis to understand the full measure of Coard's strategic thinking and full control over the OREL group, is as much a tribute to Coard's shrewdness as to the naivete of Bishop's supporters. Lewis, *Grenada,* p. 80.

23. *Grenada Documents*: Document 110, First Plenary Session, Central Committee, July 13–19, 1983. p. 7.

24. Ibid., p. 18.

25. *Grenada Documents*: Document 111, Emergency meeting of the Central Committee, August 26, 1983, p. 3.

26. *Grenada Documents*: Document 112, Extraordinary meeting of the Central Committee, 14–16 September 1983. All quotations in this section are drawn from the minutes of this meeting.

27. The call for the removal of Hudson Austin as head of the PRA is especially significant in the light of Austin's later role in the crisis. Austin, although older than Bishop, regarded Bishop as a father figure since their earliest days together in the anti-Gairy struggle. He did not vote on the joint leadership proposal (he had come late) and seems to have been drawn to support the majority at the last minute rather than out of any previous commitment to the Coard faction. That the majority proposed the removal of Hudson Austin as head of the PRA on 16 Sept. but proceeded to appoint him in charge of the Revolutionary Military Council on 20 Oct. shows that the proposals had little to do with administrative capability and performance but simply reflected Bernard Coard's changing strategic objectives. On 16 Sept. Austin's close ties to Bishop were a liability; on 20 Oct. they came an asset.

28. *Grenada Documents*: Document 113, General Membership Meeting, September 25, 1983, p. 3.

29. Ibid., p. 12.

30. Ibid.

31. Interview with Alimenta Bishop.

32. Jiri and Virginia Valenta, perhaps the leading Sovietologists to have done serious research on Grenada, fall back on the curious argument that the *lack* of action on the part of Soviets showed their true sympathies: "Had they [the Soviets] really wanted to help Bishop, they would have scheduled an official visit or extended him some other dramatic form of political or economic support." And, though acknowledging Castro's sympathies for Bishop, "There is no record of a sustained Cuban attempt to intervene in Bishop's behalf during the final phase of the coup." But they conclude that "whether or not Soviet officials were actively involved in the anti-Bishop coup . . . remains a matter of speculation." Jiri Valenta and Virginia Valenta, "Leninism in Grenada," in Jiri Valenta and Herbert J. Ellison, eds., *Grenada and Soviet/Cuban Policy* (Boulder: Westview, 1986), p. 27.

33. If "discipline" seems to have been Bernard Coard's favorite word, "manners" (West Indian lingo for harsh treatment) was Phyllis Coard's favored

expression. For a well-developed analysis on Coard's Stalinist proclivities, see Clark, "The Second Assassination of Maurice Bishop."

34. Personal interview with George Louison, Concord, Grenada, 2 Dec. 1984. Bernard Coard refers to this in his statement from the dock, Friends for Jamaica, "The Side You Haven't Heard: The Maurice Bishop Murder Trial," (New York: Mimeo, 1987).

35. Interview with Kendrick Radix.

36. In fact, Bernard Coard's own deputy—a man considered to be a bridge between the revolution and the private sector, an individual with extensive contacts with what could be considered leading potential opponents of the revolution (i.e., members of the business community), and *not* an NJM member—has stated: "Never before as in 1983, did I have such a feeling that things were settling down and that the situation was stabilizing." Interview with Lyden Ramdhanny.

37. For evidence, see "The Political Economy of the Transition" in the introduction to this book.

38. Phyllis Coard was injured as a result of the attack on the bus. The trial for the murder of Maurice Bishop and his associates was then moved to the grounds of Richmond Hill Prison, to guarantee the safety of the defendants.

39. See Bernard Coard, "Methodological Problems in Analyzing the Politics of Small States," in Louis Lindsey, ed., *Methodology and Change: Problems of Applied Social Science Research Techniques in the Commonwealth Caribbean*, pp. 281–89.

40. *George Louison and Kendrick Radix Discuss Internal Events Leading to the U.S. Invasion of Grenada* (New York: Grenada Foundation, 1984), p. 3.

41. See Harold D. Lasswell, *Power and Personality* (New York: Norton, 1976); Alexander L. George, "Power as a Compensatory Value for Political Leaders," *Journal of Social Issues*, 24 (1968), pp. 29–49, as reprinted in Gordon J. Di Renzo, ed., *Personality and Politics* (New York: Andover Press, 1974), pp. 55–80.

42. Lasswell, *Power and Personality*, p. 62.

43. One of the things that seemed to bother the Coards the most about Maurice Bishop was his irregular attendance at Bernard Coard's Saturday lectures on socialism. To have the revolution's *líder máximo* attend those classes was, of course, the ultimate confirmation of Bernard Coard's preeminence as party theoretician. See Phyllis Coard's complaints about Bishop in this regard.

44. George, "Power as a Compensatory Value," p. 65.

45. Ibid., pp. 73–74.

46. *Grenada Documents*: Document 112, Meeting of the Central Committee of the New Jewel Movement, September 16, 1983, p. 43.

47. "George Louison, and Kendrick Radix," p. 32.

48. Leslie Manigat, former director of the Institute of International Relations at the University of the West Indies, where Coard taught in the early seventies, personal interview, New York City, Aug. 1984.

49. In conversations with George Louison while Bishop was under arrest, Coard told Louison "if the masses demonstrate for weeks upon weeks, they are bound to get tired after a while and get hungry and go back to work. . . .

Williams did it in 1970 in Trinidad, Gairy did it in 1974, and it could be done again." *George Louison and Kendrick Radix,* p. 34. After this prognosis turned out to be tragically false, Bernard Coard in his statement from the dock, blamed the 19 Oct. events on "herd psychology." See Friends for Jamaica, "Side You Haven't Heard," p. 26.

50. See Frederick McDermott Coard, *Bitter-sweet and Spice: These Things I Remember* (Devon: Arthur H. Stockwell, 1970).

51. Ibid., p. 110.

52. Ibid., p. 84.

53. Ibid., pp. 30–31.

54. Ibid.

55. Curiously, Bernard Coard "never talked about his father. It was almost as if he wasn't proud of his father, a man widely respected in the more conservative circles of Grenadian society." Interview with Lyden Ramdhanny. Having witnessed his father's frustration and bitterness, Bernard Coard would have little reason to be proud of him.

56. *Grenada Documents*: Document 112, Extraordinary Meeting of the Central Committee, September 17, 1983, p. 44.

57. Coard, *Bitter-sweet and Spice,* p. 9.

58. Ibid., p. 134.

59. See Friends for Jamaica, "The Side You Haven't Heard," Bernard Coard's statement from the dock, p. 20. *Shu-shu* means rumors; *tay-bay*, gossip.

60. Coard, *Bitter-sweet and Spice,* pp. 87, 93, 97.

61. According to George Louison, Bernard Coard wrote a letter to Bishop while both were students in England in which Coard told Bishop, "When I am Prime Minister of Grenada I will make you my deputy." Bishop kept the letter in his personal file. Interview with Mario Bullen, St. George's, 25 Aug. 1987. Needless to say, this is not hard evidence. However, it was widely commented in St. George's that once, when taken to the hospital, Phyllis Coard demanded special treatment from the nurses since "they were dealing with the wife of the future Prime Minister of Grenada," a comment matching the rumors encountered by Allan LeGrenade on his visit to Jamaica in 1979.

62. In the mid-sixties, when retired from the colonial service, F. M. Coard worked for Rupert Bishop's import business. Interview with Ann Bishop.

63. See James McGregor Burns, *Leadership* (New York: Harper & Row, 1978).

64. According to Fred Greenstein, *Personality and Politics* (New York: Norton, 1976), p. 57, "unstructured political situations make it easier for ego-defensive personality needs to come to the fore."

65 Lasswell, *Power and Personality,* pp.

66. See for example Lewis, *Grenada: The Jewel Despoiled.*

67. Interview with Kendrick Radix.

68. Ibid.

69. Interview with Lydon Ramdhanny.

70. *Grenada Documents*: Document 113, General Membership Meeting, September 25, p. 12.

71. Interview with Lyden Ramdhanny.

72. Interview with Alimenta Bishop.

73. *Advocate News* (Barbados), 3 Nov. 1983.

74. Sylvia Belmar, *Trinidad Guardian,* 12 Nov. 1983. Quoted in Clark, "Second Assassination."

75. The *Nation,* 24 Nov. 1983.

76. Interview with Lyden Ramdhanny.

77. Interview with Allan LaGrenade.

78. Interview with Kendrick Radix.

79. See Jay Mandle, *Big Revolution, Small Country: The Rise and Fall of the Grenada Revolution* (Lanham, Md.: North-South, 1985), p. 102.

80. See the article by social psychologist Ramesh Deosaran, "The Political Paradox of Bishop's Charisma and the Grenada Tragedy," *Trinidad Guardian,* 30 Oct. 1983.

81. Thus in postrevolutionary Grenada, Francis Alexis, a former professor of constitutional law at UWI-Barbados, and subsequently a cabinet member in the Blaize government, has been a vigorous advocate of limiting prime ministers to two five-year terms, echoing the complaints of the Coard faction that "nobody has the right to be president-for-life." See also V. S. Naipaul, "Grenada: An Island Betrayed," *Harper's Magazine,* Mar. 1984, pp. 61–72. The denunciation of Caribbean charismatic leaders is a recurrent theme in Naipaul's works.

82. See Samuel P. Huntington, *Political Order in Changing Societies* (New Haven: Yale University Press, 1968), p. 144.

83. See Tim Hector's perceptive article, "19th October, Caribbean Unity Day: The Grenada Lessons," in the *Outlet* (Antigua), 19 Oct. 1984.

8. Small States, Eastern Caribbean Security, and the Grenada Intervention

Vaughan Lewis

ONE OF THE most controversial and least understood aspects of the October 1983 military intervention in Grenada has been the role played in it by the Organization of Eastern Caribbean States. The purpose of this chapter is to examine this role and the rationale behind it.

The Grenada episode highlighted the extraordinary lack of adequate security arrangements in the Eastern Caribbean. As very small island-states—referred to by some as microstates—whose small territorial size and population and largely single-crop, outwardly oriented economies make them extremely vulnerable to foreign intervention, these states are not in a position to deploy any large-scale military forces of their own. Traditionally, military protection for the region had been provided by the United Kingdom. But with the progressive withdrawal of the British from the Caribbean, as more and more territories opted for independence, the Eastern Caribbean states have had to come to terms with the geopolitical fact that the subregion is not next to Africa (or to the United Kingdom, for that matter) but to the United States—the traditional hegemonic power in the Western Hemisphere and, since 1945, one of the world's two superpowers.

SMALL STATES IN THE CHANGING GLOBAL ENVIRONMENT

The emergence of a bipolar world was, of course, one of the most important features of the postwar international system. The newly rising superpowers—the United States and the Soviet Union—while trying to retain spheres of influence in their own geographical environment, also sought to establish their preponderance in areas previously controlled by their predecessors, the old European metropolitan powers. The revolution in communications technology has meant that this competition reaches today even the most remote areas of the world.

Ranged against these two political entities we find a large number of small countries of varying sizes and levels of development, which need to react and adjust to trends and policies substantially determined by the larger powers and the economic processes emanating from them. The old European imperial powers, now organized in the European Economic Community, as well as Japan and China, have organized themselves to offer political and economic competition to the superpowers, while recognizing a certain dependence on them. Countries like Brazil, on the other hand, are still seeking to make the final jump into the status of industrial power, while asserting considerable influence in their immediate geographical surrounding.[1]

Some of these small countries, particularly the European ones, have an extensive experience of political and economic adjustment in response to changing environments dominated by larger neighbors. In so doing, they have become acutely aware of the importance of maintaining internal cohesion and consensus on the main lines of foreign policy. The large majority of small states, however, largely newly independent and underdeveloped, have little experience in these matters. For one thing, foreign affairs has normally been the very last policy area relinquished by the departing colonial authorities. Knowledge of the intricacies of the international environment is therefore minimal, and the domestic machinery for responding to the international environment hardly exists.

THE EASTERN CARIBBEAN AND
THE INTERNATIONAL SYSTEM

The Eastern Caribbean states achieved independence in the decade between 1974 and 1983. In marked contrast with the sixties, this was a period of considerable turmoil in the world economy, one in which a number of trends that had only been barely perceptible before became clearly evident. These included:

1. The gradual disappearance of the old preferential systems in the international trade of agricultural and mineral commodities. For the Caribbean, this meant a persistent shift in its trading and investment patterns from the United Kingdom to the United States.

2. The ending of the era of fixed exchange rates and a considerable instability in the international monetary order.

3. The communications revolution, associated with the development of the microchip—and with computer technology, more generally. This has provided hitherto unprecedented access to information. Through television, people in the Caribbean today have almost instant access to events occurring throughout the rest of the world. With this access have come conflicting interpretations of this information—linked very often to conflicting ideologies, and hence conflict among the people as to what to believe.

4. The continuing instability of commodity prices, the dominant source of foreign exchange for most underdeveloped countries. In the Eastern Caribbean, the effects of changes in currency values on the price of bananas has been particularly irksome.

One earlier Caribbean response to the challenges posed by the international system was the development of regional institutions to deflect, as it were, the disturbing effects of this environment on the individual territories. The Caribbean Free Trade Area (CARIFTA) first, and the Caribbean Community (CARICOM) later, were the products of that. But the very economic instability of the late seventies in the global arena inhibited the development of the CARICOM system.[2] Currency instability, recession, and protectionism reproduced themselves also *within* CARICOM. Differing ideological orientations, masked for a while by the concept of ideological pluralism, inhibited any harmonization of foreign relations. By the late seventies, differences in ideological orientation and in development strategy had separated Guyana and Jamaica from most other CARICOM states.[3]

Two elements in the region were particularly irritating to the United States as dominant power in the Americas. One of them was the emergence of the People's Revolutionary Government in Grenada and its foreign policy based on antiimperialism, nonalignment, and close relations with other radical governments in the hemisphere, like Cuba and Nicaragua.

The second, related factor, was the prospect of the creation of some sort of alliance of states hostile to the United States stretching across the Caribbean Basin—including Nicaragua, Jamaica, Cuba, Grenada, Guyana, and Suriname.[4]

In this concern, the United States was joined by the governments of the Windward and Leeward Islands. They reacted with fear to the coup that brought to an end the government of Eric Gairy in Grenada. Military coups were new to the Eastern Caribbean and, added to the radical foreign policy postures of the PRG, put squarely on the table the question of regional security and the military and diplomatic tools needed to cope with it.

The debate, still unresolved, was whether there was a need for a collective, regional approach, as opposed to a more individual approach, with some coordination. Another issue facing the OECS states was the level of capabilities to be sought from outside, which kind of political crisis can be met with local resources, which not?

THE GRENADIAN THREAT

The execution of Maurice Bishop and his associates on 19 October 1983 and the subsequent appointment of a Revolutionary Military Council in Grenada thus brought to the fore a matter that had been debated for quite some time but on which no consensus had emerged. Such basic questions as to what exactly constituted threats to regional security, what areas were included by the latter, and what were the instruments needed to enforce it had thus been left unanswered.

But the Grenada crisis forced the Eastern Caribbean governments to come up with an answer—however harried under the circumstances of those "two weeks that shook the Caribbean," to use Tom Adams's phrase. The countries were faced with an extremely difficult situation, unprecedented in the history of our part of the world. They thus felt the need to act very quickly if the situation was to be brought under some sort of control. The governments were very much aware that the RMC could only be a very, very difficult regime, given the extent of its military capabilities. People were shocked by the use of weapons, the assassination of the political leadership, and the display of force to cow the whole population through a twenty-four hour, "shoot-to-kill" curfew. This led to the determination of the Eastern Caribbean political leaders that such things could not be allowed to continue. To do nothing would have meant to legitimize such actions. They had to be dealt with quickly and decisively.

This threat perception was not universally shared within CARICOM, partly a function of the differences in the strengths of the various countries. The capabilities of the Eastern Caribbean states are very limited, which differentiates them from some other countries in the Caribbean with greater forces at their disposal and greater capacity to dispose of those forces to protect themselves. In this regard, there are two views in the region: one is that in certain kinds of crisis it is necessary to seek external assistance; the other is that in all crises the resolution ought to be handled indigenously. By October 1983 these debates were being postponed over and over again, so that when the crisis erupted, there was no mechanism in place. The discussion was incomplete; alternative mechanisms had to be sought.

Basically, the OECS states found themselves in a situation of having to seek assistance from outside. They were well aware that this kind of action was precedent setting, but it was considered that the situation itself was also unprecedented and precedent setting. Extraordinary steps had to be taken—in this case inviting a third party, that is to say, and extra-CARICOM party, to use military force to remove the individuals who took over the government of Grenada on 19 October.

The governments were aware that they themselves were party to the charters of the international institution that proscribed the use of force except in very well-defined circumstances. But the governments were also aware that the nature of self-defense was subject to different definitions depending on where you are sitting and what your strength is at any given time. They were aware of the position of humanitarian intervention in international societies and in international law. And it is really that rubric of humanitarian intervention that characterizes the intervention, with precedent in international law.

THE POLITICS OF INTERVENTION

The OECS was aware that it was going into an alliance, as it were, with governments much stronger than those of its member states. One of the main considerations, therefore, was to establish it in such a way that there could be some degree of control over the events as they evolved once the decision was taken to go for an intervention with the assistance of external forces.

And the OECS countries were able to hold their unanimity, to hold their coherence in the face of the tremendous onslaught, not only from groups within the region but internationally and in the international institutions. This was made possible by something that is often overlooked: the tremendous support of the people throughout the region, including those of Grenada, for the intervention. After the Grenada intervention, every single government that participated in it had to go to their parliaments to ask for approval of that action. And *in every instance, the opposition voted in favor of the government resolution.* There were opposition leaders who wanted to oppose it, but they didn't dare actually do it. For better or for worse, the fact is that the overwhelming majority of the people in the Eastern Caribbean were in favor of the Grenada intervention—and the governments were acutely aware of this.

BEYOND MILITARY SECURITY

It is a normal thing for a state to establish security arrangements for its domestic order—in other words, to have an army. Jamaica has an army, and nobody has proposed its abolition. But many people are questioning the right of the Eastern Caribbean states to set up some sort of military force. The late prime minister of Barbados, Tom Adams, proposed at one point the creation of a regional army. As he saw it, one way to minimize the impact of the military on society was to regionalize it, implying a regionalization of the political control of it. But this was not something that found favor among a majority of the Eastern Caribbean leaders. In any event, talk about a supposed "militarization" of the subregion is grossly exaggerated; what we are talking about is 300 troops. When the West Indies Federation was founded it had an army, and nobody questioned its existence.

The very questioning of the right of the OECS states to set up their own military forces underscores that within CARICOM there is still no agreement as to whether there is a regional environment in need of

protection—as distinct from individual states with their own separate
security interests. In the Eastern Caribbean, the OECS states have taken
the regional environment approach. Certain questions follow from such
an approach. At the narrower, technical, level they refer to matters like
these: What level of security capabilities can be derived from within the
Caribbean? What level of capabilities need to be sought from outside
the region? If help is going to be provided by extraregional sources in
matters of technical assistance, how is this to be done so as to maintain
both the reality and the appearance of individual and collective regional
sovereignty? Is the extraregional environment so forthcoming as to
permit a balance in the sources of external assistance such as will maintain
this sovereignty?

At the broader level, consideration has to be given to questions such
as: What kinds of political crises should and can be met by indigenous
regional assistance? What political circumstances would require extraregional assistance? Needless to say, these discussions can be undertaken
more fruitfully in times of relative quiet, in preparation for more difficult
times, than in the middle of a crisis or its immediate aftermath.[5]

The Grenada events, however, have highlighted a number of problems that had existed for quite some time in the Eastern Caribbean and
in CARICOM more generally, and that go far beyond the security issue.
The trade question is one of them, one that has had much greater
salience for the day-to-day lives of Caribbean people than the Grenada
affair. But the main point is that in the Eastern Caribbean, perhaps more
than elsewhere, a close examination of the instruments available for
national development is needed. And if those instruments are not appropriate as national instruments, ways in which the use of those instruments can be maximized collectively have to be sought.

The current debate on the subject is not an easy one. Having just
become independent, many of these countries need and desire to use
national instruments. And this problem is exacerbated by the very difficult international climate. All the countries of the OECS are faced with
what we might call a fiscal crisis of the state. The governments simply
do not have the resources to do what the people require and what in
some measure the people were promised would be forthcoming after
independence. Yet, the small size of these countries requires a regional
mechanism for approaching many issues. Human rights is one of them.
In the seventies, when the New Jewel Movement was in the opposition,
it benefited from the Legal Aid Foundation and the Caribbean Bar
Association, which served to call attention to the human rights situation
in Grenada at the time. This was an important institutional framework
for dealing with these issues. Today, there is a tremendous need for a
Caribbean court of appeals that could deal, for example, with some of
the wider regional problems and make decisions about them.

NOTES

1. For a more elaborate discussion of these changes in the international system, see Vaughan Lewis, "The World We Live In," St. Lucia Independence Lecture, Central Library, Castries, St. Lucia, 26 Feb. 1986 (mimeo).

2. For a general review of CARICOM problems at the beginning of the 1980s and some proposals for their resolution, see *The Caribbean Community in the 1980's* (Georgetown, Guyana: CARICOM Secretariat, 1981).

3. On the Jamaican case, see Vaughan Lewis, "The Small State Alone: Jamaican Foreign Policy 1977–1980," *Journal of Interamerican Studies and World Affairs* 25 (1983).

4. See Vaughan Lewis, "The Caribbean Experience of the 1970's: Some Lessons in Regional and International Relations," *Social and Economic Studies* 32 (1983).

5. For a general discussion of the security problems of small states, with some specific references to the Eastern Caribbean situation, see *Vulnerability: Small States in the Global Society,* Report of a Commonwealth Consultative Group (London: Commonwealth Secretariat, 1985).

9. The Restoration of Electoral Politics in Grenada

Selwyn Ryan

O NE OF THE declared objectives of the Grenada invasion of October 1983 was the restoration of democracy, as that term is understood in the Westminster tradition of its hybrid versions.

Following the seizure of power by the New Jewel Movement in 1979, Maurice Bishop stated that Grenada had seen the last of the Westminster model in action. He labeled Westminster type elections as they were conducted in Grenada as "rum and corned beef" affairs and indicated that the days of parliamentary democracy were "over in Grenada."[1] A free and open election was, however, one of the most pressing demands made on the Bishop regime by the Grenadian middle class and the Caribbean political elite; in fact, there are indications that the late prime minister was preparing to move in that direction in 1983 and that his overthrow was in part precipitated by fear that this was on his agenda. It might well have been that Bishop would have won those elections. His execution by the radical Coard faction and the invasion by the American and Caribbean forces, however, preempted that demarche.

To what extent did Grenadians as a whole share the view that parliamentary elections were important? There are some empirical data that suggest that Grenadians were less concerned about the loss of the freedom to vote than they were about the loss of other civil rights. When asked in a December 1983 survey which of the policies of the People's Revolutionary Government they liked least, only 7 percent of the sampled population cited the failure to call elections as being of paramount concern. More concern was expressed about the involvement with the socialist bloc, "preventive" detection, and intimidation and interference with freedom of the press and other civil liberties (table 9.1).[2]

In the postinvasion period, there was clear evidence that most Grenadians had had their fill of politics and that they wished to have an extended period of national calm before again engaging in electoral politics. It was felt that time was needed to permit the country to recover from the shock and trauma generated by the "October crisis." A clear

Table 9.1
Grenadian Public Opinion on PRG Policies, December 1983

Policy Disliked Most	Percentage
Involvement with socialist bloc (Cuba, Russia, North Korea, etc.)	20
Intimidating or detaining opponents	15
Interference with freedom of press and other civil liberties	12
All policies	10
Failure to call elections	7
Creation of armedmilitia	5
Other	12
No opinion	19

Note: The survey question was, Which of the policies of the PRG did you dislike most?

majority of the population was of the view that the caretaker regime appointed by the governor general following the invasion should remain in power indefinitely. As table 9.2 shows, 29 percent wished to postpone elections for as many as twenty-four months or more, 15 percent for eighteen months, 22 percent for twelve months, with a mere 11 percent expressing a preference for elections within six months.[3]

Apart from the need for a period of calm and reflection, Grenadians were of the view that there were no obvious successors to Bishop and the NJM other than Gairy and the Grenada United Labour Party (GULP) and the moribund Grenada National Party (GNP) of the aging Herbert Blaize. There was also fear that elections would generate violent conflicts between supporters of Gairy and supporters of the New Jewel Movement, and between followers of Bishop and followers of the hard-line Coard factions of the NJM. The fact that it was believed that many NJM militants were still in possession of arms aggravated concern that

Table 9.2
Grenadian Public Opinion on When Elections
Should Be Held, December 1983

Length of Time	Percentage
Six months	11
One year	22
Eighteen months	15
Two years	29
Don't know	8
Other	15

Note: The survey question was, How long do you think the new caretaker administration should remain in office before elections are called? Six months, a year, two years, or more than that?

Table 9.3
Grenadian Public Opinion on the Danger of
Violence and Disorder with Elections, May 1984

Response	Percentage
Agree	42
Disagree	31
Don't know	23
No response	4

Note: The survey statement was, If elections are held this year, there is a great danger that there would be violence and disorder.

these would be used to eliminate rivals. The only party anxious to have early elections were the GULP.

The fear of elections continued into 1984. When Grenadians were asked in May 1984 whether they felt that violence would ensue if elections were to be held, 42 percent agreed and 23 percent were uncertain (table 9.3).[4] Only 37 percent of those polled felt that elections should be held in 1984 (table 9.4). Fourteen percent felt that elections would make no difference as far as helping Grenada solve its economic and other problems, while 11 percent felt that elections might in fact make things worse (table 9.5).

The caretaker government, however, was determined to leave office before the end of 1984; it was aware that important investment decisions were being postponed until it became clear what sort of regime would succeed the PRG. The realization that elections would be held in 1984 galvanized political parties and personalities into action. In May 1984, the National Democratic Party (NDP) led by George Brizan, the Grenada Democratic Movement (GDM) led by Francis Alexis, the Christian

Table 9.4
Grenadian Public Opinion on When Elections
Should Be Held, May 1984

Response	Percentage
This year	37
A year from now	28
Two years from now	15
Never	6
Don't know	10
No response	4

Note: The survey question was, Some people say that elections should be held this year. Others say that elections should be postponed for a year or more. Do you think elections should be held?

Table 9.5
Grenadian Public Opinion on the Effort of
Elections, May 1984

Response	Percentage
Elections will help a great deal	20
Elections will help somewhat	33
Elections will make no difference	14
Elections will make things worse	11
Don't know	17
No response/other	5

Note: The survey question was, Some people say that holding elections this year will help Grenada solve its problems. Others disagree with this idea. Do you think that holding elections this year will help Grenada?

Democratic Labour Party (CDLP) led by Winston Whyte, the Grenada National Party (GNP) of Herbert Blaize, the Grenada United Labour Party (GULP) of Eric Gairy, and the Maurice Bishop Patriotic Movement (MBPM) led by Kendrick Radix and George Louison, former members of the PRG, all stated their intention to contest the elections.

One of the major fears of many Grenadians was that the proliferation of political parties would permit the election on a plurality basis of either the MBPM or the GULP; repeated efforts were made to bring the center parties together into a Team for National Togetherness. It was believed that the NJM still had considerable support among the youth and that they might regroup and rally behind the MBPM. However, polling data indicate that the NJM was unlikely to be a serious contender at the polls. In the December 1983 poll, only 4 percent of those interviewed said that they would vote for the NJM (table 9.6), while 51 percent (table 9.7) felt that the party should in fact be banned and not allowed to contest the elections. There were, however, still fears that the supporters of the NJM were lying low, given the American presence, and that the results could not be relied upon to predict future political behavior.

As can be seen from table 9.6, the GULP was far from moribund at the end of l983. Eleven percent of the respondents said they would vote for Gairy, compared to 16 percent and 12 percent who said they would vote for the NDP and GNP, respectively. This suggests that if the centrist parties did not get together, Gairy could win a number of seats and even hold the balance of power if the results of the election were not conclusive. This concern led to the announcement that a merger of the NDP, GDM, and the GNP would take place. In May, Francis Alexis indicated that the parties' steering committees had agreed to Blaize's proposal for the creation of a Togetherness Team to be led by Blaize.

Despite this, the moderate parties still appeared to believe that they

Table 9.6
Grenadian Public Opinion, Party Reference,
May 1984

Party	Percentage
Grenada United Labour Party (GULP)	11
National Democratic Party (NDP)	16
New Jewel Movement (NJM)	4
Christian Democratic Labour Party (CDLP)	1
Grenada National Party (GNP)	12
Grenada Democratic Movement	3
Would not vote/Refused ballot	11
Uncertain	28
No response	10
Team for National Togetherness (if formed)	4

Note: The survey question was, If an election were held this year, which party would you vote for? Please mark on this ballot and place in this box.

Table 9.7
Grenadian Public Opinion on Banning
the New Jewel Movement,
December 1983

Response	Percentage
Agree	51
Disagree	40
Refuse to say	2
Don't know	6
No response	1

Note: The survey question was, Should the New Jewel Movement be banned?

could win without a coalition. The NDP was particularly confident of its prospects for victory. Leadership rivalries and mutual suspicions also inhibited unity. Whyte and Alexis were regarded as opportunists by some. It was also felt that Alexis, who was a lecturer at the University of the West Indies in Barbados and who had not been active in Grenadian politics during the turbulent Bishop period, was a creature of U.S. interests. There was also concern about Whyte's former Gairyite connections. It was felt that his political strength in Grenada was negligible and that the bulk of his support came from Grenadian elements in Trinidad and Tobago.

In terms of the NDP and the GNP, some members of the latter party, especially its business wing, were suspicious about Brizan's former NJM membership as well as his earlier socialist orientation.[5] The NDP, for its part, backed as it was by high school students, young professionals, and clerks, was leery of associating too openly with the GNP, which was regarded as either a "geriatric" party or one that was associated with the "ideologically backward" upper classes and business elite in Grenada. The NDP had inherited much of the support enjoyed by Bishop and was concerned that the enthusiasm of this element might evaporate if the party was seen to be too closely associated with the GNP. Herbert Blaize, the leader of the GNP, was also accused of having retired to Carriacou, leaving the struggle against the PRG to be waged by others.

These differences were of great concern to politically moderate Grenadians as well as to Washington and the Eastern Caribbean countries that had intervened militarily in Grenada. This concern was heightened when the results of further surveys in August indicated that Gairy was gaining strength and that he could well emerge with enough seats to form a government if there were multicornered electoral contests. The fear was that the NJM would hold onto the radical vote leaving approximately 40,000 votes to be divided among the five nonleft parties.

The August survey, in which as many as 2,715 persons were interviewed in all fifteen constituencies, suggested that the GULP would pose a threat in St. George's South, St. Andrew South East, and St. Patrick East, and that the party was leading in St. Andrew North East, St. Andrew North West, St. Patrick West, St. Mark, and St. John (table 9.8). On a national basis, Gairy's support was likewise shown to be greater than previous surveys had shown. When asked to indicate how they felt about the GULP, 29 percent of those who answered reported that they either "liked" the party or "liked it very much" while 32 percent "disliked" it or "disliked it very much" (table 9.9).

Twenty-five percent of the respondents said they wanted the GULP to win the election (table 9.10) compared to 38 percent who chose the parties that would eventually form the NNP (i.e., the TNU, 21 percent and the NDP, 17 percent. In terms of how they would actually vote if the elections were held then, 24 percent expressed support for the GULP, 18 percent for the TNU, and 16 percent for the NDP. In terms of persons preferred to be prime minister, Gairy was the choice of 25 percent, Blaize 19 percent, and Brizan 18 percent (table 9.11).

Gairy drew most of his active support from the least educated, those more advanced in age, and from women. Forty-eight percent of those over fifty years old endorsed Gairy, 37 percent endorsed Blaize, and 10 percent Brizan. Fifty percent of those who had "little or no education" supported him, while 25 percent supported Blaize, and 18 percent Brizan. The latter had the support of 53 percent of those who had finished secondary school. In terms of sex, 39 percent of the women chose Gairy, 27 percent Blaize, and 26 percent Brizan. In a 26 October–2 November 1984 survey, the same pattern of support emerged. Support

Table 9.8
Grenada Election Outlook, August 1984: Discriminant Analysis of Likely Voters

Area	Sample Size		Percent Undecided		Percent Estimated Turnout		Percent Estimated for GULP		Percent Estimated for NNP		Points of Estimated Margin for NNP		Sample Error	
	Aug.	Oct.	Aug.	Oct.	Aug.	Oct.	Aug.	Oct.	Aug.	Oct.	Aug.	Oct.	Aug.	Oct.
St. George's (town)	177	201	48	30	69	86	32	21	65	78	33	57	±9	±7
St. David	177	199	33	38	71	84	34	21	64	76	30	57	9	7
St. Andrew SE	191	219	33	32	80	78	48	37	49	62	1	25	9	7
St. Andrew SW	199	231	30	29	76	87	29	24	64	75	35	51	8	6
St. Andrew NE	215	225	46	32	61	80	78	37	20	63	−58	26	7	6
St. Andrew NW	189	208	31	28	74	83	62	36	38	63	−24	27	8	7
St. Patrick E	191	200	31	36	79	77	49	27	48	71	−1	44	9	7
St. Patrick W	201	194	22	21	75	88	54	38	45	62	−9	24	8	7
St. Mark	196	210	37	32	73	79	71	28	25	70	−46	42	7	6
St. John	237	200	44	34	67	77	50	29	40	62	−10	33	8	7
Carriacou	185		42		81		2		89		87		6	
St. George's NE	161	190	34	23	73	87	34	19	64	81	30	62	9	7
St. George's NW	201	236	38	26	67	82	43	34	56	65	13	31	9	6
St. George's SE	170	176	39	25	71	85	25	18	75	81	50	63	8	6
St. George's S	136	219	45	30	62	82	43	31	48	64	5	33	10	
National average	185	208	37	30	72	83	44	29	53	70	9	41	±8	±7

Note: Analysis used expressed vote intention plus statistical allocation of the undecided.

Table 9.9
Grenadian Public Opinion on the Grenada
United Labor Party, August 1984

Response	Percentage
Like very much	17
Like	12
No opinion	31
Dislike	10
Dislike very much	22
Don't know about party	1
Refuse to answer	7

Note: The survey question was, I am going to call the names of the political parties contesting the coming elections. As I call each name, please tell me how you feel about the party. Do you like the party or do you dislike it? Do you like/dislike (as appropriate) this party very much or just a little? If you have not heard of the party or have no feelings one way or another about it, you can tell me that instead.

Table 9.10
Grenadian Public Opinion, Party Preference and Party Likely to
Vote for, August 1984

Party	Prefer (percent)	Would Vote For
Grenada United Labour Party (GULP)	25	24
Team of National Unity (TNU)	21	18
National Democratic Party (NDP)	17	16
Christian Democratic Labour Party (CDLP)		1
Maurice Bishop Patriotic Movement (MBPM)	3	3
None	2	1
Uncertain	21	15
No response	11	22

Note: The survey questions were, What party do you want to win the election? And if elections were held today, who would you vote for?

for the GULP rose from 11 percent of the eighteen-to-twenty-four-year age group, to 38 percent of those in the fifty-to-sixty-five-year age group. The NNP had half the support of eighteen-to-twenty-four-year age cohort and out polled the GULP among all voters under fifty years of age. The NNP received 58 percent of those who had completed their secondary education and 68 percent of the university graduates, compared to 10 percent of the former and 3 percent of the latter, who supported the GULP. Urban voters and men were also more inclined to support the NNP than rural voters and women.

The results of the August 1984 poll showed that the GULP could

Table 9.11
Grenadian Public Opinion, Preference for Prime
Minister, August 1984

Candidate	Percentage
Gairy	25
Blaize	19
Brizan	18
Alexis	3
Whyte	3
No response	31

Note: The survey question was, The most powerful figure in Grenada after the December elections undoubtedly will be Eric Gairy or Herbert Blaize. Which one, Blaize or Gairy, would you prefer to have in control of the next government?

win the election if a coalition was not formed. And 46 percent of those polled wished to see a coalition formed, compared to 28 percent who preferred to see the parties contest the election separately. The remainder were uncertain as to their preference. The data suggest that those who wished to see the parties run separately were mainly supporters of Gairy and the MBPM. Only 4 percent wanted the latter included in a grand coalition against the GULP, while 16 percent wished to see only the centrist parties included. Sixty-three percent of those polled could not or would not say which combinations of parties they preferred, if any.

And it was in the wake of the August 1984 poll that strong pressure was brought to bear on the centrist parties by Barbados, St. Lucia, St. Vincent, Dominica, and Jamaica to attend a meeting of the moderates on Union Island off the coast of St. Vincent. It was also alleged but vigorously denied that Washington was an invisible party in the negotiations. James Mitchell, prime minister of St. Vincent, claimed that he and not the Americans was the catalyst for the meeting. Alexis, Blaize, and Brizan all deny that the Americans or the Caribbean leaders put pressure on them to agree to unite at the Union Island meeting. As Brizan noted, "all they [the OECS] did was to facilitate a discussion among the leaders of the three political parties in the country." Blaize's remarks were similar.

Reports emerging from the meeting indicate that the OECS leaders first met each leader separately to determine whether there were any areas of basic disagreement. The leaders were then met collectively and told that there was a great deal they shared in common, which could form the basis for unity. They were further told that, if they chose to remain separate and then lost the election to Gairy, the governments that had invested their prestige in the invasion would abandon them and Grenada. On the other hand, if the parties merged, political campaign support would be forthcoming. The structure of incentives brought about the hoped for unity. What emerged from the meeting was an agreement to dissolve all existing parties and replace them with the New National Party under the leadership of Blaize.[6]

Despite the agreement, rivalries still existed, especially over the number of seats each faction would be allowed to contest. This was a particularly sensitive issue, since each party had already slotted prospective candidates for certain constituencies where it was felt Gairy would be defeated. The leaders of the GDM and the NDP also had prime ministerial ambitions and were both anxious to obtain a sufficient number of seats to allow them to succeed Blaize when age and ill health would force him to depart from the political scene.[7] The crisis was eased somewhat by the fact that Winston Whyte was forced out of the coalition, thus permitting a three-way split of seats among the moderates.[8] The formula eventually agreed upon was that the GNP would contest eight constituencies, the NDP four, and the GDM three.

The creation of the NNP brought angry outbursts from the radicals, who regarded the party as the creation and creature of right-wing American and Caribbean interests. The NNP was lampooned as a non-native party. Gairy was also hostile to the NNP, which he clearly saw as the major obstacle to his hopes to regain power.

The platforms of the respective parties were predictable. All parties pledged to reduce the high cost of living, to rationalize the punitive tax structure, to upgrade the agricultural sector, which was in the doldrums, to revitalize the sagging tourism industry, to improve the road system, which was in a deplorable state and to strengthen the performances of the public utilities, particularly the electricity and telephone systems.[9]

Gairy's campaign, however, had a particularly personal dimension. Gairy reminded Grenadians of his long-standing commitment to their personal well-being as well as the many occasions on which he used his personal resources to help meet some of their basic needs. As he asked Grenadians,

> Which other political leader in the world has gone out of the way to open dozens and dozens of pre-primary schools to accommodate two to six-year-olds? Which other party in the world has had a leader who has taken money from his pocket to create day-care centers to accommodate infants while their mothers go to work? Everyone knows that respectable homes for the aged is a GULP innovation. Thousands of Grenadians who now own land own it because of the initiative of the Grenada United Labour Party.[10]

Gairy also reminded the electorate that it was he who won independence for Grenada and who had been responsible for a number of "firsts" in the island's history. As he put it, "Who won independence for Grenada before any of the other Windward or Leeward Islands dreamed of the idea? Which party was responsible for the first Organization of American States Conference ever held in the Caribbean? The Grenada United Labour Party. We successfully sponsored a "Miss World" and established the biggest water extravaganza the Caribbean has ever known, the Easter Water Parade."[11] He also boasted of his prophetic, mystic, and psychic powers and about his strong religiosity. As he said, "I often had to battle against and subdue my objective consciousness or material mind. At times logical deduction and reason were superseded by something more profound in order to accomplish some of the things I have undertaken to do."[12] He likewise reminded his "flock" that it was he who built the huge lighted cross on Richmond Hill, a symbol of Christianity and a beacon to guide ships into Grenada's harbor.

Gairy denied that he was planning any campaign of victimization as alleged or that he had any past record of victimizing his opponents. The contrary was true, he moaned. He also claimed that reports about the violence of the Mongoose Gang were much exaggerated. Also denied were reports that he had extorted money from businessmen in return for political protection and advancement or that he had squirrelled away large sums of money abroad. According to Gairy, his main concern in the post-1970 period was to smother incipient communism and subversion and promote the goal of a Christianized community. He felt that events had proven that his concern was right. As he said: "Grenadians experienced a 'change with a chain,' and were it not for President Reagan's timely Rescue Mission, Grenadians would have experienced not only the 'change with a chain' but the fork, the spade, the pick, the axe, the ration card, dungaree overalls with accommodation for females to carry children while working, mass burial of the aged, a group deemed useless by the communists, more people deemed 'counters' and liquidated for that reason."[13]

Gairy declared that he would not tolerate attempts at subversion if he were to be reelected. His regret was that he was not sufficiently alert on previous occasions.

> I regret that we were a little too in-alert in dealing with the . . . communists. I think we would be more sensitive, more alert to avert an attempt to start any subversive movements in Grenada today. I think Duffus would be very much embarrassed if you were to talk to him now on the question of his report, because all that we are saying is that those people were communists and Duffus and other people are trying to dress them in the habiliment of angels and saints, and events have proved beyond the shadow of doubt that I was correct. I was right to say that they were communists. I may have been prophetic but I want to say that

I had reasons for saying what I did say about those boys, and there was no Mongoose Gang belonging to Eric Gairy or the Grenada United Labour Party government.[14]

There was widespread agreement that Gairy had functioned as a sort of Robin Hood in Grenadian politics in the fifties and sixties and that for many, particularly the old, he still remained the "hero" in "the crowd."[15] The latter remembered him as someone who provided money, land, farming assistance, housing, food, and clothing for the underprivileged, as well as protection from the planters who would victimize them. Gairy's detractors, however, characterized him as someone who had enriched himself at the people's expense, who had brutalized his opponents, associated with right-wing regimes such as that of Pinochet in Chile, and generally associated himself with evil forces. Gairy's response was to deny all these allegations and to express regret that he had never retained a public relations expert to project a more positive image of himself and the GULP.

As the campaign proceeded, it was clear that Gairy was on the defensive. He was portrayed as the person who was primarily responsible for the Grenadian crisis and the author of the island's recent misfortunes.[16] It was also made clear that he did not have the backing of the United States, who considered him an embarrassment. Feeling threatened and besieged, he chose not to offer himself as a candidate and campaigned for GULP candidates via the press and recorded speeches as well as at house meetings.[17] Only one open-air meeting was held by GULP candidates, who were instructed to refrain from such activities.

The NNP's basic campaign plank, other than the expressed concern for revitalizing the economy and democratizing the constitution to allow for the recall of candidates and to limit the number of years any one could serve as prime minister, was the need for a religious reorientation of the society.[18] The party also stressed the need to turn back the march of socialism and the need to rebuild self-confidence among the people "who had been dragged left and right and battered by what happened in October last year."

Blaize also reiterated concern that there were many caches of arms that had not been uncovered, which could be put to use in the future. Given this, he felt that the American and Caribbean peacekeeping forces should remain until such time as Grenada had built up a credible peace-keeping capability of its own.[19] The Americans were primarily involved in training a paramilitary force (the Special Services Unit), which was to be part of a regional Eastern Caribbean force primarily concerned with the threat of insurgency. The British and the Barbadians were involved in training the police service, since the existing police service was not only undermanned and undertrained but divided in its loyalty to the Gairy and Bishop regimes.

With respect to the question of American financial and political backing for the NNP, Blaize did not deny that the NNP was in contact with the Americans. When asked whether he had any special ties with the Americans, Blaize replied in the affirmative: "We are in touch from the time that the intervention took place. We have always kept in touch with the State Department and other institutions involved in American policy making, like the Republican Institute for National Development. We have been in touch with the Democrats. And so we don't want to have ourselves tied down to any one single part of the United States. We enjoy a particularly good relationship with all of them right now."[20]

The Christian Democratic Labour Party declared that its principal aim was the uplifting and humanization of Grenadian society rather than the quest for political power. The party hoped to function as a sort of yeast in the society and to ensure that the rights and freedoms of the individual were respected. The CDLP, however, fielded only five candidates and made no claims that it could win the election. The party was hoping that it would win one or two seats, which might put it in a position to hold the balance of power if the election was deadlocked. As one spokesman put it, "if we are successful in winning a few seats, we are not going into any coalition with anybody. People who want us would come to us, we are not going."[21]

The campaign of the Maurice Bishop Patriotic Movement contained no surprises. The party disavowed the NJM leaders who were in jail, extolled the virtues of Maurice Bishop, whom it projected as the martyred hero of the revolution, and stressed the positive things achieved by the PRG. Particular emphasis was given to job creation, educational reform, bulk purchase of essential foods items, and health care. The leader of the party, Kendrick Radix, was critical of the American invasion, which he regarded as a violation of international law. He also lamented the abandonment of the many ideals and programs for which Bishop stood, as well as the hypocrisy of many who now embraced the late leader. As he complained:

> We have two sets of people. The first set who are genuine people, who fundamentally mourn the loss of our revolution that Maurice Bishop personified and, of course, Maurice Bishop himself, and we see that even with his death, we see a collapse of programs and policies which were designed to uplift, increase and improve the standard of living and the standard of life of the ordinary working people, the oppressed, women and youth and so on. Secondly, we see another group of people emerging after the crisis of October, who are shedding crocodile tears in memory of Bishop. These are the Judases today who claim that his murder was a great disaster and try to implicate a number of revolutionary fighters who fought against this rise of fascism which was led by Coard. And even using Maurice Bishop's murder to galvanize and

precipitate some support for him. They never helped in any way while he lived. For them he was a traitor. For them he was a dictator. For them Maurice Bishop was a communist, but today they invoke the fact that he was a nice man. Even President Reagan rose to his vulgarity by saying how they killed the Prime Minister of Grenada and how he was coming to rescue the people. What we have to analyze is whether or not the people were rescued or whether they were invaded, and the latter is true because they lost all their fundamental rights and freedoms which our revolution brought them. We are in oppression today.[22]

Radix was also upset about the fact that the new international airport, which the Americans had criticized and then completed, was not named after Bishop, whom he claimed was the person principally responsible for getting the project on stream. Like others on the left, he was critical of the American presence in Grenada and claimed that several MBPM candidates and party supporters had been beaten and harassed by American and Caribbean military forces.[23] He was also of the view that the elections could not be fairly conducted since they were being held "under the shadow of the guns of the occupying forces."

Radix nevertheless expressed certainty that the MBPM would emerge triumphant in the elections despite what the polls showed. As he put it,

> Our strength lies in the youth of the country, with the people who understood the revolutionary process that Maurice Bishop led in Grenada, from broad democrats and patriots, and working people as a whole. . . . Despite the millions of dollars with which they [the Americans] are buying people's heads, we are going to out-perform all the other political parties and form the government of Grenada. He enjoined his followers to move "forward on your feet, not on your knees."[24]

Radix was clearly whistling in the dark, especially since it was known that many potential supporters of the MBPM had not registered to vote, on Radix's own instructions. Radix, however, chose to place full blame on the authorities for depriving his followers of their franchise. In his view, the enumeration process was unfair.

While it may be true that there might have been some disinclination or fear on the part of NJM activists to register in the early months of the enumeration exercises, the same could not be said for the latter period. There was ample opportunity for any Grenadian who wished to be registered to ensure that is name was on the rolls. In any event, photographs were not required for the casting of ballots. Radix's request for an extension of the registration period was predictably dismissed.

The Grenada population was heavily polled prior to the actual election. Over 7,000 persons were interviewed between May and November, 1984. One of the surveys, October 26–November 2, in which 2,908 registered voters were interviewed, showed that the NNP and Blaize had gained ground since the merger had taken place. As many as 45 percent of those interviewed reported that they would support the NNP, while 24 percent indicated they would endorse the GULP. Thirty percent reported that they had not yet made up their minds. In terms of preferences for prime minister, Blaize was now a clear favorite over Gairy by a margin of two to one (66 percent to 34 percent). While the likely performances of the two major parties in fourteen constituencies surveyed was assessed (Carriacou was not surveyed, since Blaize was considered a sure winner there), the NNP was found to be leading in all. The margins were as high as forty-five percentage points in St. George's North East and St. George's South East and as low as nine in St. Andrew South East, eleven in St. Andrew North East, and ten in St. Patrick West. If sampling error (about eight percentage points plus or minus) and nonresponses are taken into account, it was possible for the GULP to win as many as seven seats. When only "likely voters" were considered, that is, those who said they would vote, eleven seats were certain NNP, and three (St. Andrew South East and North East and St. Patrick) were possible GULP seats, in that the NPP margins were less than the possible sampling error. When discriminant analysis was used to assess the results, an NNP victory in all seats appeared a distinct possibility.[25] As is revealed in table 9.12, the margin of possible NNP victory was positive, in all cases and exceeded the sampling error.

Further surveys conducted in mid-November indicate that, while the NNP continued to gain support, Gairy's strength was not declining as was widely believed. Of those who responded to interviewer probing

Table 9.12
Grenadian Public Opinion, Party Preference,
October/November 1984

Party	Percentage	Percentage (adjusted)
National Democratic Party (NNP)	30	39
Grenada United Labour Party (GULP)	18	24
Other	1	1
Uncertain	25	34
Unaware of party's candidate	1	2
No response	25	

Note: The survey question asked which party the voter would support in the upcoming election.

as to how they felt about the GULP, 32 percent indicated that they favored the party, compared to 36 percent who disliked it (table 9.13). This was an increase of three percentage points over the August survey, when 29 percent reported a favorable disposition to the party (table 9.9). By way of comparison, however, 45 percent held positive attitudes toward the NNP, while only 16 percent harbored negative attitudes (table 9.13). When asked which of the two rival leaders they preferred to see control the new government, 46 percent of the respondents chose Blaize, while 31 percent chose Gairy, (table 9.14). In terms of the party they would vote for, 30 percent of those responding said they would vote for the NNP candidate, while 18 percent said they would vote for the GULP candidate (see table 9.12). If the nonresponses are excluded,

Table 9.13
Grenadian Public Opinion on New National
Party and Grenada United Labour Party,
Mid-November 1984
(percent adjusted)

Response	NNP	GULP
Like very much	21	16
Like	24	16
No opinion	30	26
Dislike	9	20
Dislike very much	7	16
Don't know about party	10	6

Note: The survey question was, I am going to call the names of the political parties contesting the coming elections. As I call each name, please tell me how you feel about the party. Do you like the party or do you dislike it? Do you like/dislike (as appropriate) this party very much or just a little? If you have not heard of the party or have no feelings one way or another about it, you can tell me that instead.

Table 9.14
Grenadian Public Opinion, Preference for
Prime Minister, Mid-November 1984

Candidate	Percentage	Percentage (adjusted)
Blaize	35	46
Gairy	23	31
Uncertain	18	23
No response	24	

Note: The survey question was, The most powerful figure in Grenada after the December elections undoubtedly will be Eric Gairy or Herbert Glaize. Which one, Blaize or Gairy, would you prefer to have in control of the next government?

the percentages are 39 and 24, respectively. An active campaign by Gairy and his candidates might well have changed the picture somewhat; in fact, the GULP's percentage of the popular vote was 36 percent, higher than predicted in the polls.

Despite all the expressed concern about the possibility of violence, the election campaign was low key. On the weekend prior to the election, the capital city was, as one commentator put it, as "quiet as a church after service."[26] In its platform speeches, the MBPM projected itself as the party of the little man, the workers, women, and youth and characterized the NNP as the party of the privileged and the CIA. The NNP for its part caricatured the MBPM as the party of the KGB and the Libyans, who allegedly provided funds for the movement's campaign. The NNP was the best funded of all the political parties, and there were allegations that the Americans had used proxies to channel funds and political expertise to the party. This support took the form of campaign literature, T-shirts, buttons, electronic systems, and help with electioneering.[27]

As indicated above, Gairy was a "ghost" leader and never appeared on any public platform. There was even a false rumor on the eve of the election that, anticipating defeat, he had left for England. Gairy, however, expressed confidence that the GULP would win at least fourteen seats. The leader of the CDLP, Winston Whyte, was inexplicably absent during much of the last days of the campaign, giving rise to charges that he had been bought out by backers of the NNP.

The election results did not come as a surprise to anyone who had followed the campaign, though the margin of victory, fourteen to one, was not widely anticipated. The GULP was popularly favored to win at least four seats, and there was speculation that in the multicornered contests, independents or MBPM candidates might squeak through. Lyle Bullen of the MBPM was even credited with a chance to wrest the Carriacou seat from Blaize, speculation based on the assumption that the people of that outer island would show their gratefulness to the MBPM for the projects it had initiated there. As we have seen, polling data had indicated a landslide victory for Blaize in Carriacou.

The final results revealed that the NNP had won fourteen seats and was supported by 58.48 percent of the 41,041 persons who cast their vote. Thirteen of the seats were won on a majority basis and one, St. John, on the basis of plurality. The results were, however, close in four constituencies—St. Patrick East, St. Mark, St. Andrew South East, and St. John. The GULP won one seat and surprised many by obtaining 36.06 percent of the votes cast. The MBPM won a mere 4.9 percent of the votes cast, and all its candidates lost their deposits. Leon Cornwall, one of the detained supporters of the Coard faction, was critical of the MBPM strategy in the election. He felt that the MBPM, whom he described as opportunist, would have done better had they not alienated the PRG supporters. To quote him: "The PRG army and the party membership combined amounts to some 1,200 young, disciplined and energetic comrades living in every village across Grenada who, with a totally different approach by MBPM, could have worked for them in the elections."[28]

George Louison, a former cabinet minister in the PRG, obtained a mere 139 votes in the St. Mark constituency, which the NNP candidate won with 928 votes. The MBPM leader, Radix, was supported by 220 votes. Winston Whyte, the leader of the CDLP, obtained the support of only 12 voters. Blaize won the Carriacou seat with 1,662 votes and obtained 90 percent of the votes cast. His MBPM rival won a mere 147 votes. George Brizan obtained the support of 2,438, or 72 percent of the voters in the St. George's North East constituency. It is worth noting that as many as 85.3 percent of the registered electorate turned out to vote, a performance indicating that the initial disinclination to participate in the electoral process had evaporated. This may well have had to do with the formation of the NNP and the fact that the electorate was presented with sharp alternatives.

The results were enthusiastically acclaimed in Grenada and throughout the Caribbean, though some concern was expressed that there would be no meaningful opposition in the Parliament. Concern was heightened when the GULP decided to give up the St. Andrew North East seat it had won, on the ground that the elections were unfairly conducted, a charge echoed by the MBPM. Gairy claimed that a special type of indelible ink was used on the ballot paper, which erased the full support received by his party's candidates. It was a patently absurd claim for Gairy to make and may well have been directed to his illiterate supporters rather than to an intelligent audience.[29]

The U.S. government was also pleased at the outcome. President Reagan described the outcome of the elections as an "achievement of historic importance." Reagan noted that it was "the first time a country which was ruled by a Marxist Leninist regime had been returned to the democratic fold" and expressed pride that the United States had played a part in helping to achieve that outcome.[30]

The Caribbean left was demoralized by the outcome. Cheddi Jagan saw the election as "a sad day for Grenada." He was, however, of the view that the experience of Guyana, Chile, and Jamaica had shown that democracy imposed at the point of an "imperialist bayonet has no answers for the people's problems." Don Rojas, former press secretary to Maurice Bishop, was also saddened by the outcome. "The NNP victory," he declared, "would put Grenada solidly in the grasp of Washington." He also noted that the left in the Caribbean was now thoroughly demoralized and in shambles. For Rojas, the fall of the Bishop regime was a "shattering blow and a tremendous setback not only to the left in the Caribbean, but also to the world revolutionary movement." Rojas saw a link between the "Grenada fiasco" and U. S. policy in Nicaragua and Cuba and hoped that "Coard in his cell is reflecting on this."[31]

Other reflective spokesmen of the Caribbean left have also rued the consequences of the Grenada crisis. Professor Gordon Lewis, doyen of Caribbean intellectuals, remarked that "the supreme lesson of Grenada is that the Caribbean left must rediscover its conviction that socialism must go hand in hand with democracy."[32] Professor Clive Thomas of the University of Guyana also agreed that the October crisis had strengthened counterrevolutionary forces in the region.

> The execution of Maurice Bishop and others on October 19, 1983 self-destructed the Grenada Revolution. It was not the invasion, which took place after the revolution had already destroyed itself, which shattered the positional advantage of the ideology of the popular forces in the region. If the invasion had not occurred, the Grenada Revolution, with all its positive gains, would have had no continued legitimacy among the broad masses of the Caribbean peoples. The impact of the Grenada events on the immediate development of popular forces is extremely negative. The growing acceptance in the region of political pluralism has been literally replaced by a polarization of ideologies as pro-colonial sentiments have risen to the fore and now dominate the media.[33]

Thomas goes on to note that "after Grenada, no social project carried out in the name of the masses of the Caribbean people, whether by government or opposition, will receive widespread support from the popular forces, or their organizations, if it does not clearly embrace political democracy as its norm of political conduct."[34] On the vexed question of elections, Thomas, against the background of both Guyana and Grenada again reasserts the importance of "free and fair elections." The failure to hold these

> tarnished the reputation [of the NJM] in the eyes of large sections of the popular forces. This was particularly so because immediately after the successful overthrow of Gairy a pledge was made to hold free and fair elections, to uphold due process, and to protect the human rights of citizens which Gairy had so grossly and savagely violated. No regime, no matter how popular it may initially be, will be able to sustain the support of the popular forces in the region if its political rule is not grounded in constitutional legality and due legal process.[35]

The NNP for its part was enthusiastic about its performance but was fully aware that it had aroused the expectations of the electorate and thus had a burdensome and conspicuous role to play in Grenadian and Caribbean politics in the next few years. It was also aware that its performance in terms of job creation, industrial and agricultural reactivation, and the provision of social welfare would be avidly watched, and that comparisons would inevitably be made with its predecessor.

THE BLAIZE YEARS: A POSTSCRIPTUM

Over and above the unquestioned "success" of the relatively rapid return to electoral politics that took place in Grenada in the aftermath of the U.S. invasion, an appraisal of the Blaize years, the 1984–1989 period in which Grenada has been ruled by the New National Party and that old stalwart of Grenadian politics, Carriacou lawyer Herbert Blaize, should also throw some light on the more long-term prospects of the island's democratic development.

On the face of it, the first four-and-a-half years of Grenada under Blaize could not have been more different from the four-and-a-half years of Grenada under Bishop. The politics of charismatic leadership, popular mobilization, and anti-imperialism of the PRG thus gave way to low-key governance, one based on the principles of minimal government interference in the economy, on an active wooing of foreign investors, and on all-out support for the U. S. position in international affairs. Emblematic of this contrast between these two periods in the island's contemporary history is perhaps the one existing between Bishop and Blaize, themselves. The youthful dynamism of the former, who spent much of his time energizing the Grenadian population in rallies of all kinds, was replaced by the almost invisible hand of Blaize, who, nursing his illnesses both in Grenada and in U. S. hospitals, did not appear in public for months. And the PRG's vigorous denunciations of U. S. policy in the Caribbean were replaced by a no less aggressive rhetoric against the Soviet Union and "communism" in general.[36]

Less apparent than these obvious differences, though, are the considerable continuities in Grenada's politics and political economy in the 1979–1989 decade. The authoritarian streak in Grenadian political culture, which had been so apparent in the Gairy era as well as during the PRG, continued to manifest itself in the mid- and late eighties, albeit in a much more attenuated form. The 1987 decree establishing a censorship board empowered to pass judgement on all calypsos played on Radio Grenada and on public events is arguably, in a society in which the radio is the most important communications medium, at least as far-reaching an infringement of freedom of expression as the closing of a newspaper. The withdrawal of passports from former NJM members like Einstein Louison and the effective barring from jobs of Grenadians returning with medical degrees from Cuba, in a country where health care is in such short supply, show that the efforts made to overcome the divisions of Grenadian society have been rather partial and limited.[37]

And in comparison with the rest of the Eastern Caribbean states, on the other hand, what is perhaps most remarkable about Grenada during 1984–1989 is a relatively high economic growth rate fueled largely by a public investment in the island's infrastructure—investment made possible by extraordinarily high amounts of foreign aid, a pattern that closely matches that of 1979–1983.[38] Foreign investment was almost as reluctant to come to Grenada after the U.S. invasion than before it, despite the free-market ideology of the Blaize government and all the support of the U.S. Department of Commerce and other federal agencies.[39] Outward migration of Grenadians, mostly to the United States, continued at an even higher rate (2,000 per year) than had been the case under the PRG.

And even those areas where the Blaize government could claim some significant successes—such as in the growth of tourism and in the establishment of a producer's cartel with Indonesia on nutmeg and mace[40]—it was in fact reaping the benefits of initiatives undertaken by the PRG (i.e., the building of the Point Salines Airport, in the first case, and the 1979 demarche for such a cartel in the second).

Perhaps the most revealing instance of the continued dependence of Grenada on foreign aid and its effects on internal political alignments can be seen in the dynamics that led to the breakup of the ruling coalition in 1987 and the formation of a new political party, the National Democratic Congress, under the leadership of George Brizan and Francis Alexis. Upon the dramatic drop in U. S. aid from 1986 to 1987, one immediate measure taken by t he government to deal with the situation was to undertake massive layoffs of public employees, which in turn triggered heated criticism from cabinet members like Brizan and Alexis and their eventual break with Blaize.

And it is a measure of the limited impact of the centrist coalition (put together on Union Island in August 1984 to dispel the threat of a Gairy victory in the upcoming elections) on the deeper cleavages of Grenadian society and party alignments that, five years afterward, two leading contenders to succeed Herbert Blaize at the helm of the island's government were a former member of the New Jewel Movement, George Brizan, and, once again, Eric Gairy.

NOTES

1. *Caribbean Echo*, 3 Dec. 1982.
2. See a report of a survey carried out by St. Augustine Research Associates

for the *Trinidad Express,* Dec. 1983. In a poll conducted by Farley Brathwaite in Nov. 1984, 70 percent of those sampled said they were "unhappy" with the failure of the PRG to hold elections. The evidence is, however, only apparently contradictory. One might well be unhappy that elections were not held but not deem it the most critical failure of the PRG. See "Public Opinion and Political Transition in Grenada," a paper prepared for the conference on "Democracy, Development and Collective Security in the Eastern Caribbean: The Lessons of Grenada." Inter American University, San Germán, Puerto Rico, 17–19 Oct. 1985.

3. "Public Opinion and Political Transition."

4. See *Grenada Political and Social Outlook* (St. Augustine, Trinidad: St. Augustine Research Associates, 1984).

5. Brizan left the NJM in 1973, before it seized power in 1979. He was an officer in the Ministry of Education when the invasion took place. In an attempt to distance himself from his past, Brizan published a pamphlet on behalf of the NDP entitled "Why the National Democratic Party is Opposed to Communism." Among the reasons given were communism's advocacy of atheism, the tendency on the part of the party to crush political opposition, the restraints it puts on free trade unionism, its celebration of the one-party state, and its preference for state ownership of all resources. Brizan also sought to make the point that it is unfair for anyone to brand him or anyone else a Communist because they supported some of the positive programs of the NJM. Many of those programs were in place in other Caribbean and Western European countries, he noted.

6. *Trinidad Sunday Guardian,* 2 Dec. 1984 and 11 Nov. 1984.

7. Blaize was sixty-six years old and partially disabled.

8. Whyte was asked to retract a statement published in the *New Guardian* in Aug. 1984 that Blaize and Gairy had met to discuss the political future in Grenada. The statement was first published in the *New York Times.* Blaize denied the story vehemently and asked for a retraction. Whyte at first agreed to withdraw the statement but later claimed that he had no control over what appeared in the *New Guardian* and refused to apologize or withdraw the statement. Blaize denied that he made retraction a precondition of association, but Whyte nevertheless chose to withdraw. Whyte was also accused of taking disagreements about the size of the steering committee into the public realm.

9. See "A New Beginning," CDLP Manifesto; "Manifesto of the Grenada United Labour Party"; George Brizan, "The National Democratic Party: A Charter for Reconciliation, Development and Peace."

10. *Grenada Guardian,* 1 Dec. 1984.

11. Ibid.

12. Ibid. As Gairy continued, "I do not go around saying that I have psychic powers but I do say that I am inspired to do many things, the perceptions of which are sometimes illogical, sometimes considered to be impossible, and yet I am driven, as it were, by an inner force, and in every case the results have been astoundingly successful." Ibid. Gairy also claimed that it was his prophetic powers that inspired him to deny Jim Jones permission to set up a commune in Grenada as he was later able to do in Guyana. He claimed he had to withstand

a great deal of pressure from U. S. Congressman Mervyn Dymally. See *Sunday Express*, 2 Dec. 1984.

13. *Grenada Guardian*, 1 Dec. 1984.

14. *Trinidad Sunday Express*, 2 Dec. 1984. The Commission of Inquiry chaired by Justice Duffus accused Gairy in 1973 of using the Mongoose Gang to brutalize his opponents.

15. The term was used to describe Gairy by Archie Singham in his book on Grenada, *The Hero and the Crowd in a Colonial Polity* (New Haven: Yale University Press, 1968).

16. A pamphlet was circulated by the NNP asking "Who Committed These Crimes?" The answer to most of the questions was Gairy. Continued the pamphlet: "The population knows who were responsible and that is why they will never allow these Murderers, Butchers, and Potential Murderers to curse this our beloved country again. Some of those are now coming forward to be elected. These animals have no shame." See the *New National*, 30 Nov. 1984.

17. Gairy denied that he was afraid to campaign out of concern that he would be booed, harassed, or assassinated. He claimed that he was simply enjoying his human rights by choosing not to run. He went on to explain that he had won eight out of the eight elections he contested and preferred to direct the conflict from the sidelines. Gairy noted that he was, however, still the political leader of the GULP and would decide his role after the elections were held.

18. See Francis Alexis, "Towards Constitution Reform," the *New National*, 30 Nov. 1984. Alexis proposed that no one person should serve as prime minister for more than two consecutive terms and no one should serve as prime minister for more than fifteen years altogether. Provision should also be made for a people's complaint bureau and for recall of elected officials. These two provisions would, it was hoped, keep the government in continuous contact with the people.

19. With respect to the question of the threat to peace posed by armed militants, George Brizan indicated that it was possible for some "20 men with sophisticated weapons to take over the government, execute its elected leaders and say the country is now under military rule." *Trinidad Guardian*, 2 Dec. 1984.

20. *Sunday Express*, 2 Dec. 1984.

21. Ibid.

22. Ibid.

23. *Indies Times*, 1 Dec. 1984. Radix himself complained about the violation of his constitutional rights and alleged that his telephone was tapped, that his mail was opened, that his Guyanese wife was prevented from entering the country, and that he was under continuous surveillance.

24. Ibid.

25. Discriminant analysis assumes that likely voters would turn out and vote as indicated by their responses and that the "undecideds" would vote in like manner as the decided voters in terms of sex, age, education, and preference for prime minister.

26. *Trinidad Guardian*, 9 Dec. 1984.

27. Former White House aide Morton Blackwell said that he raised funds to help the NNP become a capable political force. He said that, prior to his involvement, the NNP headquarters was one room with a table, chairs, and a typewriter. NNP activists were taught how to mount a publicity campaign, identify potential support, and other fundamentals of politics. See *Trinidad Guardian*, 3 Dec. 1984.

28. *Sunday Express*, 10 Nov. 1985.

29. It is worth noting that the candidate who won the election, Marcel Peters, subsequently decided to take his seat in Parliament, much to Gairy's chagrin. He was appointed leader of the opposition. Following his expulsion from the GULP, he and the three senators whom he appointed constituted themselves the Grenada Democratic Labour Party.

30. *Trinidad Guardian*, 5 Dec. 1984.

31. *Trinidad Express*, 5 Dec. 1981.

32. See *Newsletter 4* (Autumn 1984), p. 7, Centre for Developing Area Studies, University of Montreal.

33. Summary of text of lecture delivered at Queen's University, Canada, May 1984, Ibid., p. 8.

34. Ibid.

35. Ibid.

36. In Blaize's words, "Communism kills. There is no question about it. This has been proven . . . since 1917. They kill everyone until they get a few left in control." Quoted in the *Financial Times*, 11 Dec. 1986.

37. None other than T. A. Marryshow, the grandson of the grand old man of Grenadian politics of the same name, was barred from practicing medicine. The young physician has now become the leader of the Maurice Bishop Patriotic Movement (MBPM), replacing Kendrick Radix.

38. The total amount of U. S. aid to Grenada for the 1983–89 period reached $110 million, at least three time higher than the per capita aid received from the United States by Grenada's neighbors. Most aid to Grenada was targeted to infrastructure development.

39. Foreign investment in manufacturing during the 1984–89 period was limited to three or four small plants from U. S. pharmaceutical companies (including Johnson & Johnson, Shering Plough, and Smith Kline Beckman), employing no more than a couple hundred employees.

40. Indonesia accounts for 75 percent of the world's nutmeg market, and Grenada for 23 percent. On the formation of the nutmeg producer association (which also set the price of mace) see the *Financial Times*, 28 May 1987.

Part IV

A COMPARATIVE
ASSESSMENT

10. Whither Caribbean Socialism?
Grenada, Jamaica, and Guyana in Perspective

Carl Stone

SOCIALIST TRANSFORMATION has often been seen by the left intelli-gentsia of the Caribbean as the optimal development path. That socialist vision has now been informed by various efforts within the region to break out of the limiting confines of capitalist economic management and to embrace varieties of socialist practice and policy. The experiences of Guyana in the 1970s and early 1980s, Jamaica in the 1970s, and Grenada between 1979 and 1983 are three notable efforts in this direction. They provide, in different ways, interesting evidence on the limits and potential of socialist initiatives in the Caribbean region.

What is meant by socialism? For one thing, the concept overlaps considerably different political economy structures; sharp controversy also exists over whether the label appropriately describes regimes claim-ing allegiance to the socialist ideology broadly defined. Several Marxist commentators, for example, have challenged the claims to genuine so-cialist practice by the Manley regime in Jamaica in the 1970s and by Guyana under the late Forbes Burnham.[1]

Socialism involves commitment to certain specific development ob-jectives. These include large-scale redistribution of wealth, assets, or income in favor of the majority classes and the assignment of a dominant role for the state in economic management to further the life chances of the majority and to reduce, control, or eliminate the power of capitalists. Socialist theory and practice diverge on the most effective means of achieving these common objectives and on the accompanying political structures necessary to activate socialist economic development.

Social democrats seek to operate within the framework of essentially capitalist economies, seeking to humanize them and reform them through redistributive, populist, social service, and social welfare poli-cies. More radical socialist commitments attempt to overturn the capital-ist economy and replace it with a political economy controlled by the state on behalf of the people. Theory and practice within both the reformist social democratic approach and the revolutionary Marxist-Leninist approach diverge also on the question of ownership of the means of production. Emphases vary also with respect to designs to transform the productive capacity of an economy along socialist lines as against priorities that concentrate on redistribution. Further confusion is added by the fact that socialist regimes often embrace theories and articulate principles that diverge considerably from their actual practice.

Somewhere between the reformist social democratic regimes and the Marxist-Leninist political economies are regimes that ultimately seek to move toward the latter by gradual but decisive political and policy steps that take them toward a so-called noncapitalist path.[2] This intermediary position has structural features that combine capitalist elements with initiatives toward a state-managed socialist economy.

The promise of socialist development has also been associated with the objective of reducing dependence on world capitalism and its dominant system in the region (the United States) as well as with the inter-linked objectives of greater economic self-reliance, more decisive locally controlled and inward-looking development policies, as well as greater local political autonomy, dignity, and self-respect.

Implicit in the socialist promise is the democratic claim that socialist management of power is more responsive to majority interests, is more accountable, and provides more extensive channels for mass political participation. Strategies to deepen democracy or claims in that direction invariably accompany efforts at socialist economic management. Socialist management of power, it is claimed, is able to achieve a greater deconcentration of political power.

The interest in socialist transformation and its potential has generated considerable attention due to the deeply rooted economic and social problems that remain unsolved in the English-speaking Caribbean under capitalist economic management. These include high levels of open unemployment; extreme concentration of income; distressing poverty levels among the bottom 40 percent of households; extreme dependence on and vulnerability to trade, financial, consumer, and fiscal trends within the world capitalist system; weak production structures, dependent on one or two main sources of hard-currency earnings; enormous idle capacity in agriculture; extensive foreign ownership and export of capital; weak entrepreneurial traditions, centered more on mercantile activity rather than on production; and massive outflows of skills through emigration.

Whether socialist economic management offers real solutions is an issue that remains largely unexamined beyond the rhetorical claims and assertions of the left and the equally strident counterclaims of antisocialist adversaries. To confront this issue adequately requires some conceptual clarification of the development assumptions of socialist thought and a concrete specification of the precise nature of the root causes of Caribbean economic underdevelopment.

Because Marxist and social democratic notions of development emerged as antitheses to capitalism within the core economies of the world capitalist system, both assumed that capitalism had developed a productive capability that socialist management could build on to achieve its class and social objectives. The social democrats sought to harness the income base generated by dynamic private entrepreneurs to redistribute some of it in the direction of improving the quality of life of the poor through welfare state policies. Additionally, it was thought that the creative and productive energies of private capital could be channeled more toward national development by state regulation. Marxist development thought presumes that the task of revolution lies in taking hold of the productive forces created by capitalism and using them for the benefit of the majority classes rather than for the purpose of capitalist profit generation. These essentially Western European assumptions have no basis when applied to Third World regions like the Caribbean, where the priority development task lies in building a strong and viable production base, as a long history of retarded growth through colonialism, dependence, and imperialism has left a legacy of an undeveloped productive capacity.

Two Marxist views on development in the Third World are more relevant to the Caribbean situation. The first argues for a development alternative via socialism, which would avoid the excess of materialism and acquisitiveness associated with capitalism. This type of no frills development would seek to reorganize the forces of production to meet the food, shelter, clothing, health, educational, and other welfare needs of the majority classes.[3] The goal of mass affluence, or a high material level of living, is portrayed as a capitalist design to promote overconsumption. Needs rather than wants would be satisfied, and equality assured. Such an objective is realizable within the context of the productive capability of Caribbean economies. Its advantage over the present situation in the English-speaking Caribbean is that it would reduce or eliminate much of the hard-core poverty and unemployment among the bottom 40 percent of income earners. The disadvantage is that it would have nothing to offer to the top 60 percent of income earners—except a drastically reduced standard of living.

The alternative Marxist view still clings to the idea of socialism as capable of transforming the productive capacity of Third World capitalism and of beginning to bring the full fruits of modern technology within the grasp of the world's working class.[4] Here the vision of socialism coexisting with abundance and high material standards of living is kept intact, although its realization can only occur after the collapse of the world capitalist system. Underlying this view is a Leninist faith and optimism that the world capitalist system is destined to collapse and the task of Third World development is to prepare to partake in an alternative socialist development. Here the prescription is for a development effort toward a noncapitalist path. Success or failure cannot be judged in terms of whether incomes increase or mass welfare improves. Rather, the key criterion is whether development is moved toward socialism to ensure that these countries keep pace with the unfolding pattern of inevitable world historical development from capitalism to socialism.

Underlying this socialist view of development is the idea that politics takes command of economic forces and guides them in a direction that is either historically correct or designed to put them at the service of the majority classes. In the Caribbean situation, it acquires currency as an escape route from imperialism, class exploitation, and dependency. Socialist development thought in the Third World and the Caribbean focuses on the consolidation of power, the development of an appropriate ideology, mass mobilization, mass political awareness and class consciousness, organizational development, and a historically correct view of world political alignments. The result is that an overloaded agenda of political concerns crowds out detailed and technical economic policy questions.[5] These relate to economic strategies and tactics; the nature of the existing world capitalist system and how to maximize one's development policy options within it; the level of existing productive capability and how to advance it; how to go about obtaining development financing and to improve one's position in the fields of technology and trade; and what forms of economic planning are feasible, given the political capacity and administrative resource capability. The result quite often is that conventional capitalist economic strategies are borrowed and combined with socialist political strategies, leading to development that is contradictory, internally inconsistent, and confusing to both those who lead and those who follow.[6]

Socialist development in the Caribbean can therefore be judged according to a number of criteria. These include the following:

1. Has it enhanced or improved the well-being and welfare of the majority classes?
2. Is it seeking to establish a reorganized basic-needs socialist economy, or is it working within the capitalist market economy, albeit with high levels of state regulation control or ownership?
3. Is it Marxist or social democratic in ideological alignment?
4. Is the accompanying political system liberal democratic or based on the political prescriptions of the noncapitalist path, which seeks to establish political hegemony around a strong and dominant populist or majoritarian political ideology?
5. Are the development priorities biased toward consolidation of power,

biased toward economic transformation strategies, or are they balanced evenly?

6. How do the strategies of international alignment serve or undermine the economic policy thrust, and what is optimal given existing world economic realities?

7. How far are the socialist goals (economic or political) compatible with the aspirations, values, and culture of Caribbean people?

8. How far are the economic and social objectives of socialist practice likely to address the concrete or structural economic problems in the region?

9. To what extent are socialist politics consistent with the accompanying economic policies?

In examining the attempts at socialist development in Grenada, and Jamaica, and Guyana it will be useful to compare and evaluate these regimes according to these criteria.

There are essentially three basic structural problems in English-speaking Caribbean countries. Firstly, as middle-income Third World countries, they have considerably raised their post-World War II living standards through overdependence on mineral and primary products exports (bauxite, oil, sugar, bananas, etc.) to buoyant and lucrative core capitalist markets. Major downward shifts in prices and market demand for those exports have meant drastic declines in the capacity to import. High dependence on imports (due to small size and to a legacy of economic dependence) makes the region extraordinarily vulnerable to adverse price and supply changes in international commodity or consumer goods markets. Third, import dependence combined with technological dependence mean that investment expansion to extend, enlarge, and diversify productive capacity require foreign investment, loans, credit, or aid to bring such (public or private) investment projects to fruition. Policies to address these problems all require a capacity to mobilize international or foreign resources or to penetrate overseas markets. Political and economic strategies cannot therefore be entirely inward looking (whether insular or regional), as a capacity to cope with and extract resources from the world system will clearly influence success or failure in development efforts in these microstates. Socialist development strategies mean very little if they fail to offer solutions to these problems over and above those prescriptions posed by capitalist development policy and approaches.

SOCIALISM IN GRENADA, JAMAICA, AND GUYANA

Before we can attempt to compare the results of the socialist initiatives of Grenada, Jamaica, and Guyana, it is first necessary to classify and compare their structural and policy differences and similarities in both the economic and political spheres. Table 10.1 makes such a comparison of their political profile.

The regimes differ in terms of the official ideologies they articulated. Both Guyana and Grenada projected official doctrines supportive of Marxist notions of socialist development. In the case of Guyana, the official ideology was designed for cosmetic and symbolic impact rather than as a guide to policy and practice. The Grenadian leadership was genuinely Marxist in its political-ideological objectives. The People's National Party (PNP) in Jamaica, in contrast to the People's Revolutionary Government (PRG) in Grenada and the People's National Congress (PNC) in Guyana, consistently denied any Marxist commitments due to constant harassment by the opposition anti-Marxist Jamaica Labor Party (JLP) and the strong anti-Communist sentiments in Jamaica. This problem did not arise in Guyana or in Grenada; the Guyanese parties all espoused far-left ideological doctrines; in Grenada, the de facto one-party state suppressed the articulation of anti-Marxist sentiments among segments of the political community.

Guyana remained relatively isolated from any big-power connections, having failed to establish close ties with Eastern Europe and the Soviet Union. Jamaica under Manley was very friendly with Cuba but had no close ties with the Eastern bloc. Strong and radical Third World linkages guided their nonaligned foreign policies, and in either case anti-imperialist positions on international affairs led to strained relations with Washington. Open hostility by the United States pushed Grenada into a search for close Eastern European ties, which had the self-fulfilling effect of intensifying U.S. aggression. The United States adopted a hands-off position on socialist Guyana, because the political alternative was the Marxist and pro-Moscow People's Progressive Party (PPP) led by avowed Communist Cheddi Jagan. In Jamaica, the United States sought to undermine socialism and the PNP by adverse economic policies and political destabilization in support of the pro-U.S. and anti-Communist JLP led by Edward Seaga. This factor combined with their

Table 10.1
Political Profiles of Socialist Regimes in Grenada, Jamaica, and Guyana

Political Feature	Grenada	Jamaica	Guyana
Ideology	Marxist	Social democracy	Marxist
Big power alignment	Aligned with East	Nonaligned	Nonaligned
Base of support	Youth	Class	Racial
Power structure	Party state	Liberal democracy	Party state
Political style	Participatory	Participatory	Authoritarian
Individual freedom	Low	Medium	Low

similarly close Cuban connections and Jamaica's efforts to give support to the Grenadian regime established a close bond of friendship between socialist Grenada and Jamaica under Manley. This was in contrast to the relative isolation of Guyana.

Although espousing Marxism, the Guyanese PNC mobilized its mass support on the basis of black racial support in opposition to East Indian dominance. The social base of the PNC was therefore ethnicity rather than class. In contrast, while its popularity lasted—and especially between 1976 and 1980—the Jamaican PNP's base of political support came mainly from a combination of the urban and rural poor, who rallied behind the regime's populist posturing and commitment to improve the lot of the downtrodden. On the other hand, the PNP under Manley completely alienated the middle class and capitalists. In Grenada, in turn, the PRG anchored its base of support mainly on the younger generation, who identified with the party's efforts to build a revolution and transform the country along socialist lines.

In Jamaica, as in Grenada, the small peasants were either distrustful or hostile to the socialist doctrines, while organized labor was sharply divided between antisocialist and prosocialist tendencies. In contrast to Western Europe, where organized labor and the urban working class tend to rally behind socialist parties, in both Grenada and Jamaica, the relatively privileged position of organized labor generates ambivalence toward radical doctrines for social change. As movements concentrating their membership mainly among the middle 40 percent of income earners, organized labor identified both with some socialist goals that offer working class improvements and with fears that socialist policy changes could intimidate capitalists and foment a large-scale loss of employment. Middle- and upper-income wage workers also had identity problems relating to these party movements, which derived much of their emotional grass roots support from the lumpen proletariat and the subproletariat. Further, given the low productive capacity and income level of these Third World economies, leftist parties find it impossible to establish extensive welfare state benefits to attract solid working class support. Much of their social policy thrust has to be directed toward the unemployed, the self-employed petty commodity sectors (small farmers and artisans), and the subproletariat. In both Jamaica and Grenada, the link between socialism and the working class was weak; in Guyana, race rather than class established the socialist regime's popular base of support.

The power structures of these regimes had some common features but differed in critical areas. Both Guyana and Grenada had hegemonic power structures, in which the governing parties—the PNC in Guyana and the NJM in Grenada—monopolized power that was heavily concentrated in the hands of party leaders and policymakers. Guyana had a well-established and consolidated power structure, while Grenada was in the process of consolidating power before the regime collapsed. In neither case were there any checks and balances or constitutional constraints that limited the exercise of the enormous concentration of power in the hands of party and government leaders. This concentration of power enabled "politics" to effectively take command, as the party-states asserted control, direction, and guidance over all spheres of economic and social life. This was facilitated by tight control of the mass media, the merging of party and government functions, political control over the civil service, extensive growth of the state's policy leadership, and control over the economy.

Jamaica, in contrast, operated under the restrictions of orthodox Westminster-Whitehall administrative and constitutional arrangements. The power of the relatively strong capitalist class, the influences of the articulate middle class, the constraints of the legal and constitutional limits to power, a strong opposition party, and a competitive multi-mass-media situation blocked the prospects for the large-scale concentration of power that took place in Grenada and Guyana.

All three regimes were led by flamboyant charismatic figures (Michael Manley, Forbes Burnham, and Maurice Bishop). Their power was highly personalized rather than mainly institutional; each party leader wielded enormous power and control over political and policy directions. This personalization of power limited the degree to which their political machinery could become either bureaucratized or relatively autonomous.

The political management and leadership styles of the three regimes were also quite different, with major consequences for personal freedoms. Channels for mass participation were opened up in Grenada for those who supported the regime. Genuine efforts were made to galvanize the energies of the Grenadian people in attempts to build a socialist society. In Guyana, participation was discouraged, except in limited spheres subject to tight PNC party control. Fear of opposition and the possible increase in political dissent led to a climate of political repression and denial of individual political freedoms. Left authoritarianism, in which political repression was justified in the name of socialist unity, combined with widespread corruption to destroy enthusiastic mass support for the PNC regime. Increasingly, power was consolidated through repression, manipulation of the army and the police, fear, and threats of political violence from above. The abuse of political power by party and state officials to accumulate wealth through corrupt practices also played an important role in this. An elaborate patronage system evolved in which political and policy favors were exchanged for unquestioning political loyalty.

In Jamaica, the socialist PNP's participatory management style was similar to that in Grenada. The major difference was that it had less impact, because the PNP was less in control over the society and the economy than the NJM was in Grenada. Much of the mass mobilization in Jamaica was devoted to containing political attacks from the militant opposition JLP. This limited the leadership and organizational efforts that could be channeled toward mobilization to facilitate policy implementation and economic and social reconstruction. More important, in Jamaica fear of strong antisocialist and antipopulist tendencies led to more cautious, defensive, and less open styles of leadership and considerably less of the open dialogue and communication between leaders and activist supporters that was sustained for some time in Grenada before the mobilization capacity of the regime became impaired. Opposition groups (antisocialist and socialist) were severely harassed by the military in both Guyana and Grenada, while in Jamaica there were violent contests for power between socialist and antisocialist groups. Individual political freedoms were more protected in Jamaica and were less under assault from efforts to consolidate power by the silencing of opposition voices—a situation that was widespread in both Grenada and Guyana. In Jamaica, there were fewer political prisoners, detentions without trial, or unrestrained imprisonment of political adversaries. As a consequence, fair elections could be held, resulting in the loss of power by the socialist PNP party in 1980, in contrast to Guyana, where the electoral process is rigged to perpetuate the PNC in power, and to Grenada, where the regime could only be removed at gunpoint. Not surprisingly, Manley lost power through elections, while Bishop was assassinated, and Burnham lost power only when he died from natural causes.

The economic profiles of the regimes reflect equally sharp contrasts, as can be seen from table 10.2. None of these socialist initiatives involved efforts toward creating a basic-needs economy. Grenada seemed headed in that direction, but the regime did not last long enough to evolve a noncapitalist economic structure. Neither Guyana nor Jamaica showed any signs of dismantling their capitalist market economies. In contrast to Grenada, both Jamaica and Guyana embarked on appreciable levels of state ownership. In Guyana, this development went considerably further than in Jamaica. Some 80 percent of the Guyanese economy came under state ownership or control, while in Jamaica the level was

Table 10.2
Economic Profiles of Grenada, Jamaica, and Guyana

Economic Feature	Grenada	Jamaica	Guyana
State ownership	Low	Medium	High
Economic system	Market economy	Market economy	Market economy
Socialist policy priority	Redistribution	Redistribution	State ownership
External economic ties	Core capitalist	Core capitalist	Core capitalist

in the region of 9 percent. It is therefore not surprising that some analysts have characterized state ownership in both countries as exhibiting the features of state capitalism.

The central socialist policy thrust in both Jamaica and Guyana was toward state ownership of productive assets and income redistribution. Socialist production to meet the basic needs of the majority classes was on the agenda of political discussion and articulated in rhetoric in both countries but never became the subject of significant economic policy efforts. In Grenada, concern with the consolidation of political power and national self-defense against U.S. hostility were the main concerns, and the regime did not last long enough to give birth to a socialist model of economic management. Instead, economic policies were designed to minimize dislocation and to create public sector employment for the youth without threatening the existing pattern of ownership and distribution.

Overall, efforts to put socialist politics in command in all three Caribbean countries far outweighed efforts to reorganize these economies along socialist lines. Indeed, in no case was significant progress made toward socialist economic management. In the revolutionary conditions of Grenada, socialist political consolidation had to be the first priority. In Jamaica modest social democratic reforms of the capitalist market economy was the goal, and nothing far-reaching was attempted. In Guyana state ownership merely replaced private foreign ownership. Indeed, both Jamaica and Guyana revealed more state economic initiatives guided by economic nationalism than by socialism. In Guyana bauxite was nationalized to protect the national interest against multinational companies. In Jamaica a large production levy was imposed on these companies to enhance the flow of national benefits. In Grenada there were no similar large multinational companies to take over, hence the relative absence of strong state ownership policies motivated by economic nationalist.

The combination of domestic efforts at socialist development and capitalist external economic trade ties and other links of economic dependency posed a serious limitation on how far these socialist initiatives could proceed without first reorienting these external economic linkages away from the dominant world capitalist system.

AN EVALUATION OF SOCIALIST DEVELOPMENT IN GRENADA, JAMAICA, AND GUYANA

It remains now to assess the weaknesses and strengths of these three Caribbean initiatives toward socialist development and their implications for future attempts at socialist transformation in the region.

As can be seen from Table 10.3, in both Guyana and Jamaica,

Table 10.3
Economic Indicators, Six Caribbean States, 1970s (percent)

	Per Capita GDP Growth Rates (1970–1979)	Average Annual Increase in Government Spending (1970s)	Budget Deficit as Percentage of 1978 Expenditure
Jamaica	−2.0	11.0	19
Guyana	−0.7	10.5	19
Barbados	1.4	1.9	0
Puerto Rico	0.7	5.1	
Trinidad	1.0	10.4	0
Dominican Republic	3.3	−0.9	0

Sources: World Bank, *World Tables 1980* (Washington, D.C.: World Bank, 1981); for gross domestic product and government spending; *Economic Survey of Latin America* (New York: United Nations, 1979) for budget deficits.

economic growth in the 1970s was among the worst in the region. In both countries, per capita income levels actually declined, a decline that *preceded* the 1980s economic paralysis caused in both countries by the collapse of the world bauxite market (and the consequent fall in hard currency earnings and ensuing balance of payment problems).

Both countries committed themselves to rapidly increasing public spending in a period of downturn in real income and production. The result was a massive budget deficit. In Jamaica the rationale was to sustain employment and government services and to increase transfer payments to the poor through price subsidies, state ownership of enterprises, and redistributive social projects. Although the effects were not long lasting, these policies eased the burdens on the poor in the crisis period of the 1970s. The dismantling of these policy initiatives by the antisocialist JLP in the 1980s has led to unprecedented economic hardships for the poor.

State management of production and overall economic policy regulation in Guyana and Jamaica increased significantly the management burdens on the public sector. Extensive corrupt practices, weak management systems, excessive red tape, indecisiveness, waste of resources, labor nondiscipline, and huge gaps in management and technical skills exaggerated by migration created severe problems.

State ownership in Jamaica burdened the limited foreign exchange available to the government and created a major crisis, as needed spare parts and equipment could not be imported. Consequently, public utilities virtually collapsed and disrupted the capacity of the economy to produce. Political squabbles between the socialist PNP and the private sector triggered a large-scale flight of capital and hard currency, which

left the economy considerably weakened. Weak public sector management capability and some political sabotage resulted in massive waste
and crippling inefficiency in public sector projects.

In Grenada, weak mass organizations proved incapable of carrying
out the administrative tasks and political leadership needed to sustain
popular participation in economic management. As a result, effectiveness in policy implementation was at a modest level. As in Jamaica,
organizational indiscipline and a weak work ethic multiplied the problems of managing public projects and led to waste of funds. Grenada
strenuously tried to avoid the excesses of Jamaica and Guyana by mini-
mizing state ownership and attempting more stringent fiscal management. However, as table 10.4 illustrates, all three countries ended up
with the highest budget deficits in the region by 1982.

In the Grenadian case, public spending pressures came mainly from
the capital side of the budget, as tight controls were maintained over
recurrent expenditure. For both Jamaica and Guyana, high capital
spending combined with rapid rates of growth of recurrent expenditure
tended to exacerbate the budget deficit problem. Once socialist tendencies dominate policy management, there is a high propensity to expand
public spending. Further, the rate of increase in public spending tends
to exceed the rate of growth of the economy, thereby increasing the
overall share of the public sector as a percentage of GDP. The continuation of the high budget deficit in Jamaica even after the socialist PNP
lost power at the end of 1980 testifies to the difficulties involved in
cutting such deficits once they are established. Due to IMF pressures,
the new conservative JLP government managed to reduce the deficit by

Table 10.4
Fiscal Deficit as Percentage of Government Expenditure, Ten Caribbean States,
1980–1982

	1980	1981	1982
Guyana	57	56	67
Grenada	37	59	62
Jamaica	42	37	49
St. Kitts	20	27	39
Dominica	45	33	35
Trinidad	surplus	surplus	33
Barbados	11	26	16
St. Lucia		15	16
Belize	9	20	15
Antigua	9	20	

Source: *Economic Activity in Caribbean Countries, 1982* (Santiago, Chile: Economic Commission for
Latin America, 1983), p. 17.

some 50 percent between 1982 and 1984 by drastic reductions in public sector employment.

Grenada was also more successful than either Guyana or Jamaica in avoiding negative growth or a prolonged economic downturn (table 10.5). In contrast, Grenada's pattern of economic growth between 1979 and 1982 was exceeded only by Barbados (the most dynamic of the capitalist economies in the region), Trinidad, and Dominica. Serious questions have been raised over the significance of the growth of the Grenadian economy over this period, as tourism and manufacturing as well as most areas of agriculture declined. The main growth sector was government services, which expanded from 9 percent of GDP in 1975 to over 20 percent in the early 1980s. Indeed, the much acclaimed reduction in unemployment represented absorption of labor in military and government activities.

Neither Grenada nor Jamaica showed significant improvement or reorganization of the productive base of their economies. Instead, efforts were made to consolidate political support through redistributive policies and increases in social services (health, education, etc.). Both regimes directed extensive resources at raising adult literacy, organizing state and cooperative food production, and improving access to health and educational services. Significant improvements in literacy levels in Grenada and spectacular declines in rural infant mortality rates in Jamaica resulted from these social policies. In Guyana, no matching advances in social policy accompanied the socialist thrust, thereby supporting the view that the PNC's leadership was merely using the socialist ideology as a cover for legitimizing state capitalism and self-enrichment

Table 10.5
Real Growth Rates of Gross Domestic Product,
Nine Caribbean States, 1980–1982
(percent)

	1980	*1981*	*1982*
Barbados	8	12	6
Dominica	16	8	3
Trinidad	5	4	4
Grenada	3	3	5
Belize	4	3	−0.3
St. Kitts	5	3	−0.5
St. Lucia	−0.9	0.3	−0.6
Jamaica	−0.5	3	0.2
Antigua	1	1	−7

Source. *Economic Survey of Latin America and the Caribbean, 1982* (Santiago, Chile: United Nations Commission for Latin America and the Caribbean, 1983), p. 6.

by corrupt party leaders, who appropriated the resources of the state for their own selfish private ends.

In Guyana and Jamaica, balance of payments difficulties induced by international price and market pressures led to a search for extensive foreign borrowing from capitalist sources. Conflicts between the monetarist thrust of capitalist lending agencies and the socialist policy priorities of these governments produced a situation of extreme policy conflicts and the termination of loan agreements. Jamaica was able to borrow considerably more than Guyana, but the results have been more negative than positive. Excessive borrowing was used to postpone necessary adjustments in the Jamaican economy, so the basic structural problems remain, with the added burden of a huge debt payment, which now consumes 40 percent of the national budget and more than 50 percent of hard-currency earnings.

Faced with the need for adjustment loans to tide them over difficult periods of foreign exchange crises, all three countries had to seek loans from the IMF and the World Bank. These agencies sought to the shift policy thrust of the states away from socialist goals and toward free-market structural adjustment policies and austere monetary and fiscal policies. The countries had no alternative but agree, as there are no socialist or noncapitalist equivalents of the IMF or the World Bank for short-term or development borrowing. Capitalist financial dependence, especially in periods when conservative economic policy thinking is dominant in the core capitalist countries, serves to blunt and retard socialist economic advances in small Third World countries by starving them of aid (in the case of Guyana) or doling out aid generously as a condition for forcing them back onto a capitalist path (in the case of Jamaica).

That constraint could be overcome if the core socialist economies were more outward looking toward the Third World, had less of a hard currency liquidity problem, and represented a more significant segment of world trade, financing, production, and services. The continued dominance of the world economy by the core capitalist countries and the essentially inward-looking development strategies of the Eastern bloc leaves small, developing socialist countries vulnerable to world capitalist pressures to change course or forgo the socialist path. The substantial increase in U.S. and multilateral economic aid to the English-speaking Caribbean in the 1980s was designed precisely to slow down and divert what is left of the momentum toward socialist development.

Grenada received a considerable amount of Eastern bloc aid via Cuba and showed potential to increase such external and supportive socialist linkages. However, it seemed clear that even Grenada would not be readily absorbed into the Eastern bloc simply because of its Marxist ideological commitment. It soon became evident that whatever trade and aid could be obtained from the East would not be enough for Grenada to cut its ties with capitalist core countries.

The strong Eastern bloc and Cuban political ties in Grenada were assumed by the left to be a virtual guarantee against external threats. The failure of the Cubans or the Eastern bloc to challenge militarily the subsequent U.S. invasion of Grenada underscores the dilemma of Marxist socialist efforts in the Caribbean. Encircled by anticommunist regimes and the major superpower in the region, such regimes will naturally seek protection from the Eastern bloc and attempt to secure external economic ties that can reduce dependence on world capitalist nations and institutions. But such political ties make the countries vulnerable to U. S. aggression in much the same way that Grenada was powerless to resist the U.S.-inspired and-led invasion. The lesson of Grenada is that such ideological ventures are bedeviled with geopolitical hazards.

THE PROSPECTS FOR CARIBBEAN SOCIALISM

Without such an Eastern bloc connection, there is little prospect of small middle-income Caribbean economies developing a basic-needs economy, of surviving a scaling down of Western trade, and of avoiding financial and technological dependence. The basic-needs economic model, which channels productive resources toward meeting the food, clothing, shelter, health, educational, and other social needs of the majority classes as the highest economic policy priority, is in fact the only route by which socialism in the Caribbean can bring lasting and long-term improvements in the quality of life of the Caribbean poor and unemployed.

Development of a basic needs socialist economy requires a hegemonic, one-party state, a strong dominant Marxist ideology, and a mass party or movement with a highly developed capacity for mobilization and administration. Organizational weaknesses within Caribbean leftist parties; fratricidal contentions for power among ruthless, leftist, intelligentsia; low levels of organizational discipline; and weak leadership at the grass roots level, as in Grenada, all suggest that prospects for socialist development in this direction after Grenada are not very promising.

The failure to consolidate power in Grenada and the murder of the regime's popular leader has left an indelible scar on the image of Marxist-oriented socialism. This has served to exacerbate the strong anticommunist political tendencies in the region, based on conservative and fundamentalist church influences, peasant values (which are skeptical of state ownership or control of productive assets), and the regional obsession with aping and aspiring to the materialist, acquisitive, and affluent life-style of North America. The penetration of the region by

North American media, extensive networks of family connections with the North American mainland through migration, and strong social traditions that encourage excessive consumerism, individualism, private accumulation, and upward social mobility into middle-class life-styles all render the basic needs model incompatible with the value system of most Caribbean peoples. Cuban successes at transforming the quality of life among its people through the development of a basic-needs economy (albeit with extensive Eastern bloc help) has consequently not had the big impact many expected in promoting Marxist socialism in the Caribbean.

In all three countries' efforts at installing socialist political management, inadequate thought was given to the limitations and constraints imposed by a limited administrative capacity in the public sector and the limited organizational capacity of the political parties. As a result, the enlarged public sector economic and administrative responsibilities stretched these resources beyond their limits. The result was mismanagement, inefficiency, waste of resources, and policy failures. Many of the policy failures under the PNP in Jamaica in the 1970s were rooted in this problem. Limited organizational resources led to leadership failures, communication gaps, weak capability for mobilization, and political crises, as the political management tasks under socialism grew ahead of the capacity to undertake them. In Grenada this type of organizational weakness set the stage for the factional contest for power, and disillusionment with leadership led to the Coard-Bishop division and the regime's collapse.

Core capitalist economies are becoming more and more integrated, thereby increasing the size and scope of the world economic system. This is in sharp contrast to misleading Marxist-Leninist forecasts of the impending collapse of that system. In spite of its internal crises, the world capitalist system is increasing its economic penetration of peripheral economies and using the leverage of that economic power to influence ideological and policy directions in the Third World, in general—and in the Caribbean, in particular. There are no similar countervailing socialist international economic influences. All of these factors mean that prospects for socialism in the English-speaking Caribbean are, at best, weak.

The Jamaican situation well illustrates this. In 1989 the socialist PNP led by Michael Manley experienced a resurgence of mass support and defeated the conservative governing JLP. Yet the PNP's policy prescriptions have shifted from left to center, and much of the socialist vision that inspired its confident ideological posturing in the seventies has disappeared. Problem-centered pragmatism has replaced ideological evangelism. A search for economic solutions has replaced a vision that solutions can come from placing politics in command. The PNP's vocal antiimperialism has been replaced by efforts to find an accommodation with the United States, and even the former militant anti-IMF stance has softened considerably to a stance that leaves open options for accommodation with the IMF. The 1970s emphasis on redistribution has given way to a 1980s preoccupation with production and sound economic policy management. All of this is due to the consensus in the society that the socialism of the 1970s, while grounded in good intentions, produced less than satisfactory results.

The fact is that real, lasting gains from socialism are to be realized from basic-needs economic restructuring, but the administrative, political, and political economy obstacles are formidable. Socialist approaches that seek to work within existing capitalist market economies by regulating the capitalist class, promoting state ownership, and providing redistributive social policies can ease the burdens on the poor for short periods, but the results are not long lasting unless the productive base expands and hard-currency earnings increase significantly. Further, some of these policies can actively work against diversifying and enlarging the productive base of these economies.

Socialism in the Caribbean has not produced the expected transformation by reordering the political equation in favor of the majority classes. But socialist efforts at economic management have not been significantly worse than conventional capitalist approaches. Neither ideological solution has provided any easy path toward economic recovery or transformation in the English-speaking Caribbean. The reason quite simply is that politics and ideology cannot provide solutions to problems that are essentially rooted in the structure of these economies.

Two development paths are possible in the Caribbean. Export-led growth is possible under facilitating international conditions that permit capitalist management to diversify and increase the region's hard-currency earnings through export manufacturing. Most Caribbean countries lack the dynamic capitalists needed to develop this free-enterprise model and to break out of dependence on plantation agriculture and mineral exports. Alternatively, a socialist basic-needs development model would eliminate most of the deep-rooted poverty and unemployment in the region but would offer no improvement for the top 60 percent of income earners, who would have to consume less to accommodate greater equality in income and consumption. The political obstacles to that path are therefore quite formidable. Neither capitalist nor socialist development in the Caribbean offers any easy road to transformation or easy escape route from the economic stagnation that besets the region. A few countries may make it by the capitalist route, but many will be left behind in the backwater of low income and earning capacity, as the Caribbean adjusts to the harsh realities of the world economy.

Mini- and microstates do not have the resources to develop on their own, independent of the world economic system. Their fortunes are dictated by external developments beyond their control. But strong internal management is demanded to cope with these external stresses. The ability to diversify exports, the capacity of labor and management to compete in international markets or to produce food and basic-goods import substitutes, the ability to retain earned hard currency, the capacity to adapt technology to break into capital goods production and light industry, the commitment of capitalists to plow back profits into production rather than siphon them off to Miami banks or conspicuous consumption are just some of the factors that will influence development and survival prospects in the Caribbeanto a considerably greater degree than ideology, be it socialist or capitalist.

The experience of Grenada, Jamaica, and Guyana has thus helped demystify socialism and ideology for the Caribbean.

NOTES

1. Clive Thomas in fact classifies these regimes as being state capitalist rather than socialist. Clive Thomas, "From Colony to State Capitalism" (Paramaribo, Suriname: Foundation in Arts and Sciences, 1982, mimeo.).

2. See R. A. Ulyanovsky, *Socialism and the Newly Independent Nations* (Moscow: Progress Publishers, 1974).

3. North Korea and China (under Mao) represent models of this type of no-frills socialist development. Prescription of this path for the Caribbean is set out in George Beckford and Michael Witter, *Small Garden, Bitter Weed: Struggle and Change in Jamaica* (Morant Bay, Jamaica: Maroon, 1980). The basic-needs model of socialist development is comprehensively analyzed in Carl Stone, *Profiles of Power in the Caribbean Basin* (Philadelphia: ISHI, 1986). ch. 6.

4. See for example Paul Baran, *The Political Economy of Growth* (New York: Monthly Review Press, 1957).

5. There is in fact not a single comprehensive work by a Marxist theorist that deals with the technical issues of transformation to socialism in the specific context of Caribbean economies. Clive Thomas, *Dependence and Transformation: The Economics of the Transition to Socialism* (New York: Monthly Review Press, 1984), comes close, but it deals with the issue within the general Third World framework rather than addressing the specificities of the Caribbean context.

6. This was certainly a problem of the Manley regime in Jamaica.

11. Democracy and Socialism:
Reflections on the Grenada Experience

Laurence Whitehead

DEMOCRACY

THE 1973 MANIFESTO of the New Jewel Movement criticized parliamentary elections and the Westminster system, saying "it fails to involve the people except for a few seconds once in every five years, when they make an *x* on a ballot paper." It is important to notice that this stand was adopted *before* Grenada was precipitated into independence (1974), *before* Bernard Coard and his wife returned to Grenada and took up leading roles in the movement, and *before* Bishop and Coard succeeded in winning seats in the first postindependence election (1976). It is also important to remember that, on the day the NJM took power (13 March 1979), Bishop spoke as follows on Radio Free Grenada: "In closing let me assure the people of Grenada that all democratic freedoms, including freedom of elections, religious and political opinion will be fully restored to the people."[1] Thus there was a clear promise that the NJM would establish a form of democracy more authentic and more truly participatory than the system inherited from colonialism; there was also a promise of some kind of free elections, although the NJM never wavered in its criticism of prerevolutionary electoral forms.

It is surely beyond dispute that if the New Jewel Movement had organized free and honest elections in, say, 1980 (especially before 6 November 1980), the revolutionaries would have secured a handsome majority. The same is almost certainly true for the Sandinista Front in the same period. Rather more speculatively, I would claim that Fidel Castro could have secured a clear majority for the 26 July movement if he had chosen to hold elections in 1960 (especially before the U.S. presidential elections of November 1960). In all these three cases (and also in the much more uncertain case of the plebiscite by which Allende might have strengthened his authority in Chile in mid-1971), vulnerable Marxist-influenced governments had the opportunity of profiting from

309

the procedures of "bourgeois democracy," broadening their appeal to potential domestic allies, and deflating international criticism. Despite the pragmatic advantages of adopting this course, these governments all chose not to hold elections when the moment was most favorable. Subsequently, both Allende and the Sandinistas faced elections under less favorable conditions. Neither Cuba nor Grenada diluted the purity of their principles in this way (although in mid-1983, Bishop reportedly promised the government of Trinidad that there would be a constitution and some kind of elections by 1985).

How can we explain the fact that supposedly cynical and power-seeking Marxists should refuse to hold elections as a matter of principle, even when the technique seems to offer an easy way of achieving their goals? The mere adoption of Marxist categories of analysis will hardly suffice as an explanation, since counterpart parties in Mexico, Venezuela, Chile, Uruguay, Jamaica, and Guyana vociferously demand the right to participate in honest and free elections, even though they know they cannot hope to win power that way. Similarly, of course, Communist parties of postwar Eastern Europe had no hesitation in sponsoring and winning elections that helped to consolidate them in power. In fact, espousal of Communist political models is neither a necessary nor a sufficient condition for rejecting conventional liberal-democratic norms, even when they offer a tactical advantage. There were, I would imagine, at least some periods when General Pinochet might have strengthened his legitimacy by holding and winning a more or less democratic election. The same would probably apply to Franco or Trujillo.

Clearly, the right-wing regimes just listed are among the most unsavory and antidemocratic in the demonology of the left. Why should progressives, who wish to attain a higher level of popular organization and mobilization than mere "bourgeois" democracy, act in such a way that they can be bracketed with the most repressive and demobilizing regimes? Why, in particular, should they adopt such a posture when operating in the Western hemisphere, a part of the world so strongly imbued with the traditions of political liberalism and republicanism, an area where the dominant power is famous for its use of democratic imagery to legitimize acts of imperial assertion?

The last phrase of my question begins to suggest an answer. I believe it is safe to assume that if the Cuban leadership had conducted a candid discussion of the pros and cons of holding elections around 1960, the precedent of democratic Guatemala and its inability to resist CIA-directed destabilization would have been a major consideration. Less speculatively, we can see from both the public record and the captured documents about Grenada the impact of such experiences as Allende's overthrow in Chile, Manley's electoral defeat in Jamaica, and the history of the Burnham regime in Guyana. All of these experiences seem to have suggested to the Grenadian revolutionaries that the invocation of formal democratic norms would offer little defense against external harassment. The Nicaraguans would probably cite similar examples, although in the aftermath of the Grenada invasion there was probably some rethinking among the Sandinistas, which may have contributed to their decision to hold elections on 4 November 1984 (two days before a U.S. presidential election). In a somewhat similar vein, the postrevolutionary regime in Mexico evidently decided half a century ago that, although regular elections would be held, only members of the ruling party would ever be allowed to win executive office. I believe that Mexico's choice of a democratic form void of real competitive contact was to an important extent shaped by the need to present a united front against external (i.e.,U.S.) pressures, and to resist foreign interference and interventionism—needs strongly felt to this day, although the Mexican regime is far from being Communist (let alone Marxist-Leninist) in character. The Mexican model of a dominant single-party regime ought to have satisfied most of the requirements of a realistic Grenadian leadership, but the NJM seems to have thought only in terms of two alternatives—either a "colonial-type" Westminster system or the Cuban model.

Any regime that comes to power through acts of force (including the one established by George Washington) must take into account the possibility that those who were displaced by undemocratic means will probably—if they have the chance—use the same methods against the usurpers. The ability of displaced elites to stage counterrevolutions is heavily conditioned by the availability of external support, notably in the form of arms, money, and a territorial base of operations. The Mexicans, the Cubans, the Grenadians, and most recently the Nicaraguans have all had good reason to fear that the U.S. government might supply such support, just as the fledgling United States feared British intervention through the displaced Tories in Canada. The United States was able to operate under a (for that time) relatively democratic constitution while resisting external harassment. This was at least in part because the British were more or less resigned to the outcome of 1776, and indeed a strong current of domestic opinion sympathized with U.S. aspirations.

By contrast, there has been very little sympathy within the United States for the aims of the Cuban, the Grenadian, or the Nicaraguan revolutionaries (and for many years after 1910, little sympathy for Mexican objectives either). At least since 1945 the dominant strand of thinking in Washington has always been to refuse to come to terms with any regime in the Western hemisphere that sought close relations with the USSR. So if the Cubans, the Grenadians, or the Nicaraguans—

even for thoroughly prudent reasons—considered that they might need Soviet support to bolster their revolutions against the foreseeable hostility of Washington, they would have to anticipate serious U.S.-based counterrevolutionary activity. That alone may provide a sufficient *realpolitik* explanation as to why these regimes all opted for centralized political control instead of the open pluralistic politics initially promised. In a civil war (as Abraham Lincoln among others came to recognize), the other side cannot be allowed the full exercise of their democratic rights—not, at least, until the violent challenge has been put down. Similarly, at a time of declared or undeclared international conflict, the rights of potential fifth columnists almost inevitably get sacrificed (as Japanese-Americans and victims of McCarthyism can testify).

Even before the election of Ronald Reagan to the U. S. presidency, it was in these terms that Maurice Bishop explained his emphasis on organization, mobilization, and national security (and by implication his retreat on elections). The people had to be taught "why it is imperialism *must* attack us—why it is therefore, that assassinations, terrorism, destabilization, necessary invasions, *must* be part of their agenda."[2]

The external threat is certainly the most obvious, and the most often cited, reason for dispensing with the uncertainties of an electoral test. But I would like to mention three other considerations that are less likely to receive public discussion but that may be just as important in swaying the decision. Note that these are all conventional calculations of political risk and advantage—a level of discussion somewhat removed from the ideological abstractions of the official discourse heard both in revolutionary capitals and in Washington, D. C. My view is that the ideological level of discussion provides little more than an ex post facto rationalization of decisions taken for more or less well-judged and prudent reasons.

The first unspoken consideration is that any but the most highly orchestrated election campaign will allow a degree of uncertainty and the possibility of unexpected and undesired outcomes. This is of particular concern to social revolutionaries, whose "natural" social base consists of the poor, the less educated, the less well organized, those with precarious employment, and those least accustomed to the exercise of political power. In any conventional election campaign, the professional classes, those with money and economic security, the most articulate and self-assured, those accustomed to exerting influence in public life, those are the people who will be favored, and most of them are not reliable allies of any process of social redistribution. Consider the role played in election campaigns by the establishment press. Any radical challenge in a Chilean election would have to contend with *El Mercurio*, which was not just an information-gathering agency for the middle class but a national institution with the capacity to define issues and shape agendas according to its own priorities. Similarly, Castro had to consider what role the *Diario de la Marina* would play in a Cuban election; the Sandinistas had to contend with *La Prensa;* and in a rather different idiom, the Mexicans have also faced real difficulties in managing their newspaper coverage of elections.

Within a year of taking power, Bishop confronted the equivalent issue as follows: "For several months leading up to the counter-revolutionary plot last November, a most vicious local and foreign propaganda campaign was launched against the Grenada revolution. We remember the constant lies being printed in the *Torchlight* . . . the rumors circulated alleging divisions within our party and also regarding plans by the PRG to seize people's lands, houses, goats, pigs, and so on, to ration food, to prevent 18 to 40 year olds from leaving the country."[3] To hold an election campaign while facing the hostility of the most influential press (probably with encouragement from abroad) is to run a considerable risk; to first curb the press and *then* hold an election may be safer, but it is also relatively pointless.

One phrase in the speech just quoted touches on the second, largely unspoken, consideration. However much revolutionaries may be in agreement before the seizure of power, there are bound to be major differences of opinion and ambition thereafter. Even in conditions of tightly centralized political control, it is very difficult to keep such internal divisions from bursting into public view. Madero, Carranza, and Obregón were all assassinated (not to mention many lesser figures in the Mexican revolution), and it was only with great difficulty that Cárdenas established firm enough control over the party apparatus to send Calles into exile. The Castro brothers, Guevara, Cienfuegos, and Matos, provide another example of the potential for disunity within a revolutionary elite—a potential that would have been virtually impossible to contain in an open electoral contest. The Bolivian revolutionaries tried to resolve this problem by holding elections their party was sure to win, with each of the historic leaders alternating in office, but this system broke down when the three key contenders each founded his own party of unconditional loyalists—opening the way for a military dictatorship and a partial counterrevolution. The nine *comandantes* of the FSLN have attempted a different system of power sharing, which has so far proved capable of accommodating a relatively controlled election campaign.

This brings me to the third unspoken consideration militating against elections. Once one relatively open election has been held, a precedent has been set, and even if no regular calendar of popular consultations is established, the question of elections is likely to be reopened every time a leadership conflict comes about. This is hard to reconcile with the notion of achieving an "irreversible" revolutionary victory. It implies that the achievements, the direction, and perhaps even the leadership of the revolutionary process will be up for public evaluation every few years. In Mexico and Bolivia, although the revolutionary party could always marshal an apparent electoral majority, the leadership did change from one contest to the next, and in consequence the "direction" of the process became open to drastic modification. It is only through a continuity of top leadership that one can establish with reasonable certainty the sustained application of an irreversible process. Thirty years of Soviet socialism under the leadership of Stalin, thirty years of the Cuban variant under Fidel, thirty-five years under Tito, these may all count as examples of relatively irreversible progress toward socialism, but they also required a tremendous degree of personalism incompatible with any serious electoral constraint.

Maurice Bishop was not yet thirty-five years old when, through a revolutionary seizure of power, he became prime minister of Grenada. The decision to dispense with even the formalities of election, as observed throughout the rest of the ex-British Caribbean and even under Gairy, implied that he would be prime minister for life. That is also what imitation of the Cuban and Soviet models of political organization seemed to signify. One of the advantages of democracy (even the most formalistic variants) is that it offers a way to remove an individual from leadership of the state before he reaches old age. In the absence of such a mechanism, his rivals and enemies have no recourse but to endorse his ascendancy for however long it may last (thirty to forty years would be a reasonable prediction in this case) or to try to remove him by force, with all the risks that entails for all concerned.

SOCIALISM

> The present state of the Grenada Revolution [is] National- Democratic, anti-imperialist . . . I did not say a socialist revolution as some comrades like to keep pretending that we have. Obviously we do not have a socialist revolution, and it is not socialist precisely because [of] (1) the low level of development of the productive process. You cannot have a socialist revolution with this low-level development. (2) Our working class is too small and too politically underdeveloped.[4]

According to Tony Thorndike's interview with Bobby Clarke after the invasion, Bishop was "particularly scathing about Coard's plan to nationalize nearly all businesses: it was 'totally inappropriate' and 'in variance to Grenada's circumstances.' "[5] Coard secretly resigned from the Central Committee one month after the Line of March speech. One year later (23 September 1983) when Bishop had lost his majority on the Central Committee and Coard had regained the ascendancy, he explained his side of the debate to them as follows: "The standards we are aiming for are out of harmony with the level of development of the productive forces of our country, but because of the existence of world socialism and the links we are developing with world socialism, this is possible."[6]

The evidence, therefore, is fairly strong that the power struggle between Bishop and Coard was at least partly concerned with questions of principle (what kind of socialism to aim for, and what methods to use) in addition to the obvious strong personal motivations. What then can we say, from a comparative perspective, about the relative merits of these two alternative approaches to the "building of socialism"?

The weak points in Bishop's position are easy to identify. How many governments in the Third World have proclaimed themselves to be in the early stages of a transition to socialism, only to end up with some ineffective form of state planning that is unable to regulate the real forces operating in society, most of which are incipiently capitalist? Egypt, India, Burma, Indonesia, Mexico, Jamaica, Peru, Bolivia—the list is long of countries that have at one stage or another passed through what was considered at the time to be a radical antiimperialist phase. Many have for a time flirted with some form of "noncapitalist road to development" (the variety of possible forms is remarkable), and quite a few have started on the way to a socialism that never materialized and that we can now, with hindsight, see was never even a serious possibility. Finally, there are some governments that, after starting out along Bishop's "line of march," lost patience and turned to the formerly rejected metropolitan power for assistance—Mozambique turned to South Africa, and even mainland China has moved away from the route that Mao Ze-dong advocated for over a quarter century.

But where are the examples of national democratic antiimperialist regimes that actually have succeeded in progressing to the kind of fully developed socialism Bishop claimed in his speech to be aiming for? Nicaragua may still be trying, but this is hardly an encouraging example for the Bishop position. The strategy of trying to ally with the local bourgeoisie and to appease or buy off the backward petty bourgeois classes looks like an inherently temporary and unstable solution. No matter how gently the socialist regime treats the business community, private wealth holders are bound to feel that their savings and their property rights will be more secure in a more wholeheartedly capitalist setting. The resources used to appease the petty bourgeoisie must be diverted from an incipient capital-starved socialist sector of the economy. In fact, Nicaragua would seem to demonstrate, like Cuba before it, that a sine qua non for transition to fully fledged socialism may be to disregard local socioeconomic and geopolitical realities and to wholeheartedly embrace the Soviet world system.

The comparative record, therefore, offers some quite persuasive reasons for those advocating socialism in the Third World to conclude that only the Russian-Cuban model has proved reasonably solid. This is an especially powerful consideration for those determined to eradicate unemployment and to press ahead with a radically egalitarian redistribution of income—that is, to establish an undiluted and "irreversible" socialist system. Broad alliances preclude drastic redistributionism, and they are so fragile, unstable, and capable of redirection in regressive directions that they can never give rise to an "irreversible" outcome. Nevertheless, the Soviet-Cuban route to socialism also has its own very serious inconveniences.

First of all, Moscow must be persuaded to foot the bill—an open-ended commitment that canny Russian leaders are understandably careful to fend off. Whereas most U.S. commentary on the "captured documents" has emphasized how completely the island had fallen under Soviet domination, some of the most interesting material can be read in quite a different way. The detailed provisions of most treaties and agreements with the Soviet bloc are almost laughably meager. Grenada's ambassador to Moscow reported as follows in May 1983:

> By itself Grenada's distance from the U.S.S.R., and its small size, would mean that we would figure in a very minute way in the U.S.S.R.'s global relationships. Our revolution has to be viewed as a world-wide process with its original roots in the Great October Revolution. For Grenada to assume a position of increasingly greater importance, we have to be seen as influencing at least regional events. Of all the regional possibilities the most likely candidate for special attention is Suriname. If we can be an overwhelming influence on Suriname's international behavior, then our importance in the Soviet scheme of things will be greatly enhanced . . . Another candidate is Belize.[7]

If these were the best ideas the Grenadian revolutionaries could produce to win favor in Moscow, the chances of the Coard strategy cannot be rated very highly. (In practice, of course, Moscow proved even less well-informed than Havana about the debate over socialism in Grenada, and even less capable of influencing the course of events in its supposed satellite.)

Second, as Castro stressed repeatedly first to Allende and then to the Sandinistas, even with the strongest of links to the socialist bloc it remains vital to maintain enterprise efficiency at home. This means that scarce managerial and professional skills must still be nurtured, and concessions and compromises must be made, just as under the strategy of broad alliances. If the skilled middle classes are driven out because of their political unreliability, the result can be economic defeat for the builders of socialism. This is especially the case for countries with a far narrower range of human resources than Cuba possessed in 1958. It

has proved almost fatal to the aspiring socialist regimes of ex-Portuguese Africa, and a very severe problem in Nicaragua. In Grenada, according to Bishop's Line of March speech, the problem was not in finding *competent* managers for the socialist sector, but in finding managers of any description whatever. The records of the Central Committee would tend to confirm that, even with regard to the management of its own inner party life, the NJM was tragically deficient in organizational skills.

A related drawback of the Cuban approach to socialism is that, with full employment and the suppression of market incentives, the economic structure becomes very inflexible. Even in a relatively simply economy, the only way to overcome the resulting bottleneck and inertia is by military direction of labor—the armed forces replace the "reserve army of the unemployed" as the lubricant to keep the economy adaptable. This can bring with it both very severe political problems and also surprisingly poor overall economic results.

A final objection to the Cuban-Soviet variant of socialism is that it requires a most costly and inefficient diversion of trade, investment, and exchange away from the obvious and dynamic external markets. For Cuba to obtain her oil from Baku instead of Maracaibo is an obvious anomaly, but in fact the strains of integration into the distant and unnatural market of COMECON are far more pervasive and damaging than this one example would prove. For a country as poor and backward as Grenada to willfully exclude itself from the markets of North America and Western Europe would be even more foolhardy. But if the Grenadian revolutionaries tried to preserve access to these markets, despite their commitment to an accelerated dash for socialism, they would once again be obliged to follow a strategy of conciliation, reassurances, and alliance building quite as constraining as the one Bishop was faulted for advocating.

The inference of this section is that neither Bishop's nor Coard's strategy for building socialism offered much prospect of success. The enterprise was inherently farfetched, and the likelihood of failure was always pretty high. I suspect that this almost unbridgeable gap between aspirations and objective possibilities was at the heart of the NJM's difficulties, and goes far to explain the manner of its collapse.

WHAT LESSONS?

There are different lessons to be drawn from different standpoints. Much has been made of the apparent lesson for the Socialist International (namely, that it is too easy for parties to become full members of that organization without making any real commitment to some of its key principles). The documents indicate that the NJM engaged in hypocritical factionalism within the SI. This eventually dealt a substantial blow to SI prestige and influence in the Caribbean. There are other lessons for Washington, not necessarily the ones most readily drawn by ostensibly shocked American analysts as they quote selectively from the captured documents. A good case can be made that U.S. policy played into the hands of the Coard faction and undermined the position of the more realistic and pragmatic Grenadian leaders. On this occasion a *politique du pire* turned out to Washington's advantage, but this is a very clumsy, risky, and unnecessary way to promote regional stability. A key part of the rationale for it—that Moscow and Havana had created a satellite in Grenada, which posed a serious threat to U.S. security—was hysterical overreaction and misjudgment.

Those who wish to preserve the sovereignty of Caribbean ministates, those who favor political democracy, and those who would like to see the development of a participatory form of socialism will have to analyze the failure of the New Jewel Movement with special care.

The three objectives are clearly interrelated. In order to promote any participatory version of socialism, it is necessary to regard the people you are governing with a certain degree of respect, and to allow your decisions to go before them for independent evaluation. This means the "masses" must have access to reliable information about your activities (not just whatever handouts the Central Committee may choose to release, not just the leader's speeches), and they must have *some* means for holding you accountable—even in the last analysis, for replacing you. (Within these constraints, democracy can of course take many forms: the Westminster electoral system may not be the most appropriate for a small compact island.) But unless these conditions are met in some serious way, the promise of democracy is a sham, and the regime will suffer the opprobrium and the problems of internal cohesion characteristic of a dictatorship.

Socialism with democracy is a rare find; it requires enormous patience on the part of the leadership and suffers from the danger that the not-yet-very-socialist-inclined masses may use their opportunities for democratic control to overrule the objectives of their leaders. A democratic socialist must be willing to endure such a setback and must continue pursuing his goals within the constraints set by popular understanding and support. Socialism without real democracy looks easier, but of course this route surrenders much of the moral high ground that justifies its condemnation of capitalism. In purely practical terms, as well, this approach creates as many problems and dangers as it avoids.

One problem of socialism that is particularly acute for small vulnerable excolonies such as Grenada is the difficulty of reconciling it with the preservation of sovereignty. In November 1983 Fidel Castro estimated that Cuba's aid to the NJM regime was worth more than $500 per head. Just in the first year after the U. S. invasion, Western aid has been put at $634 per head—in a country with a per capita income of $870.[8] Faced with such strong financial incentives to align with one powerful patron or the other, it would be extremely difficult for an embattled political elite to retain its autonomy and to keep its distance from potential predators. It must be said that in the Grenadian case it seems that the NJM leadership may have been more eager than their benefactors to surrender their independence and lock themselves securely into the world socialist system. If so, the fundamental reason was that the Grenadian leadership had concluded, in the course of the final power struggle, that the revolution could not make it on its own. Having first reneged on their promises of democracy, they were subsequently disposed to relinquish much of their sovereignty, all in pursuit of a particularly narrow vision of what they called socialism.

This seems to be the substance behind Fidel Castro's suggestion that "those who conspired against [Bishop] within the Grenada party, army and security forces" may have been "a group of extremists drunk on political theory."[9] However it would be unjust to the Coard faction, and a failure of analysis, to allow the final verdict to rest there. If there was revolutionary intoxication, it affected Bishop as well as his rivals. The alternative to the Coard strategy was far easier to recommend than to implement. A systematic alternative would have required Bishop to fundamentally reassess his assumptions and balance his priorities in ways that he had shown no evidence of recognizing. Even with the most foresighted and principled of leadership, it would have been an almost superhuman task to strike a stable and constructive balance between the requirements of national sovereignty, democratic participation, and socialist construction. When the objective possibilities are so out of line with the theoretical aspirations of a revolutionary elite, the structural conditions are created for a *fuite en avance,* an outburst of infantile leftism, as Castro himself has good reason to know from direct experience. None of this excuses the Coard faction from the crimes and misjudgments that may have been committed. Perhaps, however, it provides some elements of explanation beyond merely personal charges of irrationality.

NOTES

1. This is according to a text issued by the Grenadian government, and reprinted in Bruce Marcus and Michael Taber, eds., *Maurice Bishop Speaks: The Grenada Revolution 1979–1983* (New York: Pathfinder Press, 1983), p. 25.

2. Interview on 15 July 1980, in Marcus and Taber, *Maurice Bishop Speaks,* p. 111.

3. Speech on 15 Feb. 1980, quoted in ibid., p. 62.

4. For Bishop's confidential Line of March for the Party speech to the Central Committee, 13 Sept. 1982, See Michael Ledeen and Herbert Romerstein, eds., *Grenada Documents: An Overview and Selection,* vol. 1 (Washington, D. C.: Depts. of State and Defense, 1984), pp. 1–49.

5. Tony Thorndike, *Grenada: Politics, Economics and Society* (Boulder: Lynne Rienner, 1985), p. 73.

6. Ibid., pp. 150–151.

7. Paul Seabury and Walter A. McDougall, eds., *The Grenada Papers* (San Francisco: Institute for Contemporary Studies, 1984), pp. 207–08.

8. Castro's 14 Nov. 1983 speech, in Marcus and Taber, *Maurice Bishop Speaks,* pp. 326, 328; Dennis R. Gordon, "Multilateral Assistance and Economic Development in Grenada: Before and After," a paper delivered at the Twelfth International Congress of the Latin American Studies Association, Albuquerque, Apr. 1985, p. 20.

9. Marcus and Taber, *Maurice Bishop Speaks,* pp. 327–28.

12. Size, Pluralism, and the Westminster Model of Democracy: Implications for the Eastern Caribbean

Arend Lijphart

T HE PURPOSE of this chapter is to discuss the question of which form of democracy is the most suitable for countries like Grenada and others in the Eastern Caribbean area. My answer is that the consensus model of democracy—characterized by such features as power sharing, proportional representation, multipartism, and federalism—should be given serious consideration as the major alternative to the Westminster or majoritarian model, because most of the Eastern Caribbean countries are plural or deeply divided societies.

I am deliberately being cautious when I state that the consensus model "should be given serious consideration" instead of asserting that it "should be adopted." Political science is not an exact science, and I am unable to guarantee that consensus democracy will work well in these countries or that it will work better than Westminster-style democracy, but I do think that the latter is highly probable. I can also state unequivocally that it is wrong to opt for the Westminster model on the basis of the assumption that this model is the only democratic system that is available or that it is the best kind of democracy, without even looking at the alternatives. It seems to me that such ignorance of and indifference to alternative democratic models have in fact occurred frequently, both in the Eastern Caribbean and elsewhere.

My main thesis is that the consensus model of democracy has great advantages for plural and other deeply divided societies. Moreover, the various consensus-oriented devices of this type of democracy are similar to what more traditional political analysis has called checks and balances—and these have undoubted advantages in all of the newer democracies that lack strong democratic traditions and, in particular, strong informal restraints on government power. Without these restraints, the Westminster model easily spells excesses of majority power and of the power of popular leaders. It is not surprising that there is growing dissatisfaction with the Westminster model in many countries. Hence in all of the newly established democracies and democratizing regimes, especially these that have serious political divisions, the alternative consensus model should be carefully examined.

In my previous writings, I have not applied this kind of analysis to the Eastern Caribbean, but it certainly appears to be highly pertinent to this area. In fact, the names of two well-known scholars associated with the Caribbean and Caribbean studies are also prominently connected with the theory of plural societies and the critique of Westminster-style democracy: M. G. Smith and Sir Arthur Lewis.

PLURAL AND DEEPLY DIVIDED SOCIETIES

Smith developed his concept of the plural society, originally stated by J. S. Furnivall, with special reference to the British West Indies, although he was obviously well aware of the fact that the problems of pluralism are, in his own words, "clearly important well beyond the bounds of this region."[1] In his book on Grenada, he describes this country as a plural society, and he defines this term as follows: "A plural society is one in which sharp differences of culture, status, social organization, and often race also, characterize the different population categories which compose it."[2] This definition is roughly similar to my own: plural societies are "societies that are sharply divided along religious, ideological, linguistic, cultural, ethnic, or racial lines into virtually separate subsocieties with their own political parties, interest groups, and media of communication."[3]

However, I disagree with Smith's further specification that "an important feature of this societal type is the subordination of the majority to a dominant minority which is also culturally distinct. . . . The dominant minority generally exercises control through the government."[4] In my view, minority control—that is, an undemocratic regime—is only one of the possible types of government in a plural society. Another possible outcome is a nominally democratic majority control, in which the majority group uses its "democratic" voting power to impose its will on the minority; examples of this kind of majority dictatorship are Northern Ireland, Sri Lanka, and Trinidad. And finally, there is the possibility of a consensual democracy, in which all significant societal groups, majority and minority, share power; Switzerland, Malaysia, pre-1975 Lebanon, and pre-1973 Suriname exemplify this type of government.[5]

It also seems very doubtful to me that Grenada fits Smith's own definition of a plural society. While the kind of differences listed by Smith do appear in Grenada, they are certainly not as sharp and distinct as those in ethnically divided Trinidad, Guyana, and Suriname. My definition has a better fit, since I also include ideological cleavages. In the 1984 general elections in Grenada, the principal parties—the victorious New National Party, the Grenada United Labour Party, and the Maurice Bishop Patriotic Movement—were divided by deep and bitter political and ideological disagreements: these three parties represent, respectively, the current regime ushered in after the 1983 foreign intervention, the regime overthrown in the 1979 armed seizure of power, and the revolutionary regime that ruled Grenada between these two explosive events. Consequently, although Grenada may not be a plural society in the most common meaning of this term, it is certainly a deeply divided society.

THE WESTMINSTER MODEL AND THE PRINCIPLE OF EXCLUSION

The second Caribbean scholar, Lewis—his book, by a remarkable coincidence, was published in the same year as Smith's two volumes mentioned above—is the first significant critic of the Westminster model of democracy for divided societies.[6] He argues that majoritarianism is undemocratic because it is a principle of exclusion. He states that the primary meaning of democracy is that "all who are affected by a decision should have the chance to participate in making that decision, either directly or through chosen representatives." Its secondary meaning is that "the will of the majority shall prevail." If this means that winning parties may make all government decisions and that the losers may criticize but not govern, he argues, the two meanings are incompatible: "to exclude the losing groups from participation in decision-making clearly violates the primary meaning of democracy."[7] If the losers do not differ much in their policy preferences from the winners, and if they have a reasonable chance of winning the next election, their exclusion may not be a very serious problem. However, these two conditions are rarely fulfilled in divided societies: by definition, such societies are characterized by major disagreements, and the voters' loyalties are frequently quite rigid, so that alternation in office does not occur easily. Under such circumstances, exclusion from government power is not only unfair to the losing groups but, in the long run, also dangerous for winners and losers alike, since it may undermine the legitimacy and stability of the democratic regime. Lewis's analysis pertains to West Africa, not the Caribbean, but as a native St. Lucian he is, of course, a Caribbean scholar.

The outcome of the Grenadian election of 1984, which was conducted according to the majoritarian method of plurality in single-member districts, illustrates the Westminster model's tendency to concentrate power in the hands of the victorious majority and to virtually exclude the losing groups. The NNP won 58.5 percent of the vote and fourteen of the fifteen seats in the legislature (93.3 percent); the GULP won 36.1 percent of the vote and only one seat (6.7 percent); and the MBPM's 4.9 percent of the vote was insufficient for any seats. The application of proportional representation (using the most proportional formula—that of the largest remainders) would have resulted in a 9-5-1 division for the seats, instead of 14-1-0. The actual, extremely lopsided, result even exceeded the overrepresentation of the largest group predicted by the cube law. This law holds that if, in two-party systems and plurality single-member district elections, the votes received by the two parties are divided in a ratio of $a:b,$ the seats that they win will be in the ratio of $a^3:b^3$. Instead of the cube law, the 1984 Grenadian election result represents a 5.5th-power rule; the cube law would have predicted merely a 12-3-0 division of seats. Giving exclusive or nearly exclusive representation and power to one group in a deeply divided society does not produce much of an incentive for compromise and reconciliation.

The example of Grenada in 1984 is by no means unusual in the Eastern Caribbean. Table 12.1 gives the results for all of the general elections in this area that involved two-party systems and the plurality single-member district electoral method. I followed the widely accepted operational definition of a two-party system: one in which there are at least two parties, in which the two strongest parties together receive at least 90 percent of the votes, and in which the second strongest party receives at least 30 percent of the votes. Electoral results that did not conform to this definition were excluded from the analysis. All Eastern Caribbean elections have been held under the plurality method, but a few have used two-member districts; these were excluded from the analysis, too (Barbados from 1951 to 1966, Montserrat from 1952 to 1958, and St. Kitts-Nevis in 1952).

In the first column of table 12.1, the disproportionality of the electoral outcome is expressed in terms of the power to which the vote shares of the two parties have to be raised in order to equal their seat shares. In the Grenadian example used above, this means that the 58.5:36.1 ratio of votes has to be raised to the power 5.46 in order to obtain the 14:1 ratio that disproportionally favored the winning party. In order to interpret the exponents in table 12.1, one has to keep in mind that an exponent of one represents a completely proportional outcome, that higher exponents indicate increasing degrees of majority overrepresentation, and that exponents lower than one represent cases where the smaller party is overrepresented. The typical exponent associated with Westminster-style plurality elections is three—hence the term *cube law*—although in practice, British elections have yielded somewhat lower exponents.[8]

The exponents in the first column of table 12.1 vary a great deal but mainly in the range from about 1.50—not too far from a proportional

Table 12.1
Majority Overrepresentation in Seven Eastern
Caribbean Two-Party Systems, 1961–1984

| | Exponents Linking Vote-Share to Seat-Share Ratios | |
	Observed Exponent	Predicted Exponent
Antigua		
1971	2.80	3.44
1976	−45.23	3.57
1980	3.90	3.64
Barbados		
1971	3.63	3.60
1976	7.03	3.62
1981	5.20	3.54
Dominica		
1966	3.28	4.09
Grenada		
1962	2.60	4.32
1967	4.61	4.46
1972	5.26	3.86
1976	5.58	3.92
1984	5.46	3.92
Montserrat		
1961	2.96	4.05
1978	infinite	4.30
St. Lucia		
1961	3.41	4.29
1969	1.45	4.36
1974	1.93	3.67
1979	3.51	3.78
St. Vincent		
1961	23.38	4.58
1966	−6.07	4.65
1967	4.58	4.64
1972	0.00	4.04
1984	3.75	4.11

Sources: Calculated from data in Patrick Emmanuel, *General Elections in the Eastern Caribbean: A Handbook,*, ISER Occasional Paper 11 (Cave Hill, Barbados: University of the West Indies, 1979), pp. 24–72; and *Keesing's Contemporary Archives* (1979–85).

outcome—to about 5. However, there are a few striking outliers that require a brief explanation. The high 23.38 exponent in the 1961 election in St. Vincent reflects the two-to-one majority of seats won by the victorious party with only a handful more votes than the losing party. In the 1978 election in Montserrat, the winning party obtained a clear vote majority, almost twice as many as the loser, and all of the seats in the legislature—a situation that yields an infinite exponent. The two negative exponents, for Antigua in 1976 and St. Vincent in 1966, represent elections in which the winning party in terms of seats was the loser in terms of the popular vote. Finally, the zero exponent for St. Vincent in 1972 was produced by an election in which the two largest vote getters won exactly equal numbers of seats.

Leaving aside these five extreme cases and focusing on the remaining more normal elections, the overall pattern is still one of a very high degree of disproportionality: thirteen exponents are higher and only five are lower than the 3 predicted by the cube law. In fact, the average of the eighteen exponents—3.94—is in closer conformity with a fourth-power rule than with the cube law. Rein Taagepera has shown that the cube law is valid for plurality single-member district elections only under special circumstances.[9] In general, the exponent (n) for a particular election equals the logarithm of the number of voters (V) divided by the logarithm of the number of seats in the legislature (S): $n - \log V / \log S$. In Britain, the United States, Canada, and New Zealand, n has happened to be close to 3—hence the erroneous assumption that the cube law was a universal law.

The application of Taagepera's formula to the elections in table 12.1 yields the predicted exponents in the second column, ranging from 3.44 to 4.65—all well above the 3 level. At first blush, these predicted exponents still seem to deviate considerably from the actually observed ones, but the general pattern is in close agreement with Taagepera's predictions: for the eighteen nonextreme elections, the mean predicted exponent is 3.96—almost exactly the same as the actually observed mean value of 3.94. Clearly, the high degree of disproportionality in Eastern Caribbean elections is not a coincidence. It is the predictable result of the numerical relationship between the number of voters and the number of seats in the legislature, as formulated by Taagepera. Since under universal suffrage the number of voters is fairly constant, the variable that is mainly responsible for the high exponents is the small size of the legislature: in the eight Eastern Caribbean legislatures, the total number of seats ranges from seven in Montserrat to twenty-seven in Barbados.

The small sizes of these legislatures tend to weaken the losing parties in two ways—not only by allocating only a disproportionately small *percentage* of the seats to them, as explained above, but also because a small percentage in a small legislature means a very small *number* of seats. Table 12.2 classifies the sixty-eight elections held in the eight Eastern Caribbean countries from 1951 to 1984 according to the number of seats won by the party with the second largest representation in the legislature. In almost two-thirds of the elections (63 percent), the

Table 12.2
Seats Won by Second Parties in General Elections, Eight Eastern
Caribbean States, 1951–1984

	Number of Elections	Second Party Won			
		No seats	One seat	Two seats	More seats
Antigua	8	5	0	0	3
Barbados	7	0	0	0	7
Dominica	8	3	1	2	2
Grenada	9	2	1	3	3
Montserrat	9	7	0	2	0
St. Kitts and Nevis	8	2	1	3	2
St. Lucia	9	0	4	2	3
St. Vincent	10	2	1	2	5
Total	68	21	8	14	25
		Percentage			
	100	31	12	21	37

Sources: Based on data in Emmanuel *General Elections,* pp. 25–72; and *Keesing's Contemporary Archives* (1979–85).
Note: Only seats won by party-affiliated candidates are counted, and independents are disregarded.

second party won only two or fewer seats, and it won three or more seats in only slightly more than one-third of the elections (37 percent).

One important qualification that must be added is that twelve of the elections were not contested by at least two parties, and hence, by definition, no seats could be won by a second party. If we exclude these twelve elections, the percentage ratio of elections yielding weak or no second parties to those yielding stronger second parties becomes 55:45. The latter category still encompasses fewer than half of the cases. Another factor that should be taken into consideration is that in the smallest legislatures, such as those of Montserrat and St. Kitts-Nevis with seven and nine members, respectively, a second party can obviously not grow much beyond two seats before it becomes the first party. Finally, some of the elections produced three or more significant legislature parties, which shared the available seats. Nevertheless, even with all of these qualifications, we see a high frequency of deviation from the Westminster ideal of a strong majority party that governs but that is carefully watched and criticized by a vigorous opposition party. It is extremely difficult, if not impossible, to conduct such an effective opposition with only one or two seats in the legislature.

The main thrust of this chapter is to propose an alternative to the Westminster model instead of minor improvements in Westminster-style regimes, but the above analysis does suggest a relatively small reform that is worthy of serious consideration. In order to improve the electoral chances of second parties and the effectiveness of parliamentary oppositions, the sizes of the Eastern Caribbean legislatures must be expanded substantially. I shall return to this question—and I shall make specific proposals for the eight countries—in the final section of this chapter.

MAJORITARIAN VERSUS CONSENSUS DEMOCRACY

In my book *Democracies,* a comparative study of twenty-one industrialized democratic states in the 1945–1980 period, I found three factors that could explain whether these countries tended to be governed along majoritarian or consensual principles: the degree of pluralism, the size of the population, and the prevailing political-cultural heritage, especially the degree to which British traditions had exerted an influence.[10] All three variables are clearly relevant in the Eastern Caribbean: most of the countries in this area are plural or deeply divided societies, with small populations and a British colonial heritage. I shall discuss these variables in greater detail below, but at this point I should like to emphasize that the first two explanations are, from a prescriptive point of view, also justifications; that is, when we try to determine the most suitable type of democracy for a particular country, its population size and its plural or nonplural character are perfectly good and legitimate considerations. However, I would argue that the political-cultural heritage, British or non-British, should not be a criterion in choosing an appropriate form of democracy; it is an explanatory variable but not a justification.

Majoritarian and consensus democracy differ from each other with regard to eight characteristics. Let me briefly describe these differences, illustrate them with the help of the British and Swiss examples, and explain how I have operationalized them for the purpose of determining their interrelationships. Switzerland is the clearest example of the consensus model. The best example of the Westminster-majoritarian model is New Zealand rather than the United Kingdom, because—especially since about 1970—the latter has started deviating from the model to a marked degree. Richard Rose has even argued that New Zealand is now "the only example of the true British system left."[11] Nevertheless, I shall use the British example, since it is much better known, and since, after all, the Westminster model originated in Britain.

CONCENTRATION OF EXECUTIVE POWER VERSUS
EXECUTIVE POWER SHARING

In the Westminster model, executive power is concentrated in the cabinet, which is composed of the leaders of the party that has a majority, but usually not a majority of overwhelming proportions, in parliament. These one-party, bare-majority executives—exemplified by virtually all British cabinets since the Second World War—contrast with the consensual pattern of the sharing of executive power among all the major parties represented in the legislature. The Swiss seven-member national executive, the Federal Council, is such a broad coalition of all four large parties, which together control about 85 percent of the seats in the lower house. In operationalizing this variable, I have given predominant weight to the question of whether cabinets are bare- majority cabinets— "minimal winning" cabinets in the terminology of the coalition theorists—or more inclusive "oversized" cabinets, in which one or more parties are represented that are not necessary to give the cabinet a parliamentary majority. Minority cabinets form an intermediate category. British cabinets were minimal-winning ones in almost the entire 1945–1980 period. The Swiss Federal Council was oversized 100 percent of the time.

Executive Dominance Versus Executive-Legislative Balance

The British cabinet is composed of the leaders of a cohesive majority party in the House of Commons. Hence it is normally backed by a Commons majority, and it can confidently count on staying in office and getting its legislative proposals approved. In Switzerland, there is a much more equal and balanced relationship between the executive and legislature. This is at least partly due to a formal separation of powers— the Federal Council is elected by, but subsequently not responsible to, the legislature—but such a balance can also occur in regular parliamentary systems. This variable is difficult to operationalize, but the best available method is to measure the average cabinet durability. Cabinets that are durable—those that do not change frequently in terms of party composition—tend to be much more powerful vis-à-vis their legislatures than less durable executives.

Unicameralism Versus Strong Bicameralism

The pure majoritarian principle requires a unicameral legislature, since a bicameral legislature might have different majorities in the two chambers—a situation that could threaten the tenure and dominance of a one-party cabinet. The pure consensus principle demands strong bicameralism, that is, a bicameral legislature in which the two houses are roughly equal in power (symmetrical) and elected by different methods (incongruent). Legislatures in which the two chambers are asymmetrical (the second chamber being inferior to the first) or congruent (the two chambers being virtual carbon copies of each other as a result of being elected by the same methods) are intermediate cases between unicameralism and strong bicameralism. Britain is not the best example here, because its parliament is bicameral, but it obviously belongs to the highly asymmetrical category. New Zealand's unicameralism provides the better example. The two Swiss chambers exemplify strong bicameralism very well: they have equal powers, and the second chamber is a federal chamber in which the cantons have equal representation.

Two-Party Versus Multiparty System

British politics has traditionally been dominated by two large parties, although various minor parties have been represented in the House of Commons. In contrast with the British two-party system, Switzerland has a four-party system, consisting of the four major parties that are represented on the executive, as well as various minor parties. The best method for operationalizing the number-of-parties variable is the "effective number of parties" measure proposed by Markku Laakso and Rein Taagepera.[12] It counts the number of parties weighted by party size. The mean effective number of parties, based on the parties' shares of legislative seats in the 1945–1980 period, was 2.1 for Britain and 5 for Switzerland.

One-Dimensional Versus Multidimensional Party System

In the Westminster model, the two major parties differ from each other programmatically on only one dimension: socioeconomic policy. The consensus model assumes differences among the major parties not only on the above left-right issue dimension but also on one or more of the following: the religious, cultural-ethnic, urban-rural, regime support, foreign policy, and postmaterialist dimensions. In operationalizing this variable, I gave one point to a dimension of high salience and half a point to those of only medium intensity. Great Britain's score is 1 (one issue dimension, the socioeconomic dimension, with high intensity), while Switzerland's score is 3 (high-salience socioeconomic and religious dimensions and medium-salience cultural-ethnic and urban-rural dimensions).

Plurality Elections Versus Proportional Representation

The difference between the party systems of majoritarian and consensus democracies can be explained in terms of both the above difference in issue dimensions and the difference in electoral systems. The British two-party system is supported by the plurality single-member district method. Proportional representation permits multipartism, as in the Swiss case. In practice, not all plurality and majority systems are equally disproportional, and not all proportional representation systems are equally proportional. For this reason, I operationalized this variable in terms of the deviation between the parties' vote and seat shares in all elections between 1945 and 1980.

Unfortunately, proportional representation has an unfavorable reputation in the Caribbean because the example of its introduction in Guyana in 1964 looms large in people's memories. It is almost certainly true that the British government, actively supported by the United States, decided in favor of this system for Guyana in order to weaken the ruling Indian-based People's Progressive Party of Cheddi Jagan and to help Forbes Burnham's black-based People's National Congress. However, one example of external and partisan manipulation of proportional representation obviously does not warrant the condemnation of the system in general. Moreover, it should be remembered that its use in Guyana in 1964 was not so much a straight advantage for the PNC as the removal of a huge advantage that the PPP had enjoyed under the plurality rule. In 1961, the PPP had won 57 percent of the seats with 43 percent of the votes, and the PNC only 31 percent of the seats with 41 percent of the votes. In 1964, the vote percentages did not change a great deal, but they were now translated roughly proportionally into seats—taking away the PPP's former parliamentary majority.[13] Finally, the widespread fraud in Guyana, especially after 1964, should not be attributed to the principle of proportional representation. Most forms of outright electoral fraud can be practiced equally well under proportionally and plurality, and two of the most common types of electoral manipulation—malapportionment and gerrymandering—are much more serious under plurality than under proportionality. In fact, a general advantage of the latter over the former is that it virtually eliminates the entire problem of districting and its susceptibility to partisan manipulation.

Unitary and Centralized Versus Federal and Decentralized Government

The Westminster-majoritarian principle demands a unitary and centralized system, which does not allow any geographical or functional areas from which the parliamentary majority and the cabinet are barred. The consensus principle favors autonomy for various minority groups by means of federalism and decentralization. Britain and Switzerland can again serve as the examples of the divergent types. Because, in practice, federations tend to be considerably more decentralized than unitary states, I operationalized this variable simply in terms of a measure of centralization: the central government's share of total central and noncentral tax receipts in the 1970s—for instance, 87 percent in Britain and 41 percent in Switzerland.

Unwritten Versus Written and Rigid Constitutions

The optimally majoritarian constitution is an unwritten one because it does not impose any formal limitations on the power of parliament, that is, of the parliamentary majority. At the other extreme is a written constitution that is protected by judicial review and that is difficult to amend; for instance, approval by a popular referendum or, better yet, by extraordinary majorities may be required in order to change the constitution. Written constitutions that are flexible (relatively easy to amend) or that are not protected by judicial review are in intermediate positions between the two extremes. Britain is one of very few democracies with an unwritten constitution. Switzerland happens to be an imperfect example of the opposite: it has a written and relatively rigid constitution, but it lacks judicial review.

DIRECT DEMOCRACY: INITIATIVE AND REFERENDUM

The ninth characteristic of the Westminster model is exclusively representative democracy. Elements of direct democracy, such as the referendum, might interfere with the supremacy of the parliamentary majority and is therefore incompatible with majoritarianism. However, this ninth majoritarian characteristic does not differentiate the model from the consensus model of democracy—which is also based on the concept of representative instead of direct democracy. In practice, direct democracy is a rare phenomenon: of the various devices of direct democracy, such as the referendum, initiative, recall, and primary elections, only the referendum is fairly frequently used. And it is used by both majoritarian and consensus systems. Britain has held only one national referendum: on the issue of Common Market membership in 1975. Consensual Switzerland is a very frequent user of referendum, but majoritarian New Zealand is also among the fairly frequent users. For the purpose of operationalizing this variable, I constructed five categories ranging from the greatest frequency of referendums, with Switzerland as the only occupant, to the group of nine countries in which no referendums occurred between 1945 and 1980.

Two further comments are in order concerning the compatibility of the referendum with consensus democracy. First, it may be argued that referendums are basically majoritarian in their effects, because they are usually decided by popular majorities for or against. They may even be considered more majoritarian than Westminster-style representative democracy, since elected legislatures offer at least some opportunities for minorities to present their case in unhurried discussion and to engage in bargaining and logrolling. David Butler and Austin Ranney state: "Because they cannot measure intensities of beliefs or work things out through discussion and discovery, referendums are bound to be more dangerous than representative assemblies to minority rights."[14] But the referendum is not inevitably a blunt majoritarian instrument. Especially when it is combined with the popular initiative, as in Switzerland, it gives even very small minorities a chance to assert a claim against the wishes of the majority of the elected representatives. Even if the effort does not succeed, it forces the majority to pay the cost of a referendum campaign. Hence, the potential calling of a referendum by a minority is a strong stimulus for the majority to be heedful of minority views.

Second, the above discussion shows that the referendum can be a stimulus for consensus democracy— or, for that matter, can be regarded as a truly direct-democracy device—*only* if it is combined with the initiative. Of the twelve Western democracies that have used the referendum since 1945, only two provide for the popular initiative: Switzerland and Italy. It is hazardous to generalize on the basis of so little evidence, but both the logic of the referendum-plus-initiative and the Swiss example support the suggestion that it may strengthen not only the quality of democracy by encouraging more direct popular participation but also the consensual character of a democratic regime.

One final point should be made. It is a mistake to argue for or against the referendum device in terms of the quality of the decisions that it leads to. The fact that the 1962 referendum in Jamaica triggered the breakup of the Federation of the West Indies—a crucial event in the region's recent history—should not be used as evidence against the referendum, just as the British 1975 referendum, which went the other way, should not be cited in its favor. Both legislative and popular majorities can be wise as well as foolish. My argument is not that referendum will produce qualitatively superior decisions but merely that, if linked with the initiative, they are likely to strengthen consensual decisionmaking. And even on this restricted basis, I certainly do not want to argue too strongly for the referendum-plus-initiative: it can strengthen consensus democracy, but it is not at all indispensable. And as a device for bringing the government closer to the people, it is obviously of much greater value in large countries than in small ones like the Eastern Caribbean ministates.

CLUSTERS OF COUNTRIES: THREE EXPLANATIONS

Since the majoritarian and consensus models of democracy are rational, logically coherent, models, my original hypothesis was that the eight majoritarian characteristics would tend to occur together in my set of democracies and that, similarly, the eight consensual characteristics would go together—but that the ninth variable, the frequency of referendums, would not be related to the other eight characteristics. The last assumption turned out to be accurate, but the rest of the hypothesis was only partly correct. Both correlation and factor analyses clearly showed that in my twenty-two democratic regimes—I included twenty-one countries but I regarded the French Fourth and Fifth Republics as separate cases—the eight majoritarian versus consensus variables clustered in two groups.[15] This means that empirically there is not one dimension but two separate dimensions of majoritarian versus consensus democracy.

The first dimension consists of the following five variables: executive power concentration versus power sharing; executive dominance versus executive-legislative balance; two-party versus multiparty system; one-dimensional versus multidimensional party system; and plurality elections versus proportional representation. The second dimension comprises the remaining three variables: unicameralism versus strong bicameralism; unitary and centralized versus federal and decentralized government; and unwritten versus written and rigid constitutions. Since decentralization, strong bicameralism, rigid constitutions, and judicial review are all associated with the concept of federalism in the political science literature, the second dimension may also be called the federal dimension.

The standardized factor scores for the twenty-two democratic regimes on the two dimensions—which can be interpreted as averages of the original variables, weighted proportionally according to their involvement in the dimension—can be used to discover clusters of similar regimes. Table 12.3 presents a three-by-three classification, based on a division into majoritarian, intermediate, and consensual categories on each of the two dimensions. How can we account for the way in which the twenty-two regimes cluster? The table suggests three causal explanations, already briefly referred to in the beginning of this chapter:

Plural or Nonplural Society

There is a clear relationship between the degree to which the countries are plural societies and their type of regime. The plural societies (Austria, Belgium, Israel, Luxembourg, the Netherlands, and Switzerland) and those that can be considered semiplural (Canada, Finland, France, Germany, Italy, and the United States) are encountered with increasing frequency as we move from the upper left-hand cell to the lower right-hand cell. The only obviously deviant cases are Japan and Luxembourg.

Population Size

Population is linked with the second dimension of the majoritarian-consensual contrast. If the twenty-one countries are divided into eleven small and ten large countries, with a population of 10 million as the dividing line, we find that the left-hand column contains only small countries with one exception (Britain), that the right-hand column contains only large countries with two exceptions (Austria and Switzerland), and that the middle column contains small and large countries in

Table 12.3
Twenty-two Democratic Regimes Classified According to
the Two Dimensions of Majoritarian and Consensus Democracy.

Dimension I	Dimension II		
	Majoritarian	*Intermediate*	*Consensual*
Consensual	New Zealand (5) United Kingdom (4)	Ireland (4)	Australia (5) Austria[a] Canada[a] Germany[a] United States[a]
Intermediate	Iceland (3) Luxembourg[a] (1)	France, Fifth Republic (6) Norway (1) Sweden (1)	Italy (4) Japan (5)
Majoritarian	Denmark (1) Israel[a] (3)	Belgium[a] (1) Finland[a] (1) France Fourth Republic Netherlands[a] (1)	Switzerland[a] (1)

Source: Arend Lijphart, *Democracies: Patterns of Majoritarian and Consensus Government in Twenty-one Countries* (New Haven: Yale University Press, 1984).
Notes: Dimension I consists of the following variables: executive power concentration versus power sharing; executive dominance versus executive-legislative balance; two-party versus multiparty system; and plurality elections versus proportional representation. Dimension II encompasses unicameralism versus strong bicameralism; unitary and centralized versus federal and decentralized government; and unwritten versus written and rigid constitutions.
    Intermediate countries have factor scores between $-.50$ and $+.50$. Figures in parentheses are Dahl's democratic-scale types. See Robert A. Dahl, *Polyarchy: Participation and Opposition* (New Haven: Yale University Press, 1971), p. 232.
a. Plural and semiplural societies.

equal proportions. Britain is a strikingly deviant case, but Austria and Switzerland are among the larger of the small countries. Another way of highlighting this relationship is to state the median population size in each column: about 3.5 million in the left-hand column (Israel and New Zealand), about 8 million in the middle column (Sweden), and about 40 million in the right-hand column (halfway between the populations of Canada and Italy). The two very small countries with populations of less than half a million, Iceland and Luxembourg, are both in the left-hand column.

Westminster Model

The strong influence of the Westminster model in countries with a British cultural heritage is very clear with regard to the first dimension of the majoritarian-consensual contrast. Table 12.3 shows an almost perfect dichotomy between Anglo-American countries, in the top row, and all other countries, in the middle and bottom rows. The only exceptions are Austria and Germany, but especially in the latter case, we should remember the strong influence on postwar German politics of Britain and the United States as occupying powers.

IMPLICATIONS FOR EASTERN CARIBBEAN STATES

These findings have important practical implications for other countries and particularly for those in the Eastern Caribbean. They suggest the paradoxical conclusion that consensus democracy is both highly suitable and likely to meet strong resistance. Each of the above three explanations is relevant. Because the Eastern Caribbean states tend to be deeply divided societies, the consensus model of democracy appears to be more suitable for them than the majoritarian model. Consensus democracy can almost be said to have been especially designed to manage the tensions inherent in such societies. Both the first and the second dimension of consensus democracy deserve serious consideration by Eastern Caribbean states that contemplate fundamental political reforms.

The above conclusion seems to be partly contradicted by the finding concerning population size. Small countries like those in the Eastern Caribbean may not have a great need for the consensual elements belonging to the second dimension, closely associated with the concepts of federalism and decentralization. However, one special characteristic of the countries in this area suggests an important qualification: for countries consisting of two or more islands, such as St. Kitts-Nevis and Trinidad-Tobago, a federal arrangement providing a considerable degree of island autonomy and a second legislative chamber representing the islands are obviously attractive possibilities.

With regard to the desirability of the elements making up the first dimension of consensus democracy, the British political traditions in the Eastern Caribbean present a big obstacle. The British heritage exerts strong majoritarian pressure on countries whose true needs could be served better by consensual arrangements. Sir Arthur Lewis compares the British tradition's bias against coalitions, oversized cabinets, and similar consensual features to brainwashing, and he states that the leaders of plural societies burdened by a British heritage may need "much unbrainwashing" in order to "grasp their problems in true perspective."[16]

A DEFENSE OF CONSENSUS DEMOCRACY

The unbrainwashing suggested by Lewis requires a convincing argument that consensus democracy is by no means inferior to majoritarian democracy. It seems to me that it is not at all difficult to make this case. Two fundamental majoritarian suspicions of consensus democracy must be countered: that consensus democracy tends to be unstable and that it is somehow not sufficiently democratic.

The charge that consensus democracy is associated with democratic instability is usually based on the evidence that consensual cabinets are less stable—that is, have shorter lives—than majoritarian cabinets. There is indeed a strong empirical relationship between oversized cabinets and comparatively low cabinet durability; in fact, these variables are the operational indicators of the first two characteristics of consensus democracy. It is also true that durability indicates strength. What is often forgotten, however, is that strong cabinets are strong only in relation to their legislatures—not necessarily with regard to policy effectiveness. There is no logical connection between cabinet predominance and the cabinet's ability to solve society's problems. Moreover, the twenty-one democracies covered in my book *Democracies* have all shown a high degree of regime stability: they have all been continuously democratic from about 1945 until the present. In other words, regime stability is something that majoritarian and consensus democracies have in common, not something that sets them apart.

It should also be pointed out that a growing number of British scholars have come to the conclusion that majority rule is not working well in Britain. S. E. Finer, especially, has forcefully called for the introduction of such consensual rules as proportional representation and coalition government in order to end "the discontinuities, the reversals, the extremisms of the existing system and its contribution to our national decline."[17]

As far as the democratic quality of consensus democracy is concerned, I would argue, following Lewis's analysis, that it is majoritarian democracy instead of democracy that is in greater need of a defense. Because majoritarianism is a principle of exclusion, it requires a special argument and special circumstances to justify its democratic character. Only if there is a regular alternation of governments in majoritarian democracies and if the majority and minority parties are not too far apart in their policy objectives can majoritarianism claim a sufficiently democratic character. Consensus democracy is inherently more democratic as a result of its inclusive nature.

Second, the consensual elements that make up the federal dimension of consensus democracy hardly require a special defense. Can anyone seriously argue that the Federal setup of countries like the United States, Canada, West Germany, Switzerland, and Australia makes these countries less democratic than the unitary United Kingdom or New Zealand?

Third, the elements that make up the first dimension of consensus democracy may seem more difficult to defend, but this is not really so. Let us take proportional representation—the consensual characteristic that is especially important from the point of view of constitutional engineering—as an example. Compared with the plurality rule and other majoritarian electoral methods, this characteristic is far more prevalent among contemporary democracies. In countries with plurality systems, there are usually many advocates of proportional representation, whereas in countries with this system, there is virtually nobody who wants to shift from it to plurality. And the proponents of plurality make their case on a variety of grounds *except* that plurality is the more democratic method; they usually concede that proportionality is, at least in principle, more democratic.

Finally, we should apply Robert A. Dahl's ratings of political regimes by their democratic quality to our question.[18] All but one of the democracies in table 12.3 are rated by Dahl as of 1968. The practical conclusion that follows is that as a minor reform—without abandoning the Westminster model—the membership of these legislatures should be increased.

Exactly how large should the legislatures be in order for the electoral outcomes to conform to the cube law? As stated earlier, Taagepera's formula is $n = \log V / \log S$. If we want the exponent n to be 3, $\log V$ has to be three times as large as $\log S$. Since the number of voters (V) can be regarded as a constant—disregarding variations in voter turnout—the number of seats (S) must equal the cube root of the number of voters.[19] The second column of table 12.4 presents the desirable sizes that will, on the average, produce the cube law, based on the numbers of voters in the elections of about 1980. In all countries, a considerable expansion is necessary for the cube law to operate: from a 48 percent increase in Dominica to a 178 percent increase in St. Kitts-Nevis. The average increase would be about 113 percent: that is, the legislatures should on the average be more than doubled in size.

Table 12.4
Size of Legislature and Sizes Necessary for the Cube Rule
and the 2.5ᵗʰ-Power Rule to Operate in Eight Eastern Caribbean States, ca. 1980

	Legislature Size		
	Actual	*By Cube Rule*	*By 2.5ᵗʰ-Power Rule*
Antigua	17	31	62
Barbados	27	49	107
Dominica	21	31	62
Grenada	15	34	70
Montserrat	7	16	29
St. Kitts and Nevis	9	25	47
St. Lucia	17	36	75
St. Vincent	13	32	65

Sources: Calculated from data in Emmanuel, *General Elections*, pp. 25–72, and *Keesing's Contemporary Archives* (1979–85).

I should like to emphasize that this reform is in no way a substitute for proportional representation. The plurality single-member district system is inherently disproportional, and changing the size of a legislature merely affects the *degree* of disproportionality. This point is illustrated in the third column of table 12.4. Approximately another doubling in size would be necessary to reduce the cube rule to the 2.5th-power rule—which still represents a very disproportional result. It should also be stressed that expanding the legislatures will not eliminate either large swings in the exponents above and below 3 or the chance that the popular vote loser will be the winner in terms of legislative seats. These are normal features of Westminster-style politics. In short, the reform that I am proposing—in particular, the sizes of the legislatures in the second column of table 12.4—is indeed just a minor reform. It does not entail a step toward consensus democracy; it will merely make the Eastern Caribbean countries conform more closely to the Westminster model.

NOTES

1. M. G. Smith, *The Plural Society in the British West Indies* (Berkeley: University of California Press, 1965), p. xiii. J. S. Furnivall, *Colonial Policy and Practice* (London: Cambridge University Press, 1948).

2. M. G. Smith, *Social Stratification in Grenada* (Berkeley: University of California Press, 1965), p. 234.

3. Arend Lijphart, *Democracies: Patterns of Majoritarian and Consensus Government in Twenty-One Countries* (New Haven: Yale University Press, 1984), p. 22.

4. Smith, *Social Stratification in Grenada,* p. 234.

5. Arend Lijphart, *Democracy in Plural Societies: A Comparative Exploration* (New Haven: Yale University Press, 1977).

6. W. Arthur Lewis, *Politics in West Africa* (London: Allen and Unwin, 1965).

7. Ibid., pp. 64–65.

8. Markku Laakso, "Should a Two-and-a-Half Law Replace the Cube Law in British Elections?" *British Journal of Political Science* 9 (July 1979), pp. 355–62.

9. Rein Taagepera, "The Size of National Assemblies," *Social Science Research* 1 (Dec. 1972), pp. 385–401; "Seats and Votes: A Generalization of the Cube Law of Elections," *Social Science Research* 2 (Sept. 1973), pp. 257–75; "Reformulating the Cube Law for P.R. Elections," *American Political Science Review* 80 (June 1986).

10. Lijphart, *Democracies* pp. 220–21.

11. Ibid., p. 19.

12. Markku Laakso and Rein Taagepera, " 'Effective' Number of Parties: A

Measure with Application to West Europe," *Comparative Political Studies* 12 (Apr. 1979), pp. 3–27.

13. R. S. Milne, *Politics in Ethnically Bipolar States: Guyana, Malaysia, Fiji* (Vancouver: University of British Columbia Press), pp. 22–26.

14. David Butler and Austin Ranney, *Referendums: A Comparative Study of Practice and Theory* (Washington, D.C.: American Enterprise Institute).

15. Lijphart, *Democracies* pp. 211–15.

16. Lewis, *Politics in West Africa,* p. 55.

17. S. E. Finer, *Adversary Politics and Electoral Reform* (London: Wigram, 1975), p. 32.

18. Robert A. Dahl, *Polyarchy: Participation and Opposition* (New Haven: Yale University Press, 1971), pp. 231–45.

19. Taagepera, "Seats and Votes"; and "Reformulating the Cube Law for PR Elections."

Bibliography

Notes on Contributors

Grenadian Politics and Society:
A Bibliographic Guide

Jorge Heine

Contrary to what one might be inclined to believe from reading some of the recent published work about Grenadian politics, Grenadian history did not start in 1979 with the seizure of power by the New Jewel Movement, nor for that matter in 1951 with the first election, won by Eric Gairy. The island has a rich and fascinating history, albeit not one as well researched and documented as one might wish. The most recent and up-to-date historical survey is the one provided by George Brizan in his *Grenada, Island of Conflict: From Amerindians to People's Revolution, 1498–1979* (London: Zed Books, 1984). Raymond Devas in his *A History of the Island of Grenada 1498–1796* (St. George's, Grenada: Carenage Press, 1974) focuses on the early centuries of colonial rule, while Edward Cox in his much more specialized *Free Coloreds in the Slave Societies of St. Kitts and Grenada* (Knoxville: University of Tennessee Press, 1984) provides an interesting glimpse into the daily life of one sector of Grenadian society in the days of slavery. As its title indicates, Knight E. Gittens's *Grenada Handbook and Directory* (Bridgetown, Barbados: Advocate, 1946) is more a compendium of useful facts about Grenada than anything else, but the amount of information it contains is so immense that it has been mined for decades by researchers from all disciplines.

One leading Jamaican sociologist, M. G. Smith, has seen in Grenada a microcosm of the cleavages to be found in Caribbean societies more generally. He has developed a quite elaborate theoretical framework based at least partly on his findings in Grenada in the early fifties. His *Social Stratification in Grenada* (Berkeley: University of California Press, 1965) can be profitably read in conjunction with his *Kinship and Community in Carriacou and Petit Martinique* (New Haven: Yale University Press, 1962), as they clearly illustrate how different those two islets are in their social patterns from Grenada proper. Part of those findings also helped Smith to develop further his theory of the plural society, which he formally set forth in his *The Plural Society in the British West Indies* (Berkeley: University of California Press, 1974), and elaborated somewhat further in *Culture, Race and Class in the Commonwealth Caribbean* (Mona, Jamaica: University of the West Indies, Department of Extra-Mural Studies, 1984), essentially a review of the literature on the subject from the forties to the eighties.

On the period immediately preceding the Gairy years, the standard source is Patrick Emmanuel's *Crown Colony Politics in Grenada, 1917–1951,* ISER Occasional Paper #7, (Cave Hill, Barbados: University of the West Indies, 1978). Originally, the author's master's thesis, it has many useful insights into island politics in those decades as well as into the struggles of T. A. Marryshow to increase the rights of Grenadians within the crown colony system. A closer examination of the personality and leadership of Marryshow, perhaps Grenada's leading political figure during the first half of the twentieth century, though, is sadly needed. On the politics of the pre-Gairy years, George Brizan's *The Grenadian Peasantry and Social Revolution, 1930–1951*, ISER Working Paper 21 (Mona, Jamaica: University of the West Indies, 1974), is also very informative.

On Gairy's rule and Gairy himself, of course, we are lucky to have one of the best studies ever done by a political scientist on a Caribbean leader, Archie W. Singham's *The Hero and the Crowd in a Colonial Polity* (New Haven: Yale University Press, 1968). Based on the author's dissertation and on field research done in 1961–1962, it is a marvelous book. Well-written and eminently quotable, it takes a sharp, close look at the constitutional conflict between Eric Gairy and J. M. Lloyd, then administrator of Grenada—which resulted in Gairy's ouster from office in 1962. While never losing sight of the dramatis personae themselves and the dynamics of the conflict, it sets the encounter between the politician and the civil servant not only within the larger setting of West Indian society but also within the psychological and sociological peculiarities of colonial politics anywhere, relying on the Weberian concept of charisma. In so doing, it becomes a classic study of politics under colonialism. It is said that Gairy has never forgiven the author for the less than flattering picture of the "hero" portrayed in the book (one that accurately predicted Gairy's drift toward dictatorship), but we are all indebted to Singham for a first-rate contribution to our understanding of Gairyism and of the relationship between masses and leaders.

A useful collection is *Independence for Grenada: Myth or Reality?* (St. Augustine, Trinidad: Institute of International Relations, University of the West Indies, 1974), edited by the PRG's future Deputy Prime Minister Bernard Coard (then a lecturer at the IIR) and a number of colleagues. The collection, based on a conference held three weeks before Grenadian independence in 1974, has three sections. One is supposed to provide a political and social profile (although it does precious little of that), another discusses the legal and political aspects of independence in very broad terms, and the third—and by far the most useful— is dedicated to Grenadian agriculture. On the chapters on politics, the most informed and analytical is the one by Richard Jacobs, the future ambassador of the PRG to Havana and later to Moscow, who in his essay "The Movement toward Grenadian Independence" traces the development of the main political forces in Grenada in the late sixties and early seventies.

On the onset of the Grenadian Revolution and the forces leading up to it, the single most informative source is Richard Jacobs and Ian Jacobs *Grenada: The Route to Revolution* (Havana: Casa de Las Américas, 1980). Although one may disagree with the often somewhat mechanical class analysis of the authors, they show a considerable command of the conflicts in Grenadian society and their articulation by the various political actors. D. Sinclair Da Breo's *The Grenada Revolution* (Castries, St. Lucia: Management, Advertising, and Publicity Services, 1979) was probably the first book to come out on the revolution, and as such, shares the deficiencies of "instant books." More informative are two books that came out somewhat later. One of them is Ecumenical Program for Inter-American Communication and Action, *Grenada: The Peaceful Revolution* (Washington, D.C.: EPICA, 1982), a sympathetic account of the first years of the PRG. Another is David Lewis' *Reform and Revolution in Grenada*,

1950 to 1981 (Havana: Casa de Las Américas, 1984), the author's honors thesis at Brandeis University, which won the Casa de Las Américas prize for 1983.

Though the Grenadian Revolution has apparently not yet inspired any fiction writers, we do have a powerfully written set of vignettes about life under the PRG, in which the author interweaves interviews with revolutionary leaders and common people with comments and analyses of his own, making for a rich tapestry of images and commentary. Jorge Luna's *Granada, la nueva joya del Caribe* (Havana: Editorial de Ciencias Sociales, 1982), written by a Peruvian journalist then working with *Prensa Latina,* is unfortunately not available in English.

The odyssey of Fitzroy Ambursley, a Jamaican doctoral student in sociology at the University of Warwick, should also be an object lesson on the perils of premature publication. While still doing his fieldwork for his dissertation, he coedited a book with his advisor Robin Cohen (*Crisis in the Caribbean* [New York: Monthly Review Press, 1983]), which includes a chapter in which he heavily criticized the course of the revolution as petty bourgeois. He was immediately deported, and although he later engaged in some heavy self-criticism in print (in his "Maurice Bishop and the New Jewel Revolution in Grenada," *New Left Review* 142 Nov./Dec. 1983, pp. 91–96) and revised the chapter in his book in the next edition, the damage had already been done. It is unlikely that his by now completed dissertation will ever be published—which is unfortunate, since Ambursley is in many ways an imaginative and resourceful researcher.

Although collections of speeches tend to be among the most boring of nonbooks, there are occasional exceptions. Two of those are *Maurice Bishop Speaks: The Grenada Revolution 1979–1983,* edited by Bruce Marcus and Michael Taber (New York: Pathfinder Press, 1983), and *In Nobody's Backyard: Maurice Bishop's Speeches, 1979–1983,* edited by Chris Searle and with an introduction by Maurice Bishop's former attorney general, Richard Hart (London: Zed Books, 1984). In both of them the enormous eloquence of Bishop comes through with great force, making it possible to appreciate how he became the very embodiment of the revolution.

The capture of a vast amount of the PRG's official documents by the U.S. occupation forces ("one of the most important scholarly windfalls since World War II," says Mark Falcoff of the American Enterprise Institute) has led to a minor publishing industry in itself. The U.S. State Department has even started a handsomely published series, the Grenada Occasional Papers, dedicated to disseminating the speeches of Maurice Bishop and other PRG leaders. Of the various collections of documents that have been published (the rest are available on microfiche at the National Archives in Washington, D.C.), the most comprehensive is *Grenada Documents: An Overview and Selection,* Vol. 1 (Washington, D.C.: Departments of State and Defense, 1984), edited by Michael Ledeen (of subsequent fame as one of the prime movers in the Iran-Contra affair) and Herbert Romerstein. The collection is useful, though one wonders about the selection criteria used by two "specialists" who know so little about the country they are dealing with that they keep referring to Grenadians as Grenadans. Another, much shorter collection, *The Grenada Papers* (San Francisco: Institute for Contemporary Studies, 1984), edited by Paul Seabury and Walter McDougall, is prefaced by an even more militantly anti-Communist introduction than the State Department collections.

The curious mixture of total contempt for and extraordinary ignorance about Grenada with which many contributors to various books about the final crisis and the U.S. invasion approach the subject is perhaps best reflected by Harvard historian Richard Pipes. His opening comments to his contribution in Jiri Valenta and Herbert J. Ellison, eds., *Grenada and Soviet/ Cuban Policy: Internal Crisis and U.S./OECS Intervention* (Boulder: Westview, 1986) are: "There is something comic opera about dealing with a country as minuscule as Grenada—in which we find documents written by semi-literate people who give themselves airs about being revolutionary leaders." He then goes on to ask, "Why did the Soviet Union and Cuba pick Grenada?"—even though, if there is *one* thing that emerges from the PRG documents, it is that, if anything, it was the Grenadians who "picked" the Cubans and the Soviets.

Unfortunately that tone also percolates to the writings of one of the few contributors to that collection who actually knows Grenada and the Caribbean, Anthony Maingot, who starts his chapter saying that "the active phase of the 'Glorious Grenada Revolution' lasted four hours"—thus missing the point about what the PRG was all about. Ironically, perhaps the most lasting contribution of a book so marked by its almost exclusive focus on Grenada as a mere rook in East-West relations that the very specificity of the Grenadian Revolution and the West Indian condition is lost, may not be a research paper but an exercise in "imaginary realism" by Jorge Domínguez, who provides a sober assessment of Cuba's position in the Caribbean and the world more generally after the Grenada debacle.

The Valenta and Ellison book can profitably be read as a companion volume to (and mirror image of) *Granada: Historia, Revolución, Intervención de Estados Unidos* (Moscow: Soviet Academy of Sciences, 1984), which places all the blame for the breakdown of the revolution on the United States.

The military aspects of the invasion are covered in Peter M. Dunn and Bruce W. Watson, eds., *American Intervention in Grenada: The Implications of Operation "Urgent Fury"* (Boulder: Westview, 1985). Though heavy on military jargon and useful for filling in tactical aspects of the operation, it has little of the analytical insight of a work like Edward Luttwak's *The Pentagon and the Art of War: The Question of Military Reform* (New York: Simon and Schuster, 1985), which has a devastating critique of the way Operation Urgent Fury was actually handled by the U.S. military, highlighting it as a classic example of how inter-service rivalries in the U.S. armed forces stand in the way of effective military action.

Probably the best first-hand account of the invasion itself can be found in Hugh O'Shaughnessy, *Grenada: Revolution, Invasion, and Aftermath* (London: Sphere Books, 1984), in which the noted British journalist also provides an introduction to the history of Grenada as well as an account of the revolution. The regional context of the Grenadian revolution is well covered in Anthony Payne, Paul Sutton, and Tony Thorndike, *Grenada: Revolution and Invasion* (London: Croom Helm, 1984). A fact-packed monograph, strongly critical of the U.S. invasion, is *Grenada: Whose Freedom?* (London: Latin American Bureau, 1984).

Three very different perspectives on the crisis of the revolution and the subsequent invasion are provided in Cathy Sunshine, *Death of a Revolution* (Washington, D.C.: EPICA); Gregory Sandford and Richard Vigilante, *Grenada: The Untold Story* (Lanham, Md.: Madison Books, 1984); and Trevor Munroe's *Grenada: Revolution, Counterrevolution* (Kingston, Jamaica: Vanguard, 1984). Sunshine's book, a follow-up on the earlier EPICA volume on the revolution, largely sympathizes with Bishop's position in the NJM power struggle. Sandford and Vigilante, both State Department officers, undertook the first effort of the U.S. government to get its perspective on the Grenada events in book form. Munroe's book, a collection of talks given by the leader of the Jamaican Workers Party, is a defense of Bernard Coard's position. By far the most exhaustively researched and tightly argued case against Bernard Coard, placing squarely on his shoulders the responsibility for bringing the Grenadian Revolution to an end, is Steve Clark's "The Second Assassination of Maurice Bishop," in *New International* 6 (1987), pp. 11–96.

The historians' dictum "the owl of Minerva flies at dusk" is still valid, and it should therefore be not surprising that no definitive history of the Grenadian revolution has yet been published. Yet, the availability of the official PRG documents has made it possible to undertake the sort of archival work that can normally only be done decades after the events. Scholars who combine a longstanding association with Grenada, fieldwork undertaken during the PRG years, and a judicious use of the documents have thus been able to produce volumes destined to have a much longer shelf life than the instant books coming out in the wake of the invasion.

The most readable of these is Gordon K. Lewis's *Grenada: The Jewel Despoiled* (Baltimore: Johns Hopkins University Press, 1987), essentially a meditation on the unraveling of the revolution. More detailed in its appraisal of the revolution itself is Tony Thorndike, *Grenada: Politics, Economics, and Society* (Boulder: Lynne Rienner, 1985). The briefest, though in some ways the most analytical of these books is Jay Mandle's *Big Revolution, Small Country: The Rise and Fall of the Grenada Revolution* (Lanham, Md.: North-South, 1985), marred only by an excessive reliance on secondary sources. More specialized is Frederic Pryor's *Revolutionary Grenada: A Study in Political Economy* (New York: Praeger, 1986), an excellent example of the quality product that can emerge from economic analysis based on the manipulation of official government data and supplemented by extensive interviewing of the key economic actors and a careful consideration of the politics of economic decisionmaking.

Gregory Sandford has also written a follow-up work on his earlier book with Vigilante. *The New Jewel Movement: Grenada's Revolution 1979–83* (Washington, D.C.: Foreign Service Institute, U.S. Department of State, 1985) shows a more nuanced and fine-grained grasp of Grenadian politics than both Sandford's earlier book and the one evidenced in collections like the ones edited by Valenta and Ellison or Dunn and Watson. Also useful, though odd in its structure and conception, is Kai Schoenhals and Richard Melanson, *Revolution and Intervention in Grenada* (Boulder: Westview, 1985). The half of the book written by

Schoenhals provides an overview of the Grenadian revolution, and the half by Melanson analyzes U.S. policy toward it.

One thing that social scientists working on Grenada have generally lacked, for a variety of reasons, is reliable survey data about Grenadian public opinion, though Singham did some surveys for his book in the early sixties. *Political Change and Public Opinion in Grenada 1979–1984,* ISER Occasional Paper 19 (Cave Hill, Barbados: University of the West Indies, 1986), authored by Patrick Emmanuel, Farley Brathwaite, and Eudine Barriteau, is therefore an extremely important addition to the literature on Grenadian politics. Based on a 1984 survey of a 390-person sample from nine different constituencies, it provides a fascinating glimpse into Grenadian attitudes toward the revolution, its leadership, the Cuban presence, and other such subjects—many of which have little to do with what has emerged as the conventional wisdom in the wake of the denouement of the revolution.

Notes on Contributors

JORGE HEINE is senior fellow at the Centro Latinoamericano de Economía y Política Internacional (CLEPI) in Santiago, Chile, and associate professor of political science at the University of Puerto Rico, Mayagüez. He has held fellowships from St. Antony's College, Oxford and from the Social Science Research Council. His books include *The Caribbean and World Politics: Cross Currents and Cleavages* (with Leslie Manigat), *The Puerto Rican Question* (with Juan M. García Passalacqua), and *Time for Decision: The United States and Puerto Rico*. He is president of the Caribbean Studies Association for 1990–1991.

PAGET HENRY is associate professor of sociology at Brown University, and taught previously at the University of Virginia and at SUNY, Stony Brook. He is the author, most recently, of *Decolonization and Dependency in Antigua* and coeditor (with Carl Stone) of *The Newer Caribbean: Decolonization, Democracy and Development*.

WALLACE JOEFIELD-NAPIER is country economist for Grenada at the Caribbean Development Bank. He did his graduate and undergraduate work at the University of the West Indies, where he also taught economics. He is coauthor (with John Gafar) of *Trends and Patterns of Caribbean Trade*, author of *Import Structure of Barbados*, and has published numerous other monographs and articles on Caribbean economic issues.

VAUGHAN LEWIS is director general of the Organization of Eastern Caribbean States in Castries, St. Lucia. He was previously director of the Institute of Social and Economic Research at the University of the West Indies. He is the editor of *Size, Self-Determination and International Relations* and has written extensively on Caribbean international relations. He was president of the Caribbean Studies Association for 1981–1982.

AREND LIJPHART is professor of political science at the University of California, San Diego, and taught previously at the University of Amsterdam. A noted comparativist, he is best known for developing the concept of "consociational democracy" and for his studies of patterns of democratic governance. He is the author of *Democracy in Plural Societies* and, most recently, *Democracies: Patterns of Majoritarian and Consensus Government in Twenty-one Countries*, among many other books.

349

ROBERT PASTOR is professor of political science and director of Latin American and Caribbean Studies at the Carter Center at Emory University in Atlanta. He is former senior staff member for Latin America on the National Security Council (1977–1981). His books include *Condemned to Repetition: The United States and Nicaragua, Migration and Development in the Caribbean: The Unexplored Connection,* and *Congress and the Politics of U.S. Foreign Economic Policy.* He holds a Ph.D. from Harvard.

ANTHONY PAYNE is lecturer in politics at the University of Sheffield in England. He has published four books on Caribbean international relations, including *The Politics of the Caribbean Community, The International Crisis in the Caribbean, Dependency under Challenge: The Political Economy of the Commonwealth Caribbean* (coedited with Paul Sutton), and *Grenada: Revolution and Invasion* (with Paul Sutton and Tony Thorndike). He was a consultant to the House of Commons Foreign Affairs Committee for its report on the Caribbean and Central America.

FREDERIC L. PRYOR is professor of economics at Swarthmore College and has held visiting appointments at the Ecole de Hautes Etudes en Sciences Sociales in Paris and the Institute of International Relations at the University of Geneva, among other universities. A consultant to the World Bank, he is the author of six books, including *The Communist Foreign Trade System.* His latest book is *Revolutionary Grenada: A Study in Political Economy.*

SELWYN RYAN is head of the Institute for Social and Economic Research at the University of the West Indies, Trinidad-Tobago. A member of Trinidad's two constitutional reform commissions, he also heads St. Augustine Associates, a polling firm. He is the author of *Race and Nationalism in Trinidad* and of numerous articles on Caribbean politics. He was president of the Caribbean Studies Association for 1989–1990.

CARL STONE holds the chair in political sociology at the University of the West Indies, Jamaica. He writes a regular column for the *Daily Gleaner* and is also Jamaica's leading public opinion pollster. He has published nine books on Jamaican political behavior and Caribbean political economy issues, including, most recently, *Profiles of Power in the Caribbean Basin* and *Democracy and Clientelism in Jamaica.* He has received numerous awards for his scholarly contributions.

TONY THORNDIKE is head of the Department of International Relations and Politics at the North Staffordshire Polytechnic in England. He is the author of *Grenada: Politics, Economics and Society,* coauthor (with Anthony Payne and Paul Sutton) of *Grenada: Revolution and Invasion,* and author of numerous articles on Grenadian affairs and Caribbean politics more generally. He holds a Ph.D. from the University of London.

LAURENCE WHITEHEAD is official fellow at Nuffield College, Oxford University. He has published several books on Latin American political and economic affairs, including *Inflation and Stabilization in Latin America* (coedited with Rosemary Thorpe) and the four-volume collection *Transitions from Authoritarian Rule* (coedited with Guillermo O'Donnell and Philippe Schmitter).

Pitt Latin American Series

Cole Blasier, Editor